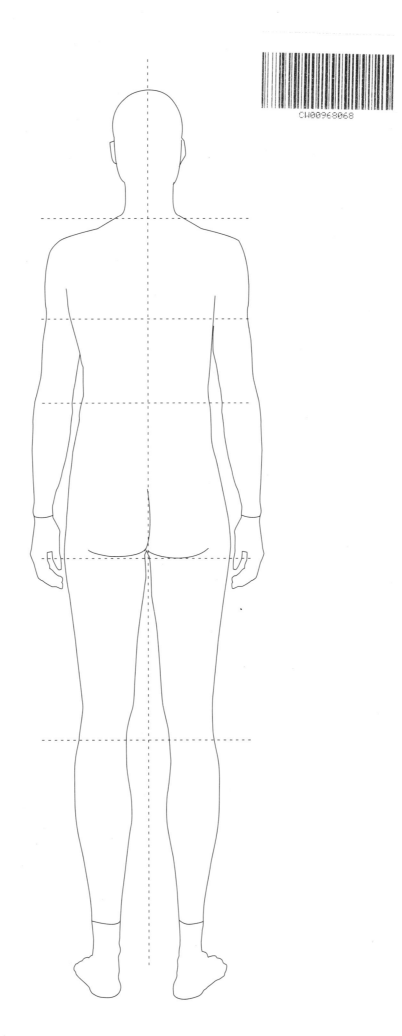

These figure templates have been provided for you to develop your designs on. Photocopy them and use the division lines to investigate the relationship between garment proportions.

# PATTERN CUTTING FOR MENSWEAR

# PATTERN CUTTING FOR MENSWEAR

**GARETH KERSHAW**

Laurence King Publishing

Published in 2013 by

Laurence King Publishing
361-373 City Road, London,
EC1V 1LR, United Kingdom

T +44 20 7841 6900
enquiries@laurenceking.com
www.laurenceking.com

Reprinted 2014, 2016, 2017 and 2019

A catalogue record for this book is available from the British Library.
ISBN: 978 1 78067 319 6

Technical drawings: Elisha Camilleri
Fashion illustrations: Thom Davies
Design: Lizzie Ballantyne, Lizzie B Design
Senior editor: Peter Jones
Picture researcher: Julia Ruxton

Printed in China


Laurence King Publishing is committed to ethical and sustainable
production. We are proud participants in The Book Chain Project®
bookchainproject.com

# CONTENTS

INTRODUCTION 7

PATTERN CUTTING IN
CONTEMPORARY MENSWEAR 8

## CHAPTER ONE

### PREPARATION FOR PATTERN CUTTING

TOOLS AND EQUIPMENT 18

STUDIO PRACTICE 20

MEASURING THE MALE FIGURE 24

TAKING MEASUREMENTS 26

MANNEQUINS 30

FIT MODELS 31

SIZE CHARTS 32

## CHAPTER TWO

### THE PATTERN CUTTING PROCESS

THE DEVELOPMENT OF THE DESIGN 36

BASIC BODY BLOCK 40

BASIC SLEEVE BLOCK 42

BASIC TROUSER BLOCK 45

CREATING A MASTER PLAN 48

HOW TO TRACE OFF A PATTERN 50

GRADING 52

PRINCIPLES OF PATTERN CUTTING 57

USING TECHNOLOGY 68

## CHAPTER THREE

### THE PATTERNS: JERSEY AND SHIRTS

LONG-SLEEVED GRANDAD VEST 74

SHORT-SLEEVED POLO SHIRT 80

HOODED SWEATSHIRT 88

CASUAL LONG-SLEEVED SHIRT 104

LUMBERJACK SHIRT 116

SHORT-SLEEVED SAFARI SHIRT 126

BIB SHIRT 138

## CHAPTER FOUR

### THE PATTERNS: TROUSERS

HIGH-WAISTED TROUSERS 150

CHINOS 158

BASIC SWEATPANTS 168

TAILORED SHORTS 176

CARGO PANTS 186

JEANS 196

## CHAPTER FIVE

### THE PATTERNS: OUTERWEAR

CAGOULE 206

FITTED DENIM JACKET 220

TRENCH COAT 232

SINGLE-BREASTED JACKET 252

DOUBLE-BREASTED JACKET 268

WAXED JACKET 288

PARKA 302

GLOSSARY 316

FURTHER READING 318

INDEX 320

PICTURE CREDITS 320

ACKNOWLEDGEMENTS 320

# INTRODUCTION

Contemporary menswear has evolved from a staple of traditional silhouettes and styles. The development of these styles has been directly influenced by social, economic and cultural requirements, played out through the many roles men have inherited: formal clothing, workwear, leisure- and sportswear. The boundaries of these styles are less clearly defined than in previous decades as trends move and change as quickly as seasons pass – Autumn/Winter-Spring/Summer. Again and again the cyclical nature of the fashion industry throws up reinterpretations of classic silhouettes.

Pattern cutting as a craft is integral to the whole fashion production process, linking the designer's concepts – a two-dimensional illustration – with the three-dimensional realisation of shape-making, proportions and silhouettes. Very few people who study fashion end up specialising in pattern technology and many who practise it have come from other disciplines. The holistic nature of the fashion industry increasingly requires practitioners to have a broad understanding and experience of most, if not all, the stages involved in the creation of clothes. A designer or practitioner who can research and conceptualize ideas, cut patterns and identify their target sizing, construct and technically finish a garment, develop, market and sell their product will be able to direct their team and product to a satisfactory conclusion. A broad skills base is needed to succeed in today's fashion industry.

This book uses generic menswear garment styles to teach the principles of pattern construction that will be encountered throughout the fashion industry. Each pattern not only offers a selection of shapes and design hints but also explores the related techniques associated with its construction and development. Working your way through each section will build your knowledge, allowing you to further explore and adapt generic styles.

Most designers / labels work towards a set of predetermined body measurements (the target consumer) or an industry-acquired size chart. These are used in conjunction with a human fit model or a size-specific mannequin or model form. Chapter 1 discusses how to take measurements to create your own size chart or use the industry charts provided. It highlights the importance of developing visual awareness of the landmark points used for taking measurements, which correlate to the human body in relationship to fit. The chapter also outlines studio practices related to sizing and technological advancements through computer-aided design (CAD) and its applications.

The designs for a garment style can be developed quickly by using the basic block template described at the beginning of Chapter 2. Tracing off the block and transferring the design development onto it creates a master plan. The master plan serves as a blueprint for the development. This process uses only half of the pattern block, thus eliminating possible duplication errors, which would result in an unbalanced pattern – the human body is generally seen as equal in proportion but not symmetrical. Even if your design is asymmetric, copying over the drafted shape to create the other side is a quick way to achieve the desired pattern style.

Where possible the different pattern pieces are kept proportional to one another but occasionally to show detail or to ensure that the text is readable this is not the case.

A modern interpretation of a classic icon, Woolrich Woolen Mills' 'Balmac' trench coat. The company's use of original fabrics (Maxima Poplin) from the Woolrich looms emphasises the functionality and detailed approach they take to creating outerwear.

# PATTERN CUTTING IN CONTEMPORARY MENSWEAR

**Pattern Cutting for Menswear brings together a collection of patterns that have become established classics of contemporary men's fashion. By working on these garment silhouettes you will learn the basic principles needed for pattern cutting. Using these styles as building blocks to explore ideas and your creative flare, you can interchange techniques and processes to develop new interpretations and solutions to your designs.**

To appreciate how far the exploration of shaping fabric to the human body has come, one needs to look at its origins. Contemporary pattern cutting is intrinsically entwined with the history of fashion. The first notions of patterns as we now know them appeared in the West in the fifteenth century as men's silhouettes began to be redefined by the demands of social organisations such as the military, royal courts and religious bodies. From these origins spring the two dominant forms of male dress construction: the first is characterised by the technique of draping and the second developed from the craft of shaping, currently known as tailoring. The latter, the most commonly used and popular technique, was to become highly prized. Guilds of tailors championed the profession and their craft was meticulously developed during the sixteenth to eighteenth centuries through numerous fitting sessions with an elite clientele in the ateliers of Western Europe. As with any craft, the greatest teacher is the practice itself: copious hours chalking, basting (loose stitching), pinning and cutting the patterns for clients of every conceivable size and shape would develop the knowledge needed to call oneself a master cutter.

More complex forms of men's clothing evolved through cutting and shaping as coat and doublet styles developed into structured jackets with opened sleeves, worn with breeches. These were first documented as simple illustrated patterns in one of the earliest books on tailoring: Juan de Alcega's *Libro de Geometría Práctica y Traça* (Madrid, 1589). Three main periods followed which shaped the evolution of men's clothes through cut, fit and construction, beginning with the civil wars of England and France in the seventeenth century. Clothes had to respond to

turbulent times: there was a societal shift from softer fabrics, to clothes produced from harsher, woollen cloth with the garment shapes made more rigid with more robust qualities that would survive the rigours of battle and the outdoor life. By the start of the eighteenth century, clothes began to reflect a more stable economic environment. The first garment of notoriety to be adopted by the aristocracy of Europe was referred to as a cassock or coat: it was a simple garment cut above the knee with two front panels and two back panels sewn to the waist with three-quarter sleeves. This style later included a collar and vented pleats and was made from silk or satin with flamboyant decorative details, creating a softer feminine silhouette. It was the forerunner of the clothing shapes we see today.

As the profession developed, M. de Garsault wrote the first serious manual to detail all the principles behind pattern construction and tailoring, *L Art du Tailleur,* published by the Académie Royale des Sciences, for the encyclopaedia *Description des Arts et Métiers* (Paris, 1769). Garsault describes the whole procedure of making the coat from start to finish, beginning with the notion of measurement taking. He introduces the use of a thin strip of paper that was cut to the required length to record the parameters of an individual client's height and width, as well as detailing construction processes with illustrated patterns that accompanied the text. Later, in 1796, an English manual was published: *The Taylor's Complete Guide or a Comprehensive Analysis of Beauty and Elegance in Dress* presented a new way to perceive the art, not too dissimilar from the present format; instructions were given on how to draw the coat with measurements made directly onto the material by following a series of illustrated diagrams. These publications brought new audiences and extended the dialogue between practitioners and their clientele.

```
Issey Miyake interprets the idea of layering
for men with a cape, Autumn 2012 collection.
Designed from the Japanese premise of 'KASANE'
- simple functionality for everyday life.
```

Modern pattern cutting developed with the industrialisation of sewing and the development of mechanical processes. From the start of the Industrial Revolution technology defined the way the clothing industry developed. Crafts men and women invented labour-saving devices to increase production. As the cultural trend towards uniformity gathered pace, the demand for standardised clothing began to outstrip supply. Replication was needed and templates (patterns) for gentlemen's clothes began to be produced. Initial attempts resulted in poorly fitting garments; the sizing of patterns would take considerable experimentation before a recognised sizing system was achieved through the use of the newly conceived 1-yard measurement tape. Laid out in inches, this gave tailors a regulated tool to record human dimensions. From these observations a mathematical drafting system was conceived, which was based on the principles of geometry and anatomical proportions.

In the first half of the nineteenth century numerous technical publications appeared to support the new drafting technique: *The Improved Tailor's Art* by J. Jacksons (1829) *Science Completed in the Art of Cutting* by W. Walker (1839) and *A Practical Guide for the Tailor's Cutting-Room* by J. Coutts. It was during this period, particularly in France, that technical

training was established; Elisa Lemonnier opened one of the first professional schools in Paris to offer cutting and tailoring among its courses. Along with the demand for cheaper clothing, in 1860 the first mail order fashion catalogues to publish paper patterns appeared; the latest styles could be bought by the middle and working classes throughout Europe and the US, bringing the ability to produce cheaper clothing to a wider audience and creating a forerunner of the ready-to-wear genre.

At the beginning of the twentieth century the craft of tailoring began to divide into specialisms – designer, pattern cutter and seamstress. It is a working model that has survived to the present day, replicated in fashion houses and garment factories all over the world. Mass production brought duplication and the development of standard sizes but fit was still of crucial importance throughout the first half of the last century. Although clothing was pre-constructed, the discerning gentleman would have it adapted to the sartorial fashions of his day. Alterations were made and silhouettes tailored through subtle changes to the cut, line or proportion of the garment.

The process of standardisation was then speeded up by the onset of the two World Wars, when standardised patterns

and size charts were needed to produce military uniforms for both officers and infantry alike. Clothing the army gave the garment industry an opportunity to review its procedures and attitudes towards sizing and construction, and this resulted in the formation of national registered organisations to regulate clothing production.

Away from the austerity of war, social hierarchy still demanded that a gentleman's wardrobe should have multiple dress options, even though a new era was dawning as the gender-role ideologies of the pre-war period were vanquished and modernism was embraced. The 1950s brought a new approach to male dress, championed by a younger generation who rebelled against the constraints of tradition. With the growing influence of American youth cultures, formal attire with its stiff silhouettes began to lose its appeal. New modes of informal dressing appeared throughout towns and cities across Europe and America. Menswear producers responded to the growth in consumerism and this new attitude by importing or recreating foreign styles associated with music, film or leisure activities (Italian tailoring, US varsity, German sportswear). Relaxed attitudes towards life brought a new direction for men's fashion assisted by technological advances in textiles and the uses of synthetic materials to create easy-wear, functional clothing.

Opposite left: Yohji Yamamoto's enigmatic approach to masculinity is portrayed in a return to his signature oversize proportions at Paris Fashion Week 2008-09.

Opposite right: Italian sensibility crafted with technical design inspires C. P. Company's relaxed tailored garments at the Via Savona, Milan Fashion Week, Autumn/Winter 2010.

Above left: A master of gender bending Thom Browne's Autumn/Winter 2012 menswear show questions masculine identity and its perceived role in society.

Above right: Walter Van Breirendock's spring 2010 menswear collection challenges fashion orthodoxy. His burly-boded biker models question our perception of masculinity.

Overleaf: Thom Browne's signature aesthetic, models wear uniformed tailored suits combining two-button jackets, Bermuda shorts and knee-socks. Spring/Summer 2011 menswear show, Paris.

Young men sought to differentiate with the restrictive forms of dress associated with the modes of work their forefathers had done. Self-expression and an individualistic approach to dress would see previous historical notions of style redefined throughout the 1960s and 70s. Activewear would contribute immensely to shaping the future of men's style through the introduction of lifestyle branding and the public promotion of health through sport. Formal, casual, leisure, sports, work, military and business clothing styles are today combined together in an eclectic attempt to redefine the ideologies of fashion. The modern man's wardrobe comprises many different clothing styles, shapes, fabrics, colours and textures forming an eclectic mix of creative ideas for different occasions (workwear, formal-wear, sportswear and casual-wear). No longer is the contemporary male restricted by the social stereotypes of a previous generation. The phenomenon of men's ready-to-wear (after 1980) brought a new perspective; men's fashion found a new language – individualism – liberated through globalised choice and the breaking down of sexual stereotypes. With the rise of new men's fashion journals and magazines such as *The Face* and *I-D*, and the reinvention of established titles such as *Esquire*, *GQ* and *Uomo Vogue*, new avenues were opened. Strict codes of dress are no longer adhered to; advertising and the media have broken the social moulds and helped to redefine the boundaries of how a man wanted to dress. Social acceptance is less of a concern; rebellion has become the way to invigorate and refresh what came before.

Contemporary pattern cutting no longer follows but increasingly defines and contributes to the innovative ideas and trends in men's fashion. What distinguishes today's craft from previous decades is not necessarily the practice or the documented techniques; the human body has remained relatively the same and the required outcomes – clothes – have kept their defining uses. It is the conceptual approach taken by contemporary fashion that has directed the views and practices of pattern cutters and designers alike.

During the 1980s and 90s, Western notions of fashion and pattern cutting took a new direction, away from the previous obsession with body-conscious image and the conventions associated with traditional forms of dress. The influence of a group of pioneering Japanese designers – Issey Miyake, Kenzo Takada, Yohji Yamamoto and Rei Kawakubo – and their sculptural design philosophy brought a new deconstructed / asymmetrical approach to notions of shape. Their garments and thus patterns were minimalist; devoid of most recognisable human features. This new aesthetic revolutionised the relationship between the perceived processes and established approaches to fashion creation of European and American

designers. It is a legacy that has defined contemporary menswear and contributed to new ideas of masculinity.

Breaking free from previous modes of thinking, a new generation of designers has established ways of encapsulating the body through shape. Martin Margiela, Rick Owens, Walter Van Beirendonck, Aitor Throup, Carol Christian Poell and Christopher Raeburn have all appropriated traditional techniques through pattern cutting, using the juxtaposition of functionality and intelligent design to reinvent hybrid genres. Cultural trends no longer appropriate generic garments alone; contemporary menswear is concerned with communicating a personal vision. Patterns have become a medium to bring new ideas into physical constructs; boundaries are redrawn as seams become structural architecture for the body, what was once hidden is now exposed. Clothes can now have an abstract relationship with the anatomy of the wearer; sleeves are turned into voluminous tubes; jackets fold into bags; coats respond to environmental changes by becoming habitable. Technology plays an increasing role within design development; computer-generated patterns, 3D shape profiling, virtual avatars and intelligent textiles continue to shape our consciousness. Questioning our identity will remain the pursuit of contemporary men's design. Centres known for their creative diversity will continue to influence and direct the evolution of the male silhouette: Milan, Paris, Antwerp, London, New York, Tokyo, all act as magnetic generators pulling in creative practitioners who respond to the ever-changing demands of global consumerism.

The future challenges to practising this craft will be the ability to generate innovative products through new vocabularies while conserving elements of the past. With the continuing advance of computer-generated solutions to pattern cutting and the replacement of learning processes that have traditionally been done by hand, the contemporary designer/ pattern cutter has to be able to retain the integrity of their creative pursuit in the face of increasingly powerful market forces. Young designers have become custodians of historical techniques through the appropriation of generic styles which are invested with inherent meanings.

```
Engineered Garments have become one of
the major brands behind the resurgence in
American sportwear. The brand's designer,
Daiki Suzuki,has a conceptual aesthetic
towards design, research, fabric and
manufacturing processes.
```

# CHAPTER ONE
# PREPARATION FOR PATTERN CUTTING

# TOOLS AND EQUIPMENT

The starting point for all pattern making is the acquisition of a good set of tools and an understanding of how to use them. Like any other trade, pattern cutting has its own specialist tools, which have been developed to aid the processes of drawing and measuring. Shown here is a selection of tools that you need to buy. As a beginner, you will not need all of them to start drafting, but most are recommended as you progress through the book.

- **Tape measure** - used to measure the circumference and length of the body. The three that are particularly useful are all dual sided with centimetres and inches: a 150cm / 60" glass fibre-coated vinyl tape will not react to changes in temperature by expanding or shrinking; a 300cm / 120" glass fibre-coated vinyl tape is useful when you are using extremely long lengths of fabric, perhaps when draping fabric on the bias; a 150cm / 60" glass fibre tailor's measure that is encased in metal at one end allows the user to hold it further away from the tip for discreet measuring around the crotch area.

- **Metre rule** - essential for starting the pattern development as it gives an uninterrupted straight line that will be longer than half the length of most human bodies. It is usually made from aluminium or steel.

- **Right-angled ruler** - 60cm x 35cm for drawing angles of 90 degrees. It is usually made from plastic, aluminium or steel.

- **Grading ruler** - 50cm with a 0.5cm grid of vertical and horizontal lines. Used for grading and adding seam allowances to patterns. It is usually made from clear plastic.

- **45-degree set square** - a large set square will help you draw angles for shoulders and darts. Buy one that has a 180-degree range printed on it so that it can double up as a protractor. It is usually made from clear plastic.

- **French curves and pattern masters** - there are many varieties to choose from. Not to be mistaken for the smaller geometry curves, these are designed to mimic the curves of the human body - neckline, armhole, waist shaping and side seams. Buy from a fashion retailer. They are made from clear plastic, aluminium or steel.

- **Hip curve** - designed to replicate the shape from the lower body, it is used to draw side seams on skirts and trousers and also to draw hems. It is usually made from metal, plastic or wood.

- **Notcher** - cuts a small rectangular shape from paper or card and is used for marking seams, ease allowances, pitch points on armholes, zip ends and for pattern alignment. It is usually made from cast metal.

- **Tracing wheel** - used to copy a pattern or garment shape through layers of fabric, card or paper. Can be bought with a wooden or plastic handle that is attached to a circular wheel with pointed needles.

- **Compass** - the best versions have an extendable arm for drawing circles or arcs.

- **Paper scissors** - pattern cutting scissors have been developed with heavy, cast-metal arms for cutting card and paper. This is the tool that you will use the most so it is important to buy a quality pair that will stay sharp for longer than normal scissors.

- **Fabric scissors** - fabric scissors come in a variety of lengths with long, slim blades on cast-metal handles. Never cut paper or card with fabric scissors as this will blunt the blades, making them tear the fabric instead of slicing through it.

- **Scalpel** - used to cut openings in patterns.

- **Eyelet punch or pattern drill** - there are many kinds of pattern drill that cut a small circle from card or paper; some only cut one size of hole while others have changeable heads to cut different sizes. Used to mark dart leg ends, button placement and pocket corners.

- **Awl** - a sharp tool used to mark holes in fabric and card.

- **Pattern hole punch** - cuts a large circular hole through card or paper to allow a pattern hook to be inserted for hanging.

- **Pattern hooks** - these are available in various sizes and are used to hold a complete set of patterns suspended from a rail.

- **Board pins** - used to hold and position patterns when drafting.

- **Dress pins** - used to secure fabric when working on the mannequin or for holding seams during construction. Buy long, industrial-quality pins.

- **Drafter's pencils** - with removable leads in sizes of 0.5 / 0.7/ 0.9 mm for drawing fine to thick lines.

- **Pattern weights** - usually made from flat rectangles of steel with attached handles for holding down patterns or fabric.

- **Manila pattern card, plain, or dot and cross pattern marker paper** - used for development, tracing and for final patterns.

- **Cutting mat**
- **Glue stick**
- **Marker pens in blue, black, green and red - ditto, biros**
- **Highlighter pen**
- **Various types of sticky tape**
- **Unpicker**
- **Pencil sharpener**
- **Eraser**
- **Tailor's chalk and dispenser**

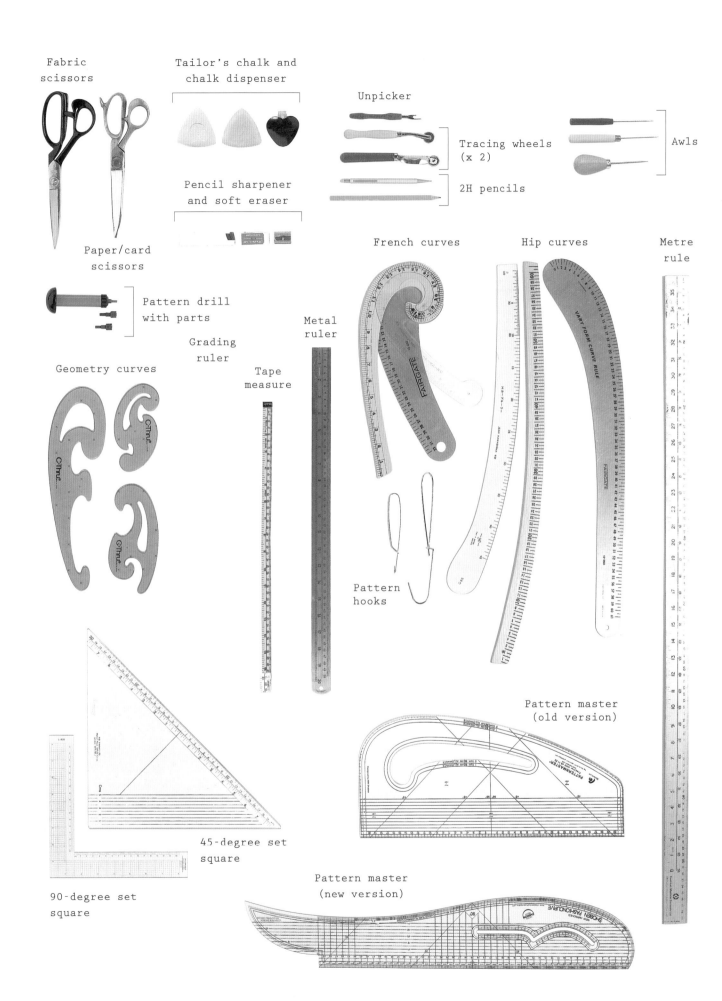

Fabric
scissors

Tailor's chalk and
chalk dispenser

Unpicker

Tracing wheels
(x 2)

Awls

2H pencils

Pencil sharpener
and soft eraser

Paper/card
scissors

French curves

Hip curves

Metre
rule

Pattern drill
with parts

Metal
ruler

Grading
ruler

Geometry curves

Tape
measure

Pattern
hooks

90-degree set
square

45-degree set
square

Pattern master
(old version)

Pattern master
(new version)

# STUDIO PRACTICE

**There are two forms of pattern making that are practised within industry: flat pattern cutting and draping. Both are equally valid routes to the development of silhouettes for garments, and each has their own individual characteristics that will appeal; the first is static and methodical, while the second is more fluid and intuitive. Both are creative and can contribute to a working process during the creation of patterns for a design.**

Flat pattern cutting is a process where the practitioner begins by using a mathematical formula and a size chart to map out a flat shape on paper or card which represents a section of the human body – the chest, arm or leg – in a basic two-dimensional form without any style lines (see page 36). These shapes, known as basic blocks, are used, together with a sketch or technical drawing of the design, to create patterns for a stylised garment through block manipulation.

Draping, also known as modelling or moulage, is a technique in which the practitioner drapes, pins, shapes, gathers and cuts the fabric directly on a model or garment stand. It is usually associated with haute couture. The process does not rely on pre-cut shapes but on the skill of the designer or pattern cutter and his or her understanding of the body. Working directly on the figure allows you to see the proportion of seam lines, panels, pockets, buttons and dart positions almost instantaneously.

Some sections of the garment industry will predominantly use the flat pattern cutting process because it is cheaper and has a shorter lead time between design and the manufacture of the garment ready for wholesale in the ready-to-wear market.

An accomplished and experienced designer or pattern cutter working for a luxury brand or haute couture house will often successfully use a combination of both draping and flat pattern cutting. This method also encourages an understanding of how flat patterns relate to the three-dimensional figure and is often used in teaching environments, too.

Although pattern making can be seen as a stand-alone specialism, it is an integral part of the production system of the modern garment industry. Most fashion brands will employ several in-house pattern cutters who will work hand in hand with the design and marketing teams and the sample machinists to develop the product through from initial concept to finished product in a studio environment. This centralised operational structure is traditional practice within the industry and offers continuity throughout the production chain.

Another commercial practice employed increasingly by many independent fashion labels, who may work within tighter financial restraints, is to outsource most of their development processes. These companies rely heavily on freelance practitioners and garment makers for the production of patterns and samples for their designs.

Key to both methods of working is the use of good communication between each element of the increasingly long production line, particularly if part or parts of that line are out of house or even in different parts of the world.

Outlined below are the two main production line processes you may come across within the industry.

Designer and pattern cutter working on a collection in a studio.

## BESPOKE AND SEMI-BESPOKE PROCESS

Bespoke, or made-to-measure as it is also known, is the production of patterns and garments for individuals made from their personal measurements; each pattern is, therefore, unique. Semi-bespoke is the production of patterns from a set of industry average measurements. The garment is manufactured to a semi-constructed stage before final adjustments are made according to the client's own measurements before finishing.

| Bespoke production chain | Description |
|---|---|
| Design sketches produced | Ideas, styles and fabric are discussed with the client. |
| Measurements taken and recorded | Once the design is chosen, the fabric is purchased and measurements are taken and recorded. |
| Pattern drafted from measurements | Measurements are used to draft basic blocks to the client's size. The block is adapted to the design. |
| Toile cut and sewn | Prototype toile is cut and sewn either from calico or the final fabric. |
| Toile fitted and adjustments made | Modifications are made to the pattern based on the fitting. Toile may be re-cut and a second fitting done before moving to the next stage. |
| Final garment cut and basted for final fitting | Final fabric cut and part assembled through basting. Fit checked on the client with possible adjustments made for proportion. |
| Final garment sewn | Machine sewing and hand finishing done according to characteristics of fabric. |
| Finishing | Buttonholes are sewn and labels attached before final pressing and dispatch. |

Senior male tailor measuring cloth in a shop.

## READY-TO-WEAR OR PRÊT-À-PORTER

Ready-to-wear, or prêt-à-porter as it is also known, is the process of producing garments en masse in a variety of sizes. This process is designed to meet the needs of a broader range of customers in terms of fit and shape. Standard measurements from industry-regulated charts are used, or specific customer data is researched through sales or gathered from external providers to create a standard size profile that fits the demographic of the target market. This mode of production now predominates over bespoke or semi-bespoke as it produces a cheaper product.

| Mass-production chain | Description |
|---|---|
| Trend research collected | Forecasting sites such as Prostyle and WGSN are consulted, previous sales are reviewed and customer profile data is collected. |
| Production / Range planned | The season's themes, looks, colours, silhouettes, fabrics and price points are agreed upon. |
| Design development | Fashion illustrations and technical flats are produced and trade shows visited to research technical advancements and to collect fabrics and trims for moodboards. |
| Designs finalised and specification document developed | Designers and garment technologists meet to produce a specification document that contains all the production information needed for manufacture. Sample fabric and trims are ordered. |
| Patterns outsourced or produced in house | Patterns are developed or adapted from previous generic styles to a sample size. |
| Samples manufactured and fitted | Samples are sewn, usually in final fabrics according to specification sheets. Printing and speciality finishes are outsourced. Samples are fitted and adaptations made. |
| Wholesale orders taken | The collection is either shown to buyers and press through a catwalk show or via private sale meetings. Often external sales agents are appointed. |
| Mass production process begins | Orders are collated into sizes and styles, delivery times are agreed and bulk fabric and trims are ordered. |
| Patterns graded | Pattern blocks are enlarged or reduced from the base sample size either manually or digitally to create a size range that meets customer and regional requirements. |
| Order dispatched to cut, make and trim (CMT) | Fabrics, trims, patterns and samples are sent with the specification document to the manufacturer. |
| Style marker and cutting | Fabric is laid out in volume and the paper pattern marker is made ready for cutting. This sheet of paper shows all the pattern pieces laid out in an arrangement so that as little fabric as possible is wasted. If the fashion company has its own in-house pattern department then a computer-aided pattern design system may be used to generate the marker, allowing the company to control the wastage. Component parts are cut en masse ready for sewing. |

Opposite: A man sews a suit jacket at a factory on the outskirts of Shanghai, China.

| Mass-production chain | Description |
| --- | --- |
| Prepare for sewing | Some styles may need fusing added to component parts before construction. Styles are then sorted into bundles of units depending on construction processes. |
| Sewing | Bundles are dispatched to the factory floor and the production line of machinists. It is very unlikely that a single machinist will sew a garment from start to finish. Teams of machinists usually sew component parts of the garment – collars, pockets – in multiple units. Each component is then passed to another team for assembly. |
| Finishing and pressing | The finishing team will trim threads and attach buttons and details. |
| Quality control and dispatch | Known as QC, this is the end of the production line where garments are measured, and sewing and details are inspected to ensure that a quality standard is upheld and customer returns minimised. The product is sorted into wholesale orders, either by size, colour and / or style, ready to be shipped. |

# MEASURING THE MALE FIGURE

The taking of accurate measurements and the creation of good size charts are vital to ensure that the result of the pattern making process is a garment that fits comfortably. This can only be done with a thorough understanding of human anatomy and the tools used to test those measurements - the garment stand and the fit model.

Body mapping is the act of physically recording the body's surface by taking measurements. These measurements are geometrically mapped out using the basic block methodology to create a shaped template pattern that, when assembled, will mirror the human form. As a continual surface the human body has no boundary lines, unlike those found on a garment. Establishing these boundary lines on the body is the first step in understanding the segmented parts of a pattern. Boundary lines always stay in the same position, no matter how a body grows upwards or outwards. Gaining an understanding of these dividing lines will help you create designs in proportion to the human form.

## MEDIAN PLANE
The median line passes longitudinally through the middle of the body from front to back, dividing it into right and left halves.

## CORONAL PLANE
This is a vertical plane at right angles to the median plane, dividing the body into front (anterior) and back (posterior) portions.

## TRANSVERSE HORIZONTAL PLANES
These lines pass horizontally through the body at right angles to the median and coronal planes, dividing the body into upper and lower portions. The chest plane runs around the largest expanse of the ribcage. The waist plane runs around the centre of the body and the hip plane runs around the widest part of the lower body.

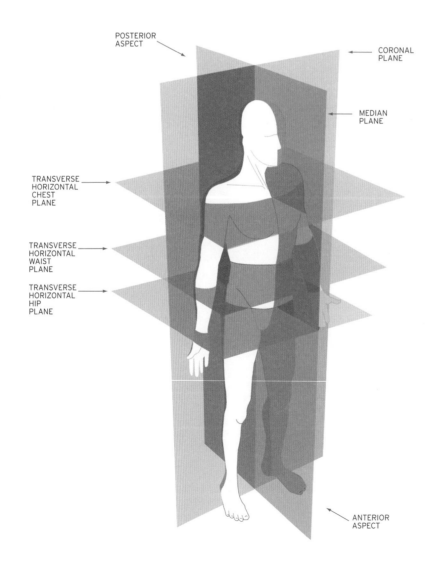

POSTERIOR ASPECT

CORONAL PLANE

MEDIAN PLANE

TRANSVERSE HORIZONTAL CHEST PLANE

TRANSVERSE HORIZONTAL WAIST PLANE

TRANSVERSE HORIZONTAL HIP PLANE

ANTERIOR ASPECT

## LANDMARK POINTS

There are various landmark points on the body that are used when taking measurements. These are extensions of the body mapping above and denote the areas of separation between the parts of the pattern.

**Top of the head or crown** - the highest point of the body
**Centre back neck point** - the protrusion of the seventh vertebra
**Shoulder neck point** - identified by the raised edge of the trapezius muscle
**Centre front neck point** - the hollow where the clavicles meet the sternum
**Shoulder point** - the most lateral aspect of the acromion
**Underarm point** - the position at which the arm joins the body under the arm

**Chest nipple point** - the point at which the nipple protrudes the most
**Elbow point** - the point at which the joint between the humerus, radius and ulna protrudes the most
**Wrist point** - the point at which the hand and wrist bones join the radius and ulna
**Seat protrusion point** - the point at which the buttocks protrude the most
**Knee point** - the middle of the patella

Refer back to the male skeletal form to start to identify the positions of these points within the bone structure. This will help you to pinpoint these landmarks accurately on your model when following the measurement steps below.

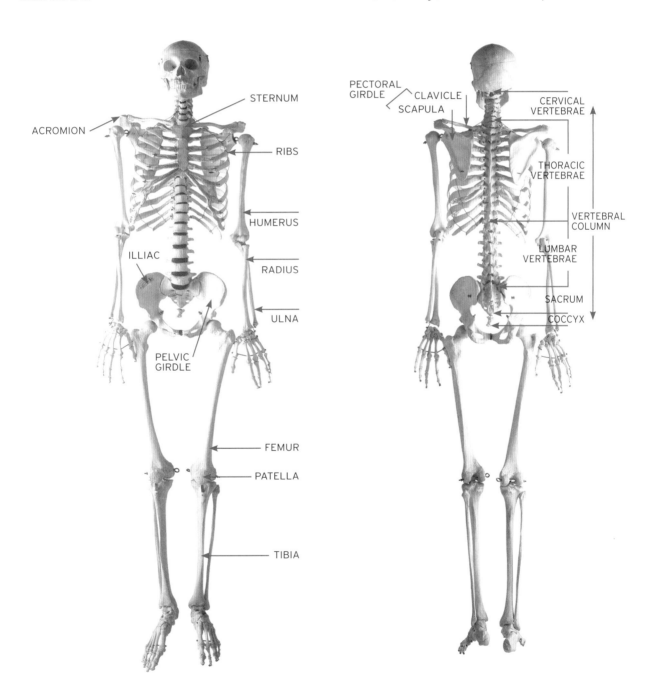

STERNUM

ACROMION

RIBS

HUMERUS

ILLIAC

RADIUS

ULNA

PELVIC GIRDLE

FEMUR

PATELLA

TIBIA

PECTORAL GIRDLE

CLAVICLE

SCAPULA

CERVICAL VERTEBRAE

THORACIC VERTEBRAE

VERTEBRAL COLUMN

LUMBAR VERTEBRAE

SACRUM

COCCYX

# TAKING MEASUREMENTS

The measurement system shown here includes the minimum landmark points needed to reproduce an accurate set of basic pattern blocks for the male figure.

## TOOLS NEEDED TO TAKE ACCURATE BODY MEASUREMENTS

- Anthropometer or a 2-metre pole or piece of wood used to gauge height
- A new cloth or fibre tape measure (cloth tape measures stretch through use, so always use a new one)
- A metre rule or stick
- A set square or right-angled ruler
- Notebook, pencil and chalk
- In order for you to take measurements accurately your fit model should not be wearing any clothes apart from a pair of fitted shorts. Make sure that the shorts are not too tight or they will distort the waistline. Ask your model to stand in an erect position, keeping his eyes looking forward in a horizontal position (so that the head does not tip up or down) with relaxed shoulders and arms falling naturally to the side and palms turned inwards to the body.

**1. Chest circumference** / fig: (A) & (B)
Place the tape around the widest point on the chest, which will be roughly level with the nipple. Make sure the tape is sitting horizontally under the armpits.

**2. (Natural) waist circumference** / fig: (A) & (B)
Place the tape horizontally around the smallest circumference of the torso between the chest and the hips.

**3. Low waist circumference** / fig: (A) & (B)
Place the tape horizontally around the abdomen, 5cm below the natural waist. This additional measurement is used when constructing a trouser block for a more casual style.

**4. Hip (seat) circumference** / fig: (A) & (B)
Place the tape at the greatest buttock protrusion keeping it parallel to the floor when passing over the buttocks.

**5. Back waist length**
(Centre back neck to the natural waist) / fig: (B)
Place the tape at the base of the neck (the last cervical vertebrae) then measure down to the natural waist point. Mark for future measurements.

**6. Centre front waist length**
(Centre front neck to the natural waist) / fig: (A)
Place the tape at the base of the neck at the front (the sternal notch), then measure down to the natural waist point. Mark for future measurements.

**7. Centre back neck to front waist length** / fig: (A) & (B)
Place the tape at the base of the centre back neck (the last cervical vertebra), then measure around the neck and over the shoulder down towards the centre front natural waist point. Mark for future measurements.

**8. Neck base circumference** / fig: (A) & (B)
Place the measure at the base of the back of the neck at the point that you identified earlier. Continue to the shoulder neck point, which can be identified by the raised edge of the trapezius muscle, mark and continue around to the front neck point, which is denoted by a hollow at the top of the chest at the centre front (sternum bone).

**9. Head circumference** / fig: (A) & (B)
Place the tape around the widest part of the head, running above the ears and over the forehead.

**10. Head length** / fig: (A)
Place the tape under the chin point with the head in a vertical position and measure up so that the measurement is taken level with the crown point on the top of the head.

**11. Across back width** / fig: (B)
Measure between the points at which the arms are connected to the body. On a pattern this is between the back pitch points.

**12. Across front width** / fig: (A)
Measure between the points at which the arms are connected to the body, where a crease is formed by the armpit. On a pattern this is between the front pitch points.

**13. Shoulder length** / fig: (A)
Place the tape at the shoulder neck point that you identified previously and measure along the top of the muscle to the shoulder point.

**14. One-piece sleeve length** / fig: (A)
Measure from the shoulder point down the arm and over the elbow to the wrist with the arm hanging naturally but slightly bent. You can also take the underarm measurement in this position by placing the tape 2cm underneath the model's armpit and measuring down to the wrist.

**15. Wrist and hand circumference** / fig: (A) & (B)
Measure around the wrist joint where the bone protrudes. Together with the width of the hand this measurement will help you establish the minimum cuff width. Measure around the widest point of the hand with fingers and thumb held as if the model is putting his arm in a sleeve.

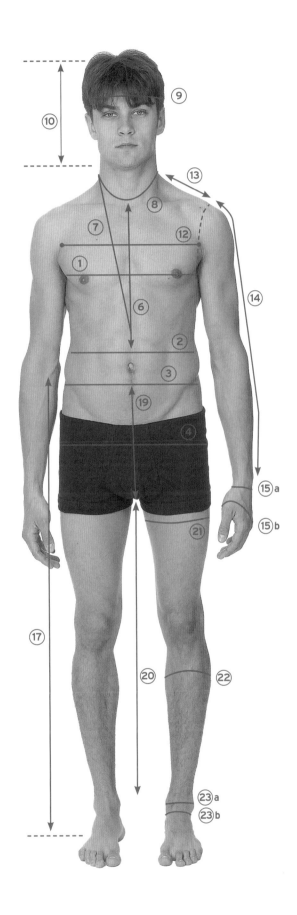

## 16. Centre back neck height from floor / fig: (B)

This measurement will allow you to gauge the proportions of all the other body length measurements and evaluate the silhouette of the garment.

To measure the model's body length accurately use an anthropometer. Ask the model to stand in an erect position with his feet together and arms hanging naturally in relaxed position. Direct the model's head into an upright position where his eyes and ears are on the same horizontal plane.

Lower the arm of the anthropometer down onto the centre back neck point. Take the height reading from the dial on the anthropometer. If you don't have an anthropometer, use a 2-metre pole or a piece of wood against a flat surface. If using a tape measure, make sure it is a new one.

## 17. Low waist to floor length / fig: (A)

Place the tape on the side of the body at the low waistline and measure down vertically to the floor.

## 18. Natural waist to hip length / fig: (B)

Place the tape at the natural waistline, on the side or the side back, then measure down to the hip line.

## 19. Crotch length (Centre front and centre back) / fig: (A) & (B)

Place the tape on the low waistline at the centre front. Pass between the lowest part of the crotch and up between the buttocks to the low waistline on the centre back. This measurement can also be separated into front rise and back rise.

## 20. Inside leg length / fig: (A)

Place the tape end in a central position under the crotch, then measure down the inside of the leg to the ankle.

## 21. Thigh circumference / fig: (A) & (B)

Place the tape around the widest point on the leg, 5cm below the crotch. Keep the tape parallel to the floor.

## 22. Calf circumference / fig: (A) & (B)

Place the tape around the widest point of the lower leg below the knee line. Keep the tape parallel to the floor.

## 23. Ankle and heel-foot circumference / fig: (A), (B) & (C)

Ankle - measure around the narrowest point (the medial malleolus) above the ankle. Keep the tape parallel to the floor.
Heel foot - measure around the heel passing the tape measure over the widest part (the dorsal juncture) of the foot at a 45-degree angle to the floor.

## 24. Seat depth / fig: (C)

Ask your model to sit upright with his knees at a right angle to his torso. Place the tape on the low waistline at the side and measure down vertically to the seated buttocks.

**FIGURE B**

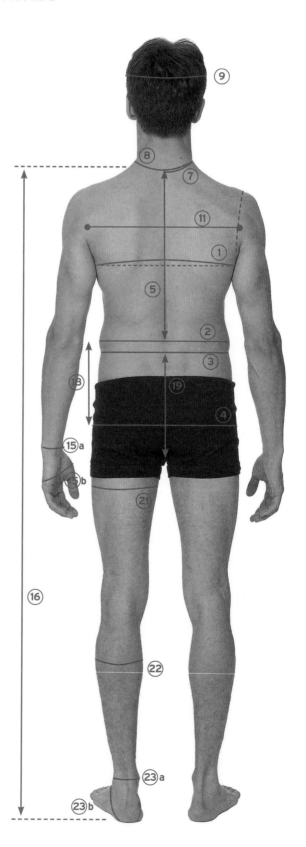

**FIGURE C**

The measurement model pictured in figures (A), (B) and (C) is a professional model working within the fashion industry. He was selected because he has an industry-endorsed average body shape for a size 38″ (96cm) chest. The summary of the model's measurements provided below was recorded by a TC2 3D Body Measurement Scanner.

**Use the information below to make comparisons with your fit model's measurements.**

| | |
|---|---|
| 1 Chest circumference | 96cm |
| 2 (Natural) waist circumference | 84cm |
| 3 Low waist circumference (5cm below natural) | 85cm |
| 4 Hip (seat) circumference | 95cm |
| 5 Centre back neck to natural waist length | 45cm |
| 6 Centre front neck to natural waist length | 40cm |
| 7 Centre back neck to front waist length | 56.5cm |
| 8 Neck base circumference | 39.5cm |
| 9 Head circumference | 58cm |
| 10 Head length | 24cm |
| 11 Across back width | 39cm |
| 12 Across front width | 36cm |
| 13 Shoulder length | 15.5cm |
| 14 One-piece sleeve length | 63cm |
| 15a Wrist circumference | 17cm |
| b Hand circumference | 25cm |
| 16 Back neck height from floor | 153.5cm |
| 17 Low waist to floor length | 103.4cm |
| 18 Natural waist to hip length | 21cm |
| 19a Front crotch length (natural waist) | 36.5cm |
| b Back crotch length (natural waist) | 37.5cm |
| 20 Inside leg length (crotch to ankle) | 73.5cm |
| 21 Thigh circumference | 55.5cm |
| 22 Calf circumference | 36cm |
| 23a Ankle circumference | 24.8cm |
| b Heel-foot circumference | 32.5cm |
| 24 Seat depth | 31.5cm |

# MANNEQUINS

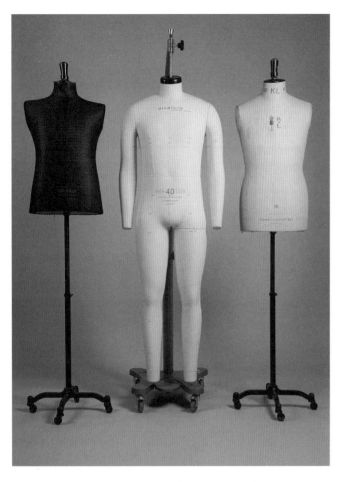

Fit mannequins or forms are used in the clothing industry for developing patterns and for fitting toiles and garments. Choosing the right one is important when establishing your size range. Modelled to represent the dimensions of the human body, they are made from fibreglass with a covering of foam and linen. They can be bought in many sizes and in different body configurations (three-quarter, full- or half-body, with or without arms).

Standard forms are three-quarter length, finishing below the hip. They are generally sold without arms and are mounted on a central metal adjustable pole, with or without wheels. These are the perfect starting point when building up a studio as you can use one to fit and assess patterns, toiles and garment silhouettes during range development. Full-body versions are available and generally hang on a pole from the crown point. They are available with removable arms and legs and collapsible shoulders.

Recent advances in 3D body scanning technology have seen the development of a new, technically superior form with an accurate body shape that is truly representative of age and customer profile. Produced from sizing data collected through surveys, these forms can be manufactured to a high level of

accuracy with collapsible shoulders, collapsible hips, removable arms and a soft abdomen. They also have measurement lines incorporated and come with an adjustable stand.

If your mannequin comes without any measurement lines, use seam tape to mark them before use. This will help you in your understanding of pattern construction as the front and back blocks represent the segmented parts of the human body. Attach the seam tape with pins or sew the landmark lines to the linen – centre front and back, neckline circumference, chest circumference, waist circumference, hip circumference, side seams, shoulder seams and armholes. To find these positions use your tape measure to divide the circumferences and lengths of the form.

Above: The evolution in the shape of the fit mannequin from three different manufacturers, all produced to a size 40". Left to right: Siegel & Stockman tailor's dummy, France, c.1960; Alvanon full-body form created using bodyscan data, US, 2005; Kennett & Lindsell's British body shape range, UK, 1980.

# FIT MODELS

When considering and selecting a fit model around which to develop a collection, it is important to identify your customer's silhouette or normal body shape first. This can be achieved by undertaking comparative research among your competitors. Take photos and collect tearsheets from magazines or from street style blogs. This information will help you identify what your consumer may look like and thus help you to select the best fit model. Remember that fashion models on the catwalk are not real customers; they are marketing tools used to project the image of the brand.

It is wise to have several fit models reflecting different male silhouettes. Once you have recruited your fit models it is important to record certain fundamental elements, such as posture, weight, eating habits and exercise routines. This will help you to make accurate judgements in future fitting sessions; if your model's shape changes you can avoid unnecessary corrections and adjustments to samples and patterns.

## POSTURE AND DROP

Posture and drop are also important factors when selecting a fit model. Unlike the mannequin, the human body may not be symmetrical.

### Posture

Posture refers to the physical manner in which the body frame is carried. Incorrect posture can affect the balance of patterns, resulting in numerous figure adjustments.

Men's ready-to-wear has traditionally offered a wider range of fitting groups with short, medium and tall heights accommodated. Increasingly retailers have categorised these into five general silhouettes:

- **Slim** - straight back with low muscle definition on chest, abdomen and lower body;
- **Regular / normal** - a flat chest and stomach with a straight back;
- **Large / athletic** - a pronounced chest with a straight back and enlarged muscle definition;
- **Stocky** - rounded shoulders with a curved back and a slightly protruding stomach and chest;
- **Obese** - a corpulent abdominal area that results in stooped shoulders and a curved back.

As your product may appeal to one or more of these figure types it is important that you can identify these variations, giving you the ability to make corrections to your patterns and thus achieve a better fitting garment for your customer.

The following are some of the most common posture variations that will also affect the balance of a garment.

| |
|---|
| **Normal**  The head and neck are held centrally over the shoulders, which sit back and down. The chest is slightly lifted above a taut stomach. Arms hang naturally with elbows bent forward over a straight back. |
| **Erect** The chest is lifted, which creates an arched upper back, thus shortening the upper back length and increasing the front chest length from the prominence of the chest to base of the neck. |
| **Rounded / slumped back** The head is slumped forward with curved shoulders and a rounded upper back and hollow chest, which leads to a narrow chest with increased back length and width. |
| **Sloped or square shoulders** Sloping shoulders will require an increase in the pitch of the shoulder slope from the armhole, while square shoulders will need a decrease in the pitch. |

### Drop

Drop is the term used to describe the ratio between the circumference of the chest and that of the waist. Identifying this will help you to visualise the silhouette of the figure: a larger waist than chest will give you a triangular silhouette; a waist that is the same as the chest will lead to a rectangular silhouette.

Designer Yohji Yamamoto conducting a fit session as he prepares for his Spring 2011 menswear show.

# SIZE CHARTS

All the size charts provided are to create proportionally balanced patterns, which would be adjusted to the individual requirements during the sampling process.

**SAMPLE CHINESE BODY SIZE CHART**

| Code | Body Measurements | | | | | | | | | | | Grade |
|------|-------------------|------|------|------|------|------|------|------|------|------|------|------|
| 1 | Chest circumference | 72 | 76 | 80 | 84 | 88 | 92 | 96 | 100 | 104 | 108 | 4 |
| 2 | (Natural) waist circumference | 62 | 66 | 70 | 74 | 78 | 82 | 86 | 90 | 94 | 98 | 4 |
| 3 | Low waist circumference | 65 | 69 | 73 | 77 | 81 | 85 | 89 | 93 | 97 | 101 | 4 |
| 4 | Hip (seat) circumference | 71 | 75 | 79 | 83 | 87 | 91 | 95 | 99 | 103 | 107 | 4 |
| 5 | Back waist length | 42.2 | 42.5 | 42.8 | 43.1 | 43.4 | 43.7 | 44 | 44.3 | 44.6 | 44.9 | 0.3 |
| 6 | Centre front waist length | 39.2 | 39.5 | 39.8 | 40.1 | 40.4 | 40.7 | 41 | 41.3 | 41.6 | 41.9 | 0.3 |
| 7 | Front waist from centre back neck | 56 | 57 | 58 | 59 | 60 | 61 | 62 | 63 | 64 | 65 | 1 |
| 8 | Neck base circumference | 37 | 38 | 39 | 40 | 41 | 42 | 43 | 44 | 45 | 46 | 1 |
| 9 | Head circumference | 56.2 | 56.5 | 56.8 | 57.1 | 57.4 | 57.7 | 58 | 58.3 | 58.6 | 58.9 | 0.3 |
| 10 | Head length | 24 | 24.2 | 24.4 | 24.6 | 24.8 | 25 | 25.2 | 25.4 | 25.6 | 25.8 | 0.2 |
| 11 | Across back width | 36 | 37 | 38 | 39 | 40 | 41 | 42 | 43 | 44 | 45 | 1 |
| 12 | Across front width | 32 | 33 | 34 | 35 | 36 | 37 | 38 | 39 | 40 | 41 | 1 |
| 13 | Shoulder length | 13.2 | 13.5 | 13.8 | 14.1 | 14.4 | 14.7 | 15 | 15.3 | 15.6 | 15.9 | 0.3 |
| 14 | One-piece sleeve length | 58 | 58 | 58 | 58 | 58 | 58 | 58 | 58 | 58 | 58 | 0 |
| 15 a | Wrist circumference | 14.8 | 15 | 15.2 | 15.4 | 15.6 | 15.8 | 16 | 16.2 | 16.4 | 16.6 | 0.2 |
| 15 b | Hand circumference | 20.8 | 21 | 21.2 | 21.4 | 21.6 | 21.8 | 22 | 22.2 | 22.4 | 22.6 | 0.2 |
| 16 | Body length | 125.8 | 128.2 | 130.6 | 133 | 135.4 | 137.8 | 140.2 | 142.6 | 145 | 147.4 | 2.4 |
| 17 | Low waist to floor length | 97.8 | 98 | 98.2 | 98.4 | 98.6 | 98.8 | 99 | 99.2 | 99.4 | 99.6 | 0.2 |
| 18 | Low waist to hip length | 18 | 18 | 18 | 18 | 18 | 18 | 18 | 18 | 18 | 18 | 0 |
| 19 a | Front crotch length | 35.3 | 35.5 | 35.7 | 35.9 | 36.1 | 36.3 | 36.5 | 36.7 | 36.9 | 37.1 | 0.2 |
| 19 b | Back crotch length | 33.9 | 34.5 | 35.1 | 35.7 | 36.3 | 36.9 | 37.5 | 38.1 | 38.7 | 39.3 | 0.6 |
| 20 | Inside leg length | 69.4 | 70 | 70.6 | 71.2 | 71.8 | 72.4 | 73 | 73.6 | 74.2 | 74.8 | 0.6 |
| 21 | Thigh circumference | 37.2 | 39 | 40.8 | 42.6 | 44.4 | 46.2 | 48 | 49.8 | 51.6 | 53.4 | 1.8 |
| 22 | Calf circumference | 31.6 | 32.5 | 33.4 | 34.3 | 35.2 | 36.1 | 37 | 37.9 | 38.8 | 39.7 | 0.9 |
| 23 a | Ankle circumference | 22.2 | 22.5 | 22.8 | 23.1 | 23.4 | 23.7 | 24 | 24.3 | 24.6 | 24.9 | 0.3 |
| 23 b | Heel-foot circumference | 30.2 | 30.5 | 30.8 | 31.1 | 31.4 | 31.7 | 32 | 32.3 | 32.6 | 32.9 | 0.3 |
| 24 | Seat depth | 31 | 31 | 31 | 31 | 31 | 31 | 31 | 31 | 31 | 31 | 0 |

## SAMPLE US BODY SIZE CHART

| Code | Body Measurements | 34" | 36" | 38" | 40" | 42" | 44" | Grade |
|---|---|---|---|---|---|---|---|---|
| 1 | Chest circumference | 84.9 | 90.7 | 96.5 | 102.3 | 108.1 | 113.9 | 5.8 |
| 2 | (Natural) waist circumference | 69.7 | 75.5 | 81.3 | 87.1 | 92.9 | 98.7 | 5.8 |
| 3 | Low waist circumference | 72.2 | 78.0 | 83.8 | 89.6 | 95.4 | 101.2 | 5.8 |
| 4 | Hip (seat) circumference | 84.9 | 90.7 | 96.5 | 102.3 | 108.1 | 113.9 | 5.8 |
| 5 | Centre back neck to natural waist length | 48.9 | 49.2 | 49.5 | 49.8 | 50.1 | 50.5 | 0.32 |
| 6 | Centre front neck to natural waist length | 44.8 | 45.8 | 46.7 | 47.7 | 48.6 | 49.6 | 0.95 |
| 7 | Centre back neck to front waist length | 53.5 | 54.5 | 55.5 | 56.5 | 57.5 | 58.5 | 1 |
| 8 | Neck base circumference | 35.6 | 36.8 | 38.1 | 39.4 | 40.6 | 41.9 | 1.27 |
| 9 | Head circumference | 56.4 | 56.7 | 57.0 | 57.3 | 57.6 | 57.9 | 0.3 |
| 10 | Head length | 25.1 | 25.3 | 25.5 | 25.7 | 25.9 | 26.1 | 0.2 |
| 11 | Across back width | 38 | 39 | 40 | 41 | 42 | 43 | 1 |
| 12 | Across front width | 36 | 37 | 38 | 39 | 40 | 41 | 1 |
| 13 | Shoulder length | 15.3 | 15.6 | 15.9 | 16.2 | 16.5 | 16.9 | 0.32 |
| 14 | One-piece sleeve length | 62.6 | 62.9 | 63.2 | 63.5 | 63.8 | 64.2 | 0.32 |
| 15 a | Wrist circumference | 16.5 | 17.2 | 17.8 | 18.4 | 19.1 | 19.7 | 0.64 |
| 15 b | Hand circumference | 21.6 | 21.8 | 22.0 | 22.2 | 22.4 | 22.6 | 0.2 |
| 16 | Back neck height from floor | 160.5 | 160.7 | 160.9 | 161.1 | 161.3 | 161.5 | 0.2 |
| 17 | Low waist to floor length | 105.8 | 106.1 | 106.4 | 106.7 | 107 | 107.4 | 0.32 |
| 18 | Natural waist to hip length | 20 | 20 | 20 | 20 | 20 | 20 | 0 |
| 19 a | Front crotch length | 32.5 | 33.4 | 34.3 | 35.2 | 36.1 | 37 | 0.9 |
| 19 b | Back crotch length | 34.6 | 35.5 | 36.4 | 37.3 | 38.2 | 39.1 | 0.9 |
| 20 | Inside leg length | 80.5 | 80.9 | 81.3 | 81.7 | 82.1 | 82.5 | 0.4 |
| 21 | Thigh circumference | 53.4 | 55.9 | 58.4 | 60.9 | 63.4 | 66.0 | 2.52 |
| 22 | Calf circumference | 34.6 | 35.6 | 36.5 | 37.5 | 38.4 | 39.4 | 0.95 |
| 23 a | Ankle circumference | 21.3 | 22.1 | 22.9 | 23.7 | 24.5 | 25.3 | 0.79 |
| 23 b | Heel-foot circumference | 32.4 | 32.7 | 33.0 | 33.3 | 33.6 | 33.9 | 0.3 |
| 24 | Seat depth | 28.0 | 28.0 | 28.0 | 28.0 | 28.0 | 28.0 | 0 |

## SAMPLE EUROPEAN BODY SIZE CHART

| Code | Body Measurements | EU34 | EU36 | EU38 | EU40 | EU42 | EU44 | Grade |
|---|---|---|---|---|---|---|---|---|
| 1 | Chest circumference | 88 | 92 | 96 | 100 | 104 | 108 | 4 |
| 2 | (Natural) waist circumference | 72 | 76 | 80 | 84 | 88 | 92 | 4 |
| 3 | Low waist circumference | 76 | 80 | 84 | 88 | 92 | 96 | 4 |
| 4 | Hip (seat) circumference | 90 | 94 | 98 | 102 | 106 | 110 | 4 |
| 5 | Centre back neck to natural waist length | 44.1 | 44.4 | 44.7 | 45 | 45.3 | 45.6 | 0.3 |
| 6 | Centre front neck to natural waist length | 39.9 | 40.2 | 40.5 | 40.8 | 41.1 | 41.4 | 0.3 |
| 7 | Centre back neck to front waist length | 55.1 | 56.1 | 57.1 | 58.1 | 59.1 | 60.1 | 1 |
| 8 | Neck base circumference | 38 | 39 | 40 | 41 | 42 | 43 | 1 |
| 9 | Head circumference | 56.7 | 57 | 57.3 | 57.6 | 57.9 | 58.2 | 0.3 |
| 10 | Head length | 24.8 | 25 | 25.2 | 25.4 | 25.6 | 25.8 | 0.2 |
| 11 | Across back width | 37 | 38 | 39 | 40 | 41 | 42 | 1 |
| 12 | Across front width | 32 | 33 | 34 | 35 | 36 | 37 | 1 |
| 13 | Shoulder length | 13.7 | 14 | 14.3 | 14.6 | 14.9 | 15.2 | 0.3 |
| 14 | One-piece sleeve length | 64 | 64 | 64 | 64 | 64 | 64 | 0 |
| 15 a | Wrist circumference | 17.2 | 17.4 | 17.6 | 17.8 | 18 | 18.2 | 0.2 |
| 15 b | Hand circumference | 21.6 | 21.8 | 22 | 22.2 | 22.4 | 22.6 | 0.2 |
| 16 | Back neck height from floor | 154.4 | 154.6 | 154.8 | 155 | 155.2 | 155.4 | 0.2 |
| 17 | Low waist to floor length | 111.3 | 111.5 | 111.7 | 111.9 | 112.1 | 112.3 | 0.2 |
| 18 | Natural waist to hip length | 20 | 20 | 20 | 20 | 20 | 20 | 0 |
| 19 a | Front crotch length | 25.9 | 26.7 | 27.5 | 28.3 | 29.1 | 29.9 | 0.8 |
| 19 b | Back crotch length | 29.5 | 30.3 | 31.1 | 31.9 | 32.7 | 33.5 | 0.8 |
| 20 | Inside leg length | 83.4 | 83.8 | 84.2 | 84.6 | 85 | 85.4 | 0.4 |
| 21 | Thigh circumference | 52.7 | 54.5 | 56.3 | 58.1 | 59.9 | 61.7 | 1.8 |
| 22 | Calf circumference | 35.1 | 36 | 36.9 | 37.8 | 38.7 | 39.6 | 0.9 |
| 23 a | Ankle circumference | 24.4 | 24.7 | 25 | 25.3 | 25.6 | 25.9 | 0.3 |
| 23 b | Heel-foot circumference | 32.4 | 32.7 | 33 | 33.3 | 33.6 | 33.9 | 0.3 |
| 24 | Seat depth | 30" | 30" | 30" | 30" | 30" | 30" | 0 |

CHAPTER TWO

# THE PATTERN CUTTING PROCESS

# THE DEVELOPMENT OF THE DESIGN

There are five stages in the development of a design in pattern cutting: the basic block pattern, the master plan or pattern, the design development pattern, the designer pattern from which the toiles are cut and, finally, the production pattern.

**How pattern blocks relate to the body**

The boundary lines of the basic pattern blocks - bodice, sleeve, trouser - and their alignment to the male figure. Use this template to assist you in your design development when determining proportional placement of style features on your silhouette.

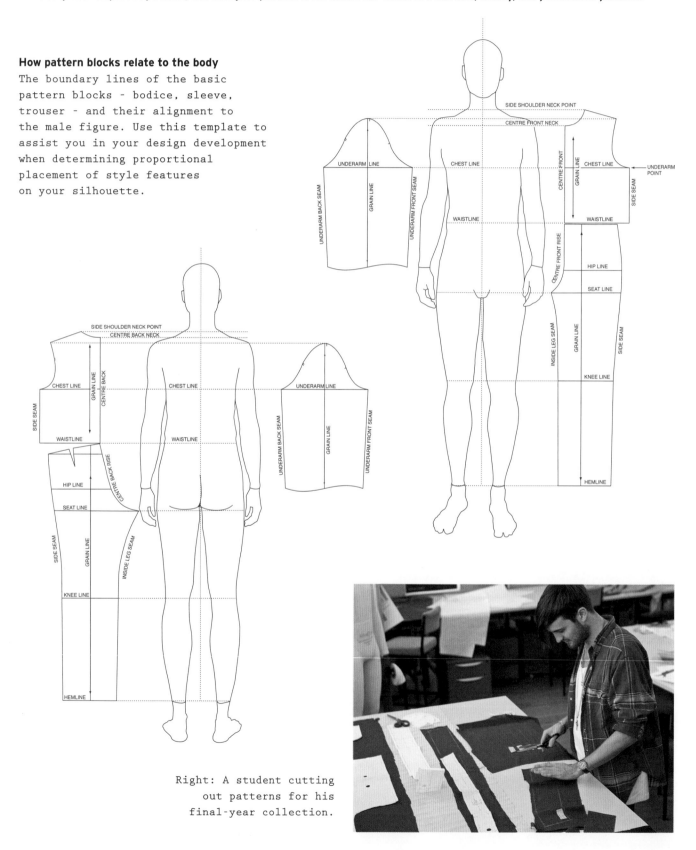

Right: A student cutting out patterns for his final-year collection.

## THE BASIC BLOCK

When developing any pattern, the first stage is to create a basic block. Drafted from a size chart or from the company's fit model's measurements, these patterns offer only the basic pattern shape, broadly following the contours of the body. For menswear the following basic blocks are usually needed:

- Basic body block, consists of a front and a back body shape
- Basic sleeve block, which can be one or two piece
- Basic trouser block, which consists of a front and back leg shape

All patterns in the book are based on these three basic blocks (see pp. 40-47). Once the basic block has been created, it is made up as a toile and fitted. After any necessary adjustments are made, the block is then cut from heavy card or thin plastic with no seam allowance.

The exception to the rule is the tailored two-piece sleeve, which is drafted direct with no block used (see Trench coat pp. 244-45).

## THE MASTER PLAN OR PATTERN

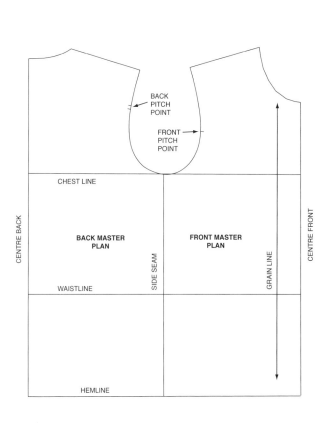

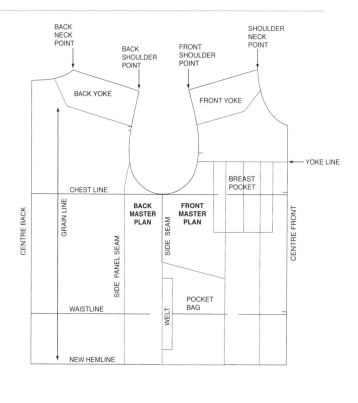

A master plan for pattern development is, like an architectural blueprint, the starting point for any design. The master plan begins from the basic pattern blocks that hold no design features. It allows visual pattern planning and design details can be investigated for positioning or depth before the basic blocks are adapted.

Start each pattern by selecting the appropriate block or blocks from which you can then create a master plan; a jacket design, for example, might start with both the basic block and the sleeve block.

The master plan (above left) is created by tracing around the shape of the block onto pattern drafting paper following the instructions on pages 48-49. The style details of the design, such as yokes, style lines, darts and pockets, are then drawn onto the master plan (above right).

Most master plans are traced from half of the block, and one side of the pattern is then developed before being copied, or mirrored, to create the other side of the pattern piece (see p. 50). This saves time in the pattern making process and serves to eliminate possible errors in duplicating design features from one side of the pattern to the other. The human body is generally symmetrical and, therefore, shape and silhouette development need only be done to one half of the body if the design is balanced. Even if the design is asymmetric, drafting one half of the pattern and then copying over the drafted shape to create the other side before working on the full front or back body pattern is a quick way to achieve the desired style.

Pattern shapes are then traced off the master plan, which is never cut but instead left intact for reference, serving as a blueprint and record of the pattern development.

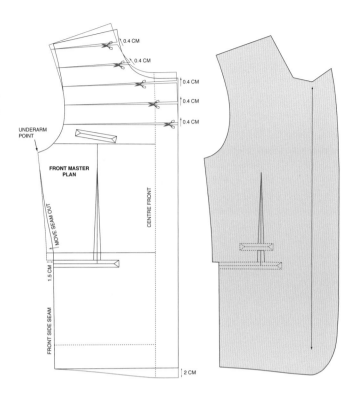

## DESIGN DEVELOPMENT PATTERNS

While developing the pattern, it may be necessary to trace off shapes from the master plan for further development – these are called design development patterns. Complicated design features may need to be slashed and spread (see p.56) to add fullness or pleats, or panel shapes may need to be opened up through pivoting techniques (see p.56) to achieve cylindrical silhouettes on the final pattern. When tracing the pattern shapes from the master plan all marks made on the master plan, such as notches or seam allowance, should also be transferred to the development pattern. Once the pattern shapes have been developed, these development patterns can then be taped to another piece of paper before the designer pattern is traced off.

## DESIGNER PATTERNS

The pattern shapes may be either traced directly from the master plan or from design development patterns onto pattern cutting paper to create the designer pattern. The designer pattern is then used to create a toile, sample or test garment for fitting prior to production.

At this stage patterns that have been designed in half, and that need to be created as shapes with a left-, and right-hand side, are copied or mirrored. Annotation is also added, such as grain lines, notches and drill holes for darts, together with seam allowances (see pp. 50–51).

In this book designer patterns are shown in blue; patterns for linings are shown in pink.

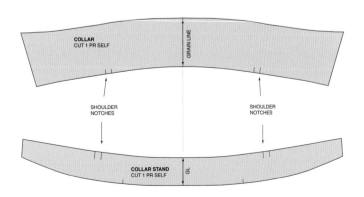

## PRODUCTION PATTERNS

Once the toile or sample garment has been approved the production patterns are traced from the designer patterns. These are then graded (see pp. 52-53) and used for mass garment manufacture. They are cut from card with all annotations added. Every part of the garment will have a corresponding pattern piece.

### Left and right patterns
In this book, all the master plans and pattern developments start with the pattern shape for the right-hand side of the garment as you would see it if you were the wearer, and this is how all the patterns are labelled. If you are looking at the pattern, or a pair of patterns, from the front, the right pattern would be on the left and vice versa.

Left: Production patterns.

Below: A woman uses a band blade to cut multiple garment pieces.

# BASIC BODY BLOCK

The method introduced here is a guide to developing the basic men's body block with no annotation or seam allowances. All the measurements given are an approximation of a UK standard size 38 (chest circumference 96cm plus 12cm full body garment ease = 108cm), which is generally regarded as a medium in the industry. The half front body block is developed on top of the half back body block and will need to be traced off and mirrored over separately before following the pattern adaptations in subsequent chapters. These blocks will serve as a starting point for all the drafts in this book (except trousers) or for your own designs. You can also use measurements from the size charts on pages 32-33 to make the block in a different size to fit your model or male mannequin.

**Measurements used for this size 38 block**
Chest circumference = 96cm
Full garment ease = 12cm

Half chest circumference = 48cm
Half ease = 6cm
Quarter chest circumference = 24cm
Quarter ease = 3cm

**Armhole (scye) depth**
Small = 21cm; Medium = 22cm; Large = 23cm; X-large = 24cm
(grade increment = 1cm)

**Measurements needed to draft block**
Quarter chest circumference = 24cm
Armhole (scye) depth = 22cm
Centre back neck to waist = 45.5cm
Waist to hip = 20cm
Garment length = 65.5cm
Half across back measurement = 20cm
Neck base circumference = 39cm

## STEP 1

### DEVELOPING THE BASIC BODY BLOCK FRAME

- Cut a large piece of drafting paper slightly longer than the length of your torso or fit model.
- Using a metre ruler, draw a vertical line down the left-hand side of your drafting paper; mark at the top of this line and label (0).
- From (0) measure down 2cm, mark and label (1). This is the centre back neck point.
- From (1) measure down 22cm (armhole depth) mark and label (2). This is a variable measurement dependent on the figure type and arm girth.
- From (1) measure down 45.5cm (back neck to waist), mark and label (3).
- From (1) measure down 65.5cm (garment length), mark and label (4). The garment length is a variable measurement dependent on the silhouette you want to create. In this instance, it is determined by adding the centre back neck to back waist measurement (45.5cm) to the waist to hip measurement (20cm)
- From (2) square across a quarter of the chest measurement plus a quarter of the garment ease 27cm; mark and label (5) (chest line).
- Repeat this from (0): square across a quarter of the chest measurement plus a quarter of the garment ease 27cm; mark and label (6).
- From (3) square across a quarter of the chest measurement plus quarter the garment ease 27cm; mark and label (7) (waistline). From (4) square across a quarter of the chest measurement plus quarter the garment ease 27cm; mark and label (8) (hip line).
- Join points (6) (5) (7) and (8) with a straight line; this will become your side seam.
- From (1) square out a fifth of the neck base circumference plus 0.7cm = 8.5cm; mark and label (9).

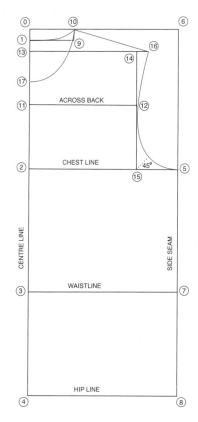

- From (9) square up 2cm and label (10). Using a French curve, draw in the back neckline from (10) to (1).
- The measurement (1) to (11) is half the measurement (1) to (2) = 11cm; mark and label (11).
- Square out from (11) half the across back measurement 20cm; mark and label (12). This is a variable measurement and 1-2cm of ease may need to be added depending on the amount of ease added to the chest circumference. If the armhole shape is too deep or flat at the underarm, add

ease to the across back measurement; this will narrow the underarm and extend the shoulder length.

- From (1) square down an eighth of the armhole depth minus 0.75cm (2cm); mark and label (13).
- From (13) square across the same measurement from (11) to (12) half the across back measurement plus ease if needed; mark and label (14).
- From (14) square down through (12) until you reach the line (2) to (5); mark and label (15).
- At (14) square out 1.8cm, mark and label (16); this is your front and back shoulder point. Draw a line from (10) front and

back shoulder neck point to (16); this is your front and back shoulder seam.
- From (15) at a 45-degree angle measure out 3cm; mark.
- Draw in the armhole shape from (16) using the whole French curve, draw a line that passes through (12), continuing down to pass through the mark you made from (15) to finish at (5). This is the front and back armhole.
- From (1) measure down a fifth of the neck base circumference minus 0.8cm (7cm), mark and label (17). Using the cylindrical part of a French curve draw a line from (10) to (17). This is the front neckline.

## STEP 2
### TRACING OFF THE FRONT AND BACK BLOCKS

- Cut a large piece of drafting paper slightly longer than the block you have just developed and twice the width.
- Draw a vertical line down the centre of the piece of paper longer than the body block. This will be the side seam line for the front and back body blocks once traced.
- Place the new paper over the master pattern you have just drafted, aligning the side seams together. To the left-hand side trace the body block off with the back neckline from the master pattern. Turn over the piece of paper so that the back body block is now aligned to the right side of the seam line.
- Trace around the same body block, drawing in the front neckline. Turn over the paper and retrace around the

front body block so that you have both sides of the body block marked on one side.
- Mark the back and front pitch points on the body blocks you have just traced, measure up 11cm from (15) on the back body block where it intersects the back armhole line. Make two marks and label *back pitch point*.
- Measure up 8cm from (15) on the front body block where it intersects the front armhole line. Mark and label *front pitch point*.

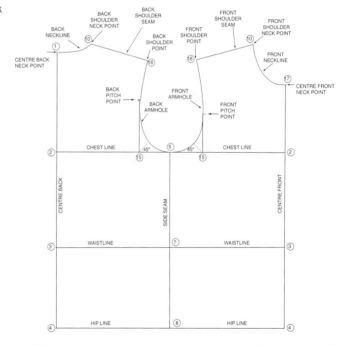

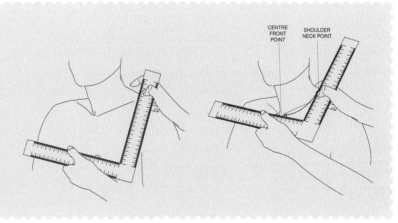

### Calculating the width and depth of the front neckline

To measure the position of the front shoulder neck point and the centre front neckpoint, through which to draw the front neckline, hold a right-angled ruler against the neck of your fit model or mannequin, keeping it horizontal to the ground. This will give you the depth of the CF neck.

# BASIC SLEEVE BLOCK

The method introduced here is a guide to developing the basic men's sleeve block with no annotation or style lines. All the measurements given here are for a sample size 38". This block will serve as a starting point for all the drafts in this book, or for your own designs. You can also use measurements from the size charts on pages 32–33 to make the block in a different size, or use your own measurements taken from your fit model or male mannequin.

**Measurements used for this sleeve block, corresponding to a size 38" body block**

Armhole = 49cm + 2.5cm ease = 51.5cm
Sleeve length to wrist = 70cm
Crown point to elbow length = 41cm
Upper biceps circumference = 35.5cm

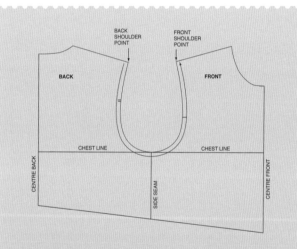

**Taking the armhole measurement from the basic body block**

The armhole measurement needs to be taken from your basic body block. Place a tape measure at the back shoulder point and walk it round the curve up to the front shoulder point.

If you are developing your basic blocks to your own measurements, just replace the armhole measurement above with the one you have taken.

STEP 1
## DEVELOPING THE BASIC SLEEVE BLOCK

- Cut a large piece of drafting paper slightly longer than the length of your sleeve measurement or the arm length of your fit model.
- Using a metre rule, draw a vertical line down the left-hand side of the drafting paper; make a mark at the top of this line and label it (1). This is the *back underarm seam*.
- From (1) square across 35.5cm to the right (the circumference of the biceps); make a mark and label it (3).
- From (1) square down 70cm (the length of the sleeve); make a mark and label it (2). Square across from (2) and down from (3) to create a rectangle.
- Divide the width of the rectangle vertically into four narrower equal-sized rectangles, naming the lines between them, from the left, *back line*, *centre line* and *front line*. Label the long side of the rectangle on the right-hand side *front underarm seam*. Label the top of the centre line (4).
- From (1) measure down one third of the armhole measurement – 17.1cm – which is the height of the sleeve head; make a mark and label it (5). This is the *back underarm point*. Square across to intersect the front underarm seam from (3); make a mark and label it (6). This is the *front underarm point*. The line you have drawn is the *underarm line*. Label the point where this line intersects the *back line* as (7) and the *front line* as (8).
- From (7) measure up 10cm (one sixth of the armhole measurement of 8.5cm + 1.5cm = 10cm); draw a notch and label it (A). This is the *back pitch point*.
- From (8), measure up 8.5cm (one sixth of the armhole measurement); draw a notch and label it (B). This is the *front pitch point*.

**Shape of the armhole**

The front pitch point is lower than the back pitch point to allow for the deeper curve at the front of the sleeve. This accommodates the shape of the sleeve and also allows the arm to move forward.

- Now you will draw in the curved sleeve head.
- Draw a straight line from (5) to (A); halfway along this line square down 0.5cm; connect (5) to (A) with a hollow curve through this point.
- Draw a straight line from (A) to (4); halfway along this line square up 1.5cm; connect (A) to (4) with a raised curve through this point.
- Draw a straight line from (4) to (B); halfway along this line square up 2cm; connect (4) to (B) with a raised curve through this point.
- Draw a straight line from (B) to (6); halfway along this line square down 1cm; connect (B) to (6) with a hollow curve through this point.
- Divide the length of the sleeve below the sleeve head in half (subtract the sleeve head height from the sleeve length (70cm - 17.1cm = 52.9cm) and divide in half (52.9cm / 2 = 26.45cm). Measure 26.45cm from (5) down the back underarm seam and mark, then square across. From this line measure 2.5cm back up towards the underarm line and make a mark and square across. This is the *elbow line*.
- Notch the crown point by measuring 0.5cm from (4) along the sleeve head towards the front pitch point.

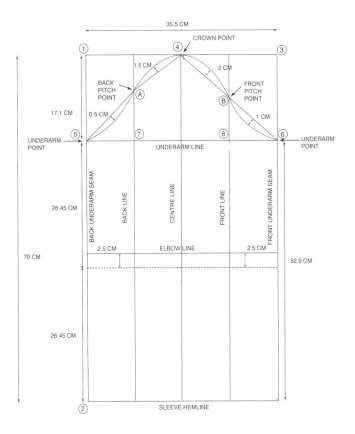

### Measuring the sleeve head and adding ease
At this point you should measure your newly drafted sleeve head, which should be 2.5cm larger than the armhole. This ease is distributed during construction between the pitch points to give shape to the sleeve head. You can add more or less ease depending on your sleeve shape, fabric or design.

## STEP 2
### SHAPING THE UNDERARM SEAMS
- Measure in 2cm from both back and front underarm seams at the sleeve hemline and mark.
- From both points redraw the new back and front underarm seam lines back up the underarm points to create a tapered sleeve shape.

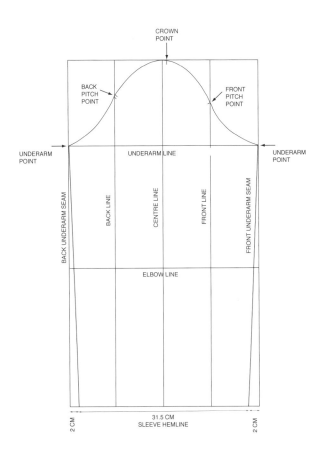

## STEP 3

### TO SHAPE THE SLEEVE HEMLINE FOR THE ADDITION OF A CUFF

**Adding a cuff to a sleeve**

The sleeve hemline is shaped for the addition of the cuff panel with a curve that is concave on the back sleeve and convex on the front. This is to balance the cuff shape around the cylindrical shape and hinged movement of the arm.

- From the centre line, divide the width of the new sleeve hemline at the front and back of the sleeve in half and mark.
- On the back sleeve hemline, measure down 0.5cm from this point and mark; and on the front measure up 0.5cm and mark.
- From the corner of the back underarm seam, draw a convex curve to the centre line through the point on the back, then reverse and draw a concave curve to the front underarm seam through the point on the front.

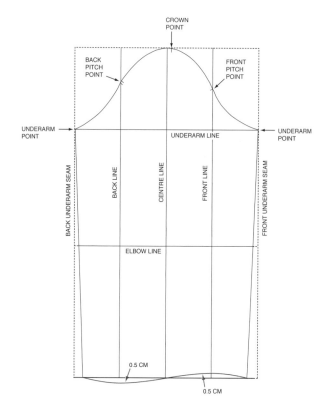

# BASIC TROUSER BLOCK

The method introduced here is a guide to developing the basic men's trouser block with a 2cm back waist dart for shape above the buttocks and a 4cm front pleat for ease of movement. The silhouette is straight with no annotation or style lines added. All the measurements given are for a sample size 32" (81cm) waist, which accompanies a size 38" (96.5cm) chest. This block will serve as a starting point for all the trouser drafts in this book, or for your own designs. You can also use measurements from the size charts on pages 32–33 to make the block in a different size, or use your own measurements taken from your fit model or male mannequin.

The modern man has diligently followed fashion when it comes to how he wears his trousers, pants and jeans. From high-waisted to low-riding, the waistline seems to be in a state of cultural flux. The natural waist in most men is the smallest measurement around the circumference of the abdomen or stomach. Generally most trousers are designed to sit between this and the hip – the most comfortable point for movement, with the waistband line being dropped 5cm below the natural waist on average, depending on the design.

**Measurements used for this size 32" (81cm) trouser block**
Waist circumference = 81cm + 3cm ease = 84cm
Total hip circumference = 96cm + 10cm ease (2.5cm ease on each of the four panels) = 106cm.
Front hip measurement = 48cm
Back hip measurement = 58cm
Crotch depth = 26cm
Outside leg measurement = 107cm
Inside leg measurement = 81cm

## STEP 1
### DEVELOPING THE BASIC TROUSER BLOCK FRAME

- Cut a large piece of drafting paper slightly longer than the length of your trouser design or the leg length of your fit model.
- Using a metre rule, draw a vertical line down the right-hand side of the paper; make a mark at the top and label it (1). This is the *outside leg* or *side seam*. Square across to the left. This is the *waistline*.
- From (1) measure down 26cm; make a mark and label it (2). This is the *crotch depth*.
- From (2) measure down 81cm; make a mark and label it (3). This is the length of the *inside leg*. Square across to the left. This is the *hemline*.
- From (1) measure down 17cm; make a mark and label it (4).
- From (4) square across to the left one quarter of the hip circumference minus 2.5cm to find the front hip measurement (26.5cm – 2.5cm = 24cm); make a mark and label it (5). This is the *hip line*.
- From (2) square across to the left one quarter of the hip circumference minus 2.5cm (26.5cm – 2.5cm = 24cm); make a mark and label it (6). This is the *crotch line*.
- From (6) measure up 26cm; make a mark and label it (7). This line is the *centre front*.
- From (6) square across to the left one quarter of the measurement from (4) to (5) minus 1cm (6cm – 1cm = 5cm) make a mark and label it (8).
- From (8) measure down 81cm to intersect with the hemline; make a mark and label it (9). This is the *inside leg seam*.

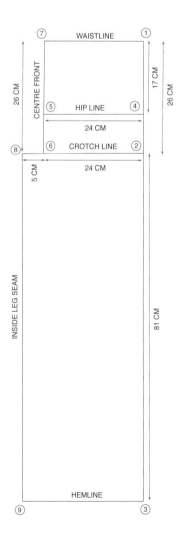

## STEP 2

### DEVELOPING THE FRONT TROUSER BLOCK

- To find the waist measurement, you need to work back from the wider front hip measurement. From (7) measure across 9cm towards the side seam; make a mark and label it (A). From (A) square down to the hemline and label it *grain line*. This will also become one side of the pleat.

- From (A) continue to measure across 4cm for the pleat; make a mark and label it (B). The pleat width can be adjusted according to the fit required.

- From (B) measure across the remainder of the front hip measurement minus 1.5cm (11cm – 1.5cm = 9.5cm) and label it (C). Shape down to (4). This is the *side seam*.

- To shape the crotch, measure out 3cm from (6) at a 45-degree angle and make a mark. Draw a curved line from (5) to (8) passing through this point.

- Make a mark where the grain line passes through the crotch line and label it (D), and another where the grain line meets the hemline and label it (E).

- To find the knee line, divide the measurement from (D) to (E) along the grain line (which is also the inside leg measurement) in half; make a mark and then measure up 8cm; make a mark and label it (F); square across 11cm towards the inside leg and 12cm towards the outside leg or side seam. This is the *knee line*.

- To create the hem width, from (E) square across 11cm towards the inside leg and make a mark and 11cm towards the side seam and make a mark.

- Draw the *inside leg seam* and the *side seam* as gentle curves from these points back to (8) and (4) respectively, passing through the points you marked at each end of the knee line.

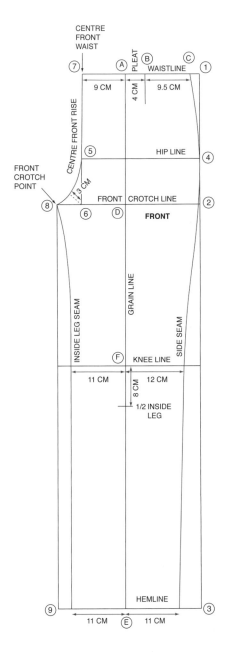

## STEP 3
### DEVELOPING THE BACK TROUSER BLOCK

- The back trouser block is developed over the front and then the two are separated when both are traced onto separate pieces of paper.
- From (7) measure up 5cm; make a mark and label it (10). Then square across to the right to a point beyond (1).
- From (1) measure out 5cm; make a mark and label it (J). Square up to meet the line you drew from (10).
- From (8) measure down 1.5cm; make a mark and label it (11). Do the same from (2) and label the mark (13). Square across from (11) to (13). This is the *back crotch line*.
- From (11) measure out 9cm; make a mark and label it (12). This is the *back crotch point*.
- From (10) measure across 4.5cm; make a mark and label it (G). This is the *centre back waist*.
- From (G) draw a 25.5cm line to (J). This is the back waist measurement including the dart width of 2cm.
- From (G) measure 14cm along the line you have just drawn; make a mark and label it (H). This marks the centre of the dart.
- From (H) square down 8.5cm; mark and label it (I). This is the length of the dart. From (H) measure out 1cm on both sides. Draw a line from each point to (I) to create the dart legs.
- Measure up 0.4cm from the top of both dart legs and redraw the waistline back to (G) and (J). This will keep a straight line along the waistline when the dart is taken in.
- To shape the crotch, continue the centre front line down from (5) through (6) to meet the new back crotch line; make a mark and label it (14). From (5) measure up 3cm; make a mark and label it (K). From (14) measure out 6.5cm at a 45-degree angle and make a mark. With a French curve draw a line from (12) to (K) passing through this point and continue up with a straight line to (G). This is the *centre back rise*.
- At the knee line from (F) measure out 13.5cm towards the inside leg and 13.8cm towards the side seam and mark.
- At the hemline from (E) measure out 12.5cm towards the inside leg and 13.5cm towards the side seam.
- From the back crotch point at (12) draw a curved line down to the mark at the knee line and continue with a straight line down to the mark at the hemline. This is the *inside leg seam*.
- At (13) measure out 2cm; make a mark and label it (L).
- From the waistline at (J) draw a curved line passing through (L) to the mark you made at the knee line, continuing with a straight line down to the mark you made at the hemline. This is the *side seam*.

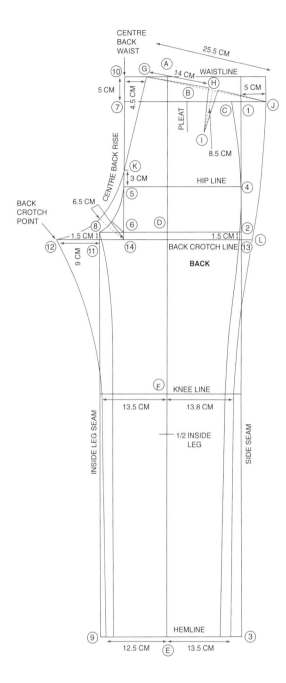

# CREATING A MASTER PLAN
## FROM A BASIC BLOCK

To adapt each block into the final pattern, the first stage is to create a master plan onto which the various features of the design are drawn. In each case, you will need to ensure that you draw the master plan onto a piece of paper that is large enough for you to draw additional elements onto the outside of the block.

### TO CREATE A MASTER PLAN FROM THE BASIC BODY BLOCK

- Cut a large piece of drafting paper slightly longer than the length of the shirt, jacket or coat you want to develop.
- Using a metre rule, draw a vertical line down the centre of the drafting paper labelling it *side seam*.
- Using a set square, draw a horizontal line through the middle of the vertical line, labelling it *waistline*.
- Place the front block to the right side of the vertical line, lining up the waistline and the side seam.
- Draw round the block, making sure that you indicate all the notches marked, and transfer the grain line. Label it *front master plan* and also label the *centre front*.
- Place the back block to the left side of the vertical line, lining up the waistline and side seam.
- Draw round the block as before. Label it *back master plan* and also label the *centre back*.
- If the block you have chosen has chest line and hip line indicated, transfer these to the master plan and label them *chest line* and *hip line*.

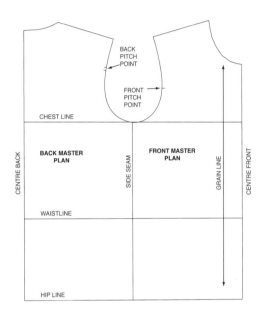

### TO CREATE A MASTER PLAN FROM THE SLEEVE BLOCK

- Cut a large piece of drafting paper slightly longer than the length of the sleeve you want to develop.
- Draw a vertical line down the centre of the drafting paper, longer than the sleeve block, and label it *centre line*.
- One quarter of the way down use a set square to draw across a horizontal line through the centre line and label it *underarm line*.
- Align the centre line and the underarm line on the sleeve block with the centre line and the underarm line drawn on the paper.
- Draw round the basic sleeve block, making sure that you indicate all the notches, the front and back pitch points and the crown point.

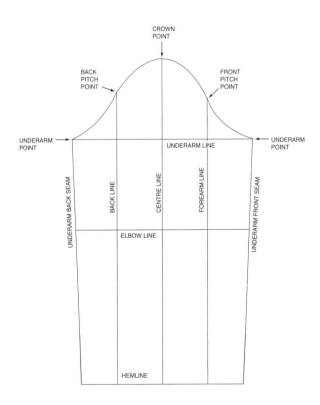

## TO CREATE A MASTER PLAN FROM THE TROUSER BLOCK

- Cut a large piece of drafting paper slightly longer than the length of the trouser you want to develop.
- Using a metre rule, draw a vertical line down the centre of the drafting paper, longer than the trouser block, and label it *centre grain line*.
- One quarter of the way down use a set square to draw across a horizontal line through the centre grain line and label it *crotch line*.
- Align the centre grain line and the crotch line on the basic trouser leg blocks with those you have drawn on the paper.
- Draw around the blocks, making sure that you indicate the notches, waist dart and hip line.
- It is important that you align the front and back trouser blocks horizontally.

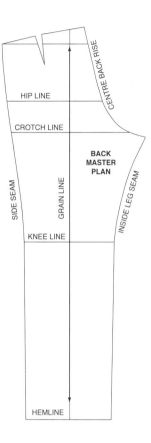

### Assessing the design

Before starting to create any pattern you should first assess the design using a menswear mannequin or fit model. The block that you have selected might be longer or shorter than the design you are developing. Analyse by taking a measurement from your fit model or mannequin and by consulting your size chart or even using competitors' garments as comparison.

Look at design features such as the placket on a shirt or the closure on a cuff. Look at the length and consider the way that a garment might be worn. Shirts, for example, are generally tucked into jeans, trousers or shorts, so the length of the block that you have selected might need to be extended. Refer back to your mannequin, samples or drawings and photos that you may have collected. For example, the yoke at the back of a shirt would start part way down the back shoulder; to find this position you can attach a piece of cotton tape to your mannequin to help you assess the proportions against your design drawings.

# HOW TO TRACE OFF A PATTERN FROM THE MASTER PLAN OR DEVELOPMENT PATTERNS

## TRACING HALF THE PATTERN SHAPE FROM THE MASTER PLAN AND THEN CREATING THE FULL PATTERN SHAPE

Collars, stands, yokes and some body panels are developed as half patterns on the master plan. When complete they will need to be mirrored to create the full pattern shape. When doing this, the centre of the pattern is usually aligned on the centre front or centre back lines.

- Using opaque paper placed over the master plan or development pattern, trace off the half pattern shape, leaving enough room on the paper to the other side of the pattern shape to fold the paper in half down the centre front or centre back.

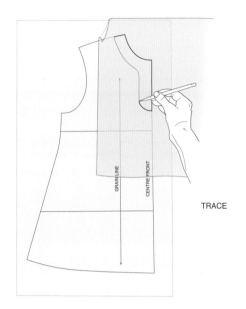

TRACE

> ### Adding details to one half of the pattern only
> If a detail, such as a pocket, appears on only the right side of the pattern, add it before mirroring (and then avoid copying it during the mirroring process); if it appears on the left-hand side, add it after the pattern has been mirrored.

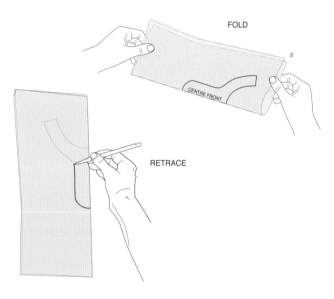

FOLD

- Transfer all the annotation marked on the master plan, including the grain line, notches and drill holes.
- Add seam allowance in accordance with the construction process (see p. 60).
- Fold the paper in half down the centre front or centre back line.
- Turn the paper over and retrace the pattern shape on the other side to create the full pattern shape. Add all the annotation necessary to complete the pattern.

RETRACE

## TRACING COMPLETE PATTERN PIECES DIRECTLY FROM THE MASTER PLAN

Some pattern pieces, such as a sleeve or a pocket, can be traced directly from the master plan or from a development pattern.

- Using opaque paper placed over the master plan or development pattern, trace off the pattern shapes.
- Transfer all the annotation marked on the master plan, including the grain line, notches and drill holes.
- Add seam allowance in accordance with the construction process (see p. 60).

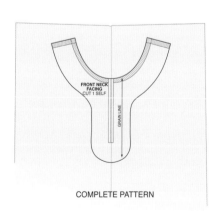

COMPLETE PATTERN

## ANNOTATION

Annotation is the technical language placed on the pattern to communicate information about the pattern, garment or its construction to the manufacturer. It should be written onto each production pattern piece clearly and centrally, or it can be marked on using a range of symbols. The language used varies between countries, manufacturers, fashion labels and pattern makers. Some of the annotation can also be written onto the master plan or development patterns during the pattern cutting process, such as the grain line, drill holes or notches.

Listed below are basic annotations used throughout the industry.

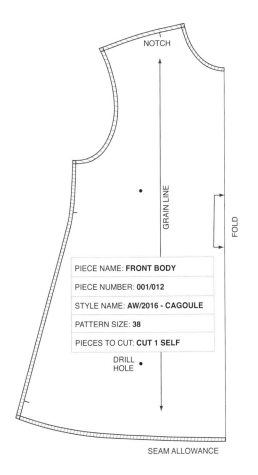

PIECE NAME: **FRONT BODY**

PIECE NUMBER: **001/012**

STYLE NAME: **AW/2016 - CAGOULE**

PATTERN SIZE: **38**

PIECES TO CUT: **CUT 1 SELF**

### Piece name
This identifies the pattern shape; whether it is a sleeve, the front right or front left body panel, or a pocket bag.

### Style identifying number or name
This could be an abbreviation, such as AW/001 (Autumn/Winter collection style number 1), or could include the name of the theme of the collection.

### Piece number
Since many patterns are made from several pattern pieces, this identifies the pattern piece within the set. It is either written as 1/7 or 1 of 7, meaning piece one in a set of seven.

### Pattern size
This is the size of the garment: 'S' (88cm, 92cm), 'M' (96cm, 100cm), 'L' (104cm, 108cm).

### Number of pieces to be cut from each pattern piece
This is abbreviated to the following symbols:
**(Self)** – Cut the pattern from the main fabric for the garment
**(Cut 1 PR Self)** – Cut one pair (right and left) from the main fabric for the garment
**(Cut 1 Self)** – Cut a single pattern piece from the main fabric
**(Cut 1 Mirrored)** – cut one of this pattern piece flipped over onto its other side.
You can also add additional information for cutting patterns from fusing or lining fabric (Cut 1 Self & 1 Fusing).
Asymmetric designs need to be marked with the abbreviation RSU (right side up), meaning place the pattern right side up on the right side of the fabric.

### Fold line or symbol
Indicates that the pattern should be folded along this line.

### Grain line
The grain line indicates the direction in which you want the pattern shape to be placed on the fabric. Most pattern pieces are placed on the straight grain, which runs parallel to the selvedge of the fabric (see p. 57).

### Seam allowances
Seam allowances can be drawn on the pattern, can be indicated by notches, or the instruction can simply be written on the pattern – '2cm seam', for example. If there is no seam allowance, use the abbreviation NSA.

### Notches and drill holes
Notches and drill holes are used to convey the construction process of the garment.
Notches are made in the edge of the pattern for seam alignment, panel placement or to indicate an area of ease.
Drill holes are used to indicate pocket placements, button positioning and dart lengths. Place the drill hole 0.5cm to 1cm before the tip of a dart or the corner of a pocket position so that the mark is not seen from the front of the finished garment.

# GRADING

Once the pattern is made, an understanding of grading and the use of technology in the pattern cutting studio and in industry will ensure that your patterns are transferred accurately for use in production.

## GRADING

At its most basic, grading is the technique of increasing the size of a garment pattern. It is not, however, a process of enlarging patterns to fit the idiosyncrasies of individual figures; those adjustments need to be carried out while adapting the block or in construction. Instead, grading is a system used in conjunction with a size chart to create proportional enlargements of a garment to best fit your customer base.

The grading of clothes began to appear in the middle of the nineteenth century as a very simple system that relied on measurements of height and circumference to enlarge and shrink the garment in proportional increments to create small, medium and large sizes. Not until the commercialisation of the ready-to-wear market after the 1950s did a sizing system that offered consistency of proportion begin to be adopted by manufacturers. The modern grading system is a process of adding growth values to a base pattern. Incremental measurements (the variable distance between two fixed points on a pattern) define intervals between sizes. Growth values have been defined within the clothing industry through the collection of measurement data on growth ratios (circumferences of the body and variable heights of the body) related to age and figure types. Grading can be performed both manually and by computer.

Incremental growth is recorded along two axes which are given numerical values, or co-ordinates. These are written as (Y), which is vertical movement plus or minus, and (X), which is horizontal movement plus or minus. These axes are at right angles to each other and the point at which they intersect is called the zero point. In the figure above values (measurable distances) are added to the X and Y co-ordinates which are applied to the cardinal points on the perimeter of a pattern to map out the next size or sizes.

To establish the cardinal point of a one-size grade, from the zero point take the required measurement horizontally (X); then square up the required measurement vertically (Y); connect (Y) to the zero point to create the grade line.

Grade rules dictate the growth between sizes. The starting point, or base size, represents the size that you used when developing the pattern. It may not have been the smallest size in the customer range, in which case you will have to grade both down and up.

The manual grading technique outlined here is shown on basic block patterns without any style lines or adaptations. Once you have understood the principles of growth related to specific areas of the male body you should be able to apply them successfully to your styled patterns. The instructions are for a one-size grade up for the basic body, sleeve and trouser blocks with a 4cm increment between sizes. Consult the size charts (pp. 32–33) for different grade values.

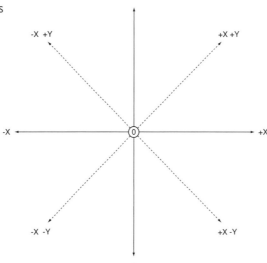

Right: Back pattern showing growth increments between sizes S to XXL.

## BACK BODY BLOCK

**Mark (1)** at the centre back neck point and measure up vertically (Y) value = 0.8cm

**Mark (2)** at the shoulder neck point measure up vertically (Y) value = 0.8cm and horizontally out (X) value = 0.25cm

**Mark (3)** at the shoulder point and measure up vertically (Y) value = 0.6cm and horizontally out (X) value = 0.5cm

**Mark (4)** at the back pitch point and measure up vertically (Y) value = 0.3cm and horizontally out (X) value = 0.5cm

**Mark (5)** at the underarm point and measure horizontally out (X) value = 0.9cm

**Mark (6)** at the waistline point and measure up vertically (Y) value = 0.4cm and horizontally out (X) value = 0.9cm

**Mark (7)** at the hemline point and measure horizontally out (X) value = 0.9cm and down vertically (Y) value = 0.4cm

**Mark (8)** at the centre back hemline and measure down vertically (Y) value = 0.4cm

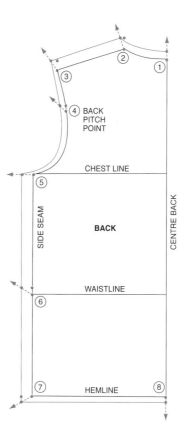

## FRONT BODY BLOCK

**Mark (1)** at the centre front neck point and measure up vertically (Y) value = 0.6cm

**Mark (2)** at the shoulder neck point measure up vertically (Y) value = 0.8cm and horizontally out (X) value = 0.25cm

**Mark (3)** at the shoulder point and measure up vertically (Y) value = 0.7cm and horizontally out (X) value = 0.5cm

**Mark (4)** at the front pitch point and measure up vertically (Y) value = 0.35cm and horizontally out (X) value = 0.5cm

**Mark (5)** at the underarm point and measure horizontally out (X) value = 1.1cm

**Mark (6)** at the waistline point and measure up vertically (Y) value = 0.4cm and horizontally out (X) value = 1.1cm

**Mark (7)** at the hemline point and measure horizontally out (X) value = 1.1cm and down vertically (Y) value = 0.4cm

**Mark (8)** at the centre front hemline and measure down vertically (Y) value = 0.4cm.

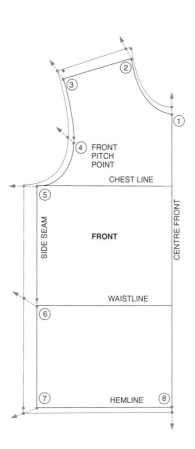

## SLEEVE BLOCK

**Mark (1)** at the back underarm seam hemline and measure horizontally out (X) value = 0.6cm and vertically down (Y) value = 0.3cm

**Mark (2)** at the front underarm seam hemline and measure horizontally out (X) value = 0.6cm and vertically down (Y) value = 0.3cm

**Mark (3)** at the back underarm line and measure horizontally out (X) value = 0.8cm

**Mark (4)** at the front underarm line and measure horizontally out (X) value = 0.8cm

**Mark (5)** at the front pitch point and measure horizontally out (X) value = 0.4cm

**Mark (6)** at the back pitch point and measure up vertically (Y) value = 0.3cm and horizontally out (X) value = 0.2cm

**Mark (7)** at the crown point and measure up vertically (Y) value = 0.6cm

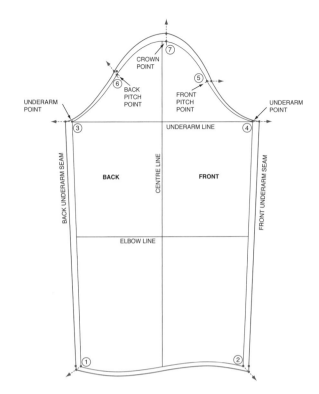

## FRONT TROUSER BLOCK

**Mark (1)** at the centre front waist point and measure up vertically (Y) value = 0.4cm and horizontally out (X) value = 0.35cm

**Mark (2)** where the hip line meets the centre front rise point measure up vertically (Y) value = 0.1cm and horizontally out (X) value = 0.35cm

**Mark (3)** at the front crotch point and measure horizontally out (X) value = 0.6cm

**Mark (4)** at the inside leg seam knee point and measure down vertically (Y) value = 0.5cm and horizontally out (X) value = 0.25cm

**Mark (5)** at the side seam knee point and measure down vertically (Y) value = 0.5cm and horizontally out (X) value = 0.25cm

**Mark (6)** at the inside leg seam hem point and measure down vertically (Y) value = 1cm and horizontally out (X) value = 0.25cm

**Mark (7)** at the side seam hem point and measure down vertically (Y) value = 1cm and horizontally out (X) value = 0.25cm

**Mark (8)** where the hip line meets the side seam point and measure up vertically (Y) value = 0.1cm and horizontally out (X) value = 0.65cm

**Mark (9)** where the waistline meets the side seam point and measure up vertically (Y) value = 0.4cm and horizontally out (X) value = 0.65cm

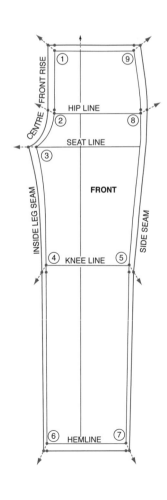

## BACK TROUSER BLOCK

**Mark (1)** at the centre back waist point and measure up vertically (Y) value = 0.4cm and horizontally out (X) value = 0.3cm.

**Mark (2)** where the hip line meets the centre back rise point measure up vertically (Y) value = 0.1cm and horizontally out (X) value = 0.3cm

**Mark (3)** at the back crotch point and measure horizontally out (X) value = 0.7cm

**Mark (4)** at the inside leg seam knee point and measure down vertically (Y) value = 0.5cm and horizontally out (X) value = 0.25cm

**Mark (5)** at the side seam knee point and measure down vertically (Y) value = 0.5cm and horizontally out (X) value = 0.25cm

**Mark (6)** at the inside leg seam hem point and measure down vertically (Y) value = 1cm and horizontally out (X) value = 0.25cm

**Mark (7)** at the side seam hem point and measure down vertically (Y) value = 1cm and horizontally out (X) value = 0.25cm

**Mark (8)** where the hip line meets the side seam point and measure up vertically (Y) value = 0.1cm and horizontally out (X) value = 0.7cm

**Mark (9)** where the waistline meets the side seam point and measure up vertically (Y) value = 0.4cm and horizontally out (X) value = 0.7cm

**Mark (10)** at the dart tip and measure up vertically (Y) value = 0.4cm and horizontally out towards the side seam (X) value = 0.25cm

**Mark (11)** at the top of the dart leg towards the side seam and measure up vertically (Y) value = 0.4cm and horizontally out towards the side seam (X) value = 0.25cm

**Mark (12)** at the top of the dart leg towards the centre back and measure up vertically (Y) value = 0.4cm and horizontally out towards the side seam (X) value = 0.25cm

**The main body growth principles**
- The centre front and centre back seams will grow in length.
- Neck and shoulder points will grow in length and width.
- Armholes will grow in length and width. To retain the balance of the sleeve the same value would be applied to the sleeve head.
- Side seams will grow in width.
- Trousers have to accommodate growth in length and width.

## Adapting patterns and blocks

Adapting the basic block into different garment styles involves a range of manipulation techniques that fit the garment to the contours of the body. These include the use of darts and style lines to help remove fabric from the block and to fit it more closely to the body, and the use of pleats and gathers to help generate fullness over the curves of the body.

Pattern cutting techniques can also be used to shape different pattern pieces and add volume.

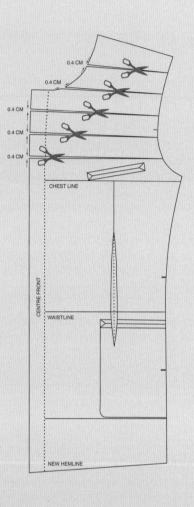

## Pivoting

Pivoting is used to redistribute volume and add in flare or a dart to a pattern piece without the need to cut through the pattern.
· Trace around the original pattern piece and then draw in the style line. Use a pattern drill to mark the end of the line.
· Pivot the pattern by placing an awl through the drill hole and then move the pattern so that the style line moves to its new position and volume is added into the pattern shape.
· Retrace the pattern with the outline of the pattern moved to its new position.

## Slash and spread

Slash and spread can also be used to add or remove volume from a pattern piece.
· Trace around the original pattern piece onto a separate piece of paper. Draw style lines equidistant from each other through the area you want to expand.
· Cut through the style lines, leaving one outer edge of the pattern attached by a few millimetres.
· Either overlap the sections evenly along the cut style lines to remove volume or open them up to add volume.
· Tape the slashed pattern to a new piece of paper and then retrace the new pattern shape.

# PRINCIPLES OF PATTERN CUTTING

### GRAIN LINE
### Straight grain
Garments are generally cut with the straight grain running down the body. The straight grain is the warp yarn, which is the yarn that runs down the length of woven fabrics parallel to the selvedge. This yarn is stronger than the weft yarn, which is the yarn that is woven horizontally across the fabric. The weft, therefore, has more give or stretch. Clothes that are cut on the straight grain are more stable and hang straighter.

### Bias grain
The bias runs at a 45-degree angle to the straight grain and to the selvedge of the fabric. Garments that are cut on the bias will stretch and therefore mould to the contours of the body, fitting many different silhouettes.

### Horizontal or cross grain
The horizontal or cross grain runs across the fabric from selvedge to selvedge. Since this grain follows the less stable weft yarn, garments cut in this direction will tend to stretch and hang softly with pleats and tucks.

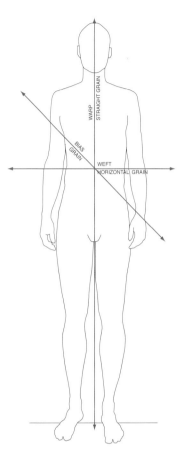

Right: The figure shows the directions of warp, weft and bias grains in relation to the body.

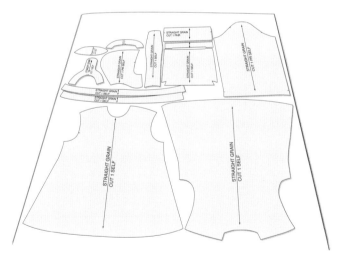

Above: Straight grain. Cagoule pattern pieces are laid along the fabric parallel to the selvedge, providing stability as the warp thread runs along the length of the garment.

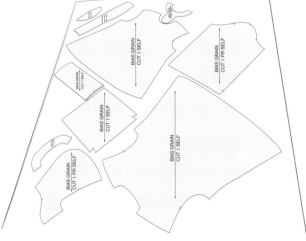

Above: Bias grain. Cagoule pattern pieces are laid along the fabric at a 45-degree angle to the selvedge, giving the garment an element of stretch as warp and weft threads at this angle are more flexible as a result of gravity and hang-weight.

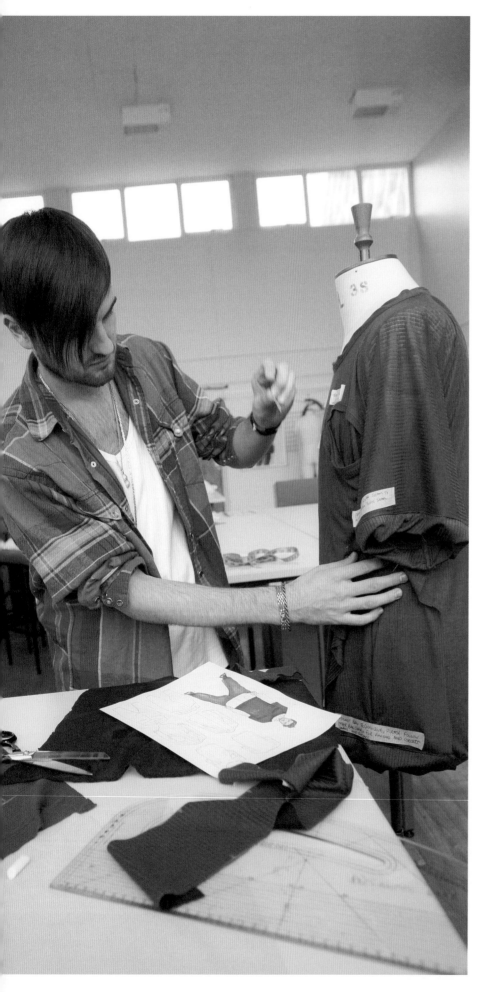

## EASE

Ease needs to be added to the measurements taken directly from the body or from a size chart to ensure that the garment is comfortable to wear.

Ease is the measurable difference between the dimensions of the human body and the garment, a difference that allows the body to move in the garment without restraint. Adding to the measurements taken from the body – to its circumference and length – when creating the pattern, creates the space. Lack of sufficient ease will cause the garment to appear tight or wrinkled when worn.

### Calculating the amount of ease

Knitted fabrics stretch and so generally require negative ease. As a result the garment is made smaller than the original measurements and uses the fabric's stretch properties to achieve its full dimensions. For most other fabrics, you will need to add ease. There are no agreed national sizing standards for the amount of ease that should be added to any particular block or style of garment. Calculating the amount of ease can be subjective and is reliant on fabric, body size, movement, function and garment style (formal-wear, workwear, sportswear). Analyse your competitors' garments, or even garments in your own wardrobe, to gain an understanding of ease.

As a general rule, ease is added to outerwear to accommodate the space needed for garments worn underneath. Ease is also added to trousers around the hip and crotch area so that the wearer can sit comfortably. It is also added to all garments at almost every point that the body moves: underarms, shoulders, chest, spine (at the back of the neck), hips, elbows and knees.

Left: A student analysing
the fit of a design on
a mannequin.

# TOLERANCE

Tolerance relates to the stability of the fabric and is measured by the amount of movement in the fabric generated through the manufacturing process. Woven fabrics generally have less movement than knitted fabrics, which have a natural stretch in their construction. The type of fibre used in a woven or knitted fabric, however, can affect the amount of tolerance – a loosely spun or natural fibre might generate greater amounts of tolerance than a more stable non-woven or synthetic fibre. Tolerances are calculated in millimetres across the width and length of the fabric. Across a whole garment they can add considerably to the amount of fabric required to achieve a comfortable fit. Assess the properties of the fabric before calculating additional allowances required for each pattern.

Allowances for tolerance and ease are calculated together and either added or taken away. By looking at the size charts on pages 32–33 and comparing the circumferential measurements you will be able to establish the ease ratio on which to base your calculations.

## Sleeve head ease

Additionally, ease is added to the sleeve head between the front and back pitch points with the greatest amount distributed over the crown point. This means that the sleeve head is generally larger than the armhole into which it will be inserted; ease allows the relatively flat shape of the sleeve to sit comfortably over the rounded shape of the shoulder point without stretching or wrinkling. Shirt sleeves generally take 0.5cm to 2cm of ease around the crown and jackets from 2cm to 4cm, depending on the type of fabric.

## Drafting the pattern with ease

Ease can be added either to the block or later to the pattern itself.

### Direct drafting

The block is drafted using measurements taken directly from the fit model or mannequin with no ease added. These blocks will fit skin-tight to the body. Ease is then added during the pattern development process to create the desired silhouette. This method is generally used for bespoke tailoring, allowing greater control over the fit of the garment.

### Drafting with ease

In this case the block is drafted to include the ease allowance, which is added to the measurements taken from the fit model, the mannequin or the commercial size chart. The block is, therefore, slightly larger than the human body at any give size. The pattern is then manipulated to create the given style. This method is used mainly in mass manufacture.

> **Ease used throughout this book**
> All the blocks in this book are drafted with basic ease given to the basic block. Ease has been added according to the style or silhouette given on each pattern. Ease has been taken away or added according to the garment design.

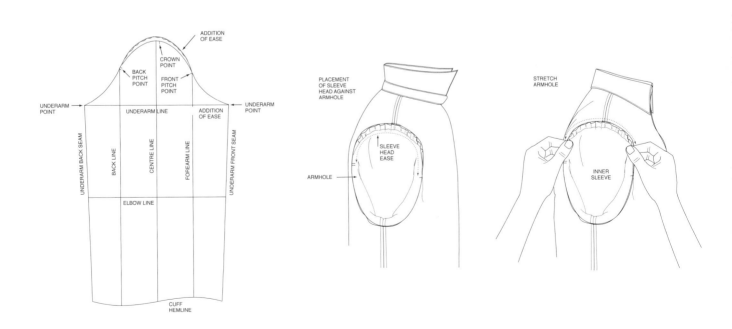

## SEAM ALLOWANCE

Seam allowance is added to the pattern once all the development is complete. Trace off the pattern shape from the master plan or development pattern and then add the seam allowance to create the final pattern. The width of the seam allowance will vary according to the fabric, style and construction technique. It is also important to consider the specialist machinery that will be used in construction before adding the seam allowance. Different machines have a different bite (the width between the needle and the cutting edge of an overlocker, for example) that can vary from 0.3mm to 1.7cm or more; the seam allowance will need to correspond to the bite. Check the lengths of the seams for corresponding pattern shapes and add alignment notches on both seams for assembly.

| Seam allowances | Light- / medium-weight fabrics | Heavyweight fabrics | Sewing machinery | Seams |
|---|---|---|---|---|
| 0.7cm | Hems, facings, necklines, collars | | Three-thread baby overlocker stitch; binding machine; single-needle lockstitch; single-needle chain-stitch | Lapfelled, welted |
| 1.0cm | Front, side, waist, shoulder and pocket seams that will be overlocked together | Armholes, sleeves, collars, facings, enclosed seams. | Single-needle lockstitch; single-needle chain-stitch; 4 / 5 thread overlocker stitch; cover-stitch | Plain superimposed |
| 1.5cm | Hem allowances | | | Capped, slotted |
| 2.0cm | Hem allowances | Side, waist seams, hem allowances | | |
| 2.5cm | Hem allowances | | | |
| 5.0cm | Double-turned or blind-hemmed seams | | Blind-hemmer | |

### Shrinkage

Some fabrics, like denim and cotton jersey, shrink when washed. A shrink test should, therefore, be carried out on any fabric likely to shrink when the garment is first washed. Cut a metre square of the fabric and mark the grain line using permanent marker or a stitching line. The fabric should then be washed using an industrial technique, or one relevant to the final product. Re-measure the metre square: this will give you the ratio by which the square has shrunk; then apply this to the pattern or block. Alternatively, make up the garment in its entirety and apply the washing technique relevant to the style. Re-measure the garment and adapt the pattern to accommodate the shrinkage ratio. A further method is to manufacture the garment from pre-shrunk fabric.

Left: Blue jersey being removed from the dyeing tank; fabric dyed before manufacture is less likely to shrink.

## FITTING

After drafting a block or pattern, a toile should be made. This is a test garment, usually made from calico, which is sewn together to check the fit. Use the toile to check the balance of the garment, fit and also the proportion of different areas of the garment in relation to each other.

### Balance

When drafting a pattern, you need to consider the relationship between the garment and the human body – the balance. Balance is achieved when the centre front and centre back lines on a jacket or shirt hang equally from both sides of the body and the side seams of a pair of trousers are perpendicular to the ground. Symmetry can be achieved by distributing volume and ease equally between the different pieces of the pattern during the drafting of the block.

Balance can, however, also be achieved by ensuring that the grain line of the pattern is marked correctly (see p. 57) and that it is aligned to the grain line of the fabric with the warp and weft threads aligned at 90 degrees to the chest line, waistline and along the centre front and centre back lines.

Gravity, which also works in conjunction with the grain line, can also affect the balance of the garment if fabric is distributed unequally around the body. Faults in the figure and poor posture can also affect balance.

**Balance control areas on the male figure**

Balance of a garment can be corrected on the patterns after fitting has occurred. Illustrated here are the two areas of the garment that affect the balance.

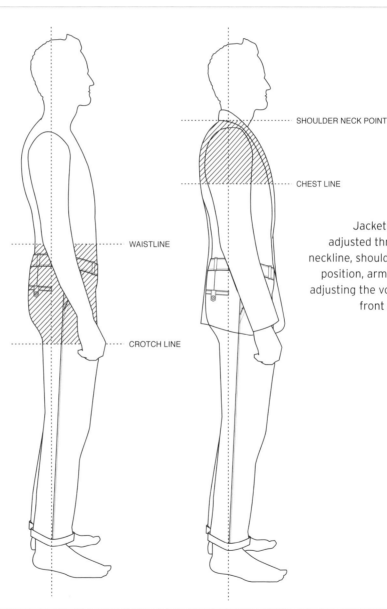

WAISTLINE

CROTCH LINE

SHOULDER NECK POINT

CHEST LINE

Trousers can be adjusted through the fit of the waist, hips and front and back crotch by adjusting the volume from front to back or vice versa.

Jackets and shirts can be adjusted through the fit of the neckline, shoulder slope and seam position, armholes and chest by adjusting the volume between the front and back patterns.

Evaluating the fit of a garment can help to rectify figure faults and problems caused by poor posture and is done through assessing the toile. Structural seam lines should fall in the expected positions on the body. Shoulders are particularly important in fitting as the clothing hangs from them. Any deviation created by wrong proportions will appear as wrinkles, creases or tightness, giving the wearer visual and physical discomfort. These areas will then need to be readdressed to reinstate the balance in the pattern and another toile will need to be made.

## Line and proportion

In menswear line refers to the structural seam lines, also called style lines, that separate the component parts that make up the garment – sleeves, yokes, collar, and front and back body panels. Proportion is the space taken (in terms of length and width) by the various pattern pieces between these lines and their relationship to each other. Together they make up the garment silhouette, the overall shape that encloses the body.

When fitting the toile you need to assess all of the above, checking to see that seams fall correctly, especially at the shoulders from which most garments hang. Any discrepancy in the balance or proportions will manifest itself as wrinkles, creases or areas of tightness that give the wearer physical discomfort or create visual distortion. Address these discrepancies by adjusting the toile, taking notes and then re-drafting the block or pattern before creating a second toile to re-test the fit.

## NECK SIZES AND COLLARS

Neck sizes vary among shirt brands and styles; minor variations in the way shirts are constructed will account for slight differences in collar fit, which can be assessed through the insertion of two fingers between the neck trunk and buttoned collar to give ease. Traditional shirt sizing is classified according to neck circumferences, which are displayed as numerical figures and take into account the sleeve length for styles worn with a button collar and tie.

Casual shirt styles are classified with descriptive sizing: Extra small, Small, Medium, Large, Extra large, which are based on corresponding chest circumference measurements. Neck opening styles are constantly in flux; they can be determined according to fashion trends or garment styles, depending on what is in vogue.

> **Collar terminology**
> The collar stand is a band that raises the collar from the neckline to the point at which the collar rolls over. It can either be incorporated into the shape of the collar itself, or it can be a separate pattern; it can be either visible or hidden.
>
> Most collars rise up from the neck edge and turn over at some point to sit on the shoulders, where they hide the neckline. The point at which they turn over is called the collar roll.

There are many variations in collar shape, both traditional and contemporary.

- A band or mandarin collar rises up from the neckline of the shirt and has a slight convex curve to the neckline and its upper edge so that it sits close to the neck. This type of collar does not have a collar roll (see Bib Shirt, pp. 138–47).
- A turned-down collar is a rolled collar. It has a convex neckline and can be attached to a stand (see Casual Long-sleeved Shirt, pp. 104–15).
- A convertible collar is a rolled collar. It also has a convex neckline and can be attached to a stand (see the Double-breasted Jacket, which has a shaped convertible collar with a hidden stand, pp. 268–87) or can be sewn straight onto the neckline.
- Straight collars are rectangular in shape with a straight neckline and are generally sewn onto the neckline without a stand. The collar rolls naturally from the centre back neck, moving in a concave line down to the centre front. They are often used in sportswear where the collar is a single layer and made from a manufactured pre-knitted rib (see Short-sleeved Polo Shirt, pp. 80–87).
- A sailor collar sits flat over the shoulders and is created by aligning the front and back body blocks at the shoulder seam and then drafting the shape on top.

## Neck Sizing Chart

| USA - Sizes | S | M | L | XL | XXL |
|---|---|---|---|---|---|
| To fit collar (inches) | 14" – 14 1/2" | 15" – 15 1/2" | 16" – 16 1/2" | 17" – 17 1/2" | 18" – 18 1/2" |

| UK - Sizes | XXS | XS | S | M | L | XL | XXL |
|---|---|---|---|---|---|---|---|
| To fit collar (inches) | 14" | 14 1/2" | 15" | 16" | 17" | 17 1/2" | 18" |
| (centimetres) | 35.5cm | 37cm | 38cm | 41cm | 43cm | 44cm | 46cm |

| European - Sizes | XS | S | M | L | XL | |
|---|---|---|---|---|---|---|
| To fit collar (centimetres) | 37-38cm | 38-40cm | 41-42cm | 43-44cm | 44-45cm | |

- A Peter Pan collar is generally used on womenswear but can be adapted with good results for men's clothing. It has a similar construction method to the sailor collar except that the shoulder seams are overlapped.
- A turtleneck or funnel collar is drafted from a rectangle whose sides are then shaped so that the upper edge is smaller than the neckline. It is generally used with stretch fabrics or can be cut from woven fabrics with a zipped or buttoned opening.

## Necklines and collar styles

There are broadly three types of neckline that are associated with different collar styles. When developing patterns you need to consider whether to lower the centre front neckline, and how much by, depending on the collar style you have chosen. In the images below the black lines represent the actual neckline, while the red lines represent the collar neckline.

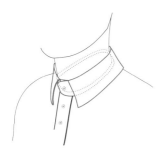

- A **high neckline** is also referred to as an English neckline. Reminiscent of the neckline of the Victorian wing-tip collar, this neckline sits close to the neck and is high at the centre front.

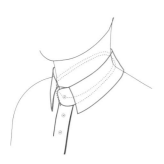

- A **mid-height neckline** is also referred to as an French-style neckline. Associated with the classic turned-down collar, this neckline sits close to the neck but is lower at the centre front.

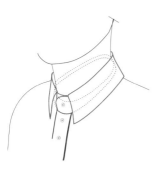

- A **low neckline** is also referred to as an Italian loose neckline. Usually associated with a cutaway or widespread collar style, this neckline sits away from the neck and is lower at the centre front, offering a loose, casual style.

Right: Suit jacket with hunting details. Junya Watanabe's Autumn 2011 show presents a distant yet familiar image of Americana.

**Classic collar styles with high and mid-style necklines.**

OFFICER COLLAR

WING-TIP COLLAR

CAMBRIDGE BOATING COLLAR

WIDE-SPREAD CUTAWAY COLLAR

CLUB COLLAR

OXFORD BUTTON-DOWN COLLAR

**Adjusting the collar**

When developing any collar that rolls over, it is important that the outer edge of the collar sits flat on the body and hides the neckline. If the outer edge of the collar is too short, it will rise up above the body when closed. If the outer edge is too long then it will bunch up and not sit flat.

The best way to evaluate how long the outer edge of the collar needs to be is to make up a calico toile of the top half of the garment with the collar sewn in to assess the fit on the mannequin. When deciding the width of your collar, make sure that it is not narrower than the stand. This will ensure that the stand will not be visible when the collar is turned over.

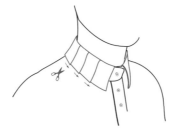

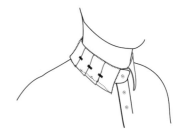

- If the outer edge is too wide, cut open the collar toile and overlap the sections evenly until the collar sits flat.

- Record the new shape by taping the sections before removing the toile and measuring the outer edge.

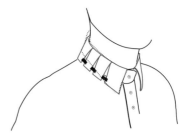

- If the outer edge is too short, cut open the collar toile into equal sections from the outer edge towards the neckline and open them out evenly until the collar sits flat on the shoulders.

- Record the new shape by taping the sections before removing the toile, then measure the outer edge of the collar.

## PLACKETS

**Grown-on placket**

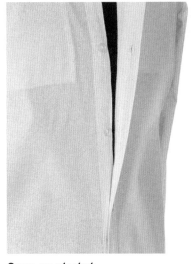

**Sewn-on placket**

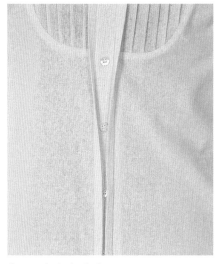

**Concealed placket**

There are many types of placket, including concealed, wrap and strap, and decorative bias, but there are only two ways to construct a placket. You can either grow on the required material that you then fold back to form the placket or you can construct it as a separate piece of material that will be sewn onto the front opening. Both are popular methods.

- Before you construct the placket, establish the diameter of the buttons you will be using. This will determine the finished width of the placket.
- Identify the fitting line, which is the line on which the buttons and buttonholes are placed, usually the centre front.
- The placket extends beyond the fitting line by approximately half the diameter of the button, or its radius plus 0.5–1cm.
- The placket is attached to both sides of the shirt and, when fastened, the left side overlaps the right. The side underneath holds the buttons and the top holds the buttonholes.

## POCKETS

There are many different styles of pocket, from patch pockets, concealed pockets that can be welted or jetted, to cargo or bellows-style pockets with gussets.

When developing the internal parts of a concealed pocket, keep in mind the job a pocket performs and the wear and tear on the integral parts. The area where a pocket is attached to the main fabric is usually reinforced with fusing to stabilise the fabric and to prevent it from stretching and becoming misshapen. The width and depth of the pocket bag itself is determined by the opening you have drawn on your master plan and the internal space available to position the pocket within the design; it should be shaped so that the bag is not caught up in any seams.

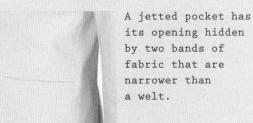

**Pocket terminology**

A flap, or welt stand, can be used to hide the pocket opening and give a tailored finish. A welted pocket is finished on the outside with one band of fabric.

A jetted pocket has its opening hidden by two bands of fabric that are narrower than a welt.

## HEMS

The hem allowance is turned up and connected to the lining during construction to create an internal facing. The hem can be fused to give rigidity.

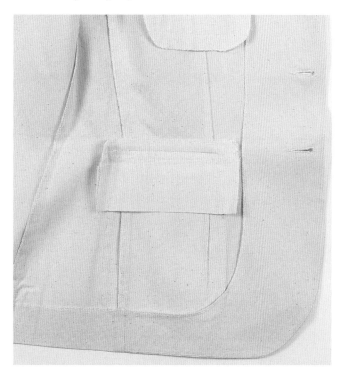

## LININGS

The job of the lining is to hide the various parts of the garment's internal construction, such as seams, fusing, interlining and pocket bags, if you have chosen not to make these a design feature.

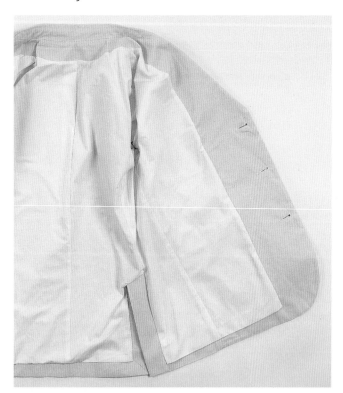

There are many different methods for constructing internal linings for jackets and coats. The lining is larger or of a similar size to the external shell of the garment, which allows for movement of the body. The linings of jackets and coats need to have ease added across the back of the shoulder blades, for example, in the form of a centre back inverted box pleat to allow for movement. Ease is frequently added to the chest front in the form of a tuck or pleat, to allow for the expansion of the chest. Lining patterns for sleeve heads and armholes are made larger to avoid pinching. Ease is also added in the form of extra length to the hems of the body and sleeve lining, to allow stretch when the body is bent over or arms raised.

## SLEEVES

The cut of the sleeve is largely determined by the sleeve head height (the distance between the crown point and the underarm line) and its relationship to the width of the underarm. A sleeve with a higher sleeve head will be tighter and the underarm shorter. This type of sleeve is often used for fitted jackets (see Single and Double-breasted Jackets,

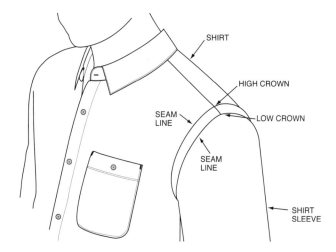

pp. 252–67 and pp. 268–87). A sleeve with a shorter sleeve head will be wider and the underarm will also be wider. This type of sleeve is used for more casual garments (see Casual Long-sleeved Shirt, pp. 104–15). When lowering the crown point to create a more casual, wider sleeve you also need, therefore, to remember to widen the underarm line.

To create a more casual sleeve first create a larger armhole on the front and back body blocks. This can be done by either lowering the armhole (see Hooded Sweatshirt, pp. 88–103) or by extending the shoulder, or both (see Casual Long-sleeved Shirt, pp. 104–15).

Take the measurement of the new armhole from the front and back body blocks by laying a tape measure held on its side around the new shape.

**Tailored two-piece**

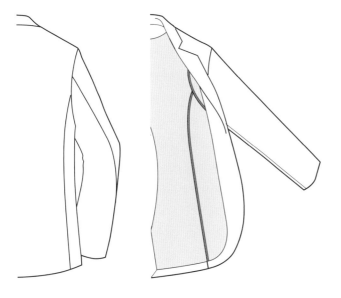

**Casual two-piece**

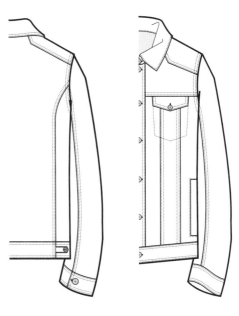

### One- and two-piece sleeves

Most sleeves are constructed from one pattern piece with a single underarm seam, and called a set-in sleeve (see Casual Long-sleeved Shirt, pp. 104–15). Tailored sleeves (see the Single-breasted Jacket, pp. 252–67), and other casual jacket sleeves (see the Fitted Denim Jacket, pp. 220–31) are made from two pieces (a top and a bottom panel).

There are two methods of drafting a pattern for a two-piece sleeve that broadly divide into the method used for tailored sleeves and for casual sleeves. The casual two-piece sleeve keeps the original sleeve head shape of the basic block as padding is not needed. The two panels needed for the sleeve (top and bottom) can therefore be drafted from the basic block. This is achieved by folding in the outer sections of the sleeve sides to give you the bottom panel. A tailored sleeve, however, has to be drafted from scratch and is developed to give you the more pronounced sleeve head needed for the padding and rolls.

### CUFFS AND CUFF GUARDS

Although not illustrated here in any depth, there are many different styles of cuff, from single cuffs to more elaborate historical designs. The single cuff used on the shirts illustrated in this book holds in the volume at the end of the sleeve, has ease added so that it fits comfortably around the wrist and can rise up when the arm moves forward.

Before adding a cuff or hem allowance to any pattern, first establish your sleeve length.

The function of the cuff guard is to finish and provide support to the opening that allows the hand to pass through the cuff. It is rectangular in shape with either a shaped or a flat end. The length of the guard can vary and it can be closed with a button midway along its length. When the guard is attached, 1cm is taken for the seam on the shirt opening.

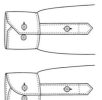 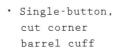
- Single-button, cut corner barrel cuff

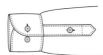
- Single-button, rounded barrel cuff

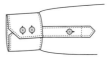
- Two-button, cut corner barrel cuff

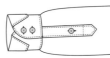
- Two-button, turned barrel cuff

# USING TECHNOLOGY

CAD / CAM are acronyms for two innovations that have revolutionised the working practices of the clothing industry. Computer-aided design and computer-aided manufacture cover a number of software and hardware solutions that are used in the pattern cutting and manufacturing processes. Clothing design and manufacturing technology has become increasingly reliant on computer-based operational systems to reduce expenditure and to respond to the ethical expectations of the consumer by using resources more efficiently. These systems have enabled brands to reduce lead times, to lower costs, to increase workforce efficiency, to communicate more effectively with manufacturers and to develop web-based profiles for customers. CAD / CAM and the internet have revolutionised all stages of the design process. The high-quality output offered by these applications has speeded up product development and enabled brands to become more competitive. The work of an entire design studio can now be contained on a single laptop, and this has changed the way designers and pattern cutters practise their craft. Style libraries, photographs and drawings, patterns, colours and textures can be scanned, modified and digitally enhanced to create range stories, moodboards and lookbooks in a matter of hours. Awareness, use and integration of the products now available is essential to any menswear brand if it wants to stay competitive in a global market.

Cagoule pattern parameters being digitised via the Gerber digitiser XLd workstation table.

A studio environment showing the AccuMark pattern design system on screen.

However, computer-aided technology has been developed to enhance the manual process of pattern cutting, not to replace it. Without the competence and knowledge gained from the practices of flat pattern cutting and draping computerised pattern-cutting technology cannot be used effectively. The advantages of using these systems are: increased speed, greater accuracy in measurement, the ability to store patterns as digital data, accurate reproduction of patterns when needed from a template library, and reduced use of space and the physical costs of paper and card. There are many CAD / CAM companies catering for small and large businesses that provide a range of solutions for the pattern cutting industry. Choosing the appropriate one for your business will require some research; information can be gathered from trade shows, web forums and other companies' experiences of the product. Most offer schemes for ongoing technical support with training, system installation and maintenance, as well as software upgrades. Software companies that provide pattern cutting solutions to larger businesses are Gerber (US), Lectra (France), Vetigraph (France), Pad System (Canada), Grafis (Germany), OptiTex (Israel), Gemini (Romania), [TC][2] (Textile Clothing Corp, US) and Alvanon (US). Companies catering for smaller pattern cutting businesses are Telestia (Greece), Fashion Cad (Australia), Wild Ginger (US), Browzwear Solutions (Singapore) and VR Software Limited (UK).

Outlined here are the basic approaches to generating patterns and the associated software and hardware products used by design and manufacturing teams throughout the apparel and educational sectors.

### Digitising and scanning patterns

Digitising is the process whereby manual patterns are mapped or traced through the use of an electronic point locator (cursor), which is moved across a digitising table; this data is converted into pattern parameters and stored for later use. The process described here is that for Gerber AccuMark software. To start, the pattern piece is placed on the digitising table with the grain line horizontal to the floor; it is secured with tape. Before the digitising process can begin certain preference tables have to be set up on the system. A storage area for the data to be saved to is created, a user environment is set up, and parameter and grade rule tables are created. Once these have been established, the process of entering the data can begin. Points on the pattern are located using the digitising cursor crosshairs and information is input by pushing the relevant keys on the cursor pad. Digitising starts by entering in the piece name, piece category and the piece description, then the rule table is selected from the alphabetical list on the table menu.

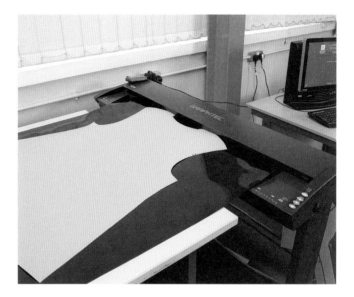

Pattern being fed through a Graphtec image scanner, which converts full-size patterns into CAD data.

Next the grain line is recorded and the process starts at the top left-hand corner on a cardinal point (shoulder tip), working clockwise, selecting the inputting code from the key pad: (AB1) – for a graded point followed by a rule number, (A) – for intermediate curves, (AB1C1) – for a graded point, rule number and notch. The digitising scanner is another method of inputting patterns into the system; patterns are passed between plastic sheets which are fed though the scanner, so it is faster than the manual process. It takes a matter of minutes for the scan to be processed into parameter data, which can be converted for checking and manipulation compatibility with Gerber AccuMark.

Piece name being entered on the menu board of the digitising table using the 16-button cursor.

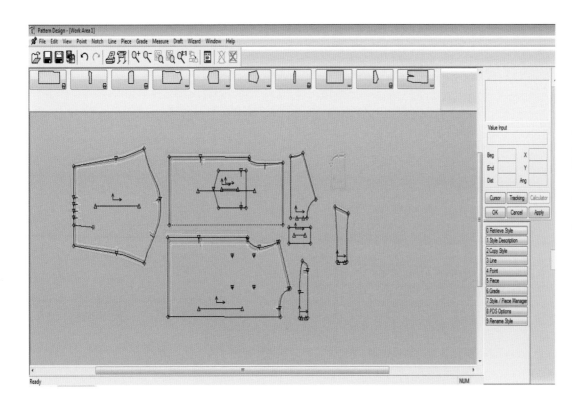

Screen shot of Gerber's AccuMark Pattern Design System (PDS) software. A shirt pattern is shown in the work area.

## Generating patterns

Patterns can also be created directly on the computer: basic blocks can be created using your landmark parameters (chest, waist, hips and body lengths) from the size charts provided. Gerber AccuMark PDS (Pattern Design System) allows you to generate new patterns or to open digitized or scanned patterns from your storage area. Menu blocks can be manipulated to add fullness, or can be stretched or shrunk for fabric tolerance; they can be scaled to change size ratios, copied to make common pieces or even mirrored to create full patterns. Seams, notches and annotations can also be applied to your pattern pieces.

## Digitally grading patterns

The principles of grading are the same for manually grading a pattern and grading a pattern on the computer. As grading by hand can be a time-consuming process, computer grading is now the process of choice for the apparel industry. With the added benefit of accuracy, patterns can be graded automatically. Like the manual method, the (X) and (Y) co-ordinates have to be assigned a measurement value. This is done through establishing a rule table to define the movement of the cardinal points of your pattern (horizontal and vertical axes). You will need to establish your incremental body growth between sizes before completing the rule table. This information can be taken from an industry-published size chart or from your own customer profiling.

## Lay planning and marker making

These two technical terms refer to parts of the production process. The lay plan is the mapping out of pattern pieces in sequential order on a piece of paper (the marker). The marker is the width and length of the fabric lay. This will be determined by the number of garments to be cut and the sizes ordered. Although manual marker making is still practised, generating markers on the computer offers considerable benefits. Material utilisation and fabric wastage can be controlled by optimising small and large sizes. Gerber AccuNest software offers an automated function where the fabric parameters and quantity are set, and then pattern pieces are selected to generate the most economical marker plan.

## Digital output

Many CAD programs for pattern cutting are now compatible with other design software, enabling pattern data to be exported and emailed around the world. Factories have the hardware to be able to print out patterns to make samples, and to make lay plans or markers in paper or card ready to be processed by single- or multi-ply vector cutting systems. The 3D Runway Creator program allows pattern data to be turned into virtual garments on avatars so that manufacturers, retailers and buyers are able to view products while they are in the development stage. Changes to style, colour and fit can be reviewed even before samples are made.

## Emerging technologies

At the forefront of apparel engineering is the advancement in digital technology and virtual software solutions for pattern generation. As the emerging market seeks to refine its production and output processes, computer-generated solutions will increasingly play a pivotal role in how the designer, pattern cutter, manufacturer and consumers interact. New software programs allow design teams and pattern cutters to view manual processes yet to be actualised. Many leading apparel companies have been developing interactive pattern design systems (PDS) that feature 3D flattening technology, a solution to flat pattern making and virtual three-dimensional prototyping. Basic pattern blocks can be rendered into full body samples which are then fitted onto a library of customisable, computer-generated

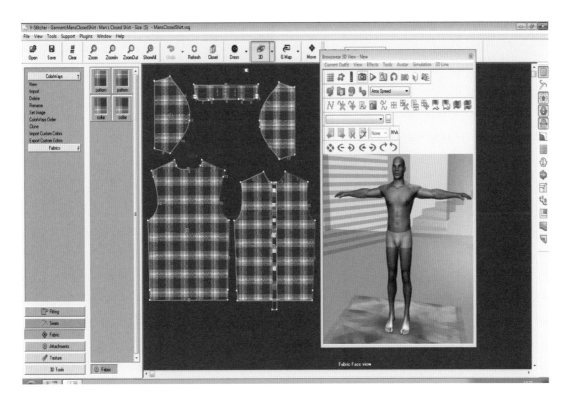

Screenshot of Browzwear's V-Stitcher 2D to 3D garment modelling software. A shirt pattern with virtual avatar is shown in the work area.

avatars, or 3D styles which can be rendered into 2D patterns. Fit, proportion, ease, tightness and other vital technical aspects of a garment can be modified. Simulated fabric and print design can be applied prior to production, reducing the need for multiple samples. Many of the Pattern Design Systems work on collaborative platforms specifically developed for the fashion industry, allowing pattern data to be easily incorporated into design or other product management programs.

## Body scanning

This new technology has changed how the apparel industry develops its size charts; research into fit and shape analysis among brand demographics has reduced the need to have multiple sizing by targeting specific body shapes. Brands and pattern cutters now have access to regional size surveying data for almost any target market or country's consumers.

Many companies now offer a range of services from fit analysis, customer profiling, demographic body surveys to basic pattern block creation based on market research. Through this new technology pattern cutters are able to influence brand positioning and capture new audiences via target sizing. Body scanning has contributed to garment creation analysis in almost every studio practice. The production of tailor-made mannequins with core realistic body shapes developed from sizing data also allows for greatly improved customer fit.

Screenshots of [TC]²'s (Textile Clothing Corp) 3D body scanning program. Measurements are extracted to generate 3D avatars and body mapping diagrams.

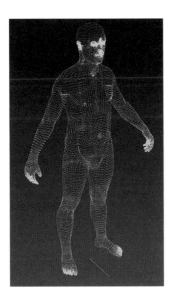
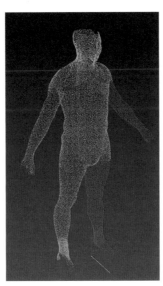
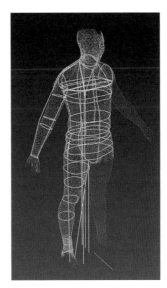
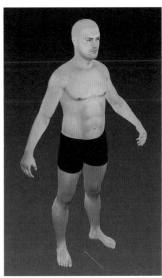

## CHAPTER THREE

# THE PATTERNS: JERSEY AND SHIRTS

# PATTERN
# LONG-SLEEVED GRANDAD VEST

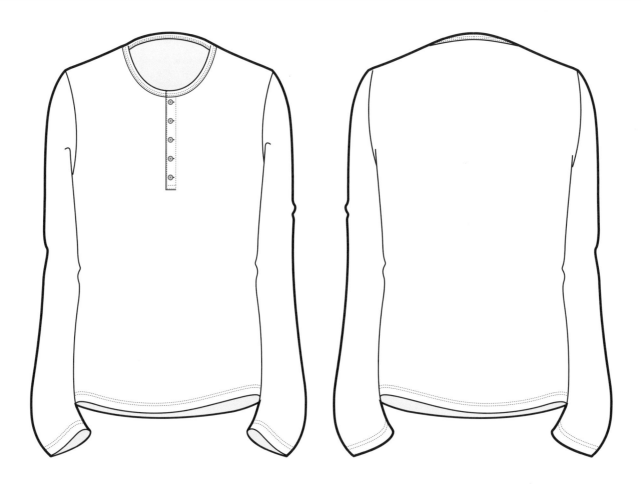

**This pattern includes development of the following features:**

Shaping the body
Lowering the neckline
Creating a front placket
Shaping the hemline
Shortening the sleeve head height
Shaping the sleeve

## STEP 1
### DEVELOPING THE MASTER PLAN

Start by selecting the basic men's body block, or by drafting the basic block according to the instructions on page 40. Cut a large piece of drafting paper slightly longer than the length of the vest you want to develop and transfer the shape of the block and all marks, labels and instructions following the directions on page 48.

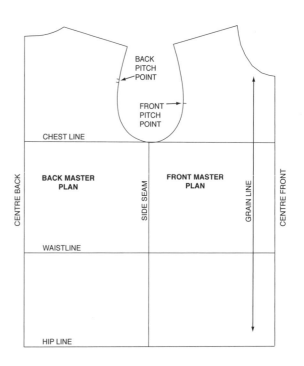

## STEP 2
### SHAPING THE BODY

- From the side seam at the waistline measure out 2.5cm on both sides and mark. From the hemline at the side seam measure out 2cm on both sides and mark.
- Connect these points with a straight line from the hemline to the waistline, then continue with a curved line to the underarm point.

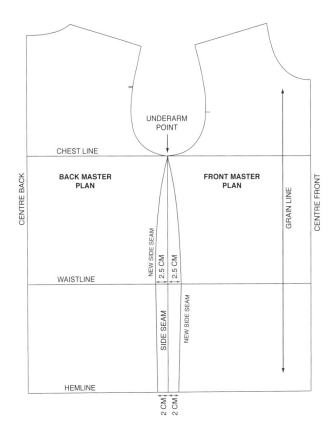

## STEP 3
### SHAPING THE HEMLINE

- Extend the centre front and back lines down 1cm at the hem and mark.
- Connect both of these points back to the bottom of the side seam with a shallow curve.
- Measure up 1.5cm along this line to indicate the hem facing and mark with a dotted fold line.

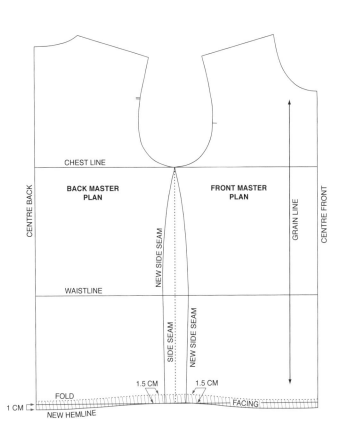

## STEP 4
### LOWERING THE FRONT NECK AND PLACKET DEVELOPMENT

- Measure down 1.5cm from the centre front neck point. Using the basic body block as a guide to the shape, draw in the new neckline.
- Continue to measure down a further 16cm – the length of the placket. From the new centre front neck point, measure back along the neckline 0.75cm and then out 0.75cm.
- At both these points, drawn a vertical line down to create a rectangular shape the length of the placket and 1.5cm wide.

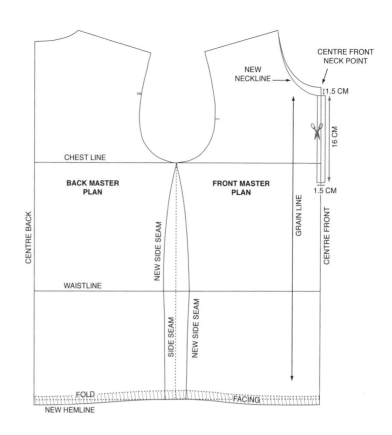

## STEP 5
### FRONT PATTERN

- Trace off the front onto a new piece of paper and, following the instructions on page 50, create the full pattern shape, which will be cut down the right-hand side of the placket to create an opening.

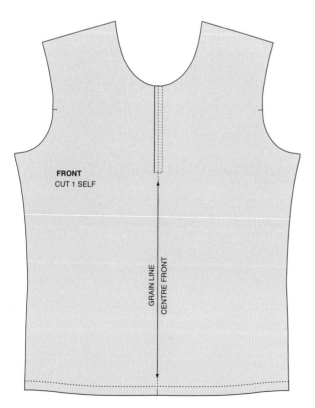

## STEP 6
### BACK PATTERN

- Trace off the back onto a new piece of paper and, following the instructions on page 50, create the full pattern shape.

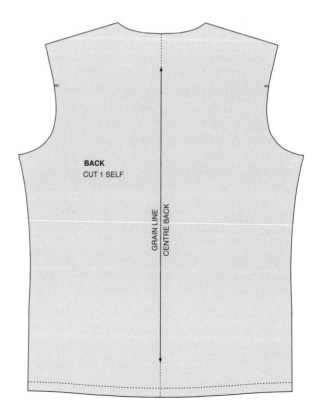

## STEP 7
### DEVELOPING THE UPPER AND UNDER PLACKET FACINGS

- Draw a rectangle 16cm long and 4cm wide.
- Indicate the 1cm seam allowance on one long side and divide the rest of the width in half to give a 1.5cm facing when folded. This will form the upper placket facing.
- Draw another rectangle 17cm long and 3.5cm wide.
- Indicate the 1cm seam allowance on the two long sides, leaving a 1.5cm facing. This will then form the under placket facing.

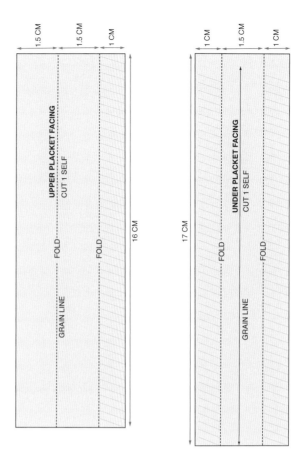

## STEP 8
### DEVELOPING THE SLEEVE MASTER PLAN

Start this development by selecting the basic men's sleeve block, or by drafting the basic sleeve block according to the instructions on page 42. Cut a large piece of drafting paper slightly longer than the length of the shirt you want to develop and transfer the shape of the block and all marks, labels and instructions, following the directions on page 48. The sleeve block that you have selected might be longer or shorter than the design you are developing. Analyse by taking a measurement from your fit model or mannequin and by consulting your size chart, or even by using competitors' garments for comparison.

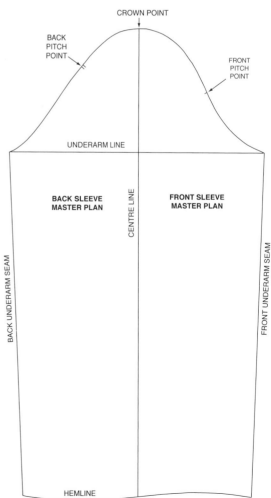

## STEP 9
### REDUCING THE SLEEVE HEAD HEIGHT

- Reduce the sleeve head by measuring 1cm down the centre line from the crown point.
- Using the basic sleeve block as a guide, draw in the new sleeve head shape.

### Ease for knitted and stretch fabrics
Knitted and stretch materials, such as jersey, fleece and Lycra, need very little or no ease allowance on the sleeve head because the ease is found in the stretch of the fabric itself. You will therefore need to reduce the sleeve head on some patterns.

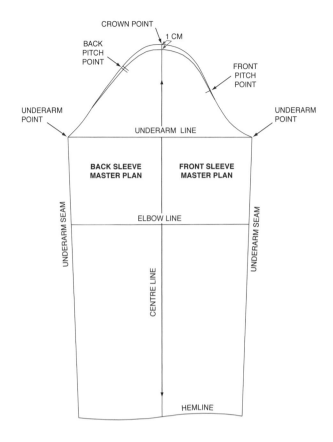

## STEP 10
### SLEEVE SHAPING

- First measure 3cm in at the sleeve hemline from both sides and mark. Repeat at the elbow line and mark.
- From the underarm point on both sides, join these new points with a curved line to the elbow line and a straight line to the hemline. These are the new underarm seams.
- At the sleeve hemline measure up 1.5cm to indicate the sleeve hem facing and mark with a dotted fold line.

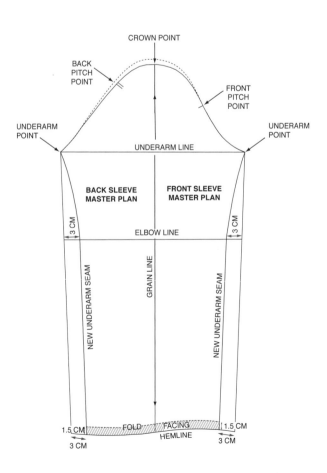

## STEP 11
### SLEEVE PATTERN

Following the instructions on page 50, trace off the sleeve pattern.

# PATTERN
# SHORT-SLEEVED POLO SHIRT

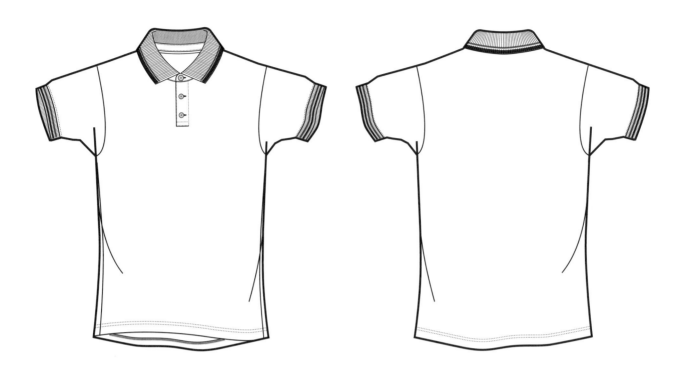

**This pattern includes development
of the following features:**

Creating a front placket

Creating a collar stand

Lowering the armhole

Widening the sleeve head

Developing a short sleeve

Incorporating a ribbed collar and cuff

## STEP 1
### DEVELOPING THE MASTER PLAN

Start by selecting the basic men's body block, or by drafting
the basic block according to the instructions on page 40. Cut
a large piece of drafting paper slightly longer than the length
of the shirt you want to develop and transfer the shape of
the block and all marks, labels and instructions following the
directions on page 48.

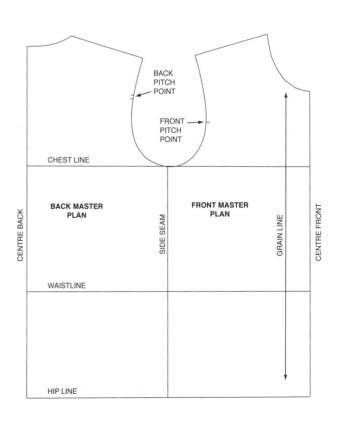

## STEP 2
### LOWERING THE ARMHOLE ON THE BODY

- Measure 2cm down the side seam from the underarm point and mark. Using the original block, recreate the shape of the armhole and transfer the back and front pitch points to their new positions on the lowered armhole.

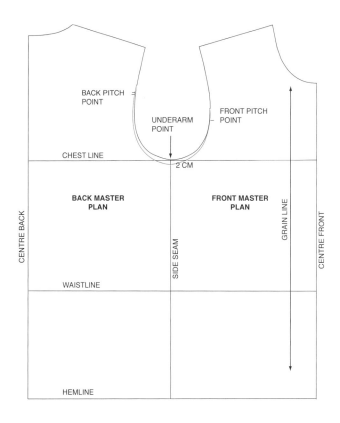

## STEP 3
### DEVELOPING THE CENTRE FRONT PLACKET AND HEM WIDTH

- From the centre front neck point measure down 10cm - the length of the placket.
- From the centre front neck point measure 1.25cm back along the neckline and then out 1.25cm.
- At both of these points draw a vertical line down to create a rectangular shape the length of the placket and 2.5cm wide.
- At the bottom of the pattern measure up 1.5cm from the hemline and draw in the hem facing line.

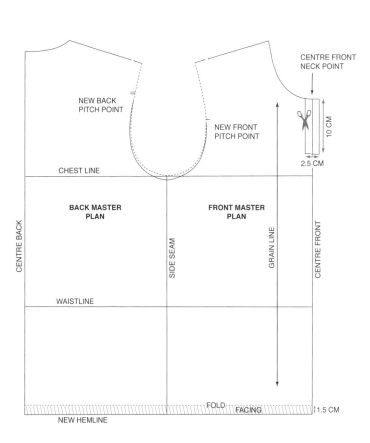

## STEP 4
## FRONT PATTERN

- Trace off the front onto a new piece of paper and, following the instructions on page 50, create the full pattern shape, which will be cut down the right side of the placket to create an opening.

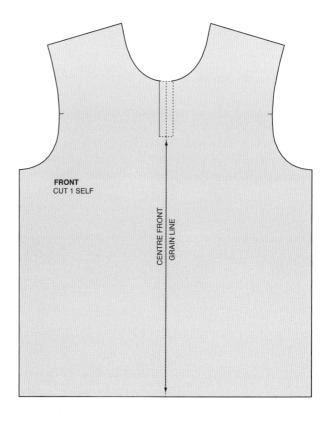

FRONT
CUT 1 SELF

CENTRE FRONT
GRAIN LINE

## STEP 5
## BACK PATTERN

- Trace off the back onto a new piece of paper and, following the instructions on page 50, create the full pattern shape.

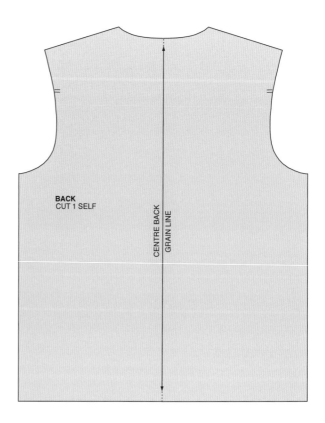

BACK
CUT 1 SELF

CENTRE BACK
GRAIN LINE

## STEP 6
### UPPER AND UNDER PLACKET FACING PATTERNS

- Draw a rectangle 12cm long by 4.5cm wide; this measurement includes a 1cm seam allowance around all four edges.
- Indicate the 1cm seam allowance around all four sides, leaving a 10 x 2.5cm facing. This will form the upper placket facing.
- Draw a rectangle 12cm long by 7cm wide; this measurement includes a 1cm seam allowance around all four edges.
- Indicate the 1cm seam allowance around all four sides and divide the rest of the width in half to give a 2.5cm facing when folded. This will form the under placket facing.

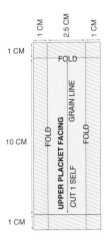

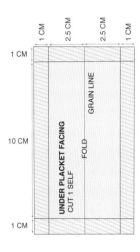

## STEP 7
### DEVELOPING A COLLAR STAND FOR A KNITTED RIBBED COLLAR

- Draw a rectangular box 2cm wide and 24.5cm long. Label the narrow side as the *centre back neck* and the long side as the *neckline*.
- From the centre back measure 8.5cm along the neckline and mark a notch. This is the half back neck measurement; the remaining 16cm is the half front neck measurement, including half the placket width, 1.25cm.
- At the front end of the collar stand measure up 1cm and make a mark. From this mark, with a shallow curve, draw a new line blending back to the shoulder notch.
- Complete the stand by drawing another new line 2cm from

the first and blending it back. Square up from the end of the new neckline to complete the front of the stand, drawing a curved line at the upper corner.
- Measure 1.25cm (half the width of the placket) from the front of the stand back towards the shoulder line, square across and label it *centre front neck*.

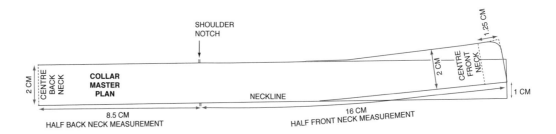

## STEP 8
### COLLAR STAND PATTERN

- Trace off the collar stand onto a new piece of paper and, following the instructions on page 50, create the full pattern shape.

**Knitted ribbed collars**
Knitted ribbed collars are piece-manufactured to order, or can be bought in specific standard neck measurements according to style and inserted between the two parts of the stand.

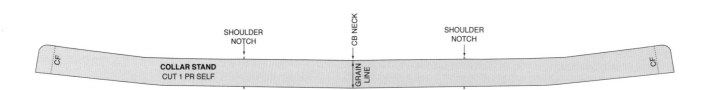

## STEP 9
### DEVELOPING THE SLEEVE MASTER PLAN

Start this development by selecting the basic men's sleeve block, or by drafting the basic sleeve block according to the instructions on page 42. Cut a large piece of drafting paper slightly longer than the length of the sleeve you want to develop and transfer the shape of the block and all marks, labels and instructions following the directions on page 48. The design illustrated is a short sleeve with a ribbed cuff. The sleeve block that you have selected might be longer or shorter than the design you are developing. Analyse it by taking a measurement from your fit model or mannequin and by consulting the size chart, or even by using competitors' garments for comparison.

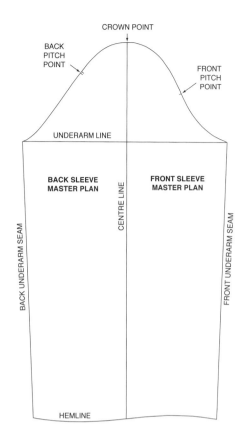

## STEP 10
### WIDENING THE SLEEVE HEAD FOR THE LOWERED ARMHOLE

**Adjusting the sleeve head to fit the armhole**
Having enlarged the sleeve circumference in Step 2, you will need to check the length of the sleeve head and increase it according to the new armhole measurement.

Measure the front and back of the original armhole on the master plan (in this case 24.5cm and 25cm respectively), then the new armhole (26.5cm and 27.5cm respectively). Compare this to the sleeve head measurement and increase the length of the sleeve head by the same amount.

Knitted materials need very little ease on the sleeve head, so in this case ease was not added to the new sleeve head measurement.

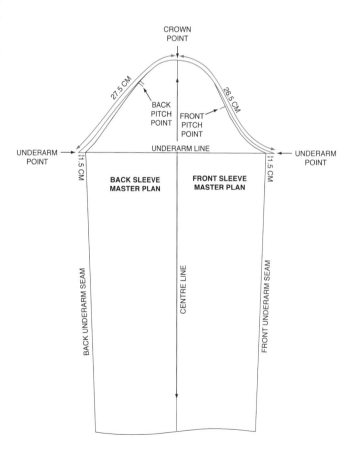

- Extend the underarm line out 1.5cm on both sides.
- Using the original sleeve block as a template, redraw the new sleeve head shape and indicate the new pitch point positions to match those on the lowered armhole.

## STEP 11
### DEVELOPING THE SHORT SLEEVE

- Measure 6cm down the centre line from the underarm line and square across the sleeve width.
- From the centre of this new line measure 15cm out to both sides and mark. This is the new sleeve cuff width.
- Join the extended sleeve head to the edge of the cuff width with a curved line on both sides.
- Continue to measure a further 1cm down the centre line and square across to create a seam to attach the knitted ribbed cuff. Both ends of this seam allowance should be extended by 1cm so that when it is folded up, the seam allowance matches the shape of the cuff.

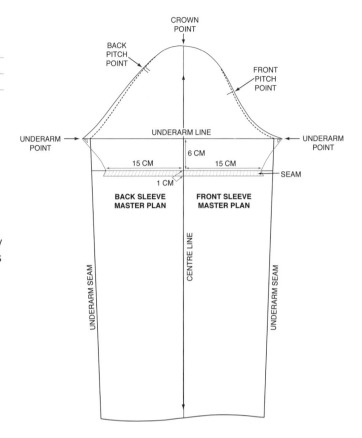

## STEP 12
### POLO SLEEVE PATTERN

- Following the instructions on page 50, trace off the sleeve pattern.

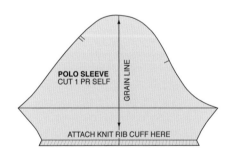

# PATTERN
# HOODED SWEATSHIRT

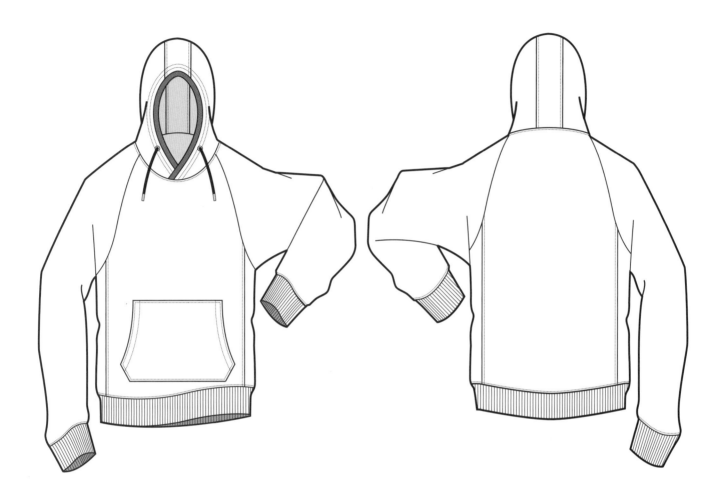

**This pattern includes development
of the following features:**

Creating a side panel

Lowering the neckline

Constructing a muff pocket

Lowering the armhole

Widening the sleeve head and lowering the crown height

Constructing a raglan panel sleeve

Reducing the length of the sleeve

Incorporating a ribbed cuff and waistband

Constructing a hood

**Assess the function of the garment**

Before embarking on any pattern development, first identify the purpose of the garment. A hooded sweatshirt is generally worn over other clothes, so you would need to make the pattern slightly larger to accommodate the clothes worn beneath it.

## STEP 1
### DEVELOPING THE MASTER PLAN

- Start by selecting the basic men's body block, or by drafting the basic block according to the instructions on page 40. Cut a large piece of drafting paper slightly longer than the length of the sweatshirt you want to develop and transfer the shape of the block and all marks, labels and instructions following the directions on page 48.

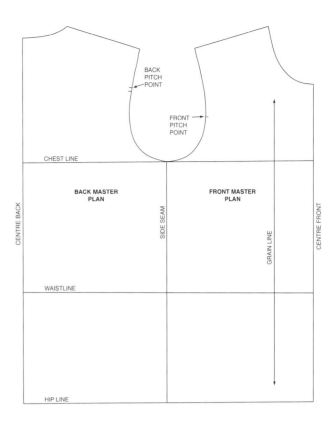

## STEP 2
### MOVING THE SHOULDER SEAM

**Raglan sleeve development**

The first stage in raglan sleeve development is to move the shoulder seam from the back of the shoulder forward to the front of the pattern. This balances the front and back pattern pieces, so that when the raglan shapes are drawn, the new shoulder seam sits centrally on the top of the shoulder.

- To move the shoulder seam forward, remove 1cm from the front shoulder seam and add 1cm to the back shoulder seam. Measure the new front shoulder seam. The back shoulder seam should be the same length, so it will extend beyond the original back shoulder neck point. You will need to redraw the back neckline, blending it back from the new back shoulder neck point.

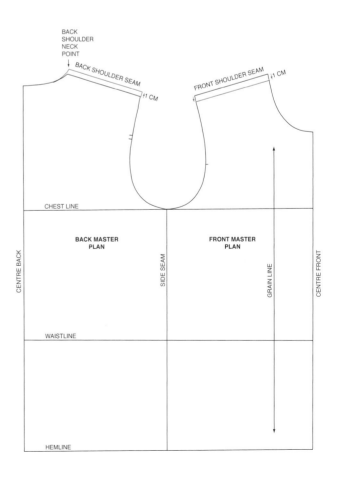

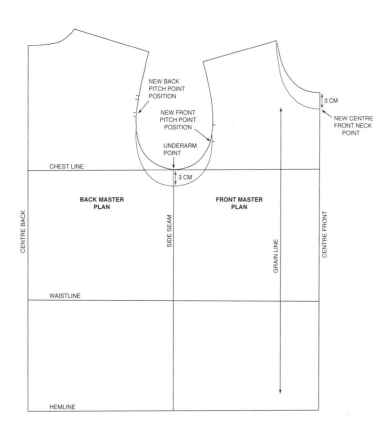

## STEP 3
### LOWERING THE ARMHOLE ON THE BODY AND CENTRE FRONT NECKLINE

- Measure 3cm down the side seam from the underarm point and mark. Using the original block as a template, recreate the shape of the armhole and transfer the back and front pitch points to their new positions on the lowered armhole.
- Measure down 3cm from the centre front neck point and mark. Using the block as a template, redraw the new lowered neckline.

## STEP 4
### CREATING THE RAGLAN SHOULDER SHAPES ON THE BODY BLOCK

- First measure 4cm down the back neckline from the back shoulder neck point and mark and 4cm down the front neckline from the front shoulder neck point and mark.
- Next measure 2cm down from the new front pitch point on the armhole and square across to the back armhole and mark. From these points draw a straight line up to each of the marks you made on the front and back necklines.
- From the back neckline measure 12cm down this line, and from the front neckline measure 10.5cm. Square up 0.5cm on each line and mark.
- With a shallow curve, draw lines from the points on the back and front necklines to the armholes, this time passing through the marks at 0.5cm.

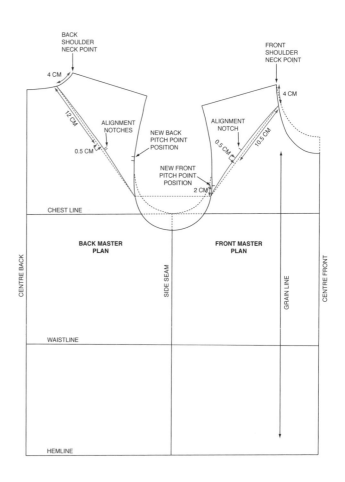

## STEP 5
## DEVELOPING THE RAGLAN SHAPE

- Trace off the shoulder shapes, which will be used to create the raglan sleeve, adding front and back notches for alignment.

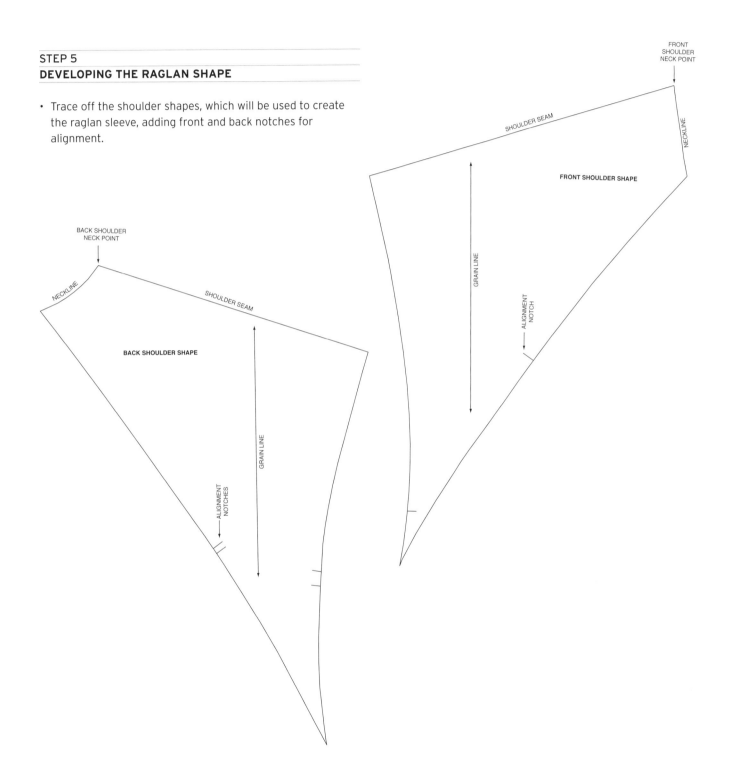

BACK SHOULDER NECK POINT

NECKLINE

SHOULDER SEAM

BACK SHOULDER SHAPE

GRAIN LINE

ALIGNMENT NOTCHES

FRONT SHOULDER NECK POINT

SHOULDER SEAM

NECKLINE

FRONT SHOULDER SHAPE

GRAIN LINE

ALIGNMENT NOTCH

## STEP 6
### DEVELOPING THE SIDE PANEL

- First measure 8cm out from the side seam along the waistline towards the centre front and centre back. Repeat at the hemline and draw two vertical lines up to the raglan style line to create the side panel.

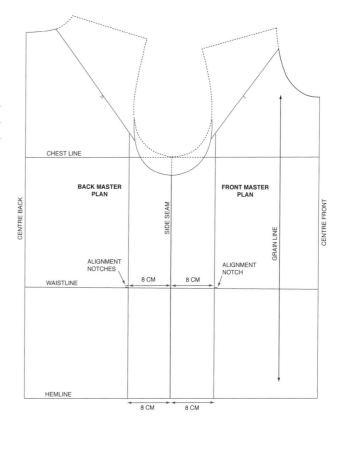

## STEP 7
### SIDE PANEL PATTERN

- Following the instructions on page 50, trace off the new side panel shape and mark the side panel stylelines with notches, two for the back and one for the front, to aid alignment during construction.

## STEP 8
### DEVELOPING THE CENTRE FRONT MUFF POCKET

- Start by developing half of the muff pocket from the centre front. Measure up 5cm from the hemline and mark, continue measuring up a further 18cm and mark. From both these points square across 14.5cm towards the side panel style line and mark. Create a rectangle by joining all four points.
- Measure in 2.5cm from the bottom left corner of the rectangle. Connect this point back to the vertical left-hand side with an angled line 5cm in length. Measure in 3cm from the top left corner. From this point, draw a shallow curved line down to connect with the top of the angled line. This will become the curved pocket opening.
- To create a facing for the front opening, measure in a further 2.5cm along the shallow curved line of the front opening, and draw in the shape of the facing.

## STEP 9
### MUFF POCKET AND FACING PATTERNS

- Trace off the muff pocket shape onto a new piece of paper and, following the instructions on page 50, create the full pattern shape.
- Following the instructions on page 50, trace off the facing pattern.

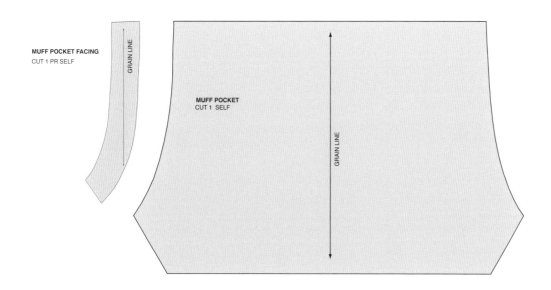

## STEP 10
### FRONT PATTERN

- Trace off the front onto a new piece of paper and, following the instructions on page 50, create the full pattern shape, adding drill holes for the muff pocket placement.

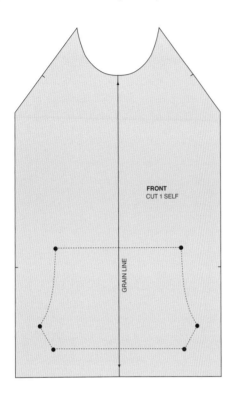

FRONT
CUT 1 SELF

GRAIN LINE

## STEP 11
### BACK PATTERN

- Trace off the back onto a new piece of paper and, following the instructions on page 50, create the full pattern shape.

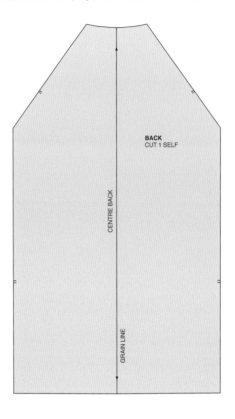

BACK
CUT 1 SELF

CENTRE BACK

GRAIN LINE

## STEP 12
### DEVELOPING THE SLEEVE MASTER PLAN

Start this development by selecting the basic men's sleeve block, or by drafting the basic sleeve block according to the instructions on page 42. Cut a large piece of drafting paper slightly longer than the length of the sleeve you want to develop and transfer the shape of the block and all marks, labels and instructions following the directions on page 48. The sleeve block that you have selected might be longer or shorter than the design you are developing. Analyse it by taking a measurement from your fit model or mannequin and by consulting the size chart, or even by using competitors' garments for comparison.

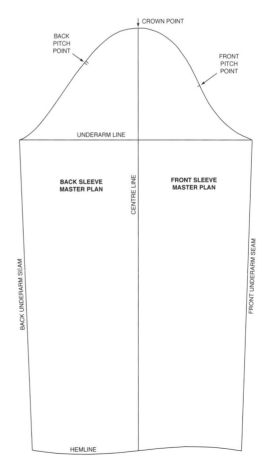

CROWN POINT

BACK
PITCH
POINT

FRONT
PITCH
POINT

UNDERARM LINE

BACK SLEEVE
MASTER PLAN

CENTRE LINE

FRONT SLEEVE
MASTER PLAN

BACK UNDERARM SEAM

FRONT UNDERARM SEAM

HEMLINE

## STEP 13

### WIDENING THE SLEEVE HEAD WITH A LOWERED CROWN AND REDUCING THE SLEEVE LENGTH

- To make the sleeve head larger, to fit the larger armhole created in Step 3, and give the finished raglan a casual fit, you will need to reduce the crown height. Measure down the centre line 2cm.
- Extend the underarm line out by up to the measurement that you lowered the armhole by, and not beyond. In this case, extend the underarm line out by 2.5cm on both sides.

**Altering the sleeve head to fit the armhole**
You must take the new measurement from the armhole so you can match it with the sleeve head plus or minus ease, depending on fabric and fit.

- Using the original sleeve block as a template, redraw the sleeve head shape and add the new back and front pitch point positions to match those on the lowered armhole. Redraw the underarm seam lines from the new points at the end of the underarm line down to the hemline at the cuff.
- Reduce the sleeve length by measuring up 10cm from the hemline and redraw the line following the shape on the original block.

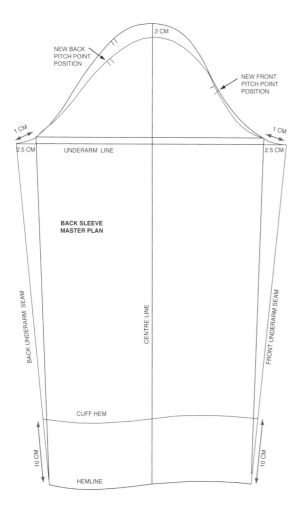

## STEP 14

### MOVING THE CENTRE LINE FORWARD TO DEVELOP THE RAGLAN SLEEVE

**Moving the centre line on the raglan sleeve**
In the same way that you adjusted the shoulder seams in Step 2, you now need to move the seam on the sleeve.

- Measure 1cm from the centre line towards the front underarm seam. At this 1cm measurement, draw a straight line from the top of the sleeve to the hem. The top of this line is the new crown point.

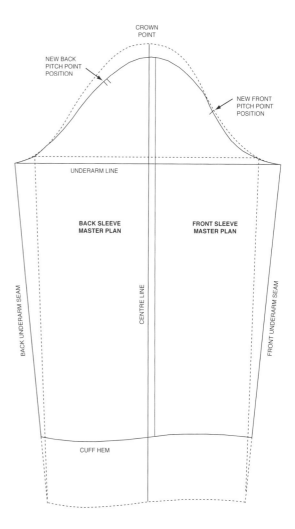

## STEP 15
### CREATING THE RAGLAN SHAPE OF THE SLEEVE

- Trace the raglan shoulder shapes from Step 4 onto the sleeve head by placing the shoulder points together at the new crown point and aligning the tips of the raglan shapes to the sleeve head lines.

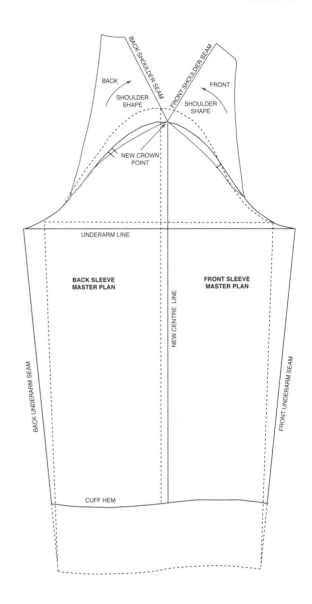

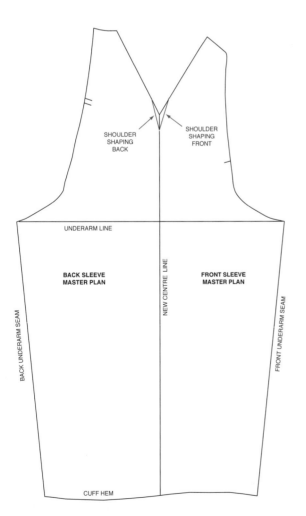

## STEP 16
### SMOOTHING OUT THE CROWN POINT

- Trace the raglan sleeve onto a separate piece of paper. To create smooth lines around the raglan sleeve head, shape the crown point so that it is less angular and smooth out the joins on the sleeve head with shallow curves. When closing the shoulder shapes the removed volume will help to avoid extra width through the shoulder seams.

## STEP 17

### CLOSING THE RAGLAN SHOULDER SHAPES ON THE SLEEVE HEAD TO CREATE A CASUAL, ONE-PIECE RAGLAN SLEEVE

- To create a one-piece raglan sleeve you have to close the front and back shoulder shape on the sleeve head. Measure the front and back shoulder seam lines from the neckline down to the crown point. Then extend the new centre line up from the crown point, to beyond the shoulder seam length.
- Trace the raglan sleeve from Step 16 onto a separate piece of paper; repeat the process for the back raglan sleeve master plan. Then place the front traced sleeve head over the original one, aligning the underarm lines. From the crown point moving up the new centre line, rotate the front shoulder seams along the centre line. Mark the sleeve width of the shoulder panel periodically as you move along the centre line until you reach the neckline; draw in the new position of the front neckline. Place the back traced sleeve head over the original one, aligning the underarm lines. From the crown point moving up the new centre line, rotate the back shoulder seams along the centre line. Mark the sleeve width of the shoulder panel periodically as you move along the centre line until you reach the neckline.
- By closing the shoulder seams you have raised the underarm line to a new position, straightening the curved shoulder line.

To establish the front and back sleeve seams, align them with the underarm line width. Once you are able to connect these three lines, redraw the sleeve length in its new position.

- Place the front and back sleeve seams at the new neckline position. To keep the same sleeve head height, measure the underarm line width, place the front shoulder seam at the new neckline, trace down the length and redraw in the new position of the front shoulder seam to the underarm line.
- Draw in the new position of the back neckline, place the back shoulder seam at the new neckline, trace down the length and redraw in the new position of the back shoulder seam to the underarm line.

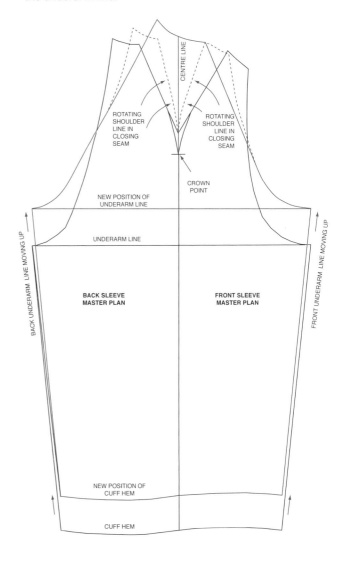

## STEP 18

### ONE-PIECE RAGLAN SLEEVE PATTERN

- Following the instructions on p. 50, trace off the final one-piece raglan sleeve pattern.

## Taking measurements for the hood

There are three measurements you need to create the pattern for the hood:

1. The front and back neck measurements, taken from the pattern - here they are 16.5cm and 9.5cm.
2. The front and back neck height, found by placing the front pattern on top of the back pattern and aligning them at the chest line, then measuring the distance between the front and back neck heights - here it is 11.5cm.
3. The vertical circumference of the head, taken for the hood opening by measuring around the face of the model's head, starting and finishing at the centre front neck point - here it is 80cm.

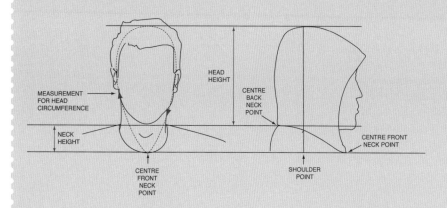

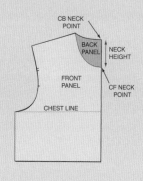

## STEP 19
### DEVELOPING THE HOOD

- Starting at the bottom left-hand side of a piece of paper, draw a 26cm horizontal line - the length of the combined back and front neck measurements.
- Square up and draw a 40cm line (half of the head circumference). Square across and then down to complete the rectangular box.
- Mark the bottom left corner and label as the *centre back neck point*.
- From the bottom left and right corners measure down 11.5cm (the neck height) and mark. Join the marks to form a rectangle.

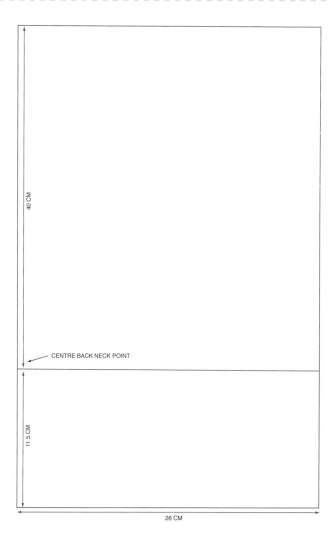

## STEP 20
## SHAPING THE HOOD

Taking the combined front and back neck measurements (26cm), use a French curve to draw the neck shape from the centre back neck point until it joins the line at the bottom of the rectangle, and mark. This is the centre front. This measurement will fall short of the bottom right corner of the rectangle.

**Design of the hood**
This hood design has a central panel. The width of the panel needs to be deducted from the hood shape at the centre back neck point and at the crown point. The overall shape of the hood is determined by the design, head size, neck opening and usage, which in this case is as outerwear.

- The central panel is 6cm wide. Remove half of the measurement from the centre back neck point and the other half from the crown point.
- From the top right corner measure down 10.5cm and square out 2.5cm. Now draw the hood shape according to the design.
- Finally, to create the pattern for the central panel, measure the back hood line – here it is 51.5cm.

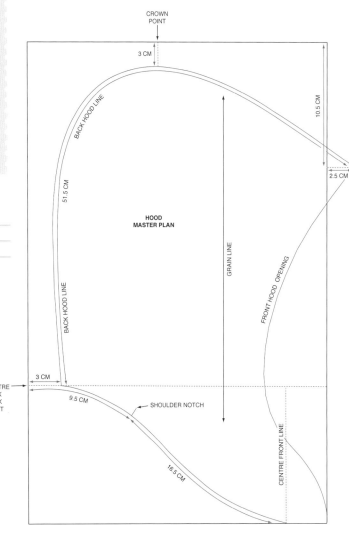

## STEP 21
## HOOD PATTERN

- Following the instructions on page 50, trace off the hood pattern.

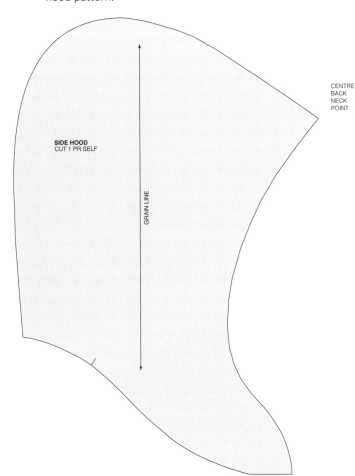

# STEP 22
## HOOD OPENING FACING STRIP AND EDGING PATTERNS

- The hood opening facing is a strip of fabric, 3cm in depth, that follows the curved shape of the hood opening. The edging finishes the hood opening.
- On the hood side panel pattern, measure in 3cm at the neckline and mark and 3cm at the top of the front hood opening and make a mark. Connect these points to create a curve 3cm in depth along the opening.
- Trace off the hood opening facing strip onto a new piece of paper and, following the instructions on page 50, create the full pattern shape.
- With a tape measure held upright measure along the outer edge of the facing strip - in this case 70cm. Draw a rectangular box 70cm long by 3cm wide and mark a fold line lengthways down the centre to create the edging.

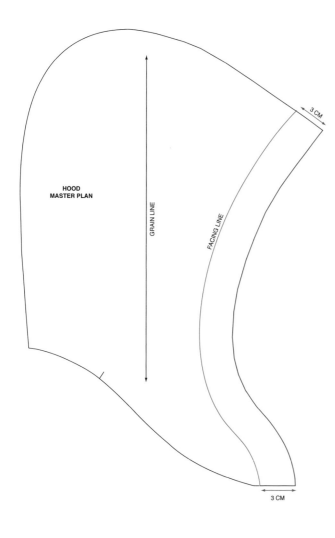

HOOD MASTER PLAN

GRAIN LINE

FACING LINE

3 CM

3 CM

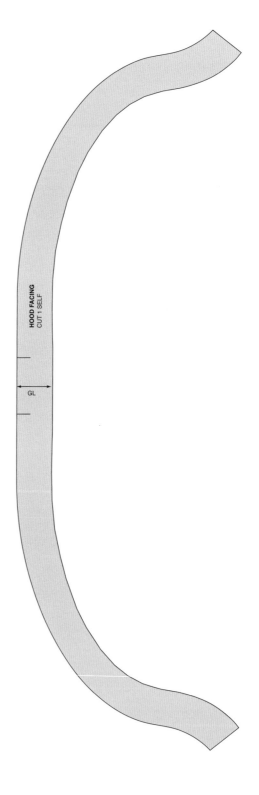

HOOD FACING
CUT 1 SELF

GL

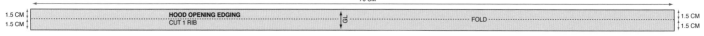

70 CM

1.5 CM
1.5 CM

HOOD OPENING EDGING
CUT 1 RIB

GL

FOLD

1.5 CM
1.5 CM

## STEP 23
## CENTRE BACK HOOD PANEL PATTERN

• Draw a rectangular box 6cm wide by 51.5cm long. This will become your final centre back hood panel.

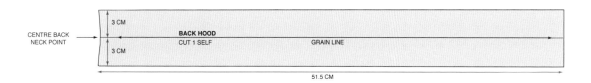

## STEP 24
## RIBBED CUFF PATTERN

• The cuff is a folded pattern. Draw a rectangular box 16cm wide and 20cm long. Mark the fold line halfway along the width.

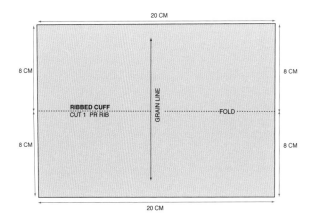

## STEP 25
## RIBBED WAISTBAND PATTERN

- The waistband is a folded pattern. Draw a rectangular box 16cm wide and 91cm long. Mark the fold line halfway along the width.

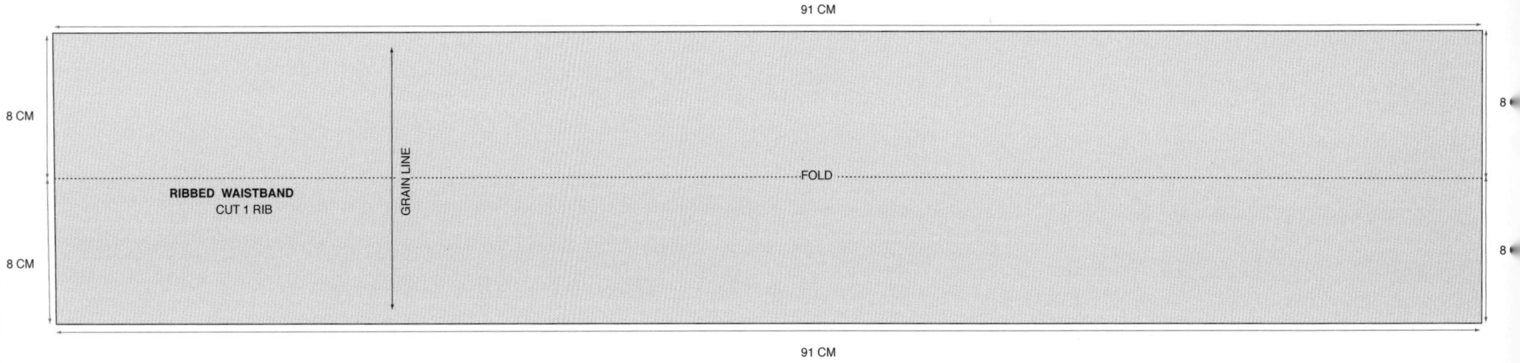

91 CM

8 CM

8

RIBBED WAISTBAND
CUT 1 RIB

GRAIN LINE

FOLD

8 CM

8

91 CM

# PATTERN
# CASUAL LONG-SLEEVED SHIRT

**This pattern includes development of the following features:**

Shaping the body

Creating a grown-on placket

Adding length to the body

Extending the shoulder, moving the shoulder
    seam and enlarging the armhole

Creating a back yoke

Creating a breast pocket

Creating a two-piece collar

Lowering the armhole

Reducing the sleeve head height

Developing a cuff with cuff guard

## STEP 1
### DEVELOPING THE MASTER PLAN

Start by selecting the basic men's body block, or by drafting
the basic block according to the instructions on page 40. Cut
a large piece of drafting paper slightly longer than the length
of the shirt you want to develop and transfer the shape of
the block and all marks, labels and instructions, following the
directions on page 48.

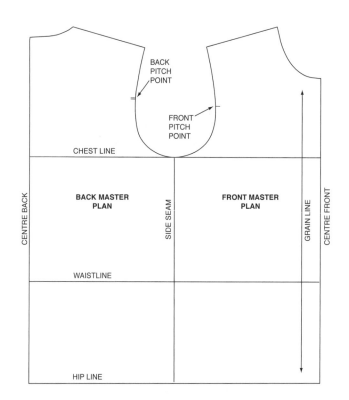

## STEP 2

### DEVELOPING THE ENLARGED ARMHOLE, EXTENDING THE SHOULDER, MOVING THE SHOULDER SEAM AND ADDING LENGTH AND WIDTH TO THE BODY

- To create the relaxed fit of this shirt style, add 2cm each to the front and back side seams. This will enlarge the armhole and give the shallower sleeve head of an extended shoulder style. You will need to reposition the front and back body blocks to add 4cm at the side seams and redraw the master plan.
- From the front shoulder point measure out 2cm over the armhole, square down 2cm and mark. At the front shoulder neck point measure 2.5cm down the neckline and draw a new line across to meet the new mark at the armhole.
- Trace this shape onto a new piece of paper and cut it out. Add the shape to the top of the back shoulder seam and trace around it. This will create a shorter shoulder on the front and a longer shoulder on the back.
- Extend the centre front and centre back lines down 6cm from the hemline and square across to create a new hemline.

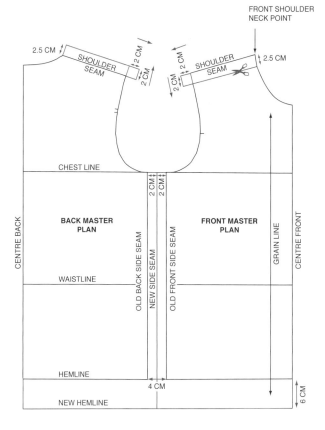

## STEP 3

### DEVELOPING THE NEW ARMHOLE AND BODY SHAPING

- Measure 2.5cm down the new side seam and make a mark. From this point on the front and back master plans, using the basic body blocks as a template, trace the new lowered armhole shape, continuing it up to connect with the new shoulders. Transfer the back and front pitch points to their new positions on the lowered armhole.
- To develop the side seam, measure out 1cm in both directions where the new side seam intersects the waistline.
- Connect both these points up to the new underarm point and down to the new hemline at the bottom of the new side seam with straight lines.
- Create a side back dart by measuring 12cm from the centre back along the chest line and the original hemline. Draw a vertical line to connect these two points.
- Measure 5cm down this new line from the chest line and mark. This point will be the starting point of the side back dart. Where the new line intersects the waistline, measure 1cm out on both sides and mark. This will become the widest point of the dart. Draw in the dart legs, connecting all the above points and the end of the dart line at the original hemline.

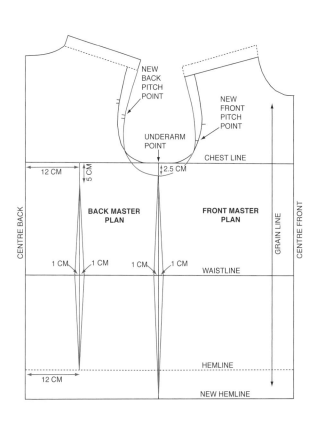

## STEP 4
### DEVELOPING THE GROWN-ON PLACKET

- The placket width in this style is 3cm and is centred over the centre front line. Measure 1.5cm out from the centre front neck point and mark, and back 1.5cm along the neckline and mark. Repeat at the hemline and connect all four marks to make a rectangle.
- Add another rectangular placket shape, 3cm wide, to the front of the first rectangle and then add a further 1cm seam allowance.
- The overall measurement of the placket excluding the seam allowance is now 6cm.

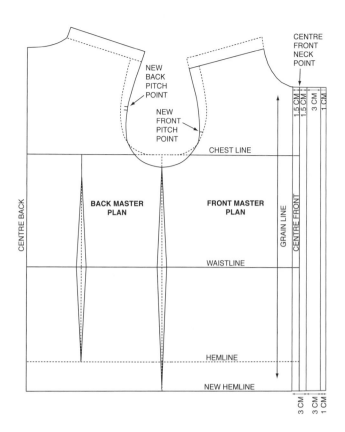

## STEP 5
### DEVELOPING THE BACK YOKE AND FRONT BREAST POCKET

- To create the back yoke measure 8cm down the centre back from the centre back neck point and mark. Measure 8cm from the new back shoulder point down the armhole and mark. Connect these two points with a straight line.
- From the front armhole measure 12cm in along the chest line and mark. At this point square up 4cm and down 7cm and draw a vertical line. At the top of the line square out 5cm on each side and mark. These points will become the pocket corners.
- Measure up 1cm from the bottom of the vertical line and square out 4.5cm to either side and mark. Join these points back to the bottom of the vertical line with straight lines. Connect these points back up to the pocket corners to create the final pocket shape.

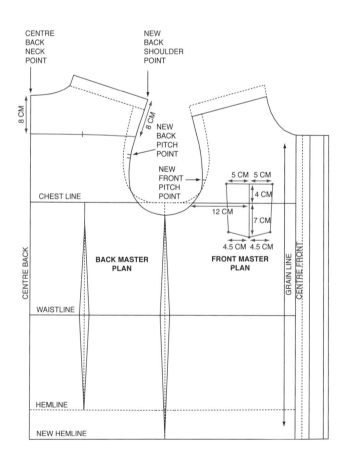

## STEP 6
## FRONT PATTERN

- Following the instructions on page 50, trace off the front pattern, indicating the breast pocket position on the right front panel with drill holes at the corners.

## STEP 7
## BACK PATTERN

- Trace off the back onto a new piece of paper and, following the instructions on page 50, create the full pattern shape.

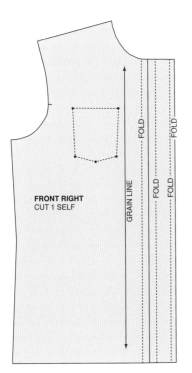
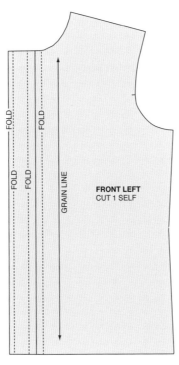
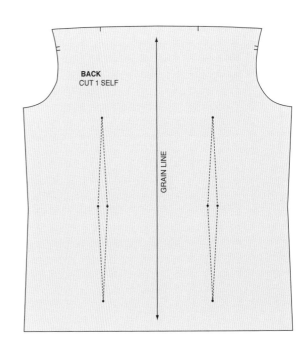

## STEP 8
## BREAST POCKET PATTERN

- Following the instructions on page 50, trace off the breast pocket pattern, adding a 2.5cm rectangular facing to the top.

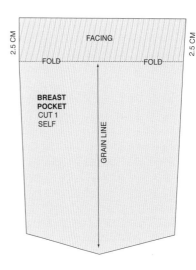

## STEP 9
## BACK YOKE PATTERN

- Trace the back yoke onto a new piece of paper and, following the instructions of page 50, create the full pattern shape.

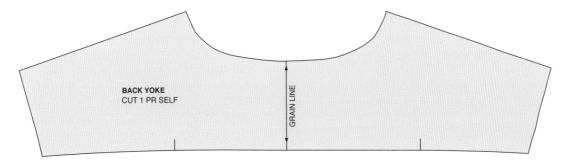

## STEP 10
### DEVELOPING THE COLLAR STAND

**Measuring half the neck from the master plan**

We will develop half the collar stand before creating the full collar stand. By taking measurements from the master plan, which is drawn in half, you will be measuring half of the neck measurement.

- On the master plan measure the length of the back neck, in this case 11cm, and the front neck from the shoulder point down past the centre front line to the point at which the placket finishes, in this case 13.5cm.
- Add these two measurements together to give half the neck measurement, in this case 24.5cm.

- On a new piece of piece of paper, draw a rectangle measuring 24.5cm by 2.5cm, which is the half neck measurement by the width of the collar stand. Label the narrow side as the *centre back neck* and the long side as the *neckline*.
- From the centre back neck, measure 11cm (the half back neck measurement) along the bottom line of the rectangle and place a notch. Label it the *shoulder notch*. Do the same 11cm along the top line of the rectangle.
- Measure up 1.5cm at the front edge of the rectangle and join this point back to the lower shoulder notch with a slight curve.
- From the shoulder notch, measure 13.5cm (the half front neck measurement) along this curved line. At the front of the curved line, square up 2.5cm (the width of the collar stand). Then draw another curved line to connect this line back to the top shoulder notch.

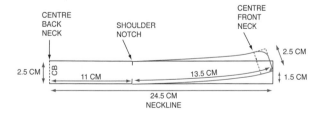

## STEP 11
### DEVELOPING THE TOP COLLAR

- Trace off the stand shape from Step 10 onto another piece of paper.
- Continue the centre back line vertically up 7.5cm from the top of the stand, square across 24cm and make a mark. This is the collar point. Connect this point back down to the centre front neck with a straight line. You have now created the basic top collar shape.
- At the collar point extend the front edge of the collar out and up by 1cm and draw a curved line back to meet the outer edge. This will give the collar a smoother shape.
- Measure up 2.5cm from the top of the stand along the centre back and make a mark. From here, square across to a point above the shoulder notch. From this point draw a curved line to meet the centre front neck, mirroring the curve of the stand. This is the inner edge of the 5cm-wide top collar shape.

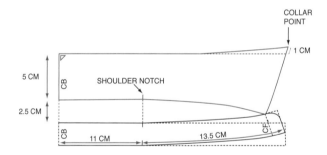

## STEP 12
### TOP COLLAR PATTERN
### COLLAR STAND PATTERN
### UNDER COLLAR PATTERN

- Trace off the collar stand pattern and, following the instructions on page 50, create the full pattern shape.
- Trace off the top collar pattern and, following the instructions on page 50, create the full pattern shape.
- The under collar is a copy of the top collar reduced by 3mm at the centre back neck, which is blended back with a line to both collar points; this reduction, when sewn, will pull the seam edge under the collar slightly so as not to be seen. Make a separate pattern for the under collar.

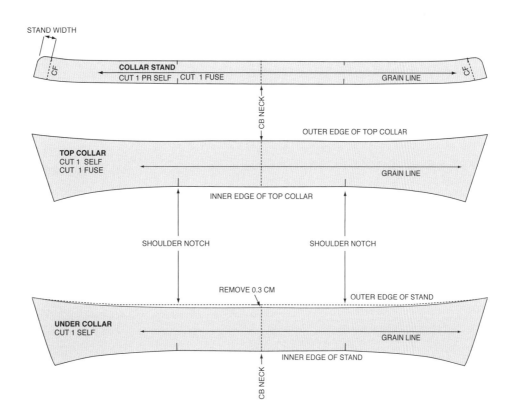

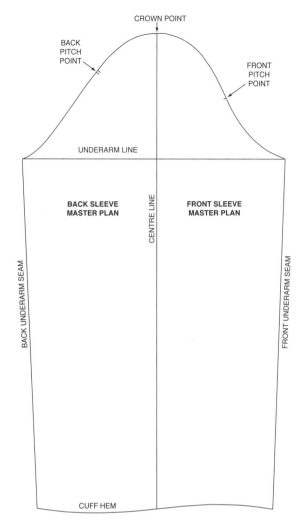

CROWN POINT

BACK PITCH POINT

FRONT PITCH POINT

UNDERARM LINE

BACK SLEEVE MASTER PLAN

CENTRE LINE

FRONT SLEEVE MASTER PLAN

BACK UNDERARM SEAM

FRONT UNDERARM SEAM

CUFF HEM

## STEP 13
## DEVELOPING THE SLEEVE MASTER PLAN

- Start this development by selecting the basic men's sleeve block, or by drafting the basic sleeve block according to the instructions on page 42. Cut a large piece of drafting paper slightly longer than the length of the sleeve you want to develop and transfer the shape of the block and all marks, labels and instructions, following the directions on page 50. The design illustrated is shaped and has a gathered tuck on the back of the sleeve for even more shaping.

**Measurements for developing the sleeve**
You will need three measurements to develop the sleeve:
1. Half the armhole measurement - measure the new armhole on the front and back patterns. In this case the front armhole is 26cm and the back 28cm. Add these measurements together (54cm) and divide in half, making 27cm.
2. Half the underarm measurement - measure the underarm line from the master plan. In this case it is 35.5cm. As this is a casual-fitting shirt you can determine the amount of ease according to the design. In this case we will add 12.5cm ease to the underarm line, making 48cm. Divide this measurement in half, making 24cm.
3. The cuff measurement, which in this case is 24cm (the wrist measurement), plus a 5cm tuck, making 29cm.

## DEVELOPING THE SLEEVE WITH A REDUCED SLEEVE HEAD HEIGHT
## AND SHAPING THE CUFF HEMLINE

- Measure 2.5cm down the centre line from the crown point to reduce the height of the sleeve head by the same amount that you lowered the armhole in Step 3.
- At an angle from the new crown point, draw out a line measuring half the new armhole – 27cm. From the centre line, draw out a line measuring half the new underarm line – 24cm. Adjust these lines until they meet to form a triangle and repeat on the other side of the sleeve. This will become the frame around which you construct the new shortened sleeve head.

- From the cuff hemline measure 13cm up the centre line and square out 14.5cm on both sides (the wrist measurement plus 5cm for the tuck) and mark. To create the shaping at the bottom of the sleeve, measure down 0.5cm on the back sleeve from the centre of the new cuff hemline and mark this point. On the front sleeve, measure up 0.5cm from the centre of the new cuff hemline and mark this point. Join the points with a curved line that is convex on the back sleeve and then reverses at the centre line so that it is concave on the front.
- Now draw in the new underarm seam lines from either end of the new cuff hemline to the new underarm points to create the sleeve shape.

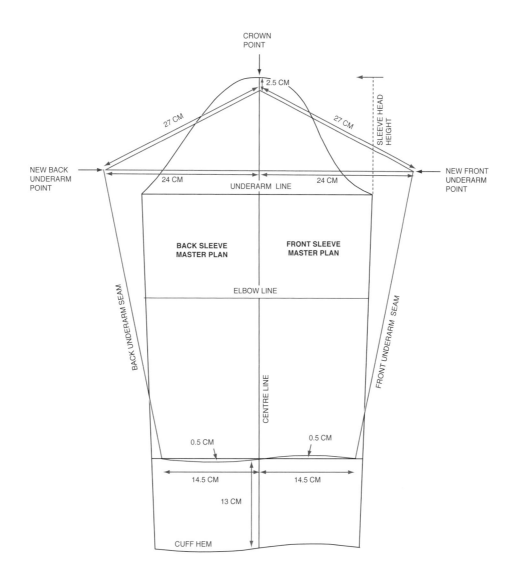

## DEVELOPING THE NEW SLEEVE SHAPE

- Add shape to the sleeve head by measuring 8.5cm from the new crown point along the diagonal line towards the new front underarm point, square out 1.3cm and mark. Then from the front underarm point measure 10cm up along the diagonal and mark. On the back measure down 9cm on the diagonal, square out 1.3cm and mark; measure 8cm up from the back underarm point and mark.

- Using a French curve, draw in shallow raised curves from the new crown point through the marks on the upper portion of the sleeve head, reversing the curves at the marks on the lower portion of the sleeve head, and finishing these hollow curved lines at the underarm points. To add in the pitch points, first measure the distance on the front and back body panels between the underarm point and the pitch points around the armhole. Then transcribe the measurements to the sleeve head, measuring from the underarm points towards the crown.
- From the back underarm seam line measure in 7.5cm along the new cuff hemline and square up 16cm. This is the cut line for the cuff guard. From the bottom of the cuff guard line, continue to measure 4.5cm and mark and a further 5cm and mark. This will become the tuck.

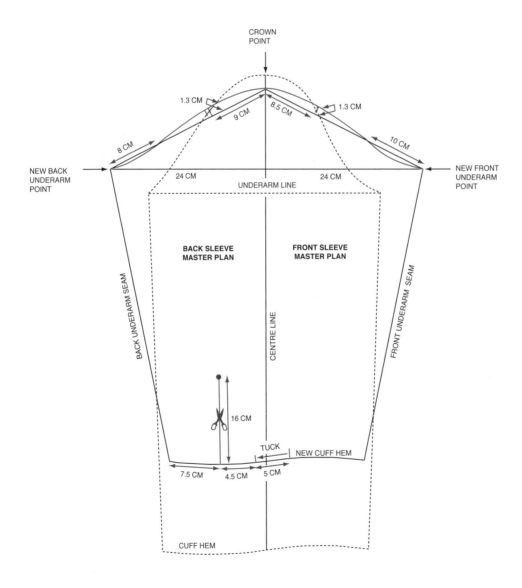

## STEP 16
## SLEEVE PATTERN

- Following the instructions on page 50, trace off the sleeve pattern, indicating the top of the cuff opening position with a drill hole.

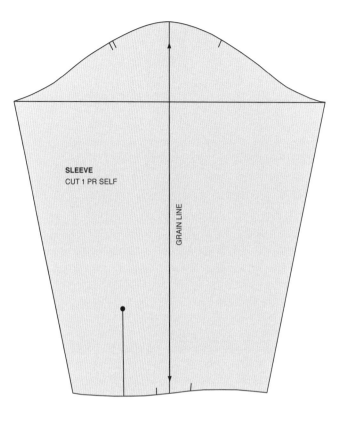

SLEEVE
CUT 1 PR SELF

GRAIN LINE

## STEP 17
## DEVELOPING THE CUFF

**Measuring the cuff**

The cuff is a double pattern piece that is sewn onto the end of the sleeve and turned inside out. The cuff shape will start and finish at the guard opening. Measure this width from the pattern, in this case 29cm, and subtract 5cm for the tuck and 1cm for the seam allowance (0.5cm on either side) on the cuff guard opening, making 23cm.

- On a separate piece of paper, draw a box 23cm long by 16cm wide to create a rectangular-shaped cuff.
- Divide the box in half lengthways, draw a line across the centre and label it *fold*.

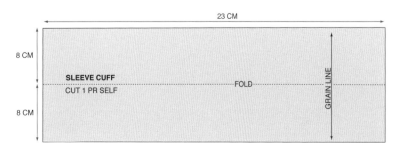

23 CM

8 CM

SLEEVE CUFF
CUT 1 PR SELF

FOLD

GRAIN LINE

8 CM

## STEP 18
### DEVELOPING THE TOP CUFF GUARD

- On a separate piece of paper, create a rectangular box 16cm long by 6cm wide.
- Divide the box in half lengthways, draw a line down the centre and label it *fold*.
- At each end square out 2cm up and 2cm down from the fold line and mark. Join these points with straight lines. This will leave you with a 1cm seam allowance on each long side.
- From the top left corner measure 2.5cm along the long side of the rectangle and square across 2cm. This small rectangular shape will be removed from the pattern.
- From the bottom right corner measure 1cm down the long side of the rectangle and mark, and measure 2cm in on the short side and mark. Join these points with an angled line.
- Now measure 1cm in along the top edge of the rectangle you drew in the top left corner and join this point to the top of the first angled line to give a pointed shape to the top of the cuff guard.

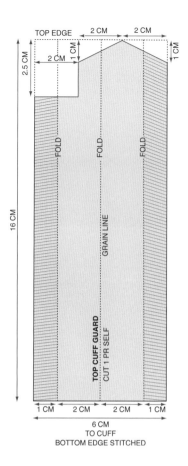

## STEP 19
### DEVELOPING THE BOTTOM CUFF GUARD

- Create a rectangular box 16cm by 6cm.
- Divide the box in half lengthways, draw a line down the centre and label it *fold*.
- At each end square out 2cm from the fold line and mark on both sides. Join these points with straight lines. This will leave you with a 1cm seam allowance on each long side.

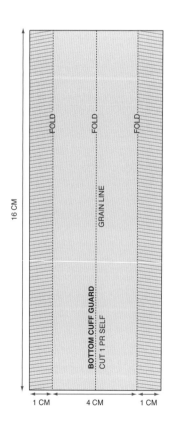

# PATTERN
# LUMBERJACK SHIRT

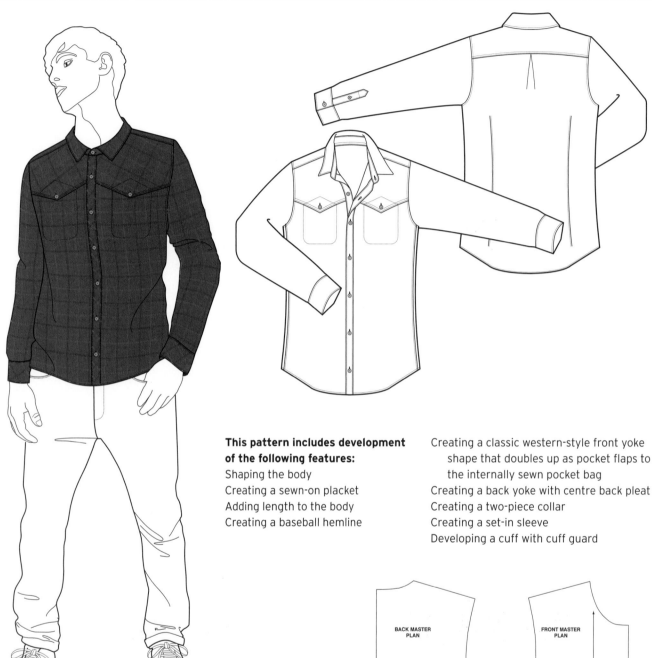

**This pattern includes development of the following features:**
Shaping the body
Creating a sewn-on placket
Adding length to the body
Creating a baseball hemline

Creating a classic western-style front yoke shape that doubles up as pocket flaps to the internally sewn pocket bag
Creating a back yoke with centre back pleat
Creating a two-piece collar
Creating a set-in sleeve
Developing a cuff with cuff guard

## STEP 1
### DEVELOPING THE MASTER PLAN

Start by selecting the basic men's body block, or by drafting the basic block according to the instructions on page 40. Cut a large piece of drafting paper slightly longer than the length of the shirt you want to develop and transfer the shape of the block and all marks, labels and instructions, following the directions on page 48.

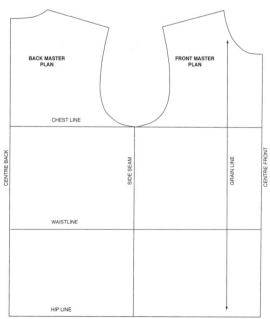

## STEP 2

### LENGTHENING THE BODY AND DEVELOPING THE BASEBALL HEMLINE

- Extend the centre front, side seam and the centre back lines down 6cm from the original hemline.
- Join these three points with a straight horizontal line to create a new hemline.
- On this new hemline measure in 4cm from the centre back and the centre front.
- From these points draw graduated curves up to meet the end of the side seam on the original hemline. You have now created a generic baseball hemline.

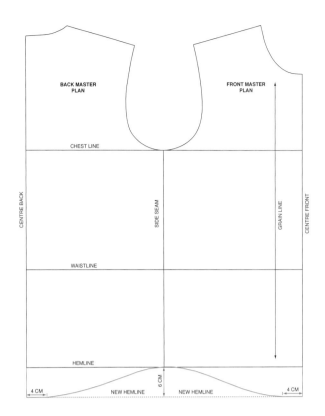

## STEP 3

### DEVELOPING THE SEWN-ON PLACKET

- The placket width is 2.5 cm and is drafted over the centre front as a template to be traced off and attached later.
- From the centre front neck point measure back 1.25cm along the neckline and mark, and measure out 1.25cm and mark; repeat this at the new hemline and connect these points with straight lines and label the outer one *fold*.
- From the outer line measure out another 2.5cm at the neckline for the placket width and mark; repeat at the hemline. Measure out another 1.5cm to create the seam allowance; repeat at the hemline. Again, join these points and label the first line *fold*.
- The overall measurement of the placket is now 6.5cm, including the seam allowance.

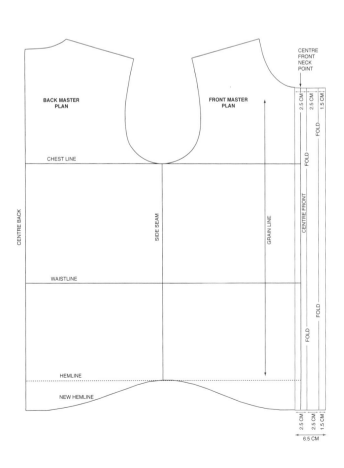

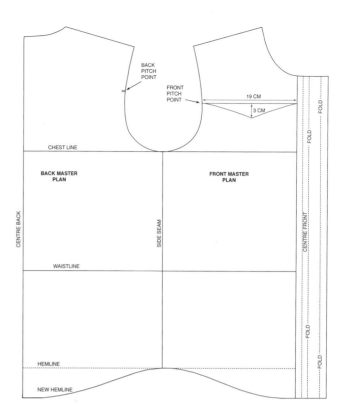

## STEP 4
### DEVELOPING THE FRONT YOKE SHAPE

- From the front pitch point on the armhole square across to meet the new placket shape.
- Measure between the front pitch point notch and the placket, in this case 19cm.
- Divide this measurement in half, in this case 9.5cm, and at this new point square down 3cm and mark. This will be the apex of the curve on the western-style front yoke.
- Draw a curved line from the front pitch point notch to the point at the apex of the curve, followed by another curved line to the point at the other end of the horizontal line you drew to the placket line.

## STEP 5
### DEVELOPING THE BREAST POCKET AND FLAP

**Pocket size**
Pocket widths generally reflect the width of a human hand or a group of fingers. The depth can depend on your design ethos or the depth of a hand from fingertip to wrist.

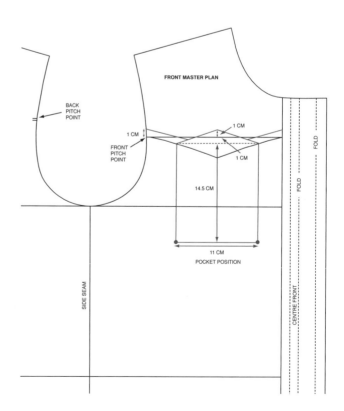

- To make a pocket 11cm wide, measure 1cm down from centre of the pitch line you drew and square out 5.5cm either side. Each end of this horizontal line should intersect the curved line of the yoke to create a triangular shape. Mirror this shape above to create a diamond shape, the apex of which sits 1cm above the horizontal pitch line. Add a 1cm-wide facing strip that follows the curve of the yoke from both sides of the diamond shape. This shape will become the concealed pocket flap described in Step 11 below.
- In this example the pocket depth is 14.5 cm measured from the middle of the diamond shape. Draw vertical lines from each point where the pocket intersects the curve of the yoke to create a rectangle 14.5cm x 11cm. Mark the lower corners of the pocket with drill holes.

## STEP 6
### DEVELOPING THE FRONT SHIRT PANEL

**Shaping for a fitted silhouette**
Side seam shaping will give the shirt a fitted silhouette. Back shaping with a dart will give you an even more fitted silhouette.

- Where the waistline intersects the side seam measure 1.5cm towards the centre front and mark.
- From the underarm point draw a slightly curved line down to meet the new point on the waistline and carry through with a curve back to the hemline at the bottom on the side seam.

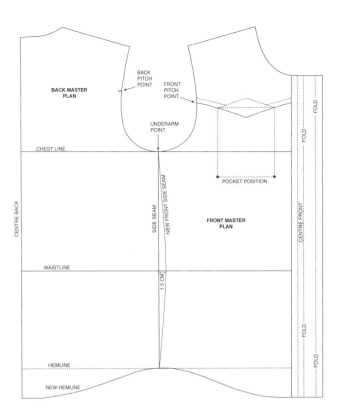

## STEP 7
### DEVELOPING THE BACK YOKE SHAPE, CENTRE BACK PLEAT AND SHAPED BACK PANEL

- From the back armhole pitch point square across to the centre back to create the back yoke panel.
- From where this line intersects with centre back measure out 2cm.
- Connect this point to the bottom of the new hemline at the centre back with a straight line. This will create half of the pleat width.
- Where the waistline intersects the side seam measure 1.5cm towards the centre back and mark.
- From the underarm point draw a slightly curved line down to meet the new point on the waistline and carry through with a curve back to the hemline at the bottom of the side seam.
- From the centre back measure 14cm along the chest line.
- From this point, square down to the original hemline.
- Measure 4.5cm down this line and mark. Measure 10cm up the line from the original hemline and mark. Where this line intersects the waistline measure out 1cm on each side and mark these points. Join all these points with straight lines to create the dart.

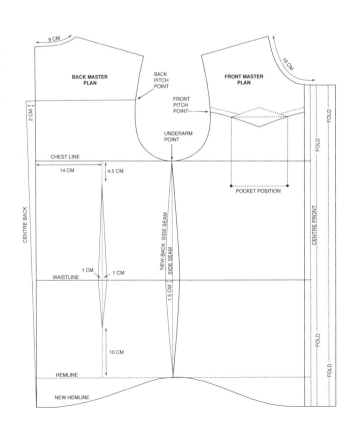

## STEP 8
### DEVELOPING THE COLLAR STAND

> **Measuring half the neck from the master plan**
> We will develop half the collar stand
> before creating the full collar stand.
> By taking measurements from the master
> plan, which is drawn in half, you will be
> measuring half the neck measurement.
> * On the master plan measure the length
>   of the back neck, in this case 9cm,
>   and the front neck from the shoulder
>   neck point down past the centre
>   front line to the point at which
>   the placket finishes when folded,
>   in this case 16cm.
> * Add these two measurements together
>   to give half the neck measurement,
>   in this case 25cm.

* On a new piece of piece of paper, draw a rectangle measuring 25cm by 2.5cm, which is half the neck measurement by the width of the collar stand. Label the narrow side as the *centre back neck* and the long side as the *neckline*.
* From the centre back neck, measure 9cm (the half back neck measurement) along the bottom line of the rectangle and place a notch. Label it the *shoulder notch*. Repeat along the top of the rectangle.
* Measure up 1.5cm at the front edge of the rectangle and join this new point back to the lower shoulder notch with a slight curve.
* From the shoulder notch, measure 16cm (the half front neck measurement) along this curved line. At the front of the curved line, square up 2.5cm (the width of the collar stand). Then draw another curved line to connect this line back to the top shoulder notch.
* From the top right corner of the stand measure along 2.5cm (the width of the placket) and from this point square across to the lower curved line. Label this *centre front neck*. Round off the top right corner with a slight curve.

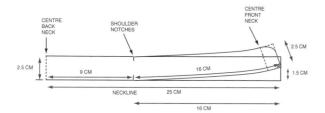

## STEP 9
### DEVELOPING THE TOP COLLAR

* Trace off the stand shape from Step 8 onto another piece of paper.
* Continue the centre back line vertically up 7.5cm from the top of the stand, square across 25cm and make a mark. Connect this point back down to the centre front line with a straight line. You have now created the basic top collar shape.
* At the collar point extend the front edge of the collar by 1cm and draw a curved line back to meet the outer edge. This will give the collar a smoother shape.
* Measure up 2.5cm from the top of the stand along the centre back and make a mark. From here, square across to a point above the shoulder notch. From this point draw a curved line to meet the centre front line, mirroring the curve of the stand. This is the inner edge of the 5cm-wide top collar shape.

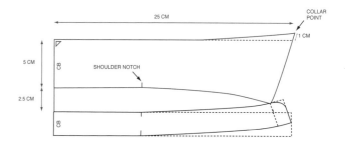

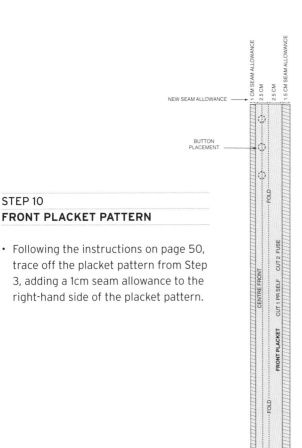

## STEP 10
### FRONT PLACKET PATTERN

- Following the instructions on page 50, trace off the placket pattern from Step 3, adding a 1cm seam allowance to the right-hand side of the placket pattern.

## STEP 11
### FRONT YOKE AND CONCEALED POCKET FLAP FACING PATTERNS

- Following the instructions on page 50, trace off the shape of the front yoke pattern from Steps 4 and 5.
- Indicate the concealed pocket flap position with a broken line.
- Trace off the flap facing pattern separately.

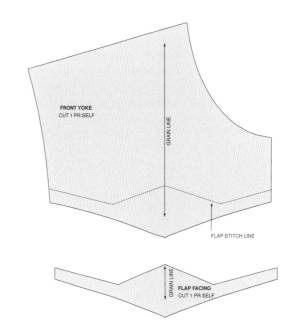

## STEP 12
### FRONT BREAST POCKET BAG PATTERN

- Following the instructions on page 50, trace off the front pocket bag pattern from Step 5.

## STEP 13
### BACK YOKE PATTERN

- Trace off the back yoke from Step 7 onto a new piece of paper and, following the instructions on page 50, create the full pattern shape.

## STEP 14
### FRONT PATTERN

- Following the instructions on page 50, trace off a copy of the lower front shirt panel from Step 7. Follow the curve from the armhole to where the curve meets the top of the pocket bag, draw a horizontal line across the pocket and then follow the curve towards the centre front. This will create the pocket opening edge under the flap.

## STEP 15
### BACK PATTERN

- Trace off the back shirt panel and, following the instructions on page 50, create the full pattern shape.

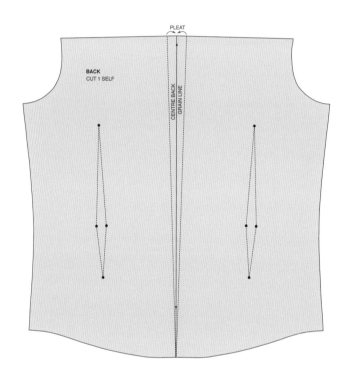

## STEP 16
### COLLAR STAND PATTERN
### TOP COLLAR PATTERN
### DEVELOPING THE UNDER COLLAR

- Trace off the collar stand pattern and, following the instructions on page 50, create the full pattern shape.
- Trace off the top collar pattern and, following the instructions on page 50, create the full pattern shape.
- The under collar is a copy of the top collar, reduced by 3mm, at the centre back neck, which is blended back with a line to both collar points; this reduction, when sewn, will pull the seam edge under the collar slightly so as not to be seen. Make a separate pattern for the under collar.

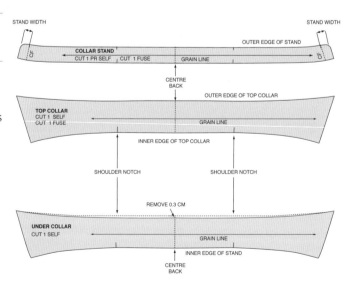

## STEP 17
### DEVELOPING THE SLEEVE MASTER PLAN

Start this development by selecting the basic men's sleeve block, or by drafting the basic sleeve block according to the instructions on page 42. Cut a large piece of drafting paper slightly longer than the length of the shirt you want to develop and transfer the shape of the block and all marks, labels and instructions, following the directions on page 48. The design illustrated is shaped and has a gathered pleat on the back of the sleeve for even more shaping. The sleeve block that you have selected might be longer or shorter than the design you are developing. Analyse by taking a measurement from your fit model or mannequin and by consulting your size chart, or even by using competitors' garments for comparison. The sleeve length is 61.5cm and the cuff measurement is calculated by adding 3cm to the wrist measurement of 25cm for a tuck, giving 28cm.

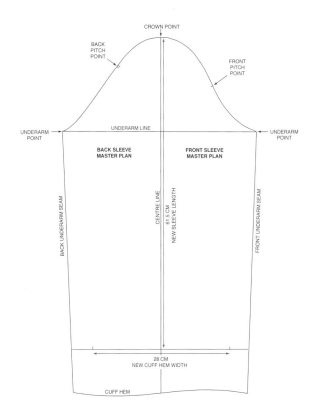

## STEP 18
### DEVELOPING THE SLEEVE SHAPE

- To create the shaping at the bottom of the sleeve, measure down 0.5cm on the back sleeve from the centre of the new cuff hemline and mark this point. On the front sleeve, measure up 0.5cm from the centre of the new cuff hemline and mark this point. Join the points with a curved line that is convex on the back sleeve and then reverses at the centre line so that it is concave on the front.
- Now draw in the new underarm seam lines to create the sleeve shape.
- From the back underarm seam line measure in 8cm along the new cuff hemline and square up 16cm. This is the cut line for the cuff guard. Measure in a further 4cm at the bottom of this line and mark and then a further 3cm and mark. This will become the tuck.

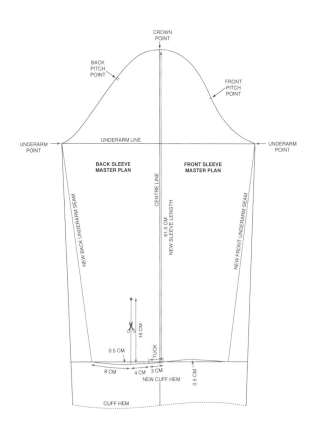

## STEP 19
### SLEEVE PATTERN

- Following the instructions on page 50, trace off the sleeve pattern.

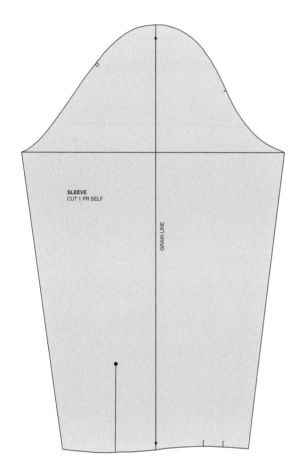

## STEP 20
### DEVELOPING THE CUFF

**Measuring the cuff**
The cuff is a double pattern that is sewn onto the end of the sleeve and turned inside out. The cuff shape will start and finish at the guard opening. Measure this width from the pattern, in this case 28cm, and subtract 3cm for the tuck and 1cm for the seam allowance (0.5cm on either side) on the cuff guard opening, making 24cm.

- On a separate piece of paper, draw a horizontal box 24cm long by 14cm wide to create a rectangular-shaped cuff.
- Divide the box in half lengthways, draw a line across the centre and label it *fold*.

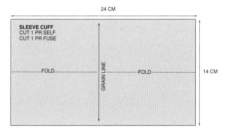

## STEP 21
### DEVELOPING THE TOP CUFF GUARD

- On a separate piece of paper, create a rectangular box 16cm long by 6cm wide.
- Divide the box in half lengthways, drawing a line across the centre and label it *fold*.
- At each end square out 2cm from the fold line on both sides and mark. Join these points with straight lines. This will leave you with a 1cm seam allowance on each long side.
- From the top left corner measure 2.5cm down the long side of the rectangle and square across 2cm. This small rectangular shape will be removed from the pattern.
- From the top right corner measure 1cm down the long side of the rectangle and mark, and measure 2cm across the short side and mark. Join these points with an angled line.
- Now measure 1cm down from the edge of the rectangle you drew in the top left corner and join this point to the top of the first angled line to give a pointed shape to the top of the cuff guard.

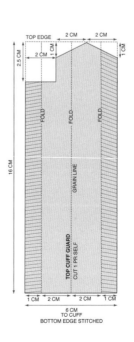

## STEP 22
## DEVELOPING THE BOTTOM CUFF GUARD

- Create a rectangular box 16cm by 6cm.
- Divide the box in half lengthways, draw a line down the centre and label it *fold*.
- At each end square out 2cm on both sides from the fold line and mark. Join these points with straight lines. This will leave you with a 1cm seam allowance on each long side.

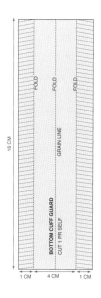

# PATTERN
# SHORT-SLEEVED SAFARI SHIRT

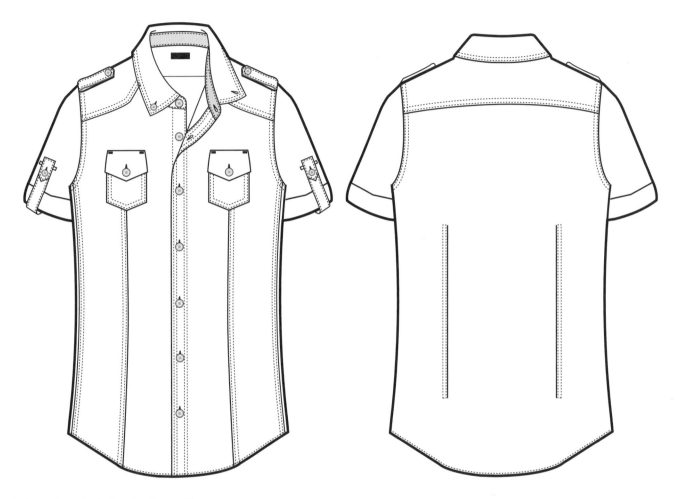

**This pattern includes development of the following features:**

Creating a darted body

Constructing a grown-on and a sewn-on placket

Adding length to the body

Creating a baseball hemline

Creating a shoulder yoke

Creating an epaulette and sleeve tab

Creating a patch pocket with flap

Creating a two-piece collar

Lowering the armhole

Reducing the sleeve head height

Developing a short sleeve incorporating a cuff

## STEP 1
### DEVELOPING THE MASTER PLAN

Start by selecting the basic men's body block, or by drafting the basic block according to the instructions on page 40. Cut a large piece of drafting paper slightly longer than the length of the shirt you want to develop and transfer the shape of the block and all marks, labels and instructions, following the directions on page 48.

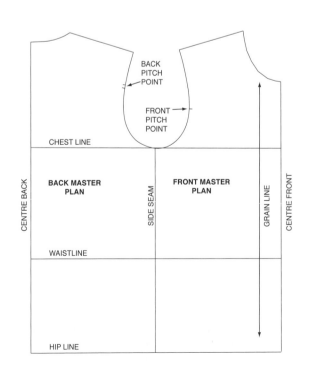

## STEP 2

### LENGTHENING THE BODY AND CREATING A GROWN-ON AND SEWN-ON PLACKET

- Extend the centre front and centre back lines down 6cm from the hemline and square across.
- The front left body panel has a grown-on placket of 2.5cm and the front right body has a sewn-on placket. You can create both from one pattern development.
- From the centre front neck point measure back 1.25cm along the neckline and mark, and measure out 1.25cm and mark; repeat this at the new hemline and connect these points with straight lines and label the outer one *fold*.
- From this line continue to measure out 2.5cm at the neckline and mark, and then a further 1.5cm for the seam width; repeat at the hemline. Again, join these points, mark and label the first line as a fold line.
- The overall measurement of the placket is now 6.5cm, including the seam allowance.

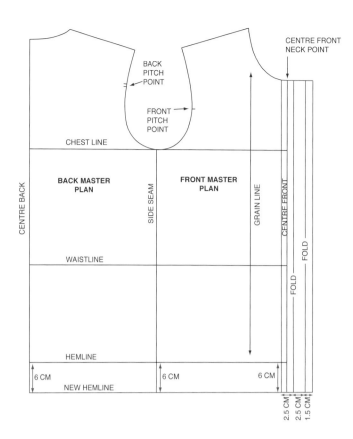

## STEP 3

### DEVELOPING THE NEW ARMHOLE, BODY AND HEM SHAPING

> **Shaping the body**
> There is no side seam shaping in this design because the side back and side front darts give enough shape to the silhouette.

- Measure 2cm down the side seam and mark. From this position on the front and back master plan, using your basic body blocks as a template, trace the new lowered armhole shape, continuing it up to connect with the shoulders. Draw in the new lowered pitch point positions.
- Create the front dart by measuring 16cm along the chest line from the old underarm point and mark, square down and draw a line to connect with the new hemline. Where this line intersects the waistline measure out 1cm on both sides and mark. This will become the widest part of the dart. Repeat at the new hemline, measuring out 0.5cm on both sides and mark. Draw in the dart legs from the chest line down, connecting all of the above points.
- Create the side back dart by measuring 11.5cm along the chest line and the original hemline from the centre back and mark. Draw a vertical line to connect these two points. Measure 5cm down this new line and mark and up 5.5cm and mark. Where this new line intersects the waistline measure out 1.5cm on both sides and mark. This will become the widest point of the dart. Draw in the dart legs, connecting all of the above points.
- Develop the hem shaping from the centre front to the side seam using a French curve. When you reach the front dart

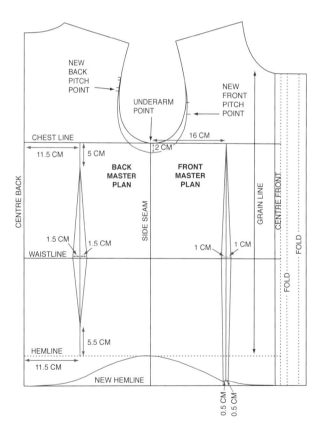

you will need to step the hemline down so that it continues in a smooth line when the dart is folded. Do this by tracing the dart legs and the hemline onto a separate piece of paper, fold the dart and then redraw the hemline. Cut it out and, when you open up the paper, you will have a template off which to trace the step. Continue to draw in the hemline up to the side seam and then back down to the centre back.

## STEP 4
### DEVELOPING THE FRONT AND BACK YOKE SHAPES

- For the back yoke shaping measure 9.5cm down the centre back line and mark, and 8cm from the back shoulder point down the armhole and mark. Connect these two points with a straight line.
- For the front yoke measure 8cm down the armhole from the front shoulder point and mark, square across 10cm and mark, and measure 4cm down the front shoulder neck point and mark. Connect all the above points with straight lines.
- Trace off the back yoke onto a separate piece of paper. Next, align the back shoulder seam you have just traced with the front shoulder seam on the master plan and trace off the front yoke shape to complete the yoke.

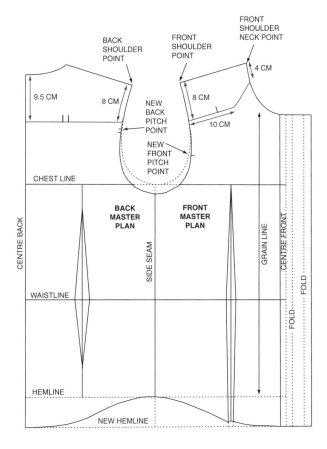

## STEP 5
### YOKE PATTERN

- Trace off the yoke onto a new piece of paper and, following the instructions on page 50, create the full pattern shape.

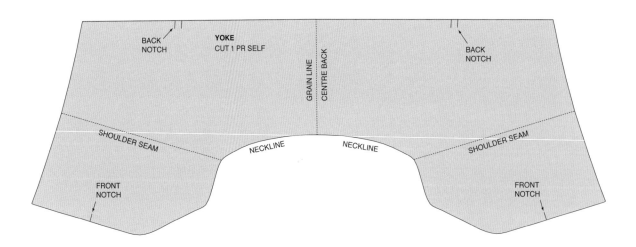

## DEVELOPING THE FRONT PATCH POCKET AND FLAP

### Front patch pocket shape
The front patch pocket is placed directly over the side front dart and is 9cm wide by 11.5cm long at the lowest point of its spade shape.

- From the dart point measure out 4.5cm on both sides along the chest line and mark to create the 9cm pocket width.
- From these points, square up 3cm and mark. Then, from the same points, square 7cm down from the chest line and mark. Measure down a further 1.5cm on the dart line and mark. Join all the above points to create the spade-shaped pocket.

### Pocket flap shape
The pocket flap is also spade shaped and is developed on top of the pocket for fit purposes. The top flap is positioned 1cm above the pocket opening edge.

- Measure up 1cm from the centre at the top of the pocket and square out 4.5cm on both sides and mark. This is the upper edge of the pocket flap.
- From the centre of this line square down 5cm and mark; this is the lowest point of the spade shape. Measure 1cm back up this line, square out 5cm on both sides and mark. Join these points up to the upper edge of the pocket flap and down to the lowest point of the spade shape.

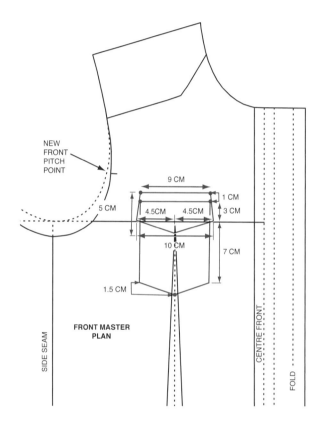

## STEP 7
## POCKET PATTERNS

- Following the instructions on page 50, trace off the pocket patterns, adding a 1cm facing to the top of the pocket flap and a 2cm facing plus a 0.5cm seam allowance to the top of the pocket bag.

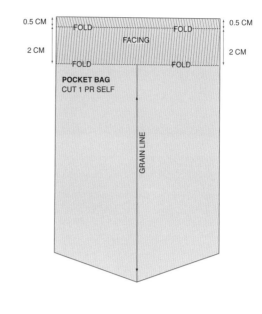

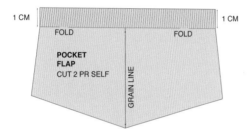

## STEP 8
## BACK PATTERN

- Trace off the back onto a new piece of paper and, following the instructions on page 50, create the full pattern shape.

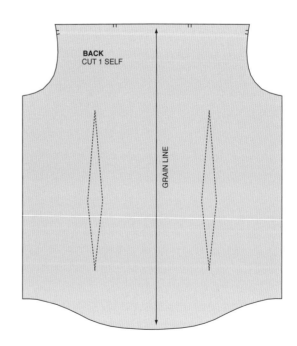

## STEP 9
### FRONT PATTERN

- The right-hand side of the front pattern has a sewn-on placket as a design feature and the left-hand side has a grown-on placket that is folded back and sewn. Following the instructions on page 50, trace off the front pattern including the placket to create the left-hand panel, and then retrace the front panel without the placket development to create the right-hand panel.

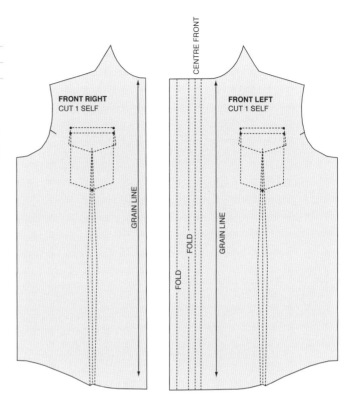

## STEP 10
### PLACKET PATTERN

- Following the instructions on page 50, trace off the placket pattern separately to be cut with fusing.

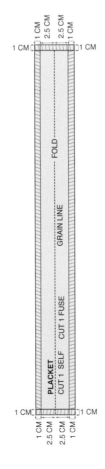

## STEP 11
### DEVELOPING THE COLLAR STAND

**Measuring half the neck from the master plan**
We will develop half the collar stand
before creating the full collar stand.
By taking measurements from the master
plan, which is drawn in half, you will be
measuring half the neck measurement.
- On the master plan measure the length
  of the back neck, in this case 8.5cm,
  and the front neck from the shoulder
  point down past the centre front
  line to the point at which the
  placket finishes when folded, in
  this case 16cm.
- Add these two measurements together
  to give half the neck measurement,
  in this case 24.5cm.

- On a new piece of piece of paper, draw a rectangle measuring 24.5cm by 2.5cm, which is the half neck measurement by the width of the collar stand. Label the narrow side as the *centre back neck* and the long side as the *neckline*.
- From the centre back neck, measure 8.5cm (the half back neck measurement) along the bottom line of the rectangle and place a notch. Label it the *shoulder notch*. Repeat along the top side of the rectangle.
- Measure up 1.5cm at the front edge of the rectangle and join this point back to the shoulder notch with a slight curve.
- From the shoulder notch, measure 16cm (the half front neck measurement) along this curved line. At the front of the curved line, square up 2.5cm (the width of the collar stand). Then draw another curved line to connect this line back to the top shoulder notch.
- From the top right corner of the stand measure along 2.5cm (the width of the placket) and from this point square across to the lower curved line. Label this *centre front neck*. Round off the top right corner with a slight curve.

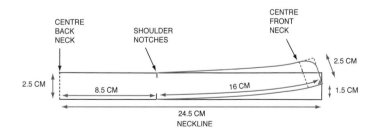

## STEP 12
### DEVELOPING THE TOP COLLAR

**Collar shape**
There are many variations in collar
shape, both traditional and contemporary.
Here we are developing a straight collar
shape. Again, only half of this pattern
will be drafted.

- Trace off the stand shape from Step 11 onto another piece of paper.
- Continue the centre back line vertically up 7.5cm from the top of the stand, square across 24cm and make a mark. This is the collar point. Connect this point back down to the centre front line with a straight line. You have now created the basic top collar shape.
- At the collar point measure up 1cm from the front edge of the collar extend the front edge of the collar by 1cm and draw a curved line back to meet the outer edge. This will give the collar a smoother shape.
- Measure up 2.5cm from the top of the stand along the centre back and make a mark. From here, square across to a point above the shoulder notch. From this point draw a curved line to meet the centre front line, mirroring the curve of the stand. This is the inner edge of the 5cm-wide top collar shape.

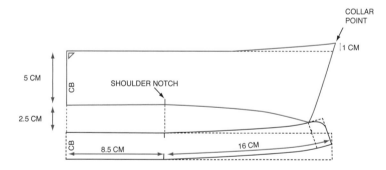

## STEP 13
## COLLAR STAND PATTERN
## TOP COLLAR PATTERN
## DEVELOPING THE UNDER COLLAR

- Trace off the collar stand pattern and, following the instructions on page 50, create the full pattern shape.
- Trace off the top collar pattern and, following the instructions on page 50, create the full pattern shape.
- The under collar is a copy of the top collar reduced by 3mm at the centre back neck, which is blended back with a line to both collar points; this reduction, when sewn, will pull the seam edge under the collar slightly so as not to be seen. Make a separate pattern for the under collar.

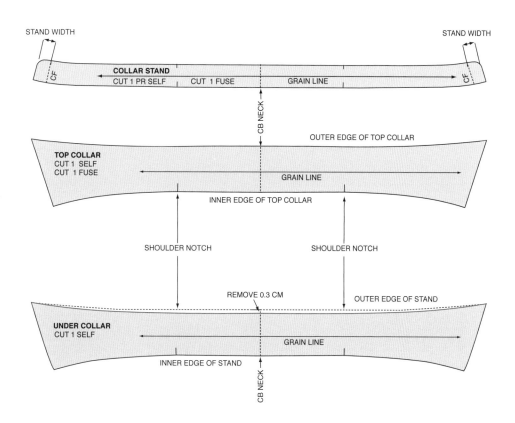

## STEP 14

### DEVELOPING THE SHOULDER EPAULETTE AND SLEEVE TAB

- For the sleeve tab, draw a rectangle 2.5cm wide by 22cm long.
- Create the point at the end of the tab by measuring 1cm back down both long sides of the rectangle and then joining these two points back to a central point.

- At the other end of the rectangle, measure in 1cm and square across for the seam allowance and then a further 2.5cm and square across for the fold line. The tab on the sleeve that the sleeve tab folds over is pre-bought herringbone cotton tape.
- For the shoulder epaulettes draw a vertical rectangle 2.5cm wide and 11.5cm long. Follow the instructions for the sleeve tab, but with a 1.5cm seam allowance and no fold line.

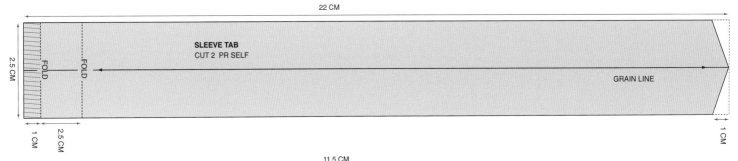

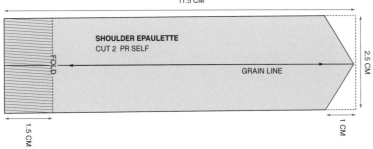

## STEP 15

### DEVELOPING THE SLEEVE MASTER PLAN

Start this development by selecting the basic men's sleeve block, or by drafting the basic sleeve block according to the instructions on page 42. Cut a large piece of drafting paper slightly longer than the length of the shirt you want to develop and transfer the shape of the block and all marks, labels and instructions, following the directions on page 48. The design illustrated has a short sleeve with turned-up cuff.

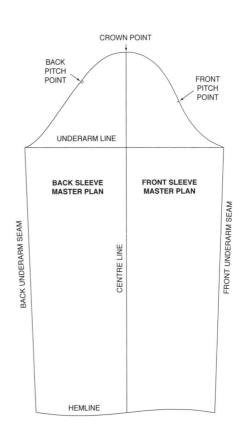

## STEP 16
### DEVELOPING THE SLEEVE WITH A REDUCED SLEEVE HEAD

**Measurements for developing the sleeve**

You will need three measurements to develop the sleeve:

1. Half the armhole measurement - measure the new armhole on the front and back patterns. In this case the front armhole is 26cm and the back 28cm. Add these measurements together (54cm) and divide in half, making 27cm.

2. Half the underarm measurement - measure the underarm line from the master plan. In this case it is 35.5cm. As this is a casual-fitting shirt you can determine the amount of ease according to the design. In this case we will add 8cm ease to the underarm line, making 43.5cm. Divide this measurement in half, making 21.75cm.

3. Half the cuff measurement, which in this case is 19.25cm.

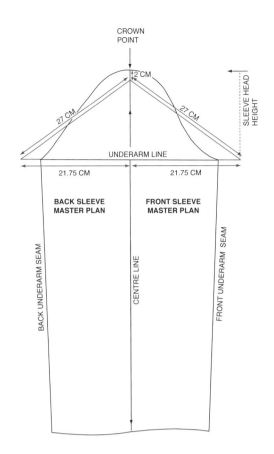

- Measure 2cm down the centre line from the crown point to reduce the height of the sleeve head by the same amount that you lowered the armhole in Step 3.
- At an angle from the new crown point, draw out a line measuring half the new armhole - 27cm. From the centre line, draw out a line measuring half the new underarm line - 21.75cm. Adjust these lines until they meet to form a triangle and repeat on the other side of the sleeve. This will become the frame around which you construct the new shortened sleeve head.

## STEP 17
### COMPLETING THE NEW SLEEVE SHAPE

- Add shape to the sleeve head by measuring 7cm from the new crown point along the diagonal line towards the new front underarm point, square out 1.3cm and mark. Then measure 6cm up along the diagonal line from the front underarm point, square 0.5cm down and mark. On the back measure 5cm down the diagonal line from the crown point, square out 1.3cm and mark; measure 8.5cm up along the diagonal line from the back underarm point, square down 0.5cm and mark.
- Using a French curve draw in shallow raised curves from the new crown point through the marks on the upper portion of the sleeve head, reversing the curves at the marks on the lower portion of the sleeve head, and finishing these hollow curved lines at the underarm points. Add in the pitch points taken from the body panels.

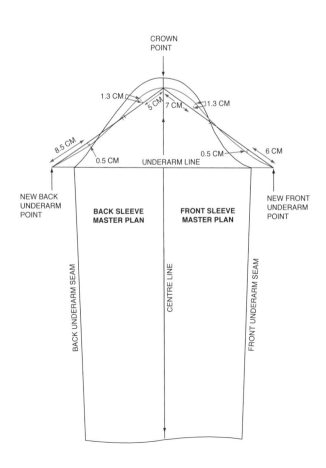

## STEP 18
### SHORTENING THE SLEEVE

- From the crown point measure 25.5cm down the centre line and square out 19.25cm on both sides. This is the new cuff hem width. Join the ends of this line back up to the underarm points with a curve.
- To add the folded cuff to the cuff hem, measure 2.5cm up from this line and square across, drawing a dotted line to meet the lines at the sides. This is the line to which the cuff will fold up. From the cuff hem continue to measure down 2.5cm and square across with another dotted line, the same width as the first dotted line. Measure a further 2.5cm down and square across with a line the same width as the cuff hem. Join all these points at the sides.
- Add a further 1cm seam to the end.

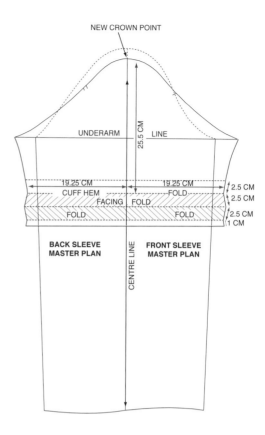

### Blending a seam
To find out how to create the steps in the curved underarm seam so that it is smooth when the cuff is folded, try folding the pattern and then drawing in the curve of the underarm seam. Either trim the seam with the paper still folded or mark with a tracing wheel, before opening out the pattern.

## STEP 19
### SHORT SLEEVE PATTERN

- Following the instructions on page 50, trace off the sleeve pattern.

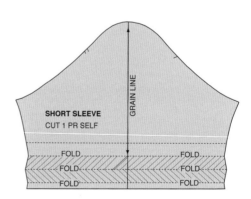

# PATTERN
# BIB SHIRT

**This pattern includes development of the following features:**

Shaping the body
Creating a concealed front placket
Adding length to the body
Shaping the hem with a lowered back
Creating a pleated bib panel
Creating a mandarin collar
Lowering the armhole
Widening the sleeve head
Developing a cuff with cuff guard

## STEP 1
### DEVELOPING THE MASTER PLAN

Start by selecting the basic men's body block, or by drafting the basic block according to the instructions on page 40. Cut a large piece of drafting paper slightly longer than the length of the shirt you want to develop and transfer the shape of the block and all marks, labels and instructions, following the directions on page 48.

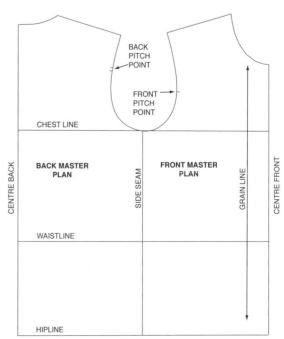

## STEP 2

### DEVELOPING THE LEFT PLACKET AND THE CONCEALED RIGHT PLACKET AND ADDING LENGTH TO THE BODY

- The hem shape in this design has a lowered back. On the front body extend the centre front and side seam lines down 6cm from the hemline and square across.
- On the back body, extend the centre back and side seam lines down 9cm from the hemline and square across.
- From the centre front neck point measure back 1.25cm along the neckline and mark, and measure out 1.25cm and mark. Repeat this at the new hemline and connect these points with straight lines. This will become the right placket width of 2.5cm.
- From the outer line measure out another 2.5cm at the neckline and mark; repeat at the hemline and join these points with straight lines. This will become the underside of the placket.

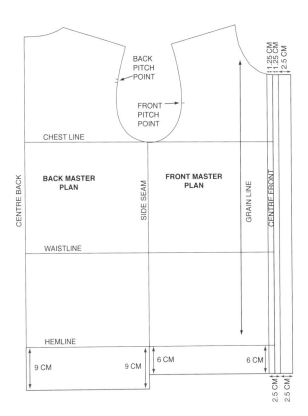

## STEP 3

### FRONT RIGHT PLACKET PATTERN

- Following the instructions on page 50, trace off the placket shape you have just developed onto a separate piece of paper, adding 1cm seam allowance on all sides to create the final front right placket pattern.

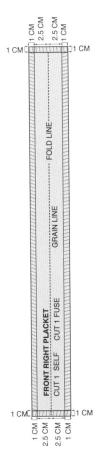

## STEP 4

### CONCEALED LEFT PLACKET PATTERN

- Trace off the placket shape from the front body twice more and position the two plackets side by side. Add 1cm seam allowance on all sides to create the final left placket pattern. The concealed placket is made by folding the placket together in the directions indicated by the arrows.

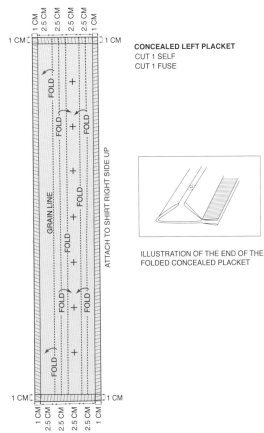

CONCEALED LEFT PLACKET
CUT 1 SELF
CUT 1 FUSE

ILLUSTRATION OF THE END OF THE FOLDED CONCEALED PLACKET

## STEP 5
### DEVELOPING THE NEW ARMHOLE, BIB AND HEM SHAPING

- Measure 2cm down the side seam and make a mark. From this position on the front and back master plan, using your basic body blocks as a template, trace the new lowered armhole shape, continuing it up to connect with the shoulders. Transfer the back and front pitch points to their new positions on the lowered armhole.
- The bib shape is developed on the front body master plan by measuring 22cm down from the centre front neck point, then squaring across 6.5cm.
- Next measure 5cm down the front shoulder seam from the front shoulder neck point. Connect this point to the line you drew previously. Draw in a shallow curve connecting the two lines at the bottom.
- Redraw the hemline with a French curve from the new lowered centre front up to the side seam on the original hemline and back down to the lowered hemline at the centre back.

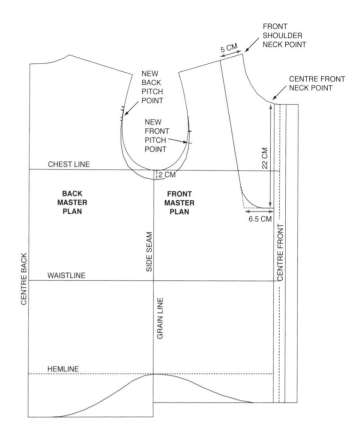

## STEP 6
### DEVELOPING THE BODY SHAPING

- To develop the side seam, measure out 1cm in both directions where the side seam intersects the waistline.
- Connect both these points with straight lines up to the new underarm point and down to the hemline at the bottom of the side seam.
- From the centre back measure 1cm along the waistline. From this point draw a straight line to the intersection of the chest line and the centre back and another line down to the new hemline.

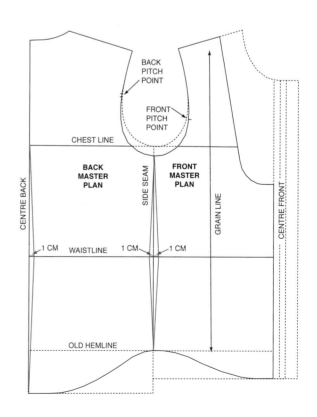

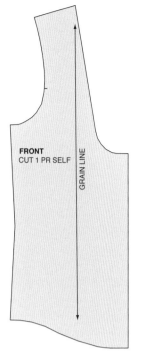

## STEP 7
### FRONT PATTERN

- Following the instructions on page 50, trace off the front body pattern.

## STEP 8
### BACK PATTERN

- Following the instructions on page 50, trace off the back body pattern.

## STEP 9
### DEVELOPING THE PLEATED BIB PANEL

**Pleating**

In a production scenario pleating would always be sourced from a professional pleater. The fabric would arrive pre-pleated to your requirements, at which stage the patterns for the pleated panels would be cut. The steps described here show how you can investigate pleating ratios yourself.

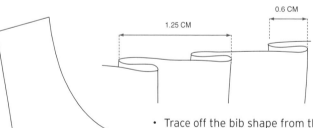

- Trace off the bib shape from the master plan onto a separate piece of paper.
- Decide on the type of pleats and their ratio. In this design we have ten knife pleats at a distance of 1.25cm apart, with a fold between each pleat of 1.2cm (0.6cm when folded).
- On another piece of paper, draw out the pleating scheme and then fold the paper into the pleats.
- With the paper still folded, place the centre front of the bib shape against the edge of the first pleat and draw around the shape. Still with the paper folded, cut out the shape and then open up the paper to reveal the pattern for the pleated bib shape.

## STEP 10
### PLEATED BIB PATTERN

- Following the instructions on page 50, trace around the pleated shape to create the bib pattern.

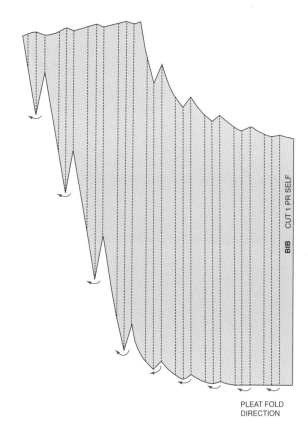

BIB   CUT 1 PR SELF

PLEAT FOLD
DIRECTION

## STEP 11
### DEVELOPING THE MANDARIN COLLAR

**Measuring half the neck from the master plan**
We will develop half the collar before creating the full collar. By taking measurements from the master plan, which is drawn in half, you will be measuring half the neck measurement.

- On the master plan measure the length of the back neck, in this case 9cm, and the front neck from the shoulder point down past the centre front line to the point at which the placket finishes, in this case 16cm.
- Add these two measurements together to give half the neck measurement, in this case 25cm.

- On a new piece of piece of paper, draw a rectangle measuring 25cm by 2.5cm, which is the half neck measurement by the width of the mandarin collar. Label the narrow side as the *centre back neck* and the long side as the *neckline*.
- From the centre back neck, measure 9cm (the half back neck measurement) along the bottom line of the rectangle and place a notch. Label it the *shoulder notch*. Repeat along the top line of the rectangle.
- Measure up 1.5cm at the front edge of the rectangle and join this new point back to the shoulder notch with a slight curve.
- From the shoulder notch, measure 16cm (the half front neck measurement) along this curved line. At the front of the curved line, square up 2.5cm (the width of the mandarin collar). Then draw another curved line to connect this line back to the top shoulder notch.
- From the top right corner of the stand measure along 2.5cm (the width of the placket) and from this point square across to the lower curved line. Label this *centre front neck*. Round off the top right corner with a slight curve.

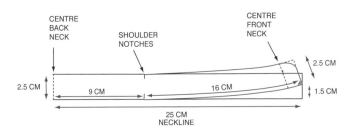

CENTRE
BACK
NECK

SHOULDER
NOTCHES

CENTRE
FRONT
NECK

2.5 CM

2.5 CM

9 CM

16 CM

1.5 CM

25 CM
NECKLINE

## STEP 12
### MANDARIN COLLAR PATTERN

- Trace off the mandarin collar onto a new piece of paper and, following the instructions on page 50, create the full pattern shape.

STAND WIDTH SHOULDER NOTCH CB NECK SHOULDER NOTCH OUTER EDGE OF STAND STAND WIDTH

CF MANDARIN COLLAR CUT 1 PR SELF CUT 1 FUSE GRAIN LINE CF

INNER EDGE OF STAND

## STEP 13
### DEVELOPING THE SLEEVE MASTER PLAN

Start this development by selecting the basic men's sleeve block, or by drafting the basic sleeve block according to the instructions on page 42. Cut a large piece of drafting paper slightly longer than the length of the shirt you want to develop and transfer the shape of the block and all marks, labels and instructions, following the directions on page 48. The design illustrated is shaped and has a gathered tuck on the back of the sleeve for even more shaping. The sleeve block that you have selected might be longer or shorter than the design you are developing. Analyse it by taking a measurement from your fit model or mannequin and by consulting the size chart, or even by using competitors' garments for comparison. The sleeve length is 61.5cm and the cuff measurement is calculated by adding 3cm to the wrist measurement of 25cm for a tuck, making 28cm.

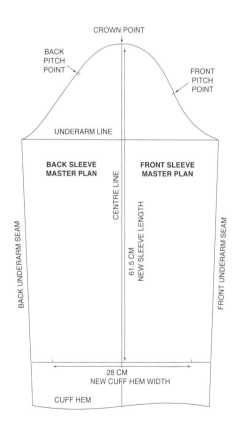

CROWN POINT

BACK PITCH POINT

FRONT PITCH POINT

UNDERARM LINE

BACK SLEEVE MASTER PLAN FRONT SLEEVE MASTER PLAN

BACK UNDERARM SEAM

CENTRE LINE

61.5 CM NEW SLEEVE LENGTH

FRONT UNDERARM SEAM

28 CM NEW CUFF HEM WIDTH

CUFF HEM

## STEP 14
### DEVELOPING THE SLEEVE FOR A LOWERED ARMHOLE

Having enlarged the sleeve circumference in Step 5, you will need to check the length of the sleeve head and increase according to the new armhole measurement.

Start by measuring the front and back of the new armhole on the body blocks (in this case 25.5cm and 27.5cm respectively). Add these measurements together (53cm) and then measure the sleeve head (51cm). The sleeve head, therefore, needs to be increased by 2cm and not beyond, allowing for the amount of ease.

- Extend the underarm line out 1.5cm on both sides so that the new sleeve head measures 53cm, the same measurement as the new armhole.
- Using the basic sleeve block as a template, redraw the new sleeve head shape, and indicate the new lowered pitch point positions.
- To create the shaping at the bottom of the sleeve, measure down 0.5cm on the back sleeve from the centre of the new cuff hemline and mark this point. On the front sleeve, measure up 0.5cm from the centre of the new cuff hemline and mark this point. Join the points with a curved line that is convex on the back sleeve and then reverses at the centre line so that it is concave on the front.
- Now draw in the new underarm seam lines to create the sleeve shape.

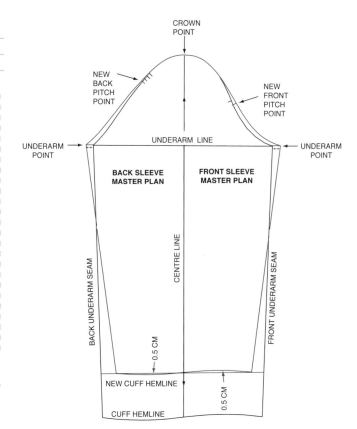

## STEP 15
### DEVELOPING THE SLEEVE

- From the back underarm seam line measure in 8cm along the new cuff hem and square up 16cm. This is the cut line for the cuff guard. Measure in a further 4cm and mark, then a further 3cm and mark. This will become the tuck.

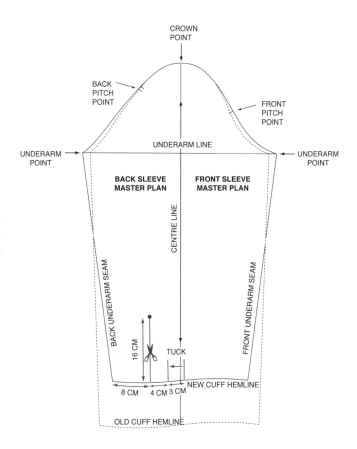

## STEP 16
### SLEEVE PATTERN

- Following the instructions on page 50, trace off the sleeve pattern.

SLEEVE
CUT 1 PR SELF

GRAIN LINE

## STEP 17
### DEVELOPING THE CUFF

**Measuring the cuff**

The cuff is a double pattern piece that is sewn onto the end of the sleeve and turned inside out. The cuff shape will start and finish at the guard opening. Measure this width from the pattern (28cm) and deduct 3cm for the tuck and 1cm for the seam allowance on the cuff guard opening, making 24cm.

- On a separate piece of paper, draw a box 24cm long by 14cm wide to create a rectangular-shaped cuff.
- Divide the box in half lengthways, draw a line across the centre and label it *fold*.

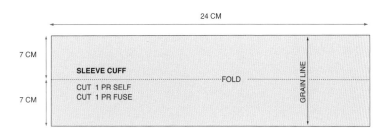

24 CM

7 CM

7 CM

SLEEVE CUFF

CUT 1 PR SELF
CUT 1 PR FUSE

FOLD

GRAIN LINE

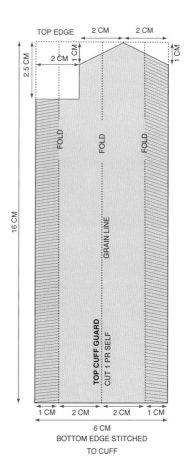

## STEP 18
### DEVELOPING THE TOP CUFF GUARD

- On a separate piece of paper create a rectangular box 16cm long by 6cm wide.
- Divide the box in half lengthways, draw down the centre and label it *fold*.
- At each end square out 2cm up and 2cm down from the fold line and mark. Join these points with straight lines. This will leave you with a 1cm seam allowance on each long side.
- From the top left corner measure 2.5cm down the long side of the rectangle and square across 2cm. This small rectangular shape will be removed from the pattern.
- From the top right corner measure 1cm down the long side of the rectangle and mark, and measure 2cm across the short side and mark. Join these points with an angled line.
- Now measure 1cm down along the right edge of the rectangle you drew in the top left corner and join this point to the top of the first angled line to give a pointed shape to the top of the cuff guard.

## STEP 19
### DEVELOPING THE BOTTOM CUFF GUARD

- Create a rectangular box 16cm by 6cm.
- Divide the box in half lengthways, draw a line down the centre and label it *fold*.
- At each end square out 2cm up and 2cm down from the fold line and mark. Join these points with straight lines. This will leave you with a 1cm seam allowance on each long side.

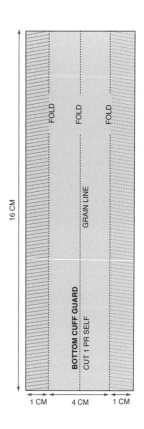

# CHAPTER FOUR
# THE PATTERNS: TROUSERS

# PATTERN
# HIGH-WAISTED TROUSERS

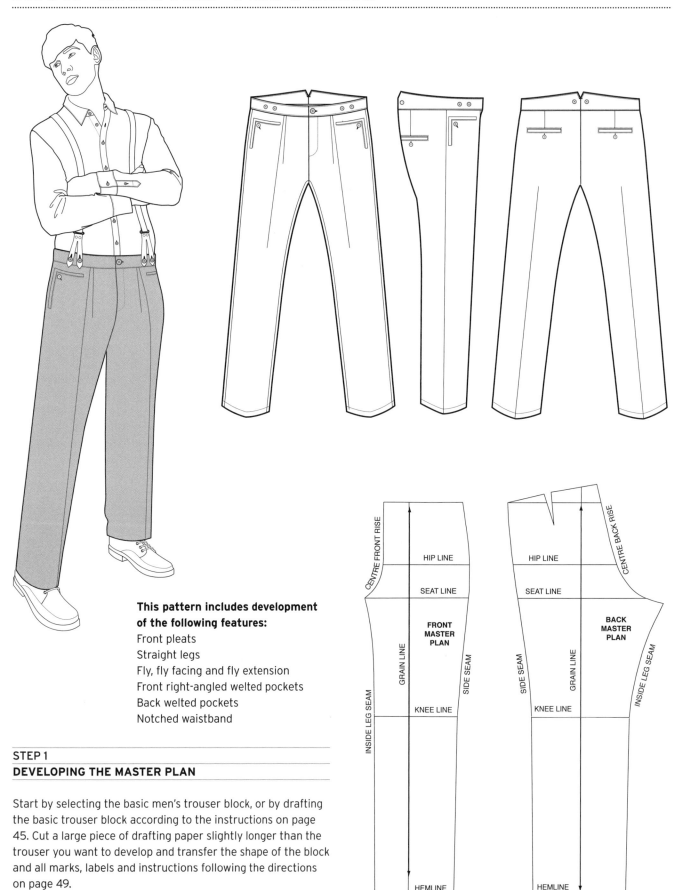

**This pattern includes development of the following features:**
Front pleats
Straight legs
Fly, fly facing and fly extension
Front right-angled welted pockets
Back welted pockets
Notched waistband

## STEP 1
### DEVELOPING THE MASTER PLAN

Start by selecting the basic men's trouser block, or by drafting the basic trouser block according to the instructions on page 45. Cut a large piece of drafting paper slightly longer than the trouser you want to develop and transfer the shape of the block and all marks, labels and instructions following the directions on page 49.

## STEP 2
## DEVELOPING THE FRONT RIGHT-ANGLED WELTED POCKET AND FLY SHAPE AND MOVING THE PLEATS

- Move the pleat lines 1cm towards the centre front along the waistline. Redraw and notch.
- Measure 4cm down from the waistline and 2cm in from the side seam and mark. From this point square down 11cm, and from the same point continue across 8.5cm towards the centre front, creating a right-angled shape. Measure in 1cm from the vertical line and draw a parallel right-angled shape to make the width of the welt opening. Square off at both ends.
- To create the fly shape, measure in 3cm from the centre front waist point and square down 17cm. At the bottom of this line measure 3cm back up and make a mark; draw a curved line from this point back down to the centre front rise.

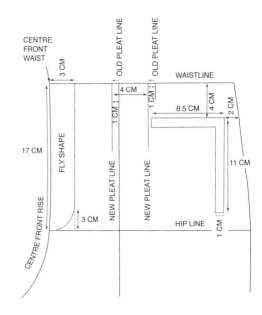

## STEP 3
## FRONT LEG PATTERN

- Following the instructions on page 50, trace off the front trouser leg pattern.

## STEP 4
## DEVELOPING THE BACK WELTED POCKET POSITION

- From the bottom of the back waist dart square out 7cm to each side. This will become the pocket opening.

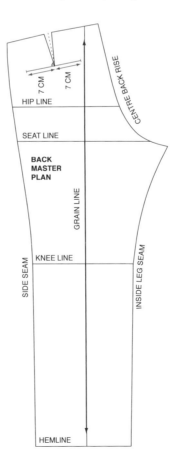

## STEP 5
## BACK LEG PATTERN

- Following the instructions on page 50, trace off the back trouser leg pattern.

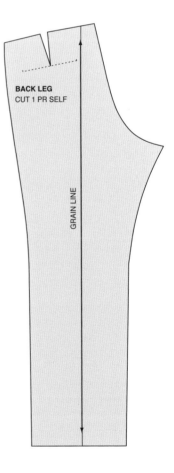

## STEP 6
### DEVELOPING THE FRONT POCKET BAG

- Measure 7cm from the side seam along the waistline and mark; square down 27.5cm and mark.
- From the bottom of this line square out 6.75cm towards the centre front and mark, and from the side seam measure in 13.5cm along the waistline and mark. Draw a line between these two points. This is the side pocket seam. From the bottom of the first line square out 6.75cm towards the side seam; from here square up 8.5cm and then square out 2cm to meet the side seam. This point is 19.5cm from the waistline, measured along the side seam.
- To create a slight angle to the side of the pocket bag, at the top of the pocket measure 1cm back along the waistline towards the side seam and redraw the side pocket seam.
- Round off all the corners.

## STEP 7
### FRONT POCKET BAG PATTERN

- Following the instructions on page 50, trace off the front pocket bag pattern.

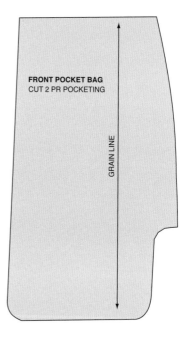

FRONT POCKET BAG
CUT 2 PR POCKETING

GRAIN LINE

WAISTLINE

13.5 CM

1 CM

7 CM

PLEAT LINE

PLEAT LINE

19.5 CM

27.5 CM

27.5 CM

CENTRE FRONT RISE

2 CM

8.5 CM

SIDE SEAM

6.75 CM

6.75 CM

## STEP 8
### DEVELOPING THE WELT SHAPE OF THE FRONT RIGHT-ANGLED POCKET

- The shape of the welt is developed on a fold so that a seam is not needed on all sides and will resemble a T shape.
- Draw an 11cm vertical line (the length of the pocket) down the centre of a piece of paper. This is the fold line.
- From the bottom of the line square out 1.4cm on each side. This is the width of the welt.

- At the top of the line square out 8.5cm on each side (the width of the pocket opening).
- From the end of each line square down 1.4cm and mark; square in from these points, ending 1.4cm from the fold, and mark. Square down and complete the end of the welt.
- Add a 1cm seam allowance to all sides of the shape to create the final pattern.

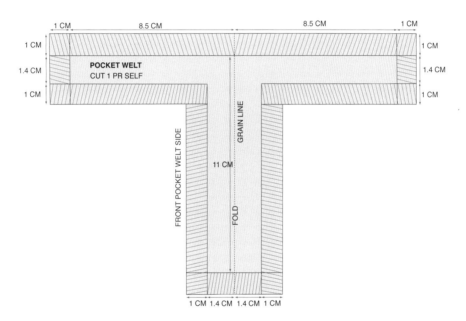

## STEP 9
### FLY FACING PATTERN

**Zips**
When developing the fly length it is important to select a zip that is 1-1.5cm shorter than the fly facing shape.

- Following the instructions on page 50, trace off the front fly facing pattern, adding a 1cm seam allowance to all sides.

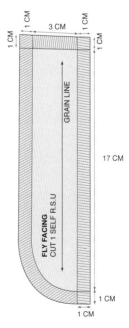

## STEP 10
## DEVELOPING THE FLY EXTENSION

**Fly extension**
The fly extension is attached to the
right side of the centre front and sits
behind the left fly facing. The facing
shape is 1cm longer to cover the bulk of
the zip end.

- On a separate piece of paper, draw a vertical box 18cm long by 8cm wide to create the rectangular-shaped fly extension.
- Divide the box in half lengthways, draw a line down the centre and label it *fold*. Add a 1cm seam allowance on all sides.

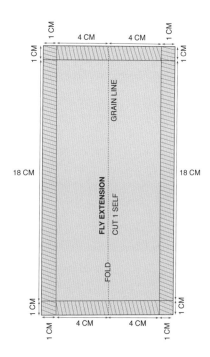

## STEP 11
## DEVELOPING THE BACK WELTED POCKET AND BAG

- The welt opening is developed at the tip of the waist dart. The pocket bag is then drawn over the back leg pattern and traced off to make individual patterns.
- From the centre of the dart at the waistline draw a 24cm perpendicular line down through the dart tip and make a mark; from this point square out 8.5cm on each side and mark. From these points square back up to the waistline to create a rectangle. This is the basic shape of the pocket bag.

- From the bottom of the dart square out 7cm on each side and mark; from these points square down 1.5cm and mark. Connect these points to create a rectangular shape. This is the welt opening, which sits 1.5cm from each side seam of the pocket bag.
- To shape the pocket bag measure 1cm in along the waistline on each side and mark. Connect these points with a shallow curve back to the side seams of the bag. From each bottom corner of the bag measure up 3.5cm and in 3.5cm and join these points with a curved line.

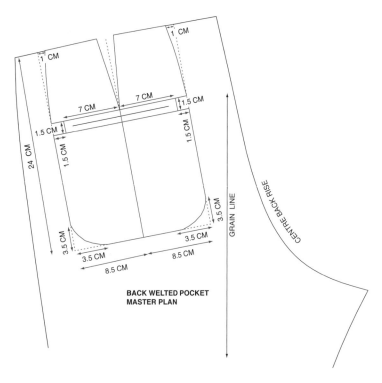

BACK WELTED POCKET
MASTER PLAN

## STEP 12
### UNDER POCKET BAG PATTERN (BACK WELTED POCKET)

**Pocket construction**
This pocket design has a self-facing strip sewn to the back of the bag so that when the pocket is open the pocketing material is not seen.

- When tracing this pattern you need to remove the dart. Following the instructions on page 50, trace off the top pocket bag pattern by placing the centre grain line on one side of the dart leg and drawing around one side of the top of the pattern before moving the grain line to the other dart leg and drawing around the other side.
- Reposition the grain line back to the centre of the dart and continue to draw the remainder of the pocket bag and welt shape.

13 CM

UNDER POCKET BAG
CUT 2 PR POCKETING

STITCH LINE            STITCH LINE

GRAIN LINE

FACING STITCH LINE

## STEP 13
### TOP SECTION OF UNDER POCKET BAG PATTERN (BACK WELTED POCKET)

- Following the instructions on page 50, trace this pattern from the waistline to the top stitch line of the welt opening, adding a 1cm seam allowance to the lower edge.

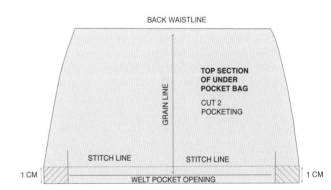

BACK WAISTLINE

TOP SECTION OF UNDER POCKET BAG
CUT 2 POCKETING

GRAIN LINE

STITCH LINE            STITCH LINE

1 CM                    WELT POCKET OPENING            1 CM

## STEP 14
### BOTTOM SECTION OF UNDER POCKET BAG PATTERN (BACK WELTED POCKET)

- Following the instructions on page 50, trace this pattern from the lower stitch line of the welt opening, adding a 1cm seam allowance to the top edge.

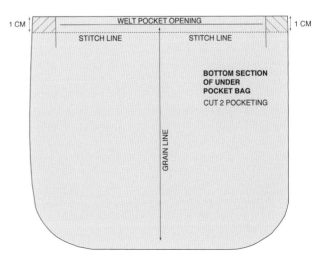

1 CM            WELT POCKET OPENING            1 CM

STITCH LINE            STITCH LINE

BOTTOM SECTION OF UNDER POCKET BAG
CUT 2 POCKETING

GRAIN LINE

## STEP 15
### DEVELOPING THE BACK POCKET SELF-FACING STRIP

- Trace the welt opening from the back trouser leg, adding 1.5cm to each end. Measure down 2cm at each end of the lower edge of this rectangular shape to create a larger rectangle measuring 17cm x 3.5cm. Add a 1cm seam allowance to the top and bottom edges to create the final pattern.

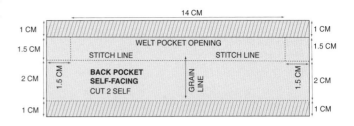

## STEP 16
### DEVELOPING THE BACK POCKET WELT STRIP

- On a separate piece of paper, draw a horizontal box 14cm long by 3cm wide to create the rectangular welt strip. Divide the box in half lengthways, draw a line across the centre and label it *fold*.
- Add a 1.5cm seam allowance to each of the shorter sides and a 1cm seam allowance to the longer sides.

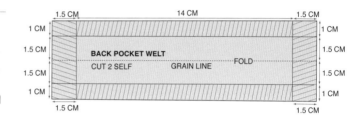

## STEP 17
### DEVELOPING THE LEFT SIDE OF THE WAISTBAND

- Draw a horizontal rectangle 41.5cm long (half the length of the full waist measurement) by 3.5cm wide (the depth of the waistband). Label the left-hand side *centre front* and the right-hand side *centre back*.
- Add alignment notches for the front pleat by measuring 8cm in from the centre front. Continue measuring 10.3cm towards the side seam, and a further 10.2cm along mark the back pleat alignment notch.
- Develop the notch shape by measuring 2.5cm up the centre back and then a further 3cm and mark. Square in 1cm and mark. Connect these two points with an angled line and draw a curved line from the top back to the side seam notch.
- Add a 1cm seam allowance to all sides to create the final pattern.

**Notched waistband**
This waistband design has a notched centre back that is reminiscent of traditional tailoring, and buttons for the attachment of braces.

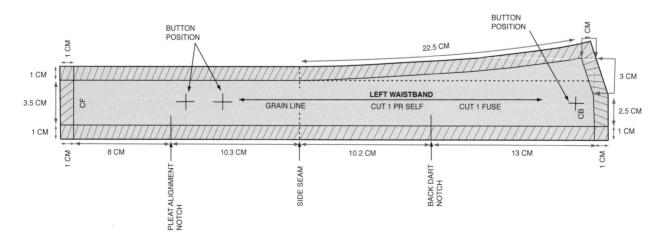

## STEP 18

### DEVELOPING THE RIGHT SIDE OF THE WAISTBAND

- Repeat the steps above, but work with the centre front on the right and the centre back on the left, or trace the left-hand side and mirror.

- Add the 4cm fly extension to the centre front then add a 1cm seam allowance to all sides to create the final pattern.

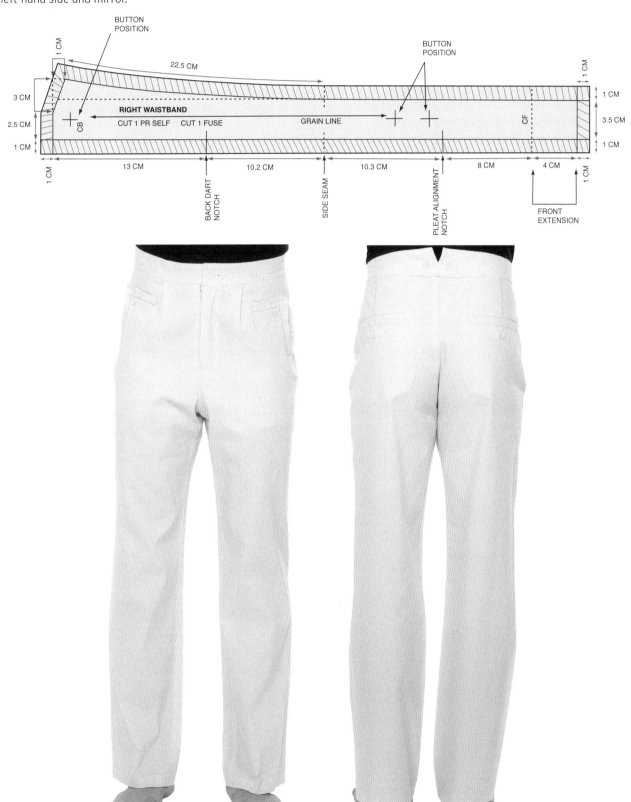

# PATTERN
# CHINOS

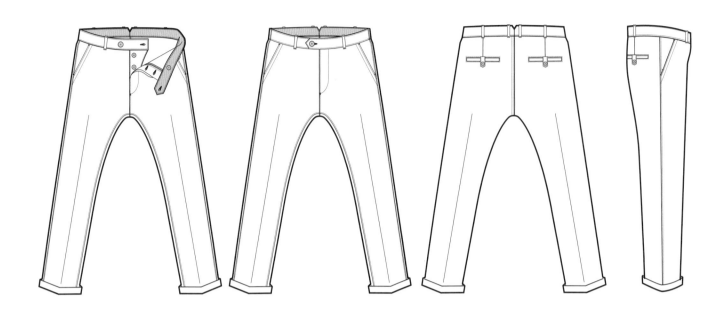

**This pattern includes development of the following features:**

Angled centre front waist and rise

Angled centre back waist

Dropped crotch

Straight legs

Front fly, fly facing and button stand and bearer

Angled side pockets

Back welted pockets

Notched waistband with front tab

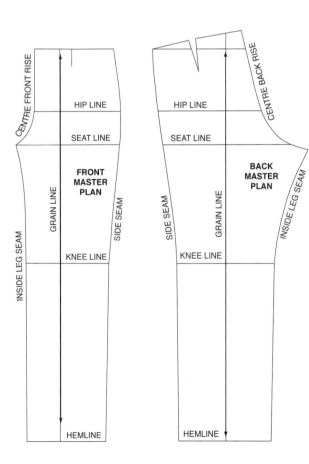

## STEP 1
### DEVELOPING THE MASTER PLAN

Start by selecting the basic men's trouser block, or by drafting the basic trouser block according to the instructions on page 45. Cut a large piece of drafting paper slightly longer than the trouser you want to develop and transfer the shape of the block and all marks, labels and instructions following the directions on page 49.

## STEP 2

### DEVELOPING THE DROPPED CROTCH, FRONT FLY, ANGLED CENTRE FRONT WAIST AND FRONT ANGLED POCKET OPENING

- Drop the seat line down 3cm from the original seat line and redraw the bottom of the front rise and the inside leg and side seams.
- Taper the hem in 2cm on both seams and redraw the lines back up to give the pant a slimmer profile.
- Remove the 4cm pleat volume by angling back the front rise. To do this, measure in 3cm from the centre front waist point and from this point square up 1cm. Connect this point back down to the dropped crotch and redraw the new waistline with a shallow curve back to the side seam. The remaining 1cm will be taken out at the centre back waist.
- To create the fly shape, measure in 4cm from the new centre front waist point and from here measure down 18cm. At the bottom of this line measure 3cm back up and make a mark; draw a curved line from this point back to the centre front rise.
- From the side seam waist point measure 4cm towards the centre front and 15cm down the side seam and connect these two points to create the angled pocket opening. Extend the pocket opening line at the waistline by 0.5cm and redraw it, blending the line back to the waistline to enlarge the opening.

**Enlarging the angled pocket opening to accommodate the width of the hand**

The pocket opening must be enlarged to allow for different hand widths or the pockets will be too tight to use and stretching will occur.

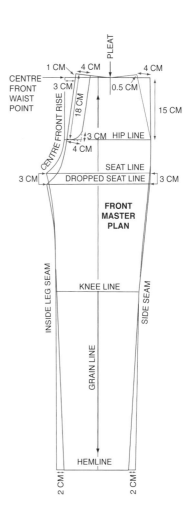

## STEP 3

### FRONT LEG PATTERN

- Following the instructions on page 50, trace off the front trouser leg pattern.

## STEP 4
### DEVELOPING THE DROPPED CROTCH, ANGLED CENTRE BACK WAIST AND WELTED POCKET POSITION

- Drop the seat line down 3cm from the original seat line and redraw the bottom of the centre back rise and the inside leg and side seams.
- Taper the hem in 1cm on both seams and redraw the lines back up to give the pant a slimmer profile.
- From the centre back waist point measure in 1cm and from this point measure up 1cm; redraw the shorter waistline and the longer back rise.
- From the bottom of the dart square out 7cm to each side. Create a rectangular box 1.5cm deep by 14cm long.

## STEP 5
### BACK LEG PATTERN

- Following the instructions on page 50, trace off the back trouser leg pattern.

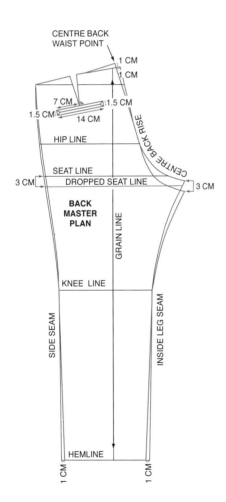

## STEP 6
### DEVELOPING THE FRONT POCKET BAG

- First recreate the original shape of the front trouser leg master plan before the shape for the angled side pocket was removed and redraw the pocket opening from Step 2 (without the extension for the enlarged opening).
- Next create the pocket bag template by measuring 12cm along the waistline from the top of the pocket opening to develop the pocket bag width. From this point square down 26cm; this is the length of the pocket bag.
- From the bottom of the pocket opening on the side seam, to create a step, measure down 4cm and from this point measure in 2cm; from here measure down a further 7cm and connect this point to the pocket length to close the bag shape.
- To create a slight angle to the side of the pocket bag, at the top of the pocket measure 1cm back along the waistline towards the side seam and redraw the pocket length. At the bottom of the pocket, round off the corners (3cm by 3cm), and round off the step.
- Develop the pocket facing depth by measuring in 3cm from the opening and connecting the waistline with the step using a parallel curved line.

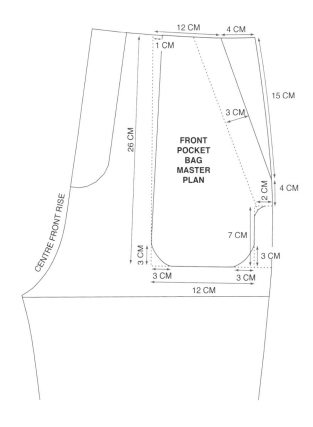

## STEP 7
### DEVELOPING THE FRONT POCKET BAG MASTER PLAN

- Trace off the pocket bag shape with the facing depth line onto a separate piece of paper, extend the pocket opening line by 0.5cm and redraw it, blending the line back to the top edge, as in Step 2.

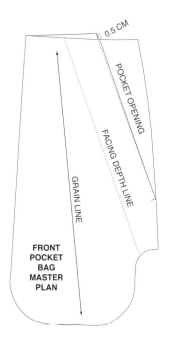

## STEP 8
## FRONT POCKET BAG COMPONENT PATTERNS

**The pocket bearer**

The pocket bearer is cut from the original fabric and is sewn to the under pocket bag, which is then sewn to the waistband and side seam behind the angled pocket opening. While the pocket opening was made longer in Step 2, the pocket bearer and under pocket bag will follow the original line of the waistline, holding the dimensions of the pocket parts together.

• Following the instructions on page 50, trace off the top pocket bag pattern and the top pocket facing from the latest development in Step 7, including the extended pocket opening. Trace off the pocket bearer and the under pocket bag without the additional shape formed by the extended pocket opening.

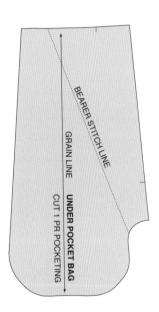

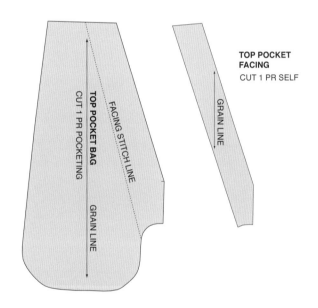

## STEP 9
## DEVELOPING THE FRONT FLY BUTTON STAND AND FRONT FLY FACING

• Following the instructions on page 50, trace off the fly shape developed in Step 2 onto a separate piece of paper. Label the straight line, *fold*; flip the fly shape over along this line and mirror it to create a single pattern shape. Add a 1cm seam allowance to all sides.
• The pattern is folded along the straight line to give double thickness to the buttonholes once positioned.
• Trace off the single fly shape from the left side of the button stand to create the fly facing pattern.

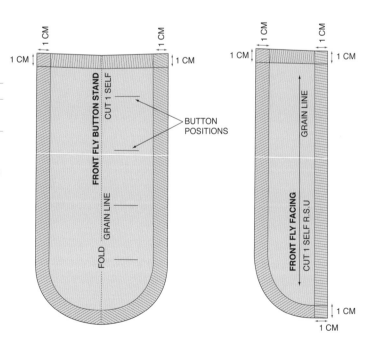

## STEP 10
### DEVELOPING THE FRONT FLY BUTTON BEARER

- Create a master plan to draw the shape of the front fly button bearer by placing the front leg patterns together at the centre front and tracing around the outline.
- The button stand and fly facing are attached to the left trouser leg and the button bearer is attached to the right trouser leg. From the centre front measure 4cm along the waistline of the left leg for the positioning of the buttons and a further 4cm for the overlap and make a mark.
- From the bottom of the fly curve draw across and up, slightly curving your line, to meet this point on the waistline.

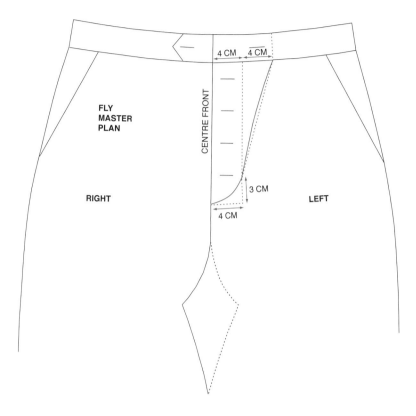

## STEP 11
### FRONT FLY BUTTON BEARER PATTERN

- Following the instructions on page 50, trace off the button bearer final pattern, adding a 1cm seam allowance to all sides.

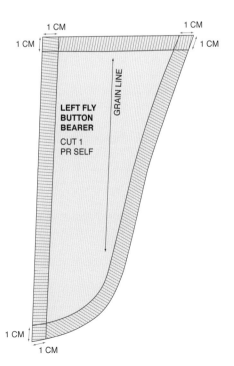

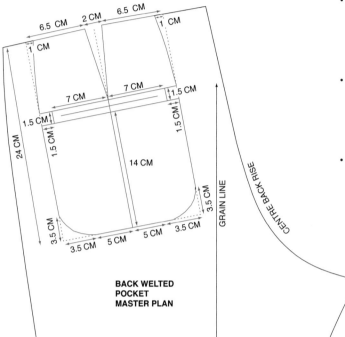

6.5 CM  2 CM  6.5 CM
1 CM       1 CM
1 CM
7 CM    7 CM
1.5 CM
1.5 CM
1.5 CM
1.5 CM
1.5 CM
24 CM
14 CM
3.5 CM
3.5 CM
3.5 CM
3.5 CM  5 CM  5 CM  3.5 CM
3.5 CM
GRAIN LINE
CENTRE BACK RISE

**BACK WELTED
POCKET
MASTER PLAN**

## STEP 12

### DEVELOPING THE BACK WELTED POCKET AND BAG SHAPE

- The welt opening is developed at the tip of the waist dart. The pocket bag parts are drawn over the back leg pattern and then traced off to make individual patterns.
- From the centre of the dart at the waistline draw a 24cm perpendicular line down through the dart tip and mark; from this point square out 8.5cm on each side and mark. From these points square back up to the waistline to create a rectangle. This is the basic shape of the pocket bag.
- From the bottom of the dart square out 7cm on each side and mark; from these points square down 1.5cm and mark. Connect these points to create a rectangular shape. This is the welt opening, which sits 1.5cm from each side seam of the pocket bag.
- To shape the pocket bag measure 1cm in along the waistline on each side and mark. Connect these points with a shallow curve back to the side seams of the bag. From each bottom corner of the bag measure up 3.5cm and in 3.5cm and join these points with a curved line.

## STEP 13

### BACK POCKET BAG BOTTOM PATTERN (BACK WELTED POCKET)

**Pocket construction**
This pocket design has a self-facing strip sewn to the back of the bag so that when the pocket is open the pocketing material is not seen.

- When tracing this pattern you need to remove the dart. Following the instructions on page 50, trace off the pocket bag pattern by placing the centre grain line on one side of the dart leg and drawing around one side of the top of the pattern before moving the grain line to the other dart leg and drawing around the other side.
- Reposition the grain line back to the centre of the dart and continue to draw the remainder of the pocket bag and welt shape.

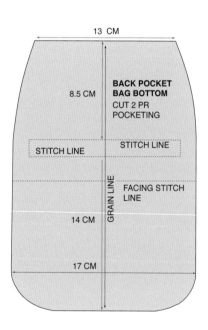

13 CM
8.5 CM
**BACK POCKET
BAG BOTTOM**
CUT 2 PR
POCKETING
STITCH LINE          STITCH LINE
GRAIN LINE
FACING STITCH
LINE
14 CM
17 CM

## STEP 14

### TOP SECTION OF UNDER POCKET BAG PATTERN (BACK WELTED POCKET)

- Following the instructions on page 50, trace this pattern from the waistline to the top stitch line of the welt opening, adding a 1cm seam allowance to the lower edge.

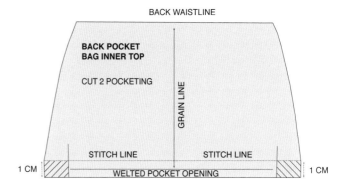

## STEP 15

### BOTTOM SECTION OF UNDER POCKET BAG PATTERN (BACK WELTED POCKET)

- Following the instructions on page 50, trace this pattern from the lower stitch line of the welt opening, adding a 1cm seam allowance to the top edge.

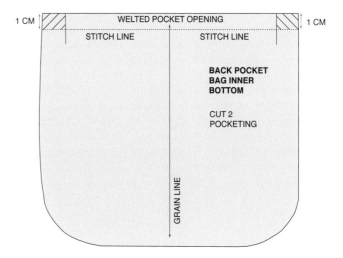

## STEP 16

### DEVELOPING THE BACK SELF-FACING STRIP

- Trace the welt opening from the back trouser leg, adding 1.5cm to each end. Measure down 2cm at each end of the lower edge of this rectangular shape to create a larger rectangle measuring 17cm x 3.5cm. Add a 1cm seam allowance to the top and bottom edges to create the final pattern.

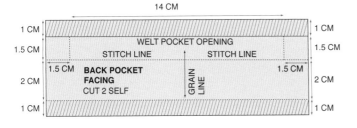

## STEP 17

### DEVELOPING THE BACK WELT STRIP

- On a separate piece of paper, draw a horizontal box 14cm long by 3cm wide to create the rectangular-shaped back welt strip.
- Divide the box in half lengthways draw a line across the centre and label it *fold*.
- Add a 1.5cm seam allowance to each of the shorter sides and a 1cm seam allowance to the longer sides.

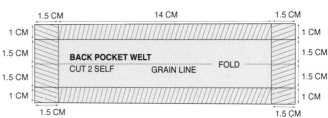

## STEP 18
### DEVELOPING THE RIGHT SIDE OF THE WAISTBAND

- This style has a notched centre back so the waistband will be drafted in two parts.
- Take the waist measurement from the front and back leg patterns to create the waistband. Draw a vertical line 3.5cm long (the depth of the waistband) and label it *centre back*. Square across 22.5cm for the back trouser width and mark the side seam. Measure a further 19cm for the front trouser

width and mark and label the *centre front*. Measure a further 8cm for the fly extension for the button bearer. Complete the rectangle.
- Develop the notch shape by measuring 2cm up the centre back and in 1cm along the top of the waistband and join these two points.
- Add a 1cm seam allowance to all sides to create the final pattern.

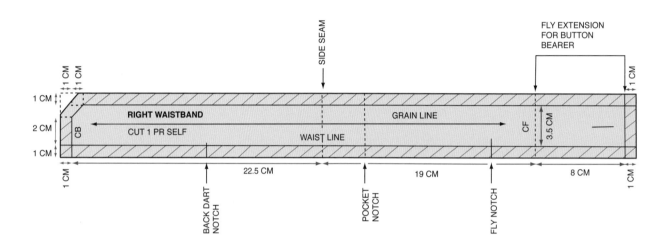

## STEP 19
### DEVELOPING THE LEFT SIDE OF THE WAISTBAND

- Use the basic waist measurement from the right waistband to create the left waistband rectangle (19cm + 22.5cm) but then add the measurement for the centre front waistband tab, which is 4cm in length with an additional 1.5cm to create the point. The waistband depth is 3.5cm.

- Develop the notch shape by measuring 2cm up the centre back and in 1cm along the top of the waistband and join these two points.
- Add a 1cm seam allowance to all sides to create the final pattern.

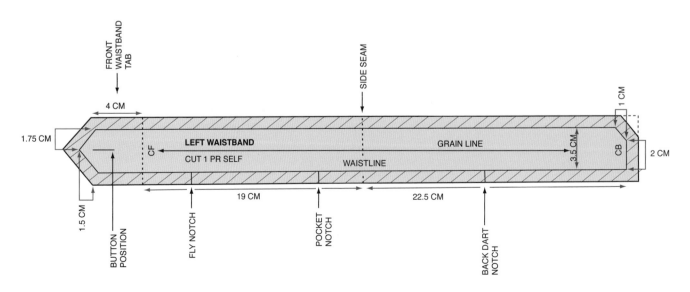

# PATTERN
# BASIC SWEATPANTS

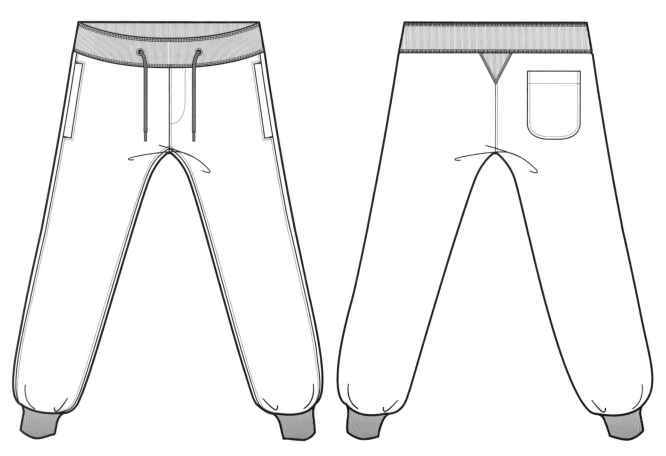

**This pattern includes development
of the following features:**

Angled centre front waist and rise

Angled centre back waist

Dropped crotch

Enlarged volume in straight legs

Stitched front fly

Side welted pockets

Back patch pocket

Drawstring ribbed waist

Centre back notch detail

Ribbed cuff at hem

## STEP 1
## DEVELOPING THE MASTER PLAN

Start by selecting the basic men's trouser block, or by drafting
the basic trouser block according to the instructions on page
45. Cut a large piece of drafting paper slightly longer than the
trouser you want to develop and transfer the shape of the block
and all marks, labels and instructions, following the directions
on page 49.

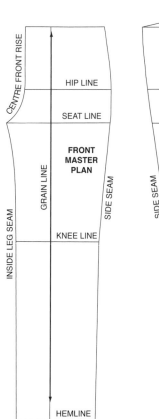

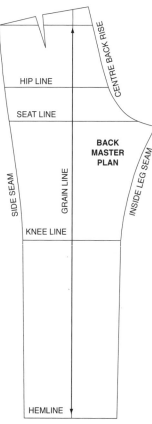

## STEP 2

### DEVELOPING THE DROPPED CROTCH, FRONT FLY AND ANGLED CENTRE FRONT WAIST

- Drop the seat line down 3cm from the original seat line and redraw the bottom of the front rise and the inside leg and side seams.
- Remove the 4cm pleat volume by angling back the front rise. To do this, measure in 3cm from the centre front waist point and from this point square up 1cm. Connect this point back down to the dropped crotch and redraw the new waistline with a shallow curve back to the side seam. The remaining 1cm will be taken out at the centre back waist.
- In this style the fly shape is stitched rather than constructed. To create the fly shape, measure in 4cm from the new centre front waist point and from here measure down 18cm. At the bottom of this line measure 3cm back up and make a mark; draw a curved line from this point back to the centre front rise.

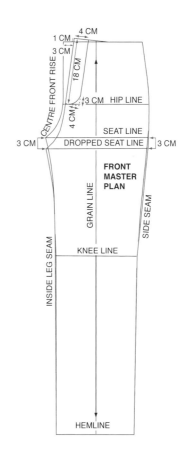

## STEP 3

### DEVELOPING THE DROPPED CROTCH, ANGLED CENTRE BACK WAIST AND WELTED POCKET POSITION

- Drop the seat line down 3cm from the original seat line and redraw the bottom of the back rise and the inside leg and side seams.
- From the centre back waist point measure in 1cm and from this point measure up 1cm; redraw the shorter waistline and the longer back rise.
- From the bottom of the dart square out 7cm to each side to create the pocket placement guide line of 14cm, for the right leg only. The top of the patch pocket is aligned against this line.

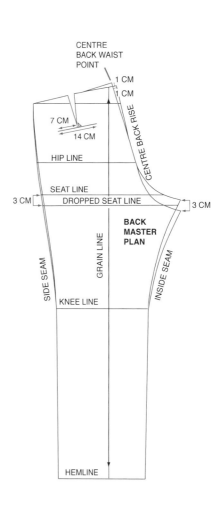

## STEP 4
### ADDING VOLUME TO THE FRONT LEG

**Pocket construction**
This pocket design has a self-facing strip sewn to the back of the bag so that when the pocket is open the pocketing material is not seen.

- Cut up the grain line and open by 2.5cm.
- From the side seam waist point measure out 1.3cm; draw in the new side seam line.

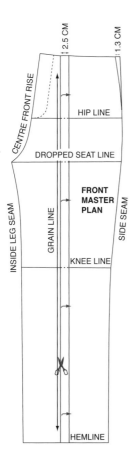

## STEP 5
### DEVELOPING THE FRONT SIDE WELTED POCKET

- From the new side seam waist point measure down 2.5cm; from this point measure in 2cm and down 15cm to the hip line. Remove a 2cm by 15cm rectangle, which will become the welted pocket opening.

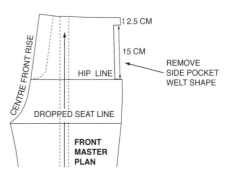

## STEP 6
### FRONT LEG PATTERN

- Following the instructions on page 50, trace off the front trouser leg pattern.

## STEP 7
### ADDING VOLUME TO THE BACK LEG

**Creating extra volume for the sweatpant silhouette in the back**

To create the sweatpant silhouette extra volume needs to be added. This is achieved by adding 2.5cm through the middle of the pattern and by keeping the dart width (2cm) but removing 0.7cm from the side seam, giving an extra 3.8cm ease in the waist of the back leg pattern.

- Cut up the grain line and open by 2.5cm.
- Remove the dart legs and continue the waistline across, keeping the volume in the pattern.
- From the side seam waist point measure in 0.7cm; draw in the new side seam line.

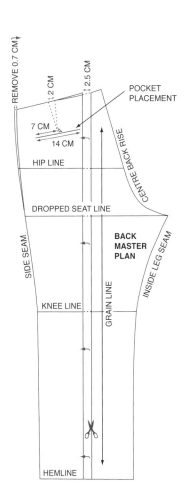

## STEP 8
### REMOVING THE CENTRE BACK NOTCH DETAIL

- To remove the V shape detail, from the centre back waist point measure 8.5cm down the back rise and mark, and 5cm along the waistline and mark. Connect these two points with a straight line.

## STEP 9
### BACK LEG PATTERN

- Following the instructions on page 50, trace off the back trouser leg pattern.

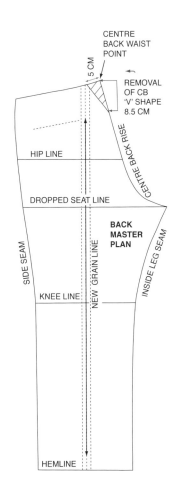

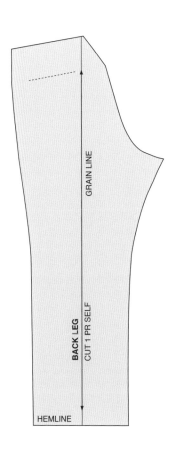

## STEP 10

### DEVELOPING THE FRONT SIDE WELTED POCKET POSITION AND BAG

- From the side seam waist point measure 13cm along the waist, and from this point square down to the hip line plus a further 8cm; from here square back to the side seam. Measure 5cm along this line and make a mark.
- From the bottom of the welt opening shape measure down 3cm along the side seam and connect this point to the 5cm point at the bottom of the pocket bag with a straight line.
- To add curves to this line, divide its measurement into four and mark. From the bottom of the line square down 0.5cm at the first mark and from the top of the line square up 0.5cm at the first mark. Draw a curved line joining these points, starting at the bottom and reversing the curve in the middle of the line.

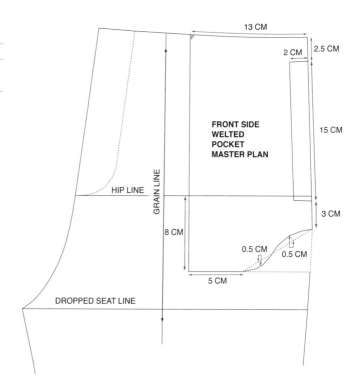

## STEP 11

### FRONT POCKET BAG PATTERN

- Following the instructions on page 50, trace off the front pocket bag pattern, and mirror it over to create both sides of the bag, with the opening on one side only.

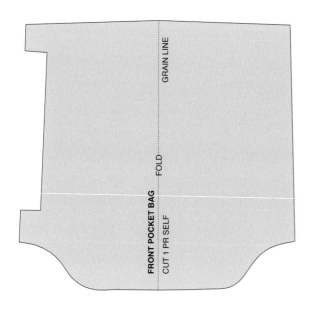

## STEP 12

### DEVELOPING THE FRONT WELT STRIP

- On a separate piece of paper, draw a horizontal box 15cm long by 4cm wide.
- Divide the box in half lengthways, draw a line down the centre and label it *fold*.
- Add a 1cm seam allowance to each side.

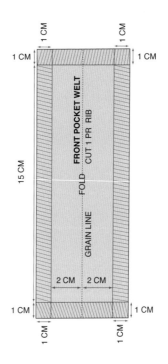

## STEP 13
### DEVELOPING THE BACK RIGHT PATCH POCKET BAG

- Use the pocket position line on the back leg pattern as the starting point for developing the patch pocket bag. From this line measure 2cm up and 1cm down at each end and join these points to create a rectangle. This is the folded facing shape.
- Continue to measure down 14cm on each side and square across. From each bottom corner of the bag measure up 4cm and in 4cm and join these points with a curved line.

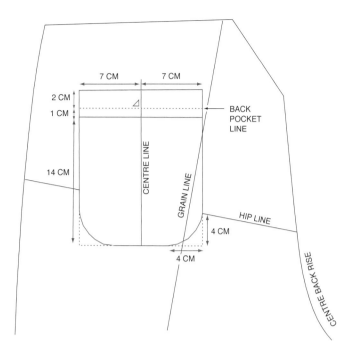

## STEP 14
### BACK RIGHT PATCH POCKET BAG PATTERN

- Following the instructions on page 50, trace off to create the back right patch pocket pattern and add on the facing shape as shown.

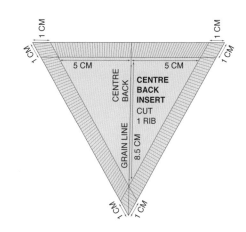

## STEP 15
### DEVELOPING THE CENTRE BACK V NOTCH STYLE DETAIL

- The centre back notch detail is purely a design feature.
- Draw a horizontal line 10cm in length and mark each end; from the centre of the line square down 8.5cm and mark. This is the centre back line.
- Connect these three points to form a triangle.
- Extend the lines out by 1cm at each end and draw a larger triangle to give 1cm seam allowance on all sides.

## STEP 16
### DEVELOPING THE RIBBED WAISTBAND

- On a separate piece of paper, draw a horizontal box 78cm long (the length of the ribbed waistband calculated according to the standard stretch calculation given below) by 10 cm wide (double the depth of the waistband).

- Divide the box in half lengthways, draw a line down the centre and label it *fold*.
- Mark cord holes for the drawstring in the bottom left and bottom right corners.
- Add a 1cm seam allowance to all sides.

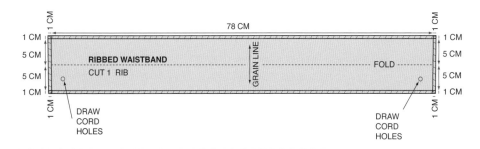

### Sizing the waistband

Before developing the waistband pattern for the ribbed jersey, it is important to calculate the amount by which you will need to reduce the waistband and this will vary depending on the stretch ratio of the rib you are using. The stretch of ribbed jersey will depend on the amount of elastic or elastane used by the manufacturer.

A standard calculation for the waistband length can be made by measuring the circumference of the waist from the front and back trouser patterns and then by dividing this measurement by four; one quarter is then subtracted from the measurement of the waist circumference.

You may have to reduce the waistband further than this standard formula, depending on the stretch of the jersey rib. Use this calculation as a starting point and check the stretch ratio before making the final waistband pattern.

## STEP 17
### DEVELOPING THE RIBBED HEM CUFF

- On a separate piece of paper, draw a horizontal box 22cm long by 16cm wide (double the depth of the hem cuff).
- Divide the box in half lengthways, draw a line across the centre and label it *fold*.
- Add a 1cm seam allowance to all sides.

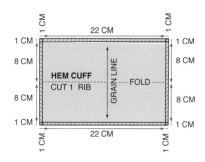

# PATTERN
# TAILORED SHORTS

 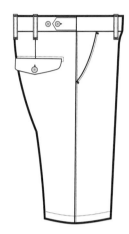 

**This pattern includes development of the following features:**
Angled centre front waist and rise
Angled centre back waist
Dropped crotch

Shortened straight legs
Front fly, fly facing and button stand and bearer
Angled side pockets
Back welted pockets with flaps
Straight waistband with side tab

---

STEP 1
### DEVELOPING THE MASTER PLAN

This shorts style is developed from the master plan of the Chinos. Start by selecting the Chinos master plan, or develop the master plan from the basic men's trouser block by following the instructions for the Chinos on pages 158-60.

The adaptations already made for the chinos style are:
Angled centre front and back waist to remove the pleat volume
Dropped crotch front and back
Front fly development
Alignment of back welted pockets

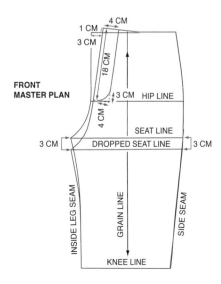 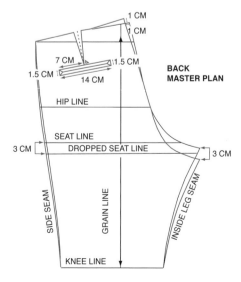

## STEP 2
### DEVELOPING THE FRONT ANGLED SIDE POCKET OPENING AND FRONT SHORTS LENGTH

- From the side seam waist point measure 4cm towards the centre front and 15cm down the side seam and connect these two points for the angled pocket opening. Extend the pocket opening line at the waistline by 0.5cm and redraw it, blending the line back to waistline to enlarge the opening.

**Enlarging the angled pocket opening to accommodate the width of the hand**
The pocket opening must be enlarged to allow for different hand widths or the pockets will be too tight to use and stretching will occur.

- From the bottom of the pocket opening measure 34.8cm down the side seam and then square out 0.8cm. Redraw the side seam back from this point.
- From the bottom of the centre front rise measure 20.5cm down the inside leg and then square out 0.8cm. Redraw the inside leg seam back from this point.
- Draw a line between the two points to form the new hemline.

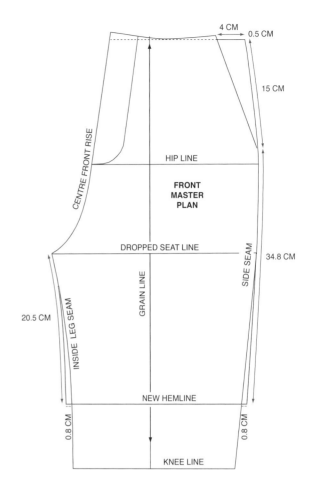

## STEP 3
### FRONT LEG PATTERN

- Following the instructions on page 50, trace off the front leg pattern.

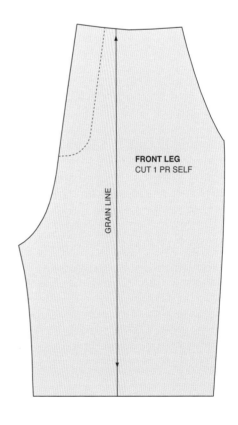

## STEP 4
### DEVELOPING THE FRONT POCKET BAG

- First recreate the original shape of the front trouser leg master plan before the shape for the angled side pocket was removed and redraw the pocket opening from Step 2 (without the extension for the enlarged opening).
- Next create the pocket bag template by measuring along the waistline a further 12cm from the opening to develop the pocket bag width. From this point square down 26cm; this is the length of the pocket bag.
- From the bottom of the pocket opening, to create a step, measure down 4cm and from this point measure in 2cm; from here measure down a further 7cm and connect this point to the pocket length to close the bag shape.
- To create a slight angle to the side of the pocket bag, at the top of the pocket measure 1cm back along the waistline towards the side seam and redraw the pocket length. At the bottom of the pocket, round off the corners (3cm by 3cm), and round off the step.
- Develop the pocket facing depth by measuring in 3cm from the opening and connecting the waistline with the step using a parallel curved line.

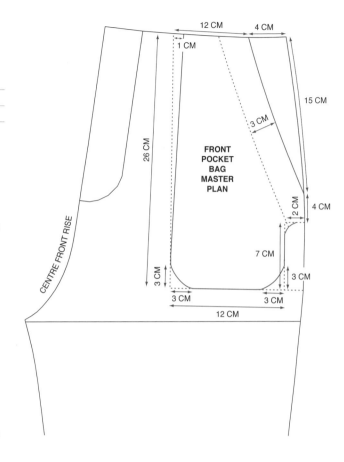

## STEP 5
### DEVELOPING THE FRONT POCKET BAG MASTER PLAN

- Trace off the pocket bag shape with the facing depth line onto a separate piece of paper, extend the pocket opening line up 0.5cm and redraw it, blending the line back to the top edge.

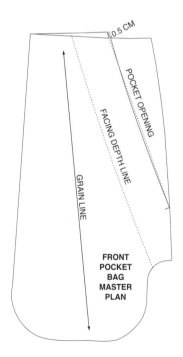

## STEP 6
### FRONT POCKET BAG COMPONENT PATTERNS

• Following the instructions on page 50, trace off the top pocket bag pattern and the top pocket facing from the latest development in Step 5, including the extended pocket opening. Trace off the pocket bearer and the under pocket bag without the additional shape formed by the extended pocket opening.

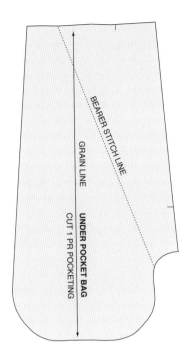

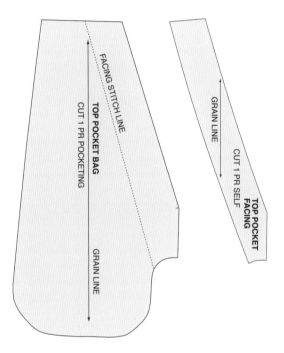

**The pocket bearer**
The pocket bearer is cut from the original fabric and is sewn to the waistband and side seam behind the angled pocket opening. It is attached to the pocketing material of the under pocket bag. While the pocket opening was made longer in Step 2, the pocket bearer and under pocket bag will follow the original line of the waistline, holding the dimensions of the pocket parts together.

## STEP 7
### DEVELOPING THE FRONT FLY FACING

• Following the instructions on page 50, trace off the fly shape developed in Step 1 onto a separate piece of paper and flip it over, adding a 1cm seam allowance to create the final fly facing pattern.

## STEP 8
### DEVELOPING THE FLY EXTENSION

• On a separate piece of paper, draw a vertical box 18cm long by 8cm wide to create the rectangular-shaped fly extension.
• Divide the box in half lengthways, draw a line down the centre and label it *fold*.
• Add a 1cm seam allowance on all sides.

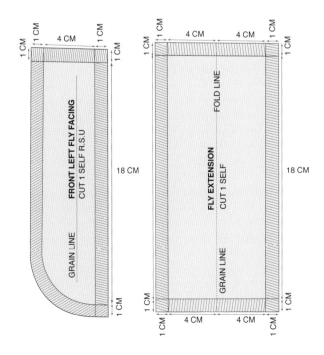

## STEP 9
### DEVELOPING THE BACK SHORTS LENGTH

- From the waistline measure 49.8cm down the side seam and then square out 0.8cm. Redraw the side seam back from this point.
- From the bottom of the centre back rise measure 20.5cm down the inside leg and then square out 0.8cm. Redraw the inside leg seam back from this point.
- Draw a line between the two points to form the new hemline.

## STEP 10
### BACK LEG PATTERN

- Following the instructions on page 50, trace off the back leg pattern.

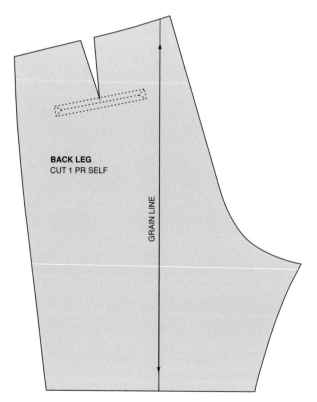

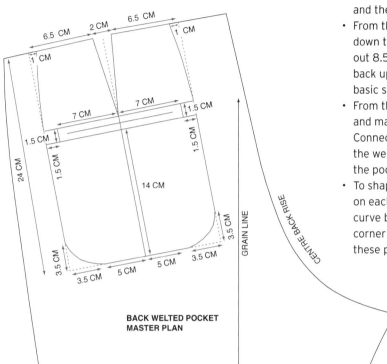

6.5 CM  2 CM  6.5 CM
1 CM
1 CM
7 CM  7 CM  1.5 CM
1.5 CM
1.5 CM  1.5 CM
24 CM
14 CM
3.5 CM  3.5 CM
3.5 CM  5 CM  5 CM  3.5 CM
3.5 CM
GRAIN LINE
CENTRE BACK RISE

**BACK WELTED POCKET
MASTER PLAN**

## STEP 11

### DEVELOPING THE BACK WELTED POCKET AND BAG SHAPE

- The welt opening is developed at the tip of the waist dart. The pocket bag parts are drawn over the back leg pattern and then traced off to make individual patterns.
- From the centre of the dart at the waistline draw a 24cm line down through the dart tip and mark; from this point square out 8.5cm on each side and mark. From these points square back up to the waistline to create a rectangle, which is the basic shape of the pocket bag.
- From the bottom of the dart square out 7cm on each side and mark; from these points square down 1.5cm and mark. Connect these points to create a rectangular shape. This is the welt opening, which sits 1.5cm from each side seam of the pocket bag.
- To shape the pocket bag measure 1cm in along the waistline on each side and mark. Connect these points with a shallow curve back to the side seams of the bag. From each bottom corner of the bag measure up 3.5cm and in 3.5cm and join these points with a curved line.

## STEP 12

### UNDER POCKET BAG PATTERN (BACK WELTED POCKET)

**Pocket construction**
This pocket design has a self-facing strip sewn to the back of the bag so that when the pocket is open the pocketing material is not seen.

- When tracing this pattern you need to remove the dart. Following the instructions on page 50, trace off the pocket bag pattern by placing the centre grain line on one side of the dart leg and drawing around one side of the top of the pattern before moving the grain line to the other dart leg and drawing around the other side.
- Reposition the grain line back to the centre of the dart and continue to draw the remainder of the pocket bag and welt shape.

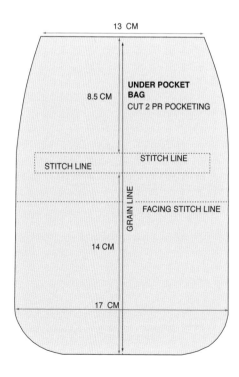

13 CM
8.5 CM
**UNDER POCKET BAG**
CUT 2 PR POCKETING
STITCH LINE  STITCH LINE
GRAIN LINE  FACING STITCH LINE
14 CM
17 CM

## STEP 13

### TOP SECTION OF POCKET BAG PATTERN (BACK WELTED POCKET)

- Following the instructions on page 50, trace this pattern from the waistline to the top stitch line of the welt opening, adding a 1cm seam allowance to the lower edge.

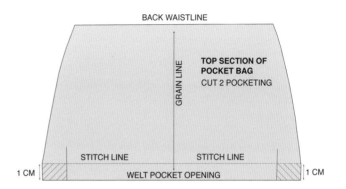

## STEP 14

### BOTTOM SECTION OF POCKET BAG PATTERN (BACK WELTED POCKET)

- Following the instructions on page 50, trace this pattern from the lower stitch line of the welt opening, adding a 1cm seam allowance to the top edge.

## STEP 15

### DEVELOPING THE BACK SELF-FACING STRIP

- Trace the welt opening from the back trouser leg, adding 1.5cm to each end. Measure down 2cm at each end of the lower edge of this rectangular shape to create a larger rectangle measuring 17cm x 3.5cm. Add a 1cm seam allowance to the top and bottom edges to create the final pattern.

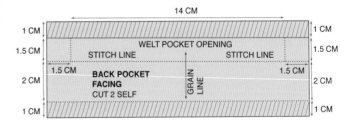

## STEP 16
### DEVELOPING THE BACK WELT STRIP

- On a separate piece of paper, draw a horizontal box 14cm long by 3cm wide to create the rectangular-shaped welt strip.
- Divide the box in half lengthways, draw a line across the centre and label it *fold*.
- Add a 1.5cm seam allowance to each of the shorter sides and a 1cm seam allowance to the longer sides to create the final pattern.

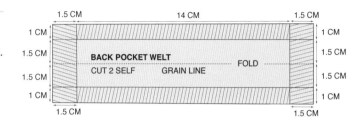

## STEP 17
### DEVELOPING THE BACK WELTED POCKET FLAP

- The pocket flap shape is developed over the back welt opening. From the top of the welt opening, at the dart point, square down 5cm and mark. From this point square across 7cm to each side and connect these two points with the top of the welt opening to create a rectangle.
- From each bottom corner measure up 2cm and connect these points back down to the centre of the bottom line to form the pointed shape of the pocket flap.
- Round off the bottom corners.
- Add a 1cm seam allowance to the top edge of the flap.

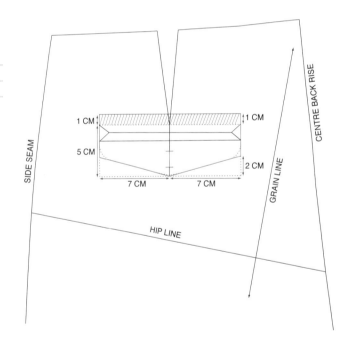

## STEP 18
### BACK WELTED POCKET FLAP PATTERN

- Following the instructions on page 50, trace off the flap pattern.

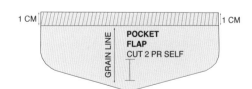

## STEP 19
### DEVELOPING THE WAISTBAND

- Create a rectangle 83cm long (the waist circumference measurement) by 7cm wide (double the waistband width). Draw a fold line lengthways across the centre. Indicate the side seams and centre back, and mark notches for the pocket opening and back darts.
- Add 4cm to the centre front for the fly extension.

- You can create the side seam tab on top of the waistband, which will allow you to define the correct proportion.
- In this case create the waist side-seam tab 6cm long by 3cm wide. Measure 1cm in from the left on each long side and connect these points to the centre of the left-hand vertical to create the pointed shape of the tab.

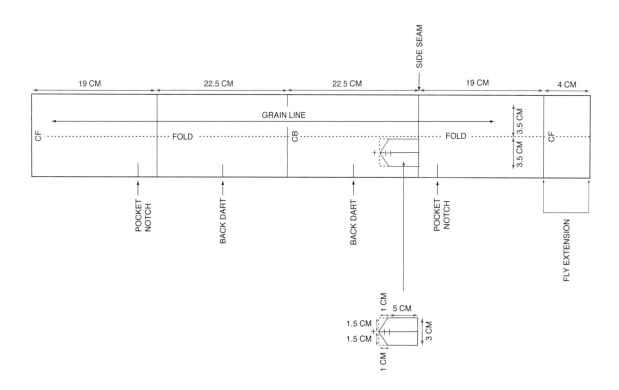

## STEP 20
## WAISTBAND PATTERN

- Following the instructions on page 50, trace off the waistband pattern, adding a 1cm seam allowance to all sides.
- Trace off the tab pattern, adding a 1cm seam allowance to all sides.

FOLD · · · · · · · · · · · GRAIN LINE · · · · · · · · · · · **WAISTBAND** CUT 1 SELF · · · · · · · · · · FOLD

**WAISTBAND TAB**
CUT 2 PR SELF

# PATTERN
# CARGO PANTS

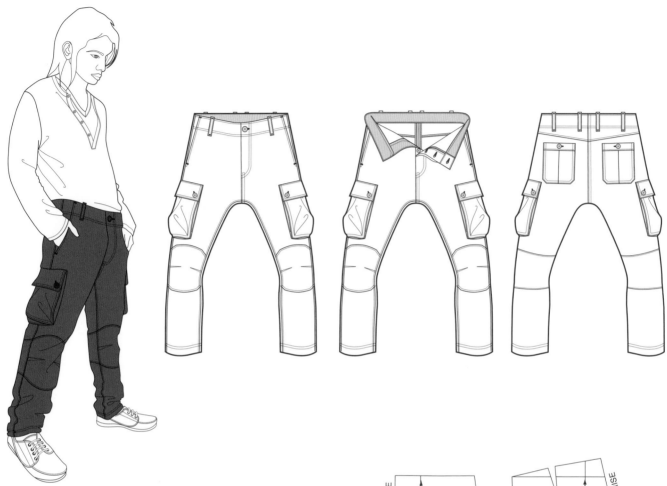

**This pattern includes development
of the following features:**

Lowered front waist and angled centre front rise

Angled centre back waist

Dropped crotch

Back yoke

Carrot leg

Shaped knee patches

Front fly, fly facing, fly extension and button stand

Angled side pockets

Back inverted box-pleat patch pocket

Cargo-style bellows pocket

Sectioned waistband

## STEP 1
### DEVELOPING THE MASTER PLAN

Start by selecting the basic men's trouser block, or by drafting the basic trouser block according to the instructions on page 45. Cut a large piece of drafting paper slightly longer than the trouser you want to develop and transfer the shape of the block and all marks, labels and instructions, following the directions on page 49.

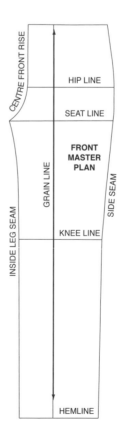

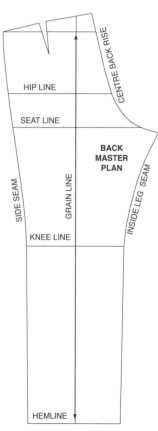

## STEP 2
### DEVELOPING THE DROPPED CROTCH, LOWERED FRONT WAIST AND ANGLED CENTRE FRONT WAIST

- Drop the seat line down 3cm from the original seat line and redraw the bottom of the front rise and the top of the inside leg and side seams.
- From the centre front waist point measure in 3cm and from this point measure down 1.5cm. Redraw the new front rise shape to the dropped crotch and redraw the new lowered waistline with a shallow curve back to the side seam. The remaining 1cm will be taken out at the centre back waist.
- On the knee line measure in 2.5cm from the inside leg seam and mark, and 0.5cm from the side seam and mark. On the hemline measure out 7cm from the grain line towards the inside leg seam and mark, and 9cm towards the side seam and mark. Redraw the new leg seams to taper the front leg silhouette.

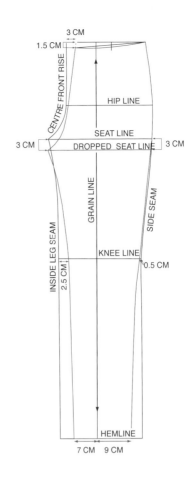

## STEP 3
### DEVELOPING THE DROPPED CROTCH, ANGLED CENTRE BACK WAIST AND BACK YOKE POSITION

- Drop the seat line down 3cm from the original seat line and redraw the bottom of the back rise and the top of the inside leg and side seams.
- From the centre back waist point measure in 1cm and from this point measure up 1cm; redraw the shorter waistline and the longer back rise.
- From the waistline measure 7cm down the centre back rise and mark, and 3.5cm down the side seam and mark; connect these points with a straight line. This is the yoke line.
- On the knee line measure in 1.5cm from the side seam and mark, and 1.5cm from the inside leg seam and mark. On the hemline measure out 11cm from the grain line towards the side seam and mark, and 10cm towards the inside leg seam and mark. Redraw the new leg seams to taper the back leg silhouette.

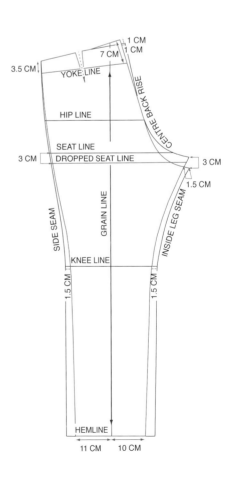

## STEP 4

### DEVELOPING THE FRONT LEG STYLING, FRONT KNEE PATCH, FLY AND POCKET POSITIONS

- To create the fly shape, measure in 4cm from the new centre front waist point and from here measure down 18cm. At the bottom of this line measure 3cm back up and make a mark, then draw a curved line from this point back to the centre front rise.
- To create the angled pocket opening, measure in 4cm along the side seam waist and connect this point back to where the hip line joins the side seam with a straight line.
- Extend the pocket opening line at the waistline by 0.5cm and redraw it, blending the line back to waistline to enlarge the opening.

**Enlarging the angled pocket opening to accommodate the width of the hand**
The pocket opening must be enlarged to allow for different hand widths or the pockets will be too tight to use and stretching will occur.

- To mark the cargo pocket position measure 6cm down from the bottom of the slit pocket opening and 8cm in from that point and mark.
- To develop the front knee patch measure 7cm up from the knee line on both the side seam and the inside leg seam and square across; measure 10cm down from the same points and square across.
- From the centre of these lines measure out 2cm; redraw, passing through these points with a curved line.

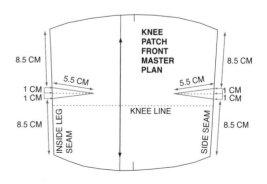

## STEP 5

### ADDING DARTS TO THE FRONT KNEE PATCH

- To add the knee darts trace off the knee patch shape onto a separate piece of paper. Divide it in half horizontally across the centre (half the patch height of 17cm). On both seams measure up 1cm and down 1cm from the centre and connect each of these points to the centre line with a 5.5cm line, forming the darts.

## STEP 6
## FRONT LEG PATTERNS

- Following the instructions on page 50, trace off the knee patch pattern and the upper front and lower front leg patterns.

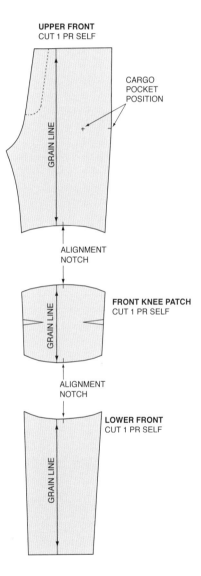

UPPER FRONT
CUT 1 PR SELF

CARGO
POCKET
POSITION

GRAIN LINE

ALIGNMENT
NOTCH

FRONT KNEE PATCH
CUT 1 PR SELF

GRAIN LINE

ALIGNMENT
NOTCH

LOWER FRONT
CUT 1 PR SELF

GRAIN LINE

## STEP 7
## DEVELOPING THE BACK LEG STYLING, BACK KNEE PATCH, BACK YOKE AND POCKET POSITIONS

- Trace off the back yoke shape onto a separate piece of paper, cut through the dart legs and close up to create the curved yoke shape.
- To remove the remaining volume left by the dart leg, measure 1cm in from the side seam along the yoke line and reshape the side seam from this point back down to the hip line.
- To mark the patch pocket position square out 7cm in each direction from the bottom of the dart horizontal to the centre back rise.
- To mark the cargo pocket position measure 6cm down from the hip line and 8cm in from that point and mark.
- To develop the back knee patch measure 7cm up from the knee line on both the side seam and the inside leg seam and square across; measure 10cm down from the same points and square across.
- Find the centre of these lines and mark. On both seams measure down 1cm from the top line and up 1cm from the bottom line and mark. Shape the knee by joining these points back to the centre points with straight lines.

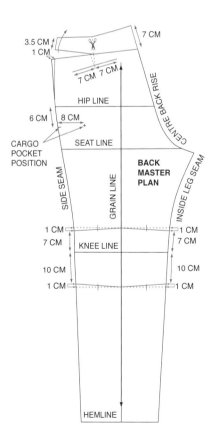

3.5 CM
1 CM

7 CM

7 CM  7 CM

HIP LINE

CENTRE BACK RISE

6 CM   8 CM

CARGO
POCKET
POSITION

SEAT LINE

BACK
MASTER
PLAN

SIDE SEAM

GRAIN LINE

INSIDE LEG SEAM

1 CM          1 CM
7 CM   KNEE LINE   7 CM

10 CM          10 CM
1 CM          1 CM

HEMLINE

## STEP 8
## BACK LEG PATTERNS

- Following the instructions on page 50, trace off the yoke pattern, the knee back pattern and the upper back and lower back leg patterns.

## STEP 9
## DEVELOPING THE FRONT FLY FACING AND BUTTON STAND

- Following the instructions on page 50, trace off the fly shape developed in Step 4 onto a separate piece of paper. Flip over the fly shape along the straight edge line and redraw to create a mirror image. Add a 1cm seam allowance to all sides.
- The pattern is folded along the straight line to give double thickness to the buttonholes once positioned.
- Trace off the single fly shape from the left side of the button stand to create the fly facing pattern.

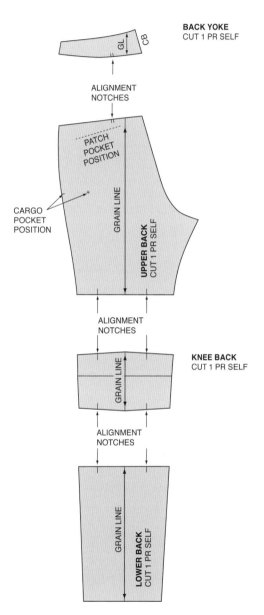

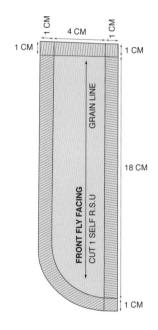

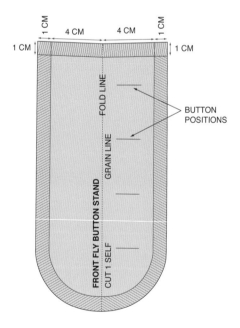

## STEP 10
## DEVELOPING THE FRONT FLY EXTENSION

**Fly extension size**
The front fly extension is wider and
longer then the fly facing and button
stand so that it will cover them both,
because multiple seams may cause
irritation to the wearer.

- On a separate piece of paper, draw a vertical box 19cm long and 9cm wide to create the fly extension.
- Divide the box in half lengthways, draw a line down the centre and label it *fold*.
- When folded and placed along the front rise the top edge of the fly extension will need to be modified to follow the angle of the waistline. Trace across and redraw.
- Add a 1cm seam allowance on all sides.

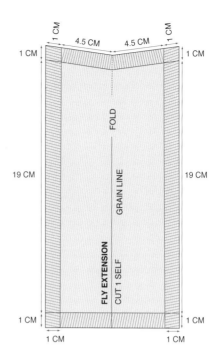

## STEP 11
## DEVELOPING THE FRONT POCKET BAG

- First recreate the original shape of the front trouser leg master plan before the shape for angled side pocket was removed and redraw the pocket opening from Step 4 (without the extension for the enlarged opening).
- Next create the pocket bag template by measuring 12cm along the waistline from the pocket opening to develop the pocket bag width. From this point square down 26cm; this is the length of the pocket bag.
- From the bottom of the pocket opening on the side seam, to create a step, measure down 4cm and from this point measure in 2cm; from here measure down a further 7cm and connect this point to the pocket length to close the bag shape.
- To create a slight angle to the side of the pocket bag, at the top of the pocket measure 1cm back along the waistline towards the side seam and redraw the pocket length. At the bottom of the pocket, round off the corners (3cm by 3cm), and round off the step.
- Develop the pocket facing depth by measuring in 3cm from the opening and connecting the waistline with the step using a parallel curved line.

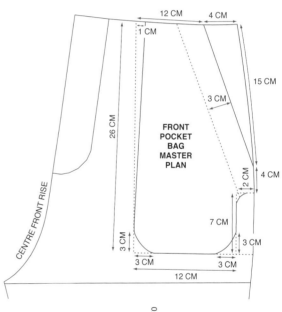

## STEP 12
## DEVELOPING THE FRONT POCKET BAG MASTER PLAN

- Trace off the pocket bag shape with the facing depth line onto a separate piece of paper, extend the pocket opening line by 0.5cm and redraw, blending the line back to the top edge.

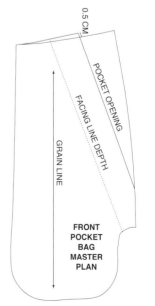

## STEP 13

## FRONT POCKET BAG COMPONENT PATTERNS

### The pocket bearer

The pocket bearer is cut from the original fabric and is sewn to the waistband and side seam behind the angled pocket opening. It is attached to the pocketing material of the under pocket bag. While the pocket opening was made longer in Step 4, the pocket bearer and under pocket bag will follow the original line of the waistline, holding the dimensions of the pocket parts together.

• Following the instructions on page 50, trace off the top pocket bag pattern and the top pocket facing from the latest development in Step 12, including the extended pocket opening. Trace off the pocket bearer and the under pocket bag without the additional shape formed by the extended pocket opening.

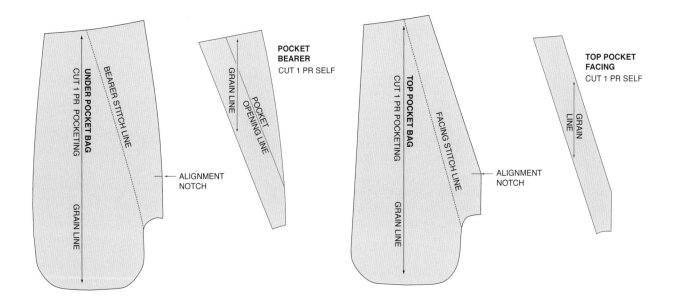

## STEP 14

### DEVELOPING THE BACK INVERTED BOX-PLEAT PATCH POCKET AND PANEL TOP

• For the patch pocket draw a rectangle 18cm wide and 17cm deep.
• From the top of the centre line measure out 1cm on both sides and mark and then a further 1cm on both sides and mark. Repeat at the bottom of the vertical line. Join all these points with dotted vertical lines and label each *fold*. The two outside lines will be folded towards the centre line to create the hidden inverted box pleat.
• From the left bottom corner measure up 2cm and mark, and measure across 2cm and mark. Join these two points to create a shaved corner. Repeat at the right bottom corner.
• Add a 1cm seam allowance on all sides.

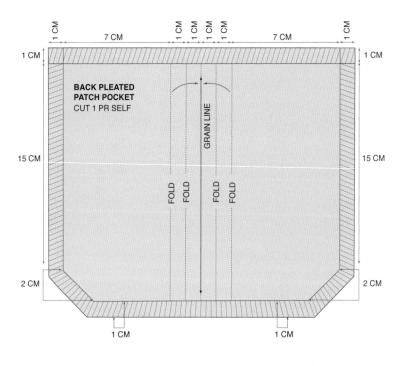

## STEP 15

### DEVELOPING THE PANEL TOP FOR THE BACK INVERTED BOX-PLEAT PATCH POCKET

- For the panel top of the patch pocket draw a horizontal rectangle 14cm long by 4cm wide. Divide it in half lengthways and draw in a dotted fold line. This will give a panel facing of 2cm.
- Add a 1cm seam allowance on all sides.

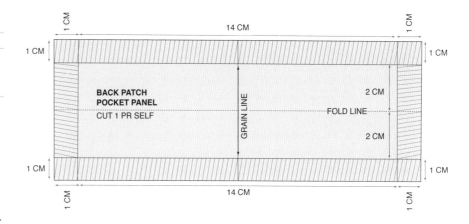

## STEP 16

### DEVELOPING THE CARGO-STYLE BELLOWS POCKET

- The bellows sides and bottom are developed onto the pocket front. Start by drawing a vertical rectangle 23cm long by 16cm wide.
- Along the top edge of this shape add a 3cm facing strip.
- To create the bellows sides, on each side of the pocket measure out 4cm from the original top line and 4cm from the bottom line and join these two points. Draw a fold line down the middle.
- For the bottom bellows strip, draw a similar 4cm rectangle at the bottom edge, with a centre fold line.
- To create the two cutaway corner shapes, draw a line at 45 degrees to each bottom corner and square out from this 2cm in each direction. Draw three sides of a 4cm square, cutting into the bellows strips. When sewn these shapes will create mitred corners when the bellows are folded.
- Add a 1cm seam allowance to all sides except the top of the bellows side panels.

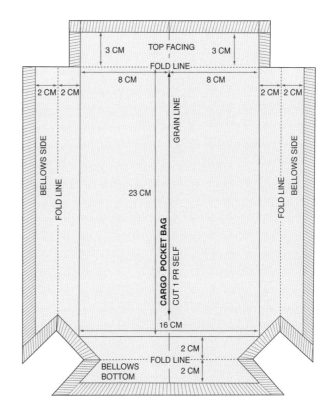

## STEP 17

### DEVELOPING THE CARGO POCKET FLAP

- To develop the pocket flap, draw a rectangle 17cm long and 12cm wide. Divide the width in half 6cm by 6cm with a dotted line the length of the pattern. This will be the fold line when constructed.
- Add a 1cm seam allowance to all sides.

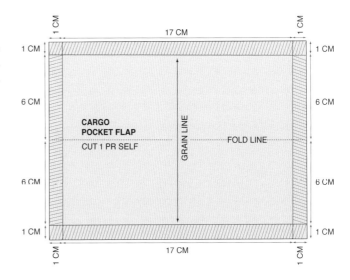

## STEP 18
### DEVELOPING THE WAISTBAND FACING

This waistband is developed in two parts. The inside facing is one full piece while the outside is segmented into parts that match the pocket openings.

- To develop the facing, on a separate piece of paper, draw a horizontal box 4cm wide by 88.5cm long (84cm waist measurement + 4.5cm fly extension), then notch the positions of the following for alignment - pockets, side seams and centre back - by measuring them from the waistline on the front and back trouser patterns.
- Add a 1cm seam allowance to all sides to create the final facing pattern.

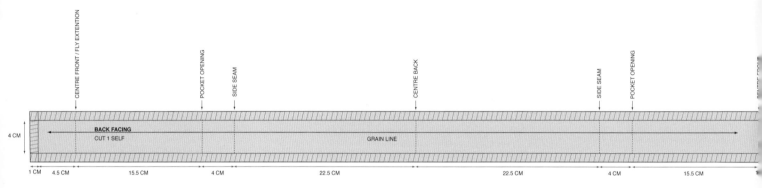

## STEP 19
### DEVELOPING THE WAISTBAND

- To develop the waistband, create separate panel patterns 4cm wide and the following in length: front left (15.5cm), pocket section left (4cm), back left (22.5cm), back right (22.5cm), pocket section right (4cm) and front right including fly extension (20cm).
- Add a 1cm seam allowance to all sides to create the final patterns.

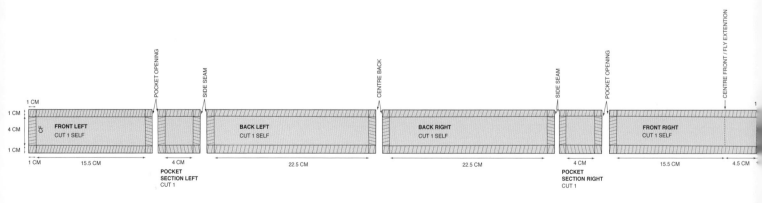

# PATTERN
# JEANS

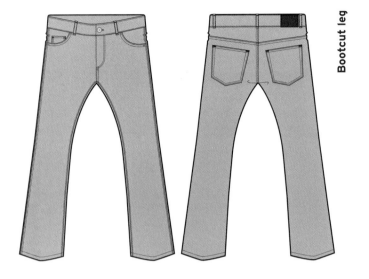

**Bootcut leg**

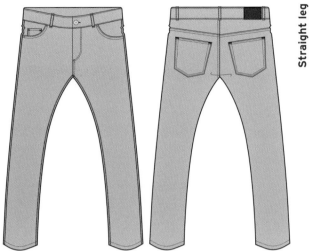

**Straight leg**

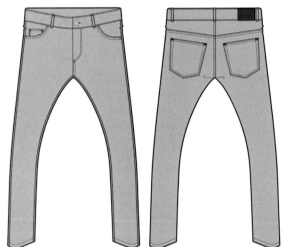

**Skinny leg**

**Carrot leg**

**Shrinkage**

Shrinkage is not included in this adaptation of the jeans pattern. All raw cotton denim shrinks when washed. A shrink test should be carried out first. Cut a metre square, apply the washing technique relevant to the final product, and re-measure the metre square: this will give you the ratio by which the square has shrunk, which you can then apply to the pattern by increasing the width and length. Alternatively, make the jeans in their entirety and then apply the washing technique relevant to the style. Re-measure the jeans and adapt the pattern to accommodate the shrinkage ratio.

**This pattern includes development of the following features:**

Lowered front waist and angled centre front rise
Raised centre back waist
Back yoke
Straight legs, bootcut legs, carrot legs, skinny legs
Jeans pocket
Coin pocket
Back patch pocket
Straight waistband

## STEP 1
### DEVELOPING THE MASTER PLAN

Start by selecting the basic men's trouser block, or by drafting the basic trouser block according to the instructions on page 45. Cut a large piece of drafting paper slightly longer than the trouser you want to develop and transfer the shape of the block and all marks, labels and instructions, following the directions on page 49.

## STEP 2
### DEVELOPING THE LOWERED FRONT WAIST AND ANGLED CENTRE FRONT RISE

- Remove the 4cm pleat volume by angling back the front rise. From the centre front waist point measure in 3cm and from this point measure down 1.5cm. Redraw the new front rise shape down to crotch point.

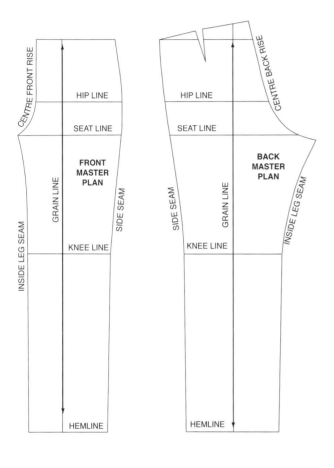

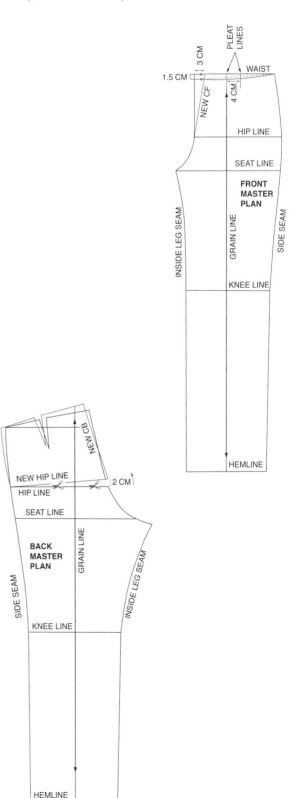

## STEP 3
### DEVELOPING THE RAISED CENTRE BACK WAIST

- From the centre back rise cut along the hip line towards the side seam. Open up the back rise 2cm and redraw the new position of the waist top.

## STEP 4

### DEVELOPING THE FRONT FLY, JEANS POCKET AND LEG SILHOUETTES

- To create the fly shape, measure in 3.5cm from the centre front waist point and from here measure down 17cm to create a rectangular fly shape. At the bottom of this line measure 2cm back up and make a mark; draw a curved line from this point back to the centre front rise.
- From the side seam waist point measure back 11cm and down 7.5cm and create a rectangle. At the bottom left corner of the rectangle measure 4cm along and 4cm up and join the points to create a rounded opening.
- The original side seam of the master plan is the side seam for the straight leg silhouette. To create the slim leg silhouette measure in 3cm from both seams along the hemline and redraw the side seams up to the seat line.
- To create the bootcut silhouette measure out 2cm from both seams along the hemline and redraw the side seams up to the knee.

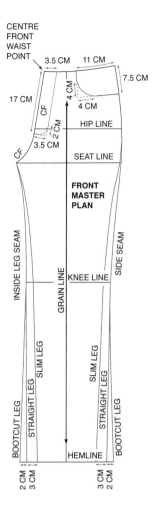

## STEP 5

### FRONT LEG PATTERN

- Following the instructions on page 50, trace off the front trouser leg pattern using the desired leg silhouette.

## STEP 6
### DEVELOPING THE BACK YOKE SHAPE AND LEG SILHOUETTES

- From the waistline, measure 8cm down the centre back rise and mark, and 3cm down the side seam and mark; connect the points with a straight line. This is the yoke line.
- Measuring along the waistline, remove 1cm from the side seam, which is extra volume left by the front pleat.
- Trace off the back yoke shape onto a separate piece of paper, cut through the dart legs and close up to create the curved yoke shape.
- To remove the remaining volume left by the dart leg, measure 0.8cm in from the side seam along the waistline and reshape the side seam from this point.
- The original side seam of the master plan is the side seam for the straight leg silhouette. To create the slim leg silhouette measure in 3cm from both seams along the hemline and redraw the side seams up to the seat line.
- To create the bootcut silhouette measure out 2cm from both seams along the hemline and redraw the side seams up to the knee.

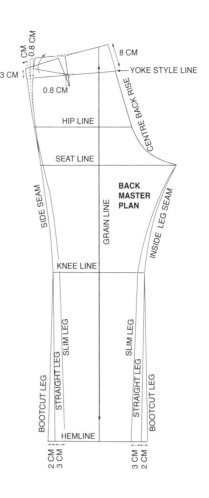

## STEP 7
### BACK LEG PATTERN

- Following the instructions on page 50, trace off the back trouser leg pattern using the desired leg silhouette.

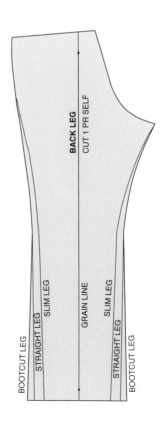

## STEP 8
### BACK YOKE PATTERN

- Following the instructions on page 50, trace off the final back yoke pattern. Seam allowance is not added as many seam variations are possible in jeans construction. The two most commonly used are flat felled seams and lapped seams; the former usually has a seam allowance of 8mm and the latter 4mm.

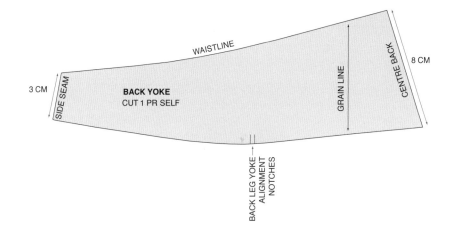

## STEP 9
### FRONT FLY FACING PATTERN

- Following the instructions on page 50, trace off the fly shape developed in Step 4 onto a separate piece of paper and flip it over, adding a 1cm seam allowance to all sides to create the final fly facing.

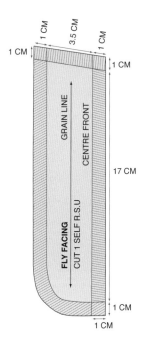

## STEP 10
### FRONT FLY EXTENSION PATTERN

**Front fly extension size**
The front fly extension is longer than the fly facing so that it will cover it, because multiple seams may cause irritation to the wearer.

- On a separate piece of paper, draw a vertical box 18cm long by 7cm wide.
- Divide the box in half lengthways, draw a line down the centre and label it *fold*.
- When folded and placed along the front rise the top edge of the fly extension will need to be modified to follow the angle of the waistline. Trace across and redraw.
- Add a 1cm seam allowance on all sides.

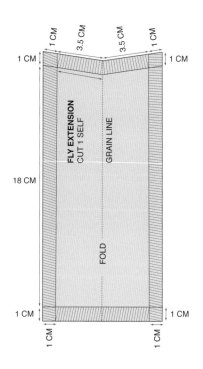

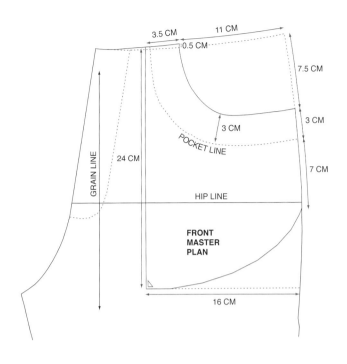

## STEP 11

### DEVELOPING THE FRONT JEANS POCKET BAG AND BEARER

- Extend the pocket opening line 0.5cm above the waistline to allow for the width of the hand. From this point measure a further 3.5cm towards the centre front to create the pocket bag width. From here square down 24cm and mark; then square back 16cm to the side seam.
- Develop the pocket opening facing and bearer depth by drawing a line 3cm from and parallel with the opening line.
- From the opening line on the side seam measure 3cm down (the facing depth) and a further 7cm and mark. Connect this point with the end of the pocket depth line using a descending curve.

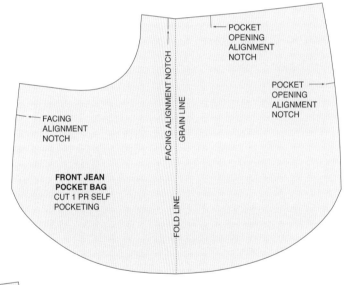

## STEP 12

### FRONT JEANS POCKET BAG AND BEARER PATTERNS

- The jeans pocket bag is constructed in one piece. Trace off the pocket bag shape from the master plan mirroring it over using the left-hand side as the fold line. Remove the pocket opening shape from the left side.
- Trace off the final pocket bearer shape from the front pocket master plan.

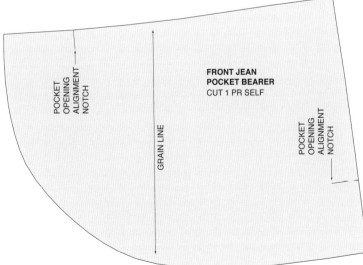

## STEP 13

### DEVELOPING THE COIN POCKET PATTERN

- Draw a rectangle 6cm wide by 10cm long. At one end, along the shorter side, mark two fold lines 1cm apart.

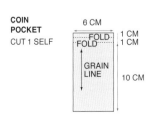

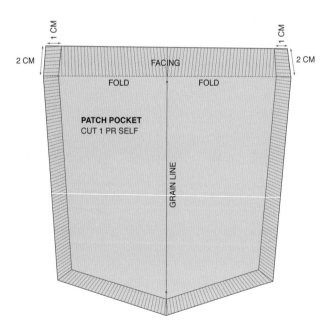

## STEP 14
### DEVELOPING THE BACK PATCH POCKET BAG

- From the centre point of the yoke line measure out 7.5cm each side and from each of these points square down 3cm and mark. Draw a line between these two points; this is the top opening of the patch pocket. From the centre point of the opening, square down 15cm and mark.
- From this point measure up 2cm and mark. Square out 6.5cm to each side, and connect these points up to the top opening line to give an angled pocket shape.
- Connect the same points down to the centre point on the bottom line.

## STEP 15
### BACK PATCH POCKET BAG PATTERN

- Following the instructions on page 50, trace off the patch pocket bag pattern and add a 2cm folded facing at the top and a 1cm seam allowance to all other sides to create the final pattern.

## STEP 16
### DEVELOPING THE WAISTBAND

- Draw a rectangle 8cm wide by 86.5cm long (81cm waist measurement plus 2cm ease plus 3.5cm fly extension measurement), with the fly extension marked at the right-hand end. Draw a fold line down the centre lengthways.
- Add a 1cm seam allowance to all sides.
- Notch the centre front, pocket openings, side seams and centre back.

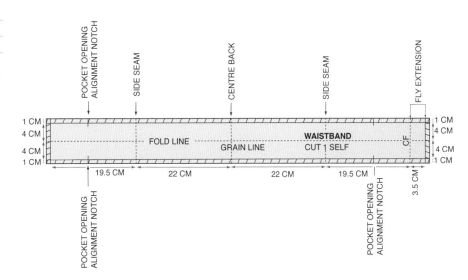

# CHAPTER FIVE
# THE PATTERNS: OUTERWEAR

# PATTERN
# CAGOULE

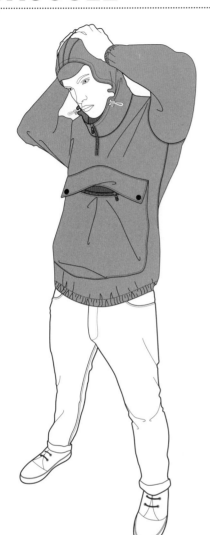

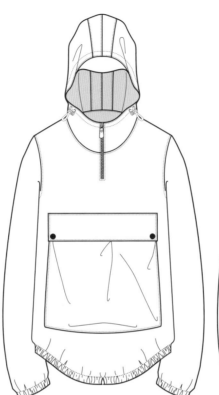

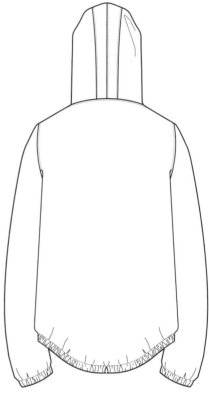

**This pattern includes
development of the following features:**

Adding volume to the front and back patterns

Enlarging the neckline

Creating a shaped and elasticated hemline

Creating a dropped shoulder with seam moved towards
   the front

Developing a centre front patch pocket with mitred
   corners, zip opening and flap

Enlarging the sleeve head

Creating a sleeve with elasticated cuffs

Developing a hood with separate front peak

## STEP 1
### DEVELOPING THE MASTER PLAN

Start by selecting the basic men's body block, or by drafting
the basic block according to the instructions on page 40. Cut
a large piece of drafting paper slightly longer than the length
of the jacket you want to develop and transfer the shape of
the block and all marks, labels and instructions, following the
directions on page 48.

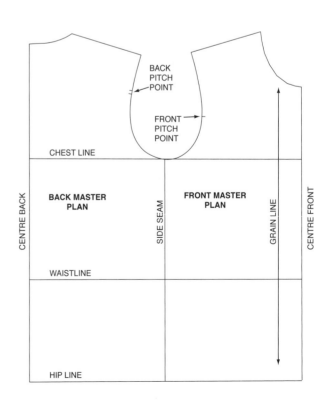

## STEP 2

### DEVELOPING THE ENLARGED NECK, DROPPED SHOULDER AND LOWERED ARM AND ADDING VOLUME TO THE SIDE SEAM

- From the centre front neck point measure down 2cm and from the front shoulder neck point measure in 0.5cm; measure in 0.5cm from the back shoulder neck point. Using the basic body block as a template draw in the new front and back necklines.
- From the front and back shoulder points measure up 0.5cm and out 2cm over the armhole and find and mark the new shoulder points.
- Open up the side seam by adding in 2cm between the front and back body panels and repositioning.
- From the chest line square down 3.5cm on each side and, starting from the underarm point, redraw the new armhole shape using the basic body blocks as a template up to the new shoulder points. Draw in the new pitch point positions.

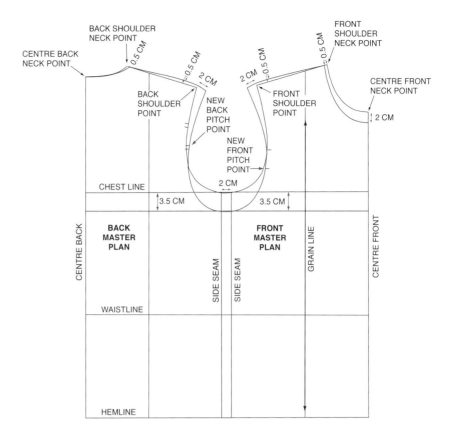

## STEP 3

### EXTENDING AND SHAPING THE HEM AND SHAPING THE SIDE SEAM

- Extend the centre front, side seam and centre back lines down 11cm from the hemline and square across to create a new hemline.
- To shape the hemline measure 3cm up the side seam and blend back towards the centre front and centre back using a French curve.
- To develop the side seam shaping, at the hemline measure 1cm into the front body and connect this point back to the new underarm point with a straight line. Repeat these steps for the back by measuring 1cm into the back body.

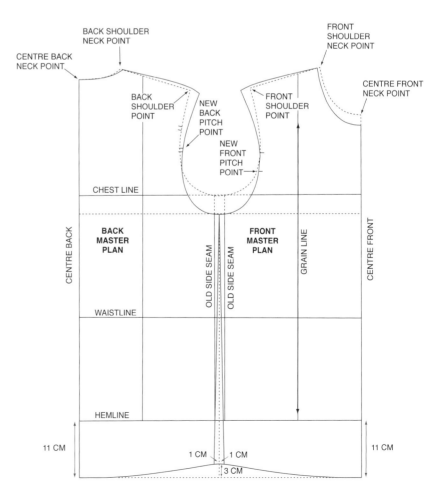

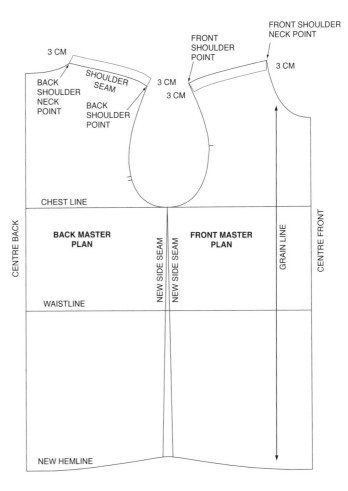

## STEP 4
### REPOSITIONING THE SHOULDER SEAM

- From the front shoulder neck point measure 3cm down the front neckline and 3cm down the armhole from the front shoulder point and draw in the new shoulder seam. Cut and remove this shape from the front body panel.
- To add the shape onto the back body panel, from the back shoulder neck point and the back shoulder point measure up 3cm and connect these points with a straight line from the back shoulder neck point, curving it down slightly to the new shoulder point.

## STEP 5
### ADDING VOLUME TO THE FRONT

- Trace off the front body panel onto a new piece of paper. Volume will be added by cutting and spreading the pattern pieces open to redefine the shape.
- From the side seam square in 9cm at two points and from the hemline draw a 35cm vertical line passing through the points. Continue to measure in a further 10cm and from the hem draw a 40cm vertical line.
- Measure 5cm down the side seam from the underarm point and connect this point with an angled line to the top of the 40cm vertical line.
- Measure down a further 6.5cm and connect this point with an angled line to the top of the 35cm vertical line.
- From the hemline cut up each line and out to the side seam, leaving the shape connected by a few millimetres.
- Starting from the centre front open each panel out 5cm at the hem.
- Redraw the new hemline with a gradual curve back towards the centre front, removing the overhanging panel corners.

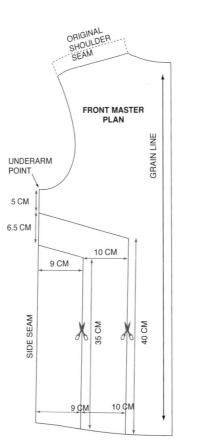

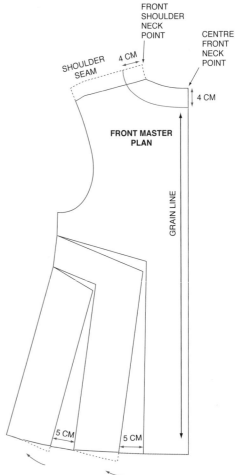

## STEP 6
### FRONT PATTERN AND DEVELOPING THE FRONT NECK FACING, PATCH POCKET BAG AND HEM FACING

- Trace off the front onto a new piece of paper and, following the instructions on page 50, create the full pattern shape. You will now develop the front neck facing and patch pocket on top of this pattern.
- The front neck facing will strengthen the zip insertion. From the front shoulder neck points measure 4cm down each shoulder seam and draw a curved line down towards the centre front following the shape of the neckline.
- From the centre front neck point measure out 0.5cm on both sides along the neckline. From these points create a rectangle 1cm wide by 12cm long; this will be cut later to allow the zip to be sewn in.

- From the bottom of the rectangle measure down 4cm along the centre front and then square out 4cm right and left; this is the width of your facing. Connect these points back up to meet the curved lines drawn previously and round off all the corners.
- To develop the pocket bag measure 6cm down from the bottom of the facing shape. From this point square out 16cm left and right. Measure 32cm down both sides to create a square.
- Measure 3cm up along the length of the hemline to create a channel to take the elastic for a gathered finish.

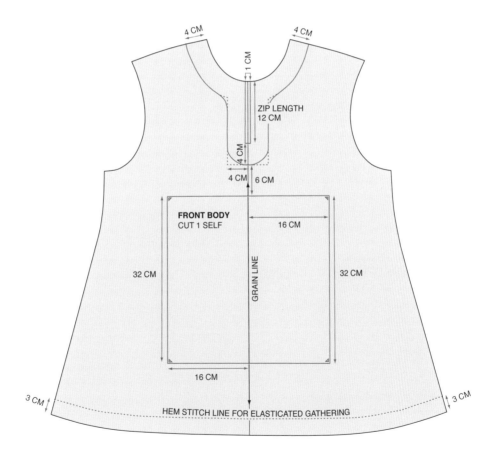

## STEP 7
### FRONT NECK FACING PATTERN

- Following the instructions on page 50, trace off the neck facing pattern, adding a 1cm seam allowance on the neckline and shoulders only.

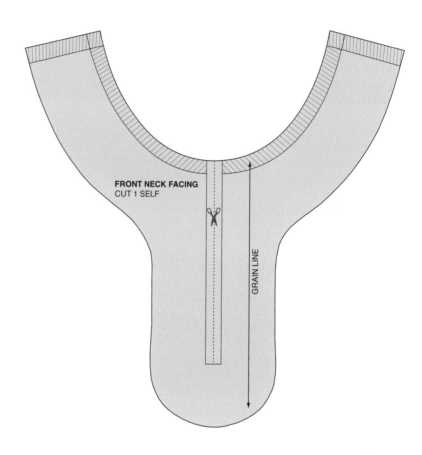

## STEP 8
### FRONT HEM FACING PATTERN

- Following the instructions on page 50, trace off the hem facing pattern, adding a 1cm seam allowance on all sides.

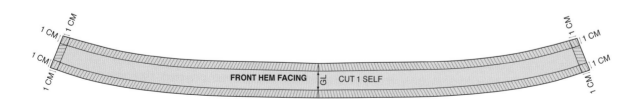

## STEP 9

### DEVELOPING THE POCKET BAG WITH MITRED CORNERS AND ZIP OPENING

- Trace off the 32cm by 32cm square from the front body, indicating the centre grain line.
- The zip opening will be inserted along a panel seam, which is created by measuring down 4cm from each top corner and squaring across. To create the zip opening draw a rectangle 26cm by 1cm, centred on the panel seam.
- To develop the mitred corners that will give the pocket a bellows effect, square out 1cm from the bottom corners and connect to the top corners to give a new angled side. From the new angled side measure in 4cm along the bottom line and mark, and from this point square down 4cm and mark. Repeat on the other side. Join the lower points on each side with a straight line to create a new pocket bottom line. Name the old bottom line *fold*. Continue to measure 1.5cm down the angled side and mark. Measure 1.5cm out from the new pocket bottom line and mark. Join these two points back to the point you marked on the original pocket bottom line (now the fold line). Repeat on the other side.

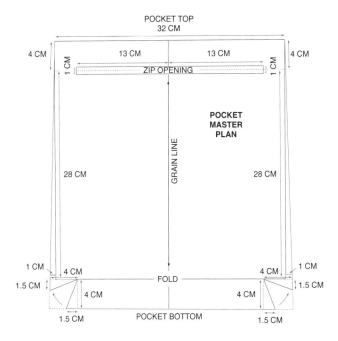

## STEP 10

### BOTTOM AND TOP POCKET BAG PATTERNS

- Following the instructions on page 50, trace off the bottom pocket bag pattern.
- Following the instructions on page 50, trace off the top pocket bag pattern.

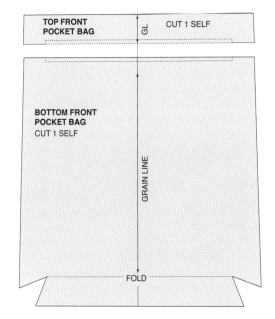

## STEP 11

### POCKET FLAP PATTERN

- On a separate piece of paper, draw a horizontal box 32cm long by 16cm wide to create a rectangular-shaped pocket flap.
- Divide the box in half lengthways, draw a line across the centre and label it *fold*.
- Add a 1cm seam allowance on all sides.

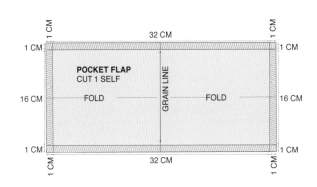

## STEP 12
### ADDING VOLUME TO THE BACK AND CREATING THE BACK NECK FACING

- Trace off the back body panel onto a new piece of paper. Volume will be added by cutting and spreading the pattern pieces open to redefine the shape.
- From the side seam square in 9cm at two points and from the hemline draw a 35cm vertical line passing through the points. Continue to measure in a further 10cm and from the hem draw a 40cm vertical line.
- From the underarm point measure 5cm down the side seam and connect this point with an angled line to the top of the 40cm vertical line.
- Measure down a further 6.5cm and connect this point with an angled line to the top of the 35cm vertical line.
- From the hemline cut up each line and out to the side seam, leaving the shape connected by a few millimetres.

- Starting from the centre back open each panel out 5cm at the hem.
- Redraw the new hemline with a gradual curve back towards the centre back, removing the panel corners that are overhanging.
- To create the back neck facing, measure 4cm down the shoulder seam from the back shoulder neck point and mark, and 4cm down the centre back from the centre back neck point and mark. Join these points with a curved line following the shape of the neckline.

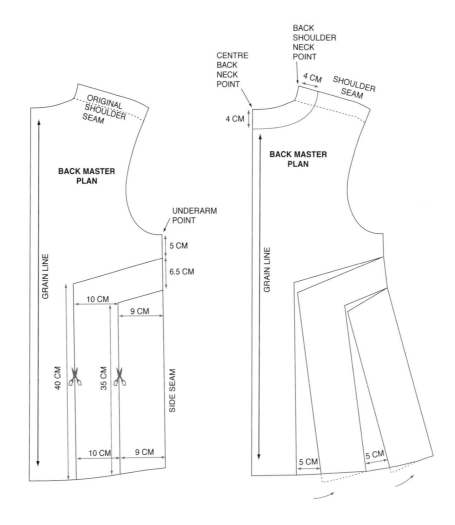

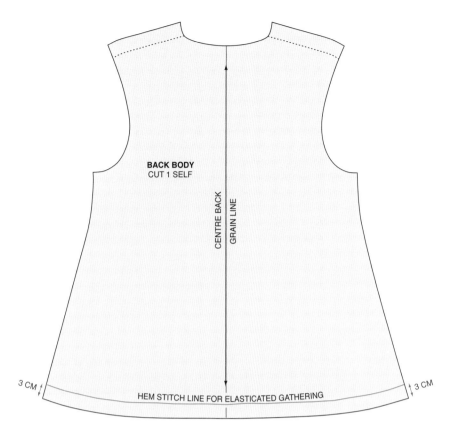

BACK BODY
CUT 1 SELF

CENTRE BACK

GRAIN LINE

3 CM

HEM STITCH LINE FOR ELASTICATED GATHERING

3 CM

## STEP 13
### BACK PATTERN AND HEM FACING

- Trace off the back onto a separate piece of paper and, following the instructions on page 50, create the full pattern shape, adding a 1cm seam allowance on the neckline and shoulders only.
- Measure 3cm up along the length of the hemline to create a channel to take the elastic for a gathered finish.

## STEP 14
### BACK NECK FACING PATTERN

- Trace off the back neck facing onto a separate piece of paper and, following the instructions on page 50, create the full pattern shape, adding a 1cm seam allowance on the neckline and shoulders only.

1 CM    1 CM                    1 CM    1 CM

GL

BACK NECK FACING
CUT 1 SELF

## STEP 15
### BACK HEM FACING PATTERN

- Trace off the back hem facing onto a separate piece of paper and, following the instructions on page 50, create the full pattern shape, adding a 1cm seam allowance on all sides.

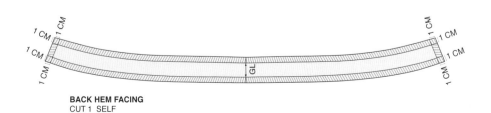

1 CM  1 CM                                              1 CM
1 CM                                                   1 CM
1 CM                GL                              1 CM

BACK HEM FACING
CUT 1  SELF

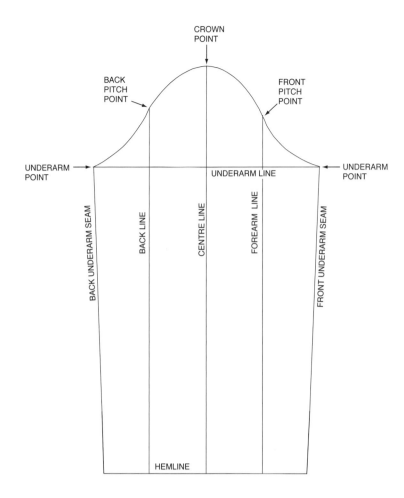

## STEP 16
### SLEEVE MASTER PLAN

Start this development by selecting the basic men's sleeve block, or by drafting the basic sleeve block according to the instructions on page 42. Cut a large piece of drafting paper slightly longer than the length of the shirt you want to develop and transfer the shape of the block and all marks, labels and instructions, following the directions on page 48. For this design the block will be altered to reflect the dropped shoulder and lowered armhole.

## STEP 17
### DEVELOPING THE SLEEVE MASTER PLAN

- Open up the master plan along the centre line by 2cm and intersecting the underarm line.
- From the crown measure down 2cm, the amount by which you dropped the shoulder on the body block.
- From the centre of the underarm line square down 1.75cm, half the amount by which you dropped the armhole. Redraw the new underarm line position, extending it by 3cm each side.
- Using the basic sleeve block head shape as a template, redraw the new sleeve head, indicating the lowered pitch points.
- Extend the sleeve hemline by 3cm to each side and draw in the new underarm seams by connecting the points back up to each end of the new underarm line.
- Extend the sleeve hemline by 3cm to each side, recreating the opposite angle to the sleeve pitch, as the hem will be folded up.
- When adapting any sleeve, check the amount of ease and adjust if necessary before copying off the final pattern.

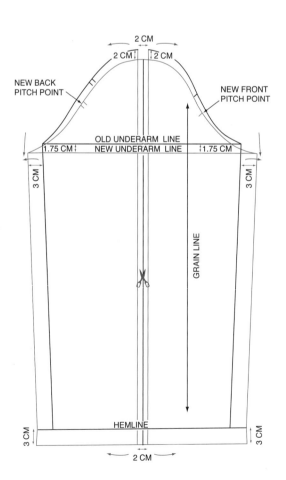

## STEP 18
### SLEEVE PATTERN

- Following the instructions on page 50, trace off the new sleeve pattern.

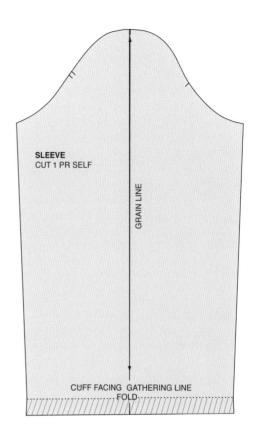

SLEEVE
CUT 1 PR SELF

GRAIN LINE

CUFF FACING  GATHERING LINE
FOLD

## STEP 19
### DEVELOPING THE HOOD

- Starting at the bottom right side of your paper mark point (A); square left 25cm (the length of the combined neck measurement) and mark point (B).
- From (A) square up 40cm (half the head circumference) and mark point (C). Complete the rectangular box and mark point (D).
- From (B) square up 7.5cm (the neck height) and then square in 7.5cm and label as *centre back line*.
- Taking half the front and back neck measurements added together (25cm) use a French curve to draw the neck shape from (A) up to a finishing point on the centre back line.
- From (A) measure up 9cm and then out 1cm and draw in a curved line.
- From (D) square down 13cm and then across 1.5cm and mark; and again from (D) square across 12.5cm and then down 3cm and mark.
- From (C) square down 6.5cm and then out 2cm and mark.
- Use these points to draw in your hood shape (determined by the design, head size, neck opening and usage).
- From the top of the hood opening, measure 12cm down the front opening and draw in the peak alignment notch.

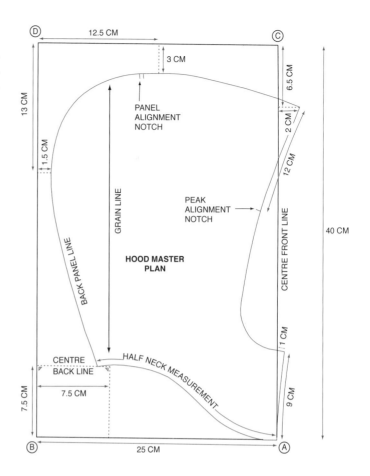

## STEP 20
### HOOD SIDE PANEL PATTERN

- Following the instructions on page 50, trace off the hood side panel pattern.

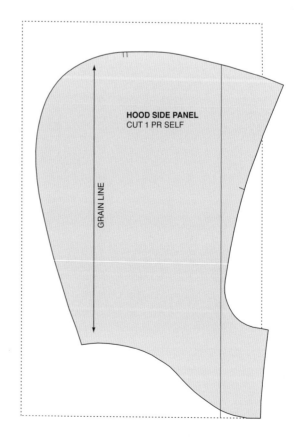

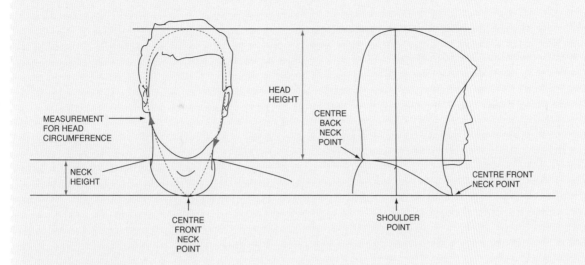

## Taking measurements for the hood

There are three measurements you need to create the pattern for the hood:

1. The front and back neck measurements, taken from the pattern - here they are 12.5cm and 12.5cm. If you are developing a hood with a centre back panel remember to deduct the panel width from the final neck measurement as well as from the crown and front opening.

2. The front and back neck height, found by placing the front pattern on top of the back pattern and aligning them at the chest line, then measuring the distance between the front and back neck heights - here it is 7.5cm.

3. The vertical circumference of the head, taken for the hood opening by measuring around the face of the model's head, starting and finishing at the centre front neck point - here it is 80cm.

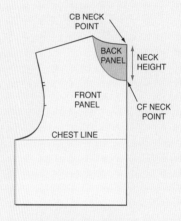

## STEP 21
## DEVELOPING THE CENTRE BACK HOOD PANEL

**Measurements for the hood panel**
The centre hood panel is 8cm wide at
the neckline and 7cm wide at the hood
opening. To find the length, measure the
back panel line on the hood master plan
to create the centre panel – here it is
52cm. The shape of the panel follows the
shape of the head, so it is narrower at
the back of the neck, wider at the crown
and then narrower again at the front of
the head – following a similar principle
to the way the segment of an orange
is shaped.

- Draw a vertical grain line 52cm long. At the top square out
  3.5cm on each side and label the line *hood front*. At the
  bottom measure out 4cm on each side and draw a slightly
  curved line reflecting the shape of the centre back neck on
  the body block; label as *neck edge*.
- From the centre of the hood front square down 18.5cm and
  then square out 5.5cm to each side: this is the widest point.
  Notch for alignment.
- On both sides connect the hood front to the neck edge,
  passing through the central notch alignment line; this shape
  will become the final centre back hood panel.

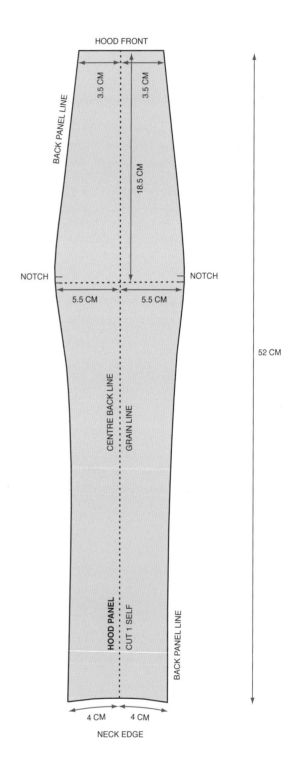

## DEVELOPING THE HOOD PEAK PATTERN

- Start by drawing a rectangular box 9cm wide by 23cm long. Divide in half widthways at 11.5cm.
- From this centre point on one side of the rectangle measure out 3.5cm and mark; on the same side of the rectangle, measure 2cm down along its width and mark. Join these points with a curved line.

- Repeat for the other half of the rectangle.
- Draw the peak curve by connecting the left and right 2cm marks with a curved line passing through the halfway point on the lower side of the rectangle.

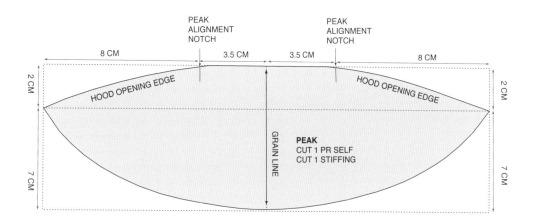

# PATTERN
# FITTED DENIM JACKET

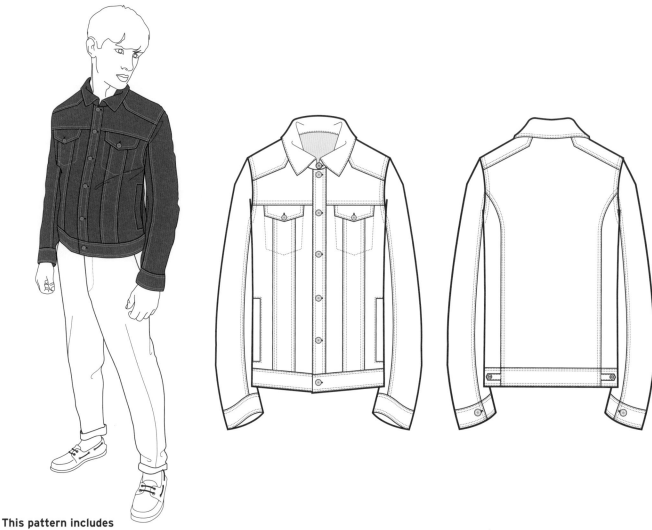

**This pattern includes
development of the following features:**

Creating front and side back panels

Creating a sewn-on front placket

Reducing the length of the body

Creating a front yoke and combined front and back
    shoulder panel

Developing side welted pockets

Developing a front breast envelope pocket

Developing a shaped convertible collar with hidden stand

Creating a waistband with tabs

Developing a casual two-piece sleeve with two-piece cuff

## STEP 1
### DEVELOPING THE MASTER PLAN

Start by selecting the basic men's body block, or by drafting
the basic block according to the instructions on page 40. Cut
a large piece of drafting paper slightly longer than the length
of the jacket you want to develop and transfer the shape of
the block and all marks, labels and instructions, following the
directions on page 48.

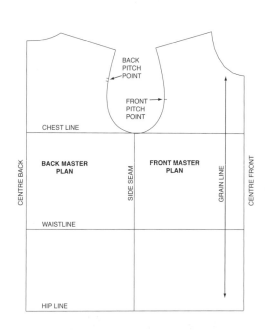

## STEP 2

### DEVELOPING THE ENLARGED NECK, REDUCED BODY LENGTH, FRONT PLACKET AND BODY PANELS

- From the centre front neck point measure down 2cm, and draw in the new neckline using the basic body block as a template.
- From the new centre front neck point measure down 47cm, and from this point square across to the centre back to reduce the body length.
- From the new centre front neck point measure back 2cm along the new neckline and mark, and measure out 2cm and mark. Repeat this at the new hemline and connect these points with straight lines to create a rectangle. This is the 4cm-wide placket.
- To create the three front panel shapes first create the front yoke. From the front neck line measure 9cm down the side of the placket and from this point square across to the back armhole and make a mark.
- From the placket measure 5.5cm along the yoke line you have just drawn and from this point square down to meet the new hemline. Continue to measure a further 7cm along the yoke line and square down to the hemline again. These are the three front panels.
- To create the back panel measure 19cm from the centre back along the hemline and mark; repeat at the chest line. Draw a vertical line through these points, at the chest line curving in towards the armhole mark made earlier.

## STEP 3

### DEVELOPING THE SHOULDER PANEL, SIDE WELTED POCKET AND BREAST ENVELOPE POCKET

- Measure 4cm down the front shoulder neck point and make a mark. Measure 7cm down the armhole from the front shoulder point and square across 10cm into the front. Join this line back up to the mark you made on the neckline.
- Measure 4.5cm from the centre back neck point along the neckline and make a mark. Measure 7cm down the armhole from the back shoulder point and square across 14cm into the back. Join this line back up to the mark you made on the neckline.
- From the centre front measure in 3cm along the yoke line to develop the breast envelope pocket. Continue to measure a further 12cm for the pocket width, and divide it in half. At each end measure down 14cm and join across the bottom to create a rectangle.
- The side welted pocket is developed from the side seam into the front body. From the hemline square 3cm up the side seam, then measure up a further 14cm and create the welt shape by drawing a 14cm by 2cm rectangle. Continue to measure up 3cm along the side seam for the height of the pocket bag, and make a mark. To develop the width of the pocket bag measure 12.5cm along the hemline from the side seam and then square up 17cm. Close the shape by joining this point to the mark on the side seam with an angled line.

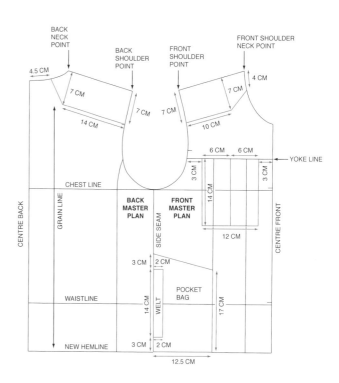

## STEP 4
### DEVELOPING THE BREAST ENVELOPE POCKET PARTS

- All the pocket parts are developed on top of each other and then traced off separately. The envelope breast pocket is stitched behind the front panels along the yoke.
- First draw the rectangular opening. From the centre of the top line of the pocket measure out 5cm on each side. Measure down 1.5cm at each end and join to create a 10cm by 1.5cm rectangle.
- Next draw the pocket flap, which will be stitched into the yoke seam and sit over the welt. From each end of the top pocket line square down 3cm and mark; from the centre of the top line square down 4cm and mark. Join the points at the sides to the central mark to create the angled pitch of the flap point.
- To shape the angled envelope pocket bag square down 12cm from the centre of the top pocket line and from this point square out on each side to meet the side lines of the pocket rectangle. According to the shape desired, on each side draw an angled line up from a point along this line to the top corner. Finish by connecting these points down to the centre line.

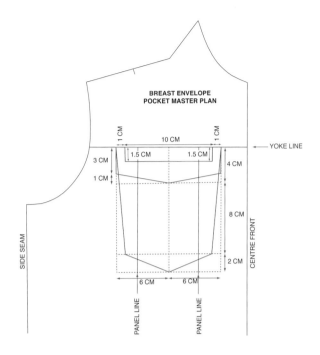

## STEP 5
### FRONT FOLDED PLACKET PATTERN

- Following the instructions on page 50, trace off the front placket shape developed in Step 2. Double over the rectangular shape and draw the fold line down the centre.

## STEP 6
### DEVELOPING THE FINAL COMBINED SHOULDER PANEL

- In this design the shoulder panels are constructed by joining the front and back shoulder panels developed in Step 3. Following the instructions on page 50, trace off the front shoulder pattern from the front block, then align the front shoulder seam with the back shoulder seam and trace off the back shoulder pattern to create the final shoulder yoke pattern.

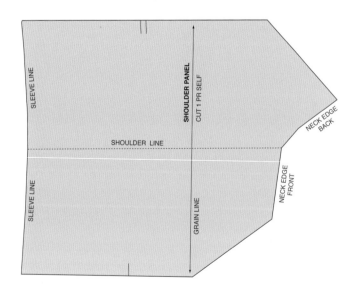

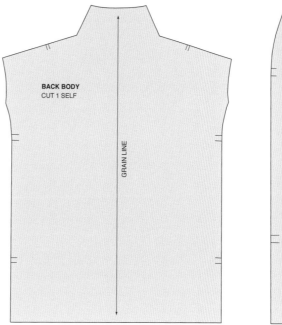

## STEP 7
### BACK AND SIDE BACK BODY PANEL PATTERNS

- Trace off the back body panel onto a new piece of paper and, following the instructions on page 50, create the full pattern shape.
- Following the instructions on page 50, trace off the side back body pattern.

## STEP 8
### FRONT YOKE BODY PANEL PATTERN

- Following the instructions on page 50, trace off the front yoke pattern developed in Step 3, adding alignment notches for the shoulder panel.

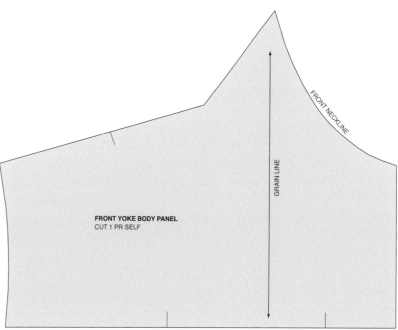

## STEP 9
## SIDE WELTED POCKET
## COMPONENT PATTERNS

- Following the instructions on page 50, trace off all the side welted pocket parts developed in Step 3.
- Start with the welt shape, doubling the width to create a 14cm by 4cm rectangle. Mark the centre fold line lengthways and add a 1cm seam allowance to all sides to create the final pattern.
- The top pocket bag has the welt rectangle removed and the bottom pocket bag is a full shape. Add a 1cm seam allowance to all sides to create the final patterns.

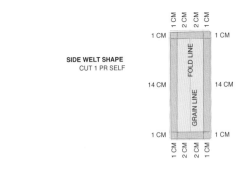

SIDE WELT SHAPE
CUT 1 PR SELF

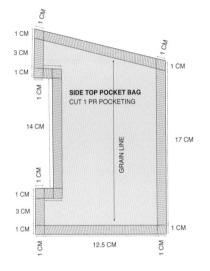

SIDE TOP POCKET BAG
CUT 1 PR POCKETING

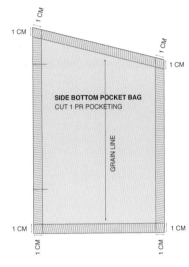

SIDE BOTTOM POCKET BAG
CUT 1 PR POCKETING

## STEP 10
## FRONT BODY PANEL PATTERNS

- Following the instructions on page 50, trace off all the front body panel patterns developed in Step 3: the centre front panel, the middle front panel and the side front panel.

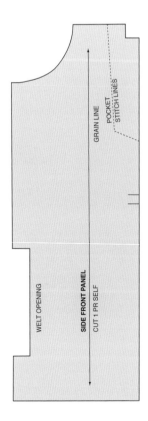

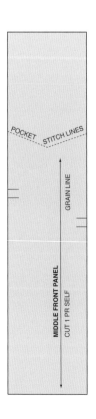

## STEP 11
### FRONT BREAST ENVELOPE POCKET COMPONENT PATTERNS

- Following the instructions on page 50, trace off the final envelope pocket parts developed in Step 4.
- Add a 1cm seam allowance on all sides to create the final envelope pocket and flap patterns.
- Add a 1 cm seam allowance to the top and sides to create the final envelope pocket facing pattern.

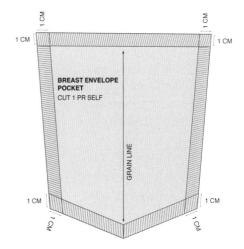

**BREAST ENVELOPE POCKET**
CUT 1 PR SELF

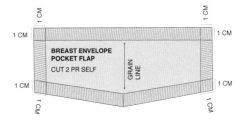

**BREAST ENVELOPE POCKET FLAP**
CUT 2 PR SELF

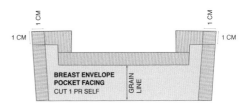

**BREAST ENVELOPE POCKET FACING**
CUT 1 PR SELF

## DEVELOPING THE FINAL WAISTBAND PARTS AND TAB

### The waistband and tab

Take the measurements of the hemline for the front and back body panels from the master plan in Step 2, including the placket width. The denim jacket in this design has a split waistband 4cm in width, with a tab inserted at the side back panel seam. The tab is developed on top of the front waistband for proportion and then removed for the final pattern.

- For the front waistband draw a rectangle 37cm long by 8cm wide (4cm doubled for the folded band). Indicate the panel lines with notches for alignment. Add a 1cm seam allowance on all sides to create the final pattern.
- For the back waistband draw a rectangle 38cm long by 8cm wide (4cm doubled for the folded band). Indicate the centre back with an alignment notch at 19cm (half the waistband length). Add a 1cm seam allowance on all sides to create the final pattern.
- For the waistband tab construct a rectangle 6cm long by 3cm wide. At one end measure back 1cm at the sides and join these points to a centre point to create an angled point. Add a 1cm seam allowance on all sides to create the final pattern.

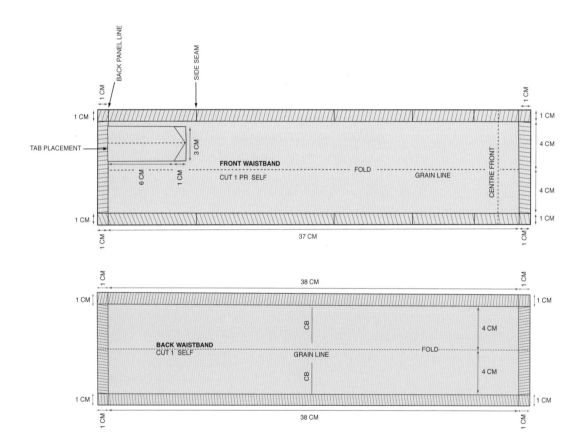

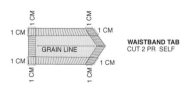

## DEVELOPING THE SHAPED CONVERTIBLE COLLAR WITH HIDDEN STAND

**Measuring half the neck from the master plan**
We will develop half the collar and stand before creating the full collar and stand. By taking measurements from the master plan, which is drawn in half, you will be measuring half of the neck measurement.

- On the master plan in Step 2 measure the length of the back neck, in this case 8.5cm, and the front neck from the shoulder point down past the centre front line to the point at which the placket finishes, in this case 17cm.
- Add these two measurements together to give half the neck measurement, in this case 25.5cm.

- Starting in the centre of the piece of paper make a mark to indicate the bottom of the centre back and label it (A). From (A) draw a 25.5cm horizontal line and mark (B) at the end.
- From (A) measure out 8.5cm (the width of the half back neck) along the line and place a notch. Name it the *shoulder notch*.
- From (A) square up 3cm and mark (G); continue up 5cm and mark (D).
- From (D) square out 25.5cm and mark (E) at the end.
- To give the collar shape, measure up 1cm from (B) and mark (F). Join this point back with a slightly curved line measuring 8.5cm to (C).
- From (E) square up 1cm and out 1cm and from these points run a straight line back down to (F) and back along to blend in with the top line towards (D). Then continue each of these lines up from the 1cm mark until they intersect. This is the collar point.
- Develop the hidden stand shape by drawing a curved line out from (G) down to meet (C).
- Trace the master plan on to a separate piece of paper and cut out the stand. Divide the stand length into four equal parts and draw vertical cut lines.
- Remove the top collar shape from the development by tracing onto a separate piece of paper. Trace the cut lines across from the stand.

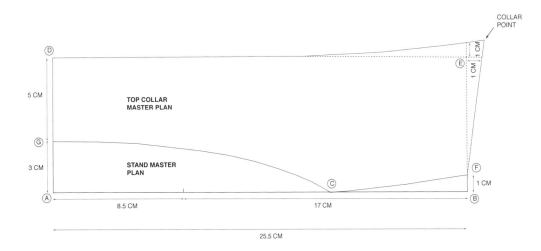

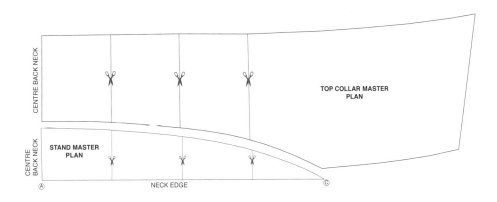

## STEP 14
### ADDING SHAPING TO THE CONVERTIBLE COLLAR AND STAND

- Cut down the vertical lines on the top collar shape, leaving them attached at the bottom by a few millimetres. Starting from the centre back open out each line by 0.4cm, curving down the top collar. From the centre back neck remove 0.9cm, the width lost when closing up the stand.

- Cut down the vertical lines on the stand shape, leaving them attached at the bottom by a few millimetres. Overlap the sections along the top edge moving them by 0.3cm towards the centre back; this will bring up the neckline.

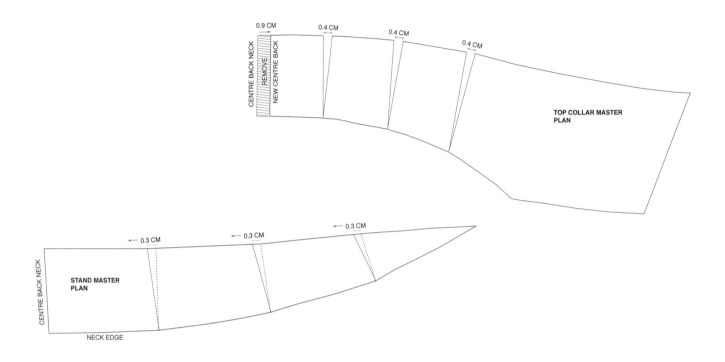

## STEP 15
### COLLAR STAND PATTERN

- Trace off the collar stand onto a new piece of paper and, following the instructions on page 50, create the full pattern shape, adding a 1cm seam allowance on all sides.

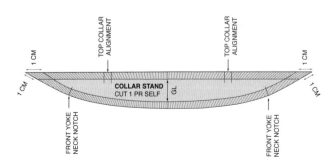

## STEP 16
## TOP COLLAR PATTERN

- Trace off the top collar onto a new piece of paper and, following the instructions on page 50, create the full pattern shape, adding a 1cm seam allowance on all sides.

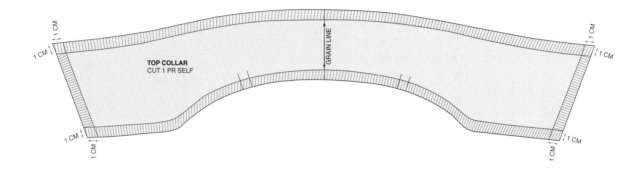

## STEP 17
## DEVELOPING THE SLEEVE MASTER PLAN

Start this development by selecting the basic men's sleeve block, or by drafting the basic sleeve block according to the instructions on page 42. Cut a large piece of drafting paper slightly longer than the length of the sleeve you want to develop and transfer the shape of the block and all marks, labels and instructions, following the directions on page 48. The design illustrated has a two-piece sleeve.

### Casual two-piece sleeve

The two-piece sleeve shown here is for a casual jacket that retains the sleeve head shape of the basic sleeve block, unlike the tailored two-piece sleeve that has a padded sleeve head. The starting point is the basic sleeve block from which two panels - top sleeve and undersleeve - are created.

For this two-piece sleeve we are going to separate the under- and top sleeve panels so that the seams align with the points at which the side back and front yoke seams meet the armhole.

- Shorten the sleeve to allow for the addition of the cuff. From the sleeve hemline measure up 9cm on each side and square across to create the new hemline.
- To find the position at which to separate the top sleeve and undersleeve panels, measure the armhole on the front master plan created in Step 2 from the front shoulder point

to the yoke line and on the back master plan from the back shoulder point to the back panel line. In this case the combined yoke measurement from the front yoke line to the back panel line is 27cm and the remainder of the armhole measures 24cm. Transfer these measurements to the sleeve by measuring down the front and back armhole of the sleeve from the crown point and marking the seam panel alignment notches.

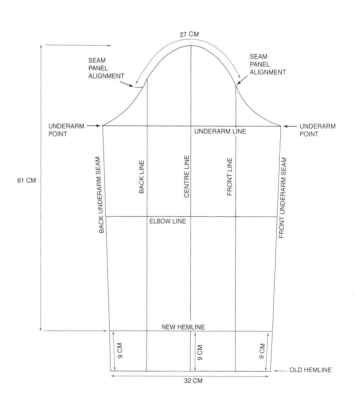

## STEP 18
### STARTING TO DEVELOP THE TWO-PIECE SLEEVE

- Divide the width of the new underarm line into four and mark. From these points square up to the same level as the crown point and down to the sleeve hemline to divide the sleeve into four sections widthways. Label the new lines *back line, centre line* and *front line* to recreate the frame of the original sleeve block.
- On the back underarm seam, mark (A) where it intersects the elbow line and (B) where it intersects the new hemline.
- On the front line, mark (C) where it intersects the new hemline and (D) where it intersects the elbow line.
- Mark (1) where the elbow line intersects the back line. The square created by points (A), (B), (C) and (D) will now be pivoted anticlockwise from (1) on the elbow line by 3cm, measured from the centre line at the hem. Do this by copying the square onto a separate piece of paper to pivot and draw in the new position.
- Square down from the back seam panel alignment notch. Trace off the triangular shape between the sleeve head and the underarm line. Flip this shape over and position it so that the back underarm point aligns at the centre line along the underarm line. Copy the shape over. Repeat from the front seam panel alignment notch.

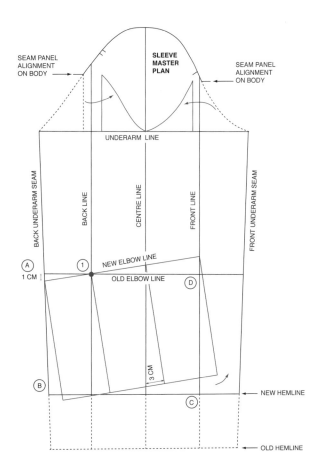

## STEP 19
### DEVELOPING THE TOP AND UNDERSLEEVE SHAPES

- To develop the top sleeve front seam square in 9cm from the front underarm seam until you intersect the new angled hemline and from this point draw a line up to connect with the front seam panel alignment notch.
- To create the top sleeve back seam continue to measure 13cm along the angled hemline, which gives the hem width. Using a curved line connect this point to the back seam panel alignment notch, passing through the elbow line.
- To develop the undersleeve shape square in 4cm from the back seam panel alignment notch and from this point draw down a curved line passing through the elbow line 2cm in from the top sleeve back seam (measured along the elbow line) connecting to the hemline.
- From the front seam panel alignment notch measure in 1.5cm to ensure that the front and back underarm seams are aligned on the centre line. (This method may differ depending on changes made to the basic sleeve block following any lowering of the armhole.) Using a curved line connect this point with the hemline, passing through the elbow line 2cm in from the top sleeve front seam (measured along the elbow line).

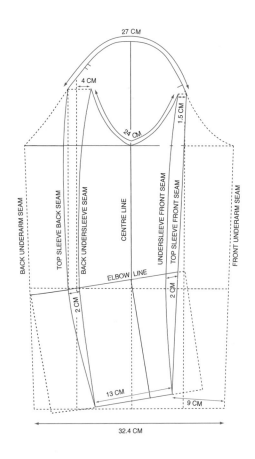

## STEP 20
### UNDERSLEEVE PATTERN

- Following the instructions on page 50, trace off the final undersleeve pattern, adding in alignment notches.

## STEP 21
### TOP SLEEVE PATTERN

- Following the instructions on page 50, trace off the final top sleeve pattern, adding in alignment notches.

## STEP 22
### TWO-PIECE SLEEVE CUFF PATTERN

- Construct a rectangle 26cm long by 8cm (4cm doubled in width for a folded cuff). Add a 1cm seam allowance on all sides to create the final pattern.

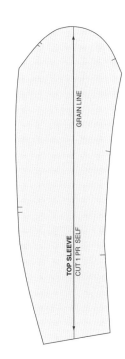

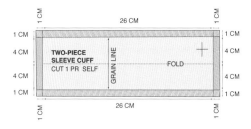

# PATTERN
# TRENCH COAT

**This pattern includes development of the following features:**

Shaping the body panels, moving the side seam to the back

Creating a double-breasted extension

Extending the hemline

Lowering the armhole

Creating a centre back vent

Developing a storm flap and epaulette

Developing front welted pockets

Developing a shaped convertible collar with hidden stand and lapel

Developing a tailored two-piece sleeve with cuff vent

Developing a full body lining

**Fitting the trench coat**

Traditionally, trench coats were produced as an outer garment to be worn over suit jackets or dress coats. Chest circumferences, neck openings, armholes, sleeve heads and sleeve lengths were all made larger to accommodate the garment underneath. Modern interpretations combined with a more casual approach to dress no longer dictate that trench coats should be oversized. When developing this style, take into account the formality or informality of the garment you are designing, together with how it may be worn.

## STEP 1
### DEVELOPING THE MASTER PLAN

Start by selecting the basic men's body block, or by drafting the basic block according to the instructions on page 40. Cut a large piece of drafting paper slightly longer than the length of the coat you want to develop and transfer the shape of the block and all marks, labels and instructions following the directions on page 48.

## STEP 2
### LOWERING THE ARMHOLE, EXTENDING THE HEMLINE AND DEVELOPING THE DOUBLE-BREASTED EXTENSION

- From the chest line square down 2.5cm on each side and starting from the new underarm point redraw the new armhole shape using the basic body blocks as a template. Transfer the back and front pitch points to their new positions on the lowered armhole.
- Extend the side seam, centre front and centre back lines down vertically from the existing hemline to the required length of the coat.
- Square across from the centre front to the centre back at the new hemline.
- To develop the double-breasted extension, square out 7.5cm from the centre front at the neckline.
- Repeat at the hemline.
- Connect the two points with a vertical line to create the double-breasted extension.

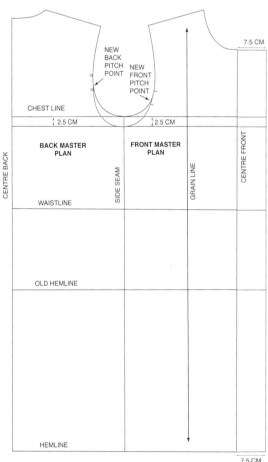

## DEVELOPING THE HEMLINE FACING, BACK VENT AND FRONT WELTED POCKET POSITION

### Developing the hemline facing, back vent and front welted pocket position

Most trench coat styles have a back vent incorporated into the design. The job of this vent is to allow freedom of movement around the leg and seat area. Sitting down in a closed garment will restrict body movement and feel uncomfortable. The length of your design will generally determine the length of the vent needed; the longer the coat or jacket, the longer the vent.

The vent extension has a diagonal line at the top so that the seams, when pressed, are not as bulky as they would be if the vent was square. A diagonal seam with less bulk creates an optical illusion, drawing your eye away from this detail. Take time to look at other examples of vents as you do your research. You will find that some are topstitched along this diagonal seam and others are sewn internally.

- Add the hem facing to the bottom of the pattern as a horizontal rectangle measuring 4cm in width.
- To develop the vent measure 5cm up the centre back from the old hemline, and from this point square out 6cm.
- From the bottom of the hemline facing, square out 6cm. Join the two points with a vertical line.
- Now measure an additional 1.5cm up the centre back line and mark.
- Draw a line from this point down to the top of the vent extension at its outside edge, creating a diagonal line at the top of the vent.
- To develop the rectangular pocket opening, measure in 23cm along the old hemline from the centre front and then square up 3cm and mark; this will be the bottom right-hand corner of the pocket opening. Create a rectangle 18cm long by 2cm wide at an angle of your choice.
- Mark each corner of the pocket opening with a drill hole.

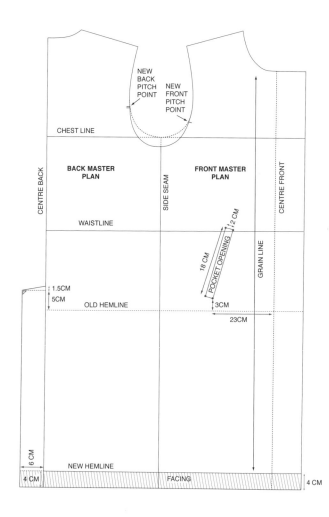

## STEP 4
## DEVELOPING THE SHAPING LINES

### Shaping the coat

To create a fitted coat you can introduce shaping into the block by moving the side seam into the back panel. Once you have extended the front panel you can create two new style lines. Shaping is created by removing the internal volume between these lines. At the hemline you can add a little flare to the design by crossing the lines over, thus adding volume by extending the circumference of the hem.

- From the side seam, measure 10.5cm along the back armhole towards the back pitch point, and draw a vertical line down from this point to the hemline.
- From the intersection of this line with the waistline, measure 3.5cm towards the centre back and 1.5cm towards the side seam and mark both points.
- Join these new points back up to the armhole with slightly curved lines.
- Label the line that defines the new back panel shape *back panel style line*.
- Label the line that defines the new front panel shape *front panel style line*.
- Continue the back panel style line down in a graduated curve until it meets the vertical line you first drew.
- At the hemline, measure out 7cm from the vertical line you first drew towards the centre back and mark.
- Continue the front panel style line down in a graduated curve until it meets this new point.

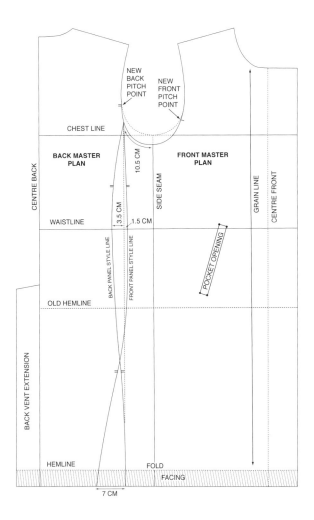

## STEP 5

**DEVELOPING THE SHAPED CONVERTIBLE COLLAR WITH HIDDEN STAND AND LAPEL
AND POSITIONING THE FRONT DART LINE**

### Break point and roll line

The point at which the front will turn
over to create a lapel is called the
break point (BP) and the line that it
turns on is the roll line. The lower
down the front your BP is, the wider
an opening you will have around the
neck silhouette.

### Collar measurements and lapel shape

To draft the lapel and shaped convertible
collar with hidden stand for a pattern
with a front neck measurement of 14.5cm,
excluding the double breast extension,
and a back neck measurement of 9.5cm,
first locate the position on the pattern
where you want your collar to break on
the new front edge line of the body
section. To work out the shape and size
of the lapel and collar, consider the
proportion of your design and the length
of the silhouette. It is always a good
idea to assess the shape of the lapel by
folding the paper back on the roll line.
Redraw and develop the shape until you
are satisfied.

- To give the front of your lapel some shape, from the neckline square out 1cm and square up 1cm. Find the new front neck point and join this point back to the neckline and down to the break point with slight curves to give the shaping for the lapel.
- From the shoulder neck point continue the shoulder seam out 2.5cm and mark point (C).
- From the break point on the front line draw a straight dotted line to (C).
- Continue this line beyond (C) for 9.5cm (the length of the back neck measurement) and mark point (A).

- Square left 2.5cm and mark point (B).
- Join points (B) and (C) with a dotted line.
- From (B) square out 2.5cm back towards the shoulder and mark point (D).
- From (D) square back into the shoulder, curving the line slightly back towards the neckline and cutting off the shoulder neck point.
- Continue the straight line from (D) through (B), extending it to the width you would like to make the collar, and mark point (E).
- At a right angle from (E) draw out the collar shape you require.
- Mark a notch at the point where the top collar joins the neckline and at the point where it meets the shoulder line.
- To position the line of the front dart, measure 4.5cm from the original side seam along the front armhole towards the front pitch point. From here draw a straight line in towards the pocket, finishing a quarter of the way up from the bottom of the pocket opening. This is the line of the dart.

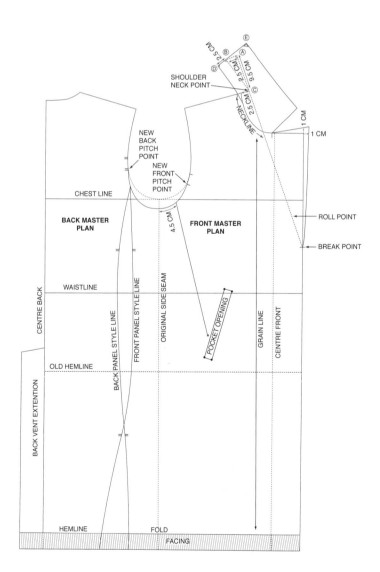

## STEP 6
## DEVELOPMENT OF THE FRONT DART SHAPING

**Rotating the pattern**
Creating and opening a dart on the front panel will allow you to introduce shaping that runs from under the arm towards the front pocket, giving the trench coat a closer fitted silhouette. This dart is achieved by opening and rotating, or pivoting, the pattern.

- Trace off the shape of the front panel from the master plan onto a separate piece of paper.
- To open the dart line at the armhole, on another piece of paper trace around the front panel starting from the end of the dart line at the pocket opening, up to the top of the dart line at the armhole and then continuing in a clockwise direction until the point directly under the end of the dart on the hemline.
- Make sure the two pieces of paper are aligned exactly, and at the pocket end of the dart line place a drill hole through both pieces of paper.
- With an awl holding the pieces of paper down at the same

point, pivot the new pattern clockwise so that the top of the dart line moves a distance of 3cm to the left.
- Trace along the dart line again, creating the second side of the dart, and continue to trace the rest of the panel shape.
- After pivoting, the hemline will be pitched lower towards the centre back line. Blend the two lines together with a shallow curve. Once the dart is closed this will bring the hemline back up into a straight line.

## STEP 7
## FRONT PANEL PATTERN

- Following the instructions on page 50, trace off the front panel pattern.

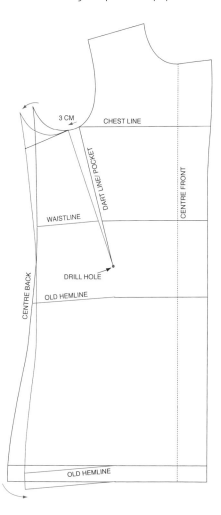

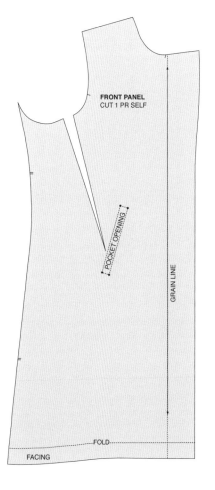

## DEVELOPING THE SHAPED CONVERTIBLE COLLAR WITH HIDDEN STAND

**The shaped convertible collar with hidden stand**
In this design the trench coat collar
has a separate stand incorporated which
allows the collar to turn over and sit
flat around the back of the neck.

- Fold a piece of paper in half and, laying the fold on the centre back of the collar on the master plan, trace off the shape of the collar (including the notches). Label the centre back. This is the collar master plan and you will be developing this in half.
- The next step is to create the stand shape. Measure 2.5cm up the centre back (the width of the collar stand). From this point draw a curved line that ends where the roll line intersects the neckline on the master plan. This ensures that the stand will not be seen when the collar is turned down.
- Place a double notch along this new line.

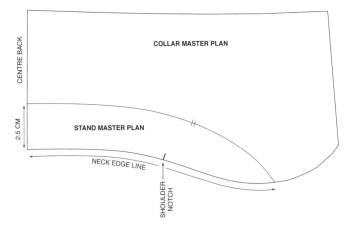

## STEP 9
## COLLAR STAND PATTERN

- Trace off the collar stand pattern onto a new piece of paper and, following the instructions on page 50, create the full pattern shape.

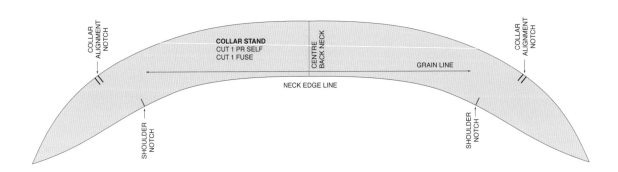

## DEVELOPING THE COLLAR USING SLASH AND SPREAD

### Slash and spread

In order to sit flat across the shoulders, the outer edge of the collar needs to be wider than the inside edge. You can use the slash and spread method to increase the length of the outer edge of the collar.

Slash and spread is a technique that allows you to introduce fullness or volume to an area of a pattern by cutting a line in the pattern and opening the two sides out at one end of the line only. Once you have introduced the volume, you can then trace off the new shape.

- Trace off the half collar shape without the stand from the collar development.
- Measure across the length of the half collar and draw lines to divide it into five equal sections.
- Cut down each line towards the stand, but do not cut right through to the edge.
- Transfer the measurements obtained from your calico toile to your paper pattern, and open out the lines on the pattern to the same distances as on the toile.
- Redraw the collar, creating a smooth curve at the outer edge.
- You may find that the collar point is too square and you need to add some shaping according to the style of the design. Continuing the curve, measure out 2cm from the edge of the collar and draw a line back to the centre front neck point.

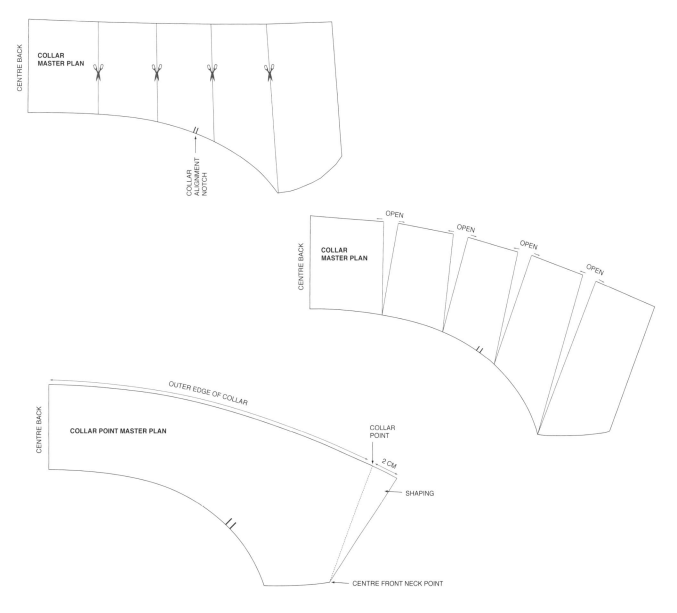

## STEP 11
### TOP COLLAR PATTERN

- Trace off the half collar pattern and, following the instructions on page 50, create the full pattern shape.

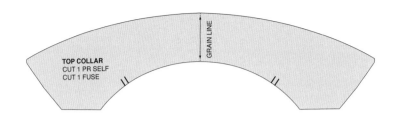

## STEP 12
### DEVELOPING THE FRONT FACING SHAPE

**Front facing**

In this design make the front facing wider than the double-breasted extension so that the button and buttonhole are cut and sewn through the main fabric, giving them support and strength.

- Develop the front facing on the front panel pattern.
- From the new front line measure in 9.5cm along the chest line, and measure in 8.5cm along the waistline, the old hemline and the new hemline.

- From the shoulder neck point measure 5cm along the shoulder seam towards the armhole.
- Draw a straight line connecting these points from the hemline up towards the shoulder seam, blending through the chest line to the marked point on the shoulder with a smooth curve.

## STEP 13
### FRONT FACING PATTERN

- Following the instructions on page 50, trace off the front facing shape to create the final pattern, adding a 1cm seam allowance to all sides.

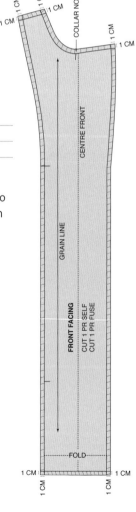

## STEP 14
## BACK PANEL PATTERN

- Following the instructions on page 50, trace off the back panel pattern.

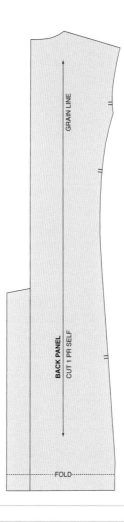

## STEP 15
## DEVELOPING THE FRONT WELTED POCKET STAND AND BAGS

### Pocket shape
The pocket bag for this trench coat is not rectangular like most patch pockets but shaped like half a human kidney. The depth and width is determined by the opening you have drawn on your master plan and the internal space available to position the pocket within the design.

- Start by creating a separate master plan on a new piece of paper. Trace round the rectangular pocket opening shape indicating the direction of the grain line next to it.
- Label the two long sides of the rectanglar box *top stitch line* and the other *bottom stitch line*. The pocket and welt stand shapes are developed from these lines.
- To develop the bag shape, square out 1cm from the top stitch line at each end and connect the points. Extend this line 1.5cm at each end.
- Starting from a right angle at each end of this line, draw a half kidney-like shape that, once constructed, will hang below the pocket opening.
- When drawing the pocket bag shape check that you do not extend it too far forward so that it interferes with the facing or button placements. This will now become your top pocket bag shape.

- To develop the shape for the welted pocket stand, which will be attached to the bottom stitch line during construction, square out 5cm from the bottom stitch line at each end and connect the points. At the top end extend the line by 1cm and connect this point back to the bottom stitch line at an angle. This will conceal the opening when sewn down.

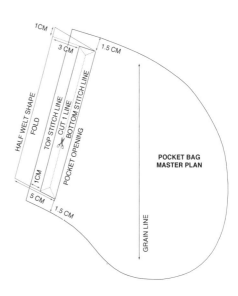

## STEP 16
### POCKET WELT PATTERN

- The welt flap shape that you have just developed is only a half pattern. Trace it off and, following the instructions on page 50, create the full pattern.

POCKET WELT
CUT 1 PR SELF
CUT 1 PR FUSE

GRAIN LINE

FOLD

## STEP 17
### TOP POCKET BAG PATTERN

- Following the instructions on page 50, trace off the pocket bag shape.

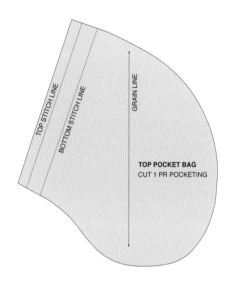

TOP STITCH LINE

BOTTOM STITCH LINE

GRAIN LINE

TOP POCKET BAG
CUT 1 PR POCKETING

## STEP 18
### UNDER POCKET BAG PATTERN

- Following the instructions on page 50, trace off the top pocket bag shape to create the under pocket bag pattern; make sure you carry over the stitch lines. The under pocket bag is smaller than the top pocket bag. To create the under pocket bag pattern, measure up 1cm from the understitch line and draw a parallel line; this is the new edge of the pattern.

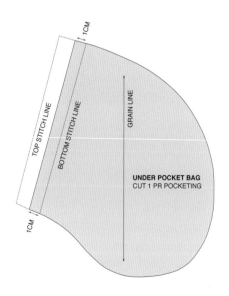

1CM

TOP STITCH LINE

BOTTOM STITCH LINE

GRAIN LINE

UNDER POCKET BAG
CUT 1 PR POCKETING

1CM

## STORM FLAP AND EPAULETTE MASTER PLAN

### Storm flap

A design feature on this trench coat style is the classic storm flap that is associated with many outerwear garments. The flap is sewn down to the front chest and to the back, leaving the armhole open. Storm flaps are open to interpretation and can be designed in many different ways.

- Cut a piece of paper large enough to cover the front and back upper body panels.
- Draw a horizontal line through the middle of the paper.
- Place the front and back body panels together at the shoulder, as you would if you were sewing them together, and position the shoulders along the seam.
- Trace round the front and back upper body from the chest line up, including the armhole.

- This is the storm flap master plan onto which you will develop the style lines.

## DEVELOPING THE STORM FLAP AND EPAULETTE

- To develop the storm flap as a half pattern with the epaulette protruding from the shoulder, start from the shoulder neck point and measure in 0.5cm along the shoulder seam, then square down 25cm towards the chest line and centre front.
- From this point square across 9cm to just below the chest line and mark. From the front underarm point measure in 3cm along the chest line and from here square up 2cm and mark.
- Connect these two points with a curve to complete the lower front edge of the storm flap.
- To draft the side of the flap around the armhole, extend the shoulder seam out 2cm. Next measure in 1cm from the back armhole along the chest line and then square up 1cm and mark. With a shallow curve, join this point to the end of the extended shoulder seam and the point at the outside edge of the front of the flap.
- To shape the lower edge of the back of the storm flap first locate the position of the lower back point. To do this measure in 9.5cm from the centre back along the chest line and square down 3cm and mark.
- Then locate the apex of the curve on the centre back by measuring 1cm up the centre back line from the chest line and mark.
- Join this point to the lower back point with a curve, representing half of the curve across the centre back. Draw a shallow curve from the lower back point to the point at the edge of the armhole curve.

- To draft the epaulette draw a 14cm line out from the shoulder seam, square down 5cm towards the front chest line and square back towards the armhole. Create the point at the end of the epaulette by measuring 2cm back down both sides and then joining these two points to a central point at the tip.

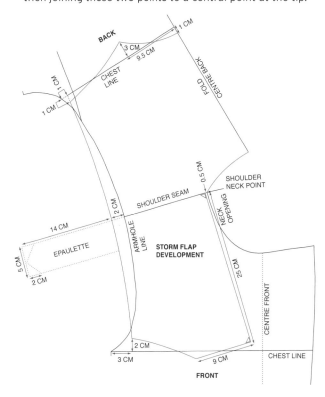

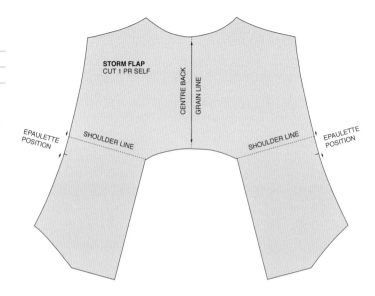

## STEP 21
### STORM FLAP PATTERN

- Trace off the storm flap onto a new piece of paper and, following the instructions on page 50, create the full pattern shape, indicating with notches the position of the epaulette.

## STEP 22
### EPAULETTE PATTERN

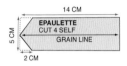

- Following the instructions on page 50, trace off the pattern for the epaulette.

## STEP 23
### DEVELOPING THE TWO-PIECE TAILORED SLEEVE

**Measurements required to develop the sleeve**

Measurements required to draft the tailored two-piece sleeve are as follows.
- Armhole 54cm + 4cm ease = 58cm. (Take this measurement from the basic body block.)
- Sleeve length to wrist = 70cm. (This measurement is taken from the crown point, running down the back of the elbow to the wrist; extra length can be added at this point to suit your design.)
- Crown point to elbow length = 41cm.
- Upper biceps circumference = 36.5cm. (This measurement is taken round the upper arm; extra width 'ease' can be added for movement.)
- Cuff measurement = 32cm. (This garment is taken from the basic tapered block. As an overgarment there is no need to reduce the cuff width.)
- Sleeve head height = 18.5cm.

- Cut a large piece of drafting paper slightly longer than the length of your sleeve or the arm length of your fit model.
- Draw a 70cm vertical line down the centre and label it *centre line*; label the top of this line (1) and the bottom (2). This is the length of the sleeve.
- From (1) measure down 18.5cm (the sleeve head height, or one third of the armhole measurement not including ease, to which you can allow tolerance of plus or minus 0.5cm) and label point (3).
- From (1) measure down 41cm (the elbow length) and label point (4).
- Divide the armhole measurement (58cm) by 6 to give 9.6cm and add 1cm volume to give 10.6cm. From (1) square out 10.6cm to the left and to the right and label these points (5) and (6).
- From (2) measure out 10.6cm to the left and to the right and label these points (7) and (8).
- Connect all points (5), (6), (7), (8), to form a rectangle.
- Divide the sleeve head height (18.5cm) by 3 to give 6.1cm. From (6) measure down 6.1cm, make a mark and label it *back pitch point*. From the back pitch point square in 2.5cm and mark point (A); this is the top point of the back seam on the undersleeve.
- From (3) square out to the left to intersect the line from (5) to (7) and mark point (B), and square out to the right to intersect the line from (6) to (8) and mark point (C). This is the underarm line.
- From (B) measure out 2.5cm and mark point (D), and measure in 2.5cm and mark point (E). From (C) measure in 1cm and mark point (F), and measure out 1cm and mark point (G).

- To establish the front pitch point on the armhole divide the sleeve head height (18.5cm) by 2 to give 9.25cm, and subtract 2cm to give 7.25cm. This will ensure a rectangular shape to the sleeve head instead of the square shape that would occur if the sleeve head were just divided in half. From (B) measure up 7.25cm, make a mark and label it *front pitch point*.
- From (4) square out to the left to intersect the line from (5) to (7) and mark point (H), and square out to the right to intersect the line from (6) to (8) and mark point (I). This is the elbow line.
- From (H) measure out 1cm and mark point (J), and measure in 4cm and mark point (K).

- From (7) measure up 2cm and from this point measure out 2cm and mark point (L); this is the top sleeve cuff point. Measure in 2cm and mark point (M); this is the undersleeve cuff point.
- The cuff circumference is 32cm. Divide this between the top and undersleeve so that the top sleeve cuff width is 18cm and the undersleeve is 14cm. This allows the top sleeve seam to fall towards the back of the arm, slightly out of view.
- From (L) draw a line 18cm long to intersect the line from (7) to (8) and mark point (N). From (M) draw a line 14cm long to intersect the line from (7) to (8) also at point (N). These are the cuff hemlines.
- Draw in the top sleeve front seam by drawing a blended line connecting the points from (L) through (J) to (D).
- Draw in the undersleeve front seam by drawing a blended line connecting the points from (M) through (K) to (E).
- Using a French curve, draw in the top sleeve head starting at (D) with a concave curve through the front pitch point where you reverse the curve to a convex curve up to (1) and back down to the back pitch point with a similar convex curve.
- Measure the length of this line and compare it to the measurement of the armhole on the front and back patterns. Here the length should be 37cm. Adjust the curves until the line is the correct measurement.
- Using a French curve, draw in the top of the undersleeve with convex curve starting at (E) up to (A).
- Again, measure this line and adjust it until it is the same measurement as the armhole on the front and back patterns – in this case 21cm.
- Draw in the back seam of the top sleeve with a blended line from the back pitch point through points (G) to (I) and continue down to (N).
- Draw in the back seam of the undersleeve with a blended line from (A) through (F) to (I) and also continue with this seam on the same line as the top sleeve down to (N).

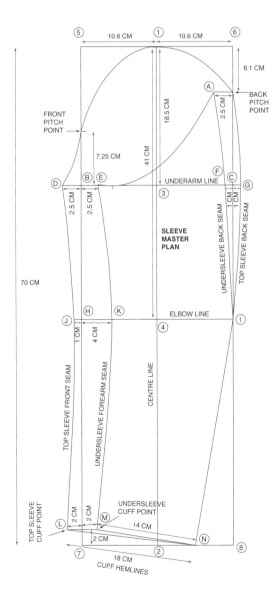

## STEP 24
### TOP SLEEVE PATTERN, FACING AND CUFF VENT

**Adding the sleeve facing**

It is important that you have already established your sleeve length before adding a sleeve facing to the bottom of your sleeve.

- Following the instructions on page 50, trace off the final top sleeve pattern, adding in alignment notches.
- From the sleeve hemline square down 3cm and draw a rectangular box. This is the sleeve facing, which will be folded up inside the sleeve.
- Extend the length of the sleeve facing by 3cm at the back seam to create a sleeve opening.
- Measure up 10cm along the back seam and create a rectangular box 3cm in width.
- Measure up a further 1.5cm and join this point to the outer corner of the box, creating an angle and shape similar to the centre back vent.
- The corner of the sleeve facing and opening can be finished with a mitred seam once folded back and attached to the sleeve lining.

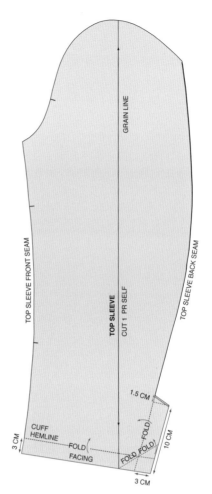

## STEP 25
### UNDERSLEEVE PATTERN, FACING AND CUFF VENT

- Following the instructions on page 50, trace off the final undersleeve pattern, adding in alignment notches.
- From the sleeve hemline square down 3cm and draw a rectangular box to create the sleeve facing.
- Extend the length of the sleeve facing by 3cm at the back seam to create the other side of the sleeve opening.
- Measure up 10cm along the back seam to create a rectangular box 3cm in width.
- Measure up a further 1.5cm and join this point to the outer corner of the box, creating an angle and shape similar to the centre back vent.
- The corner of the sleeve facing and opening can be finished with a mitred seam once folded back and attached to the sleeve lining.

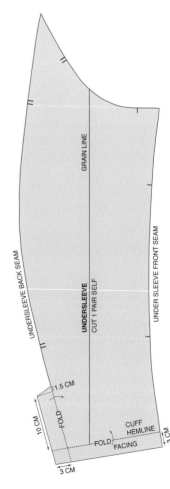

## STEP 26
### DEVELOPING THE TOP SLEEVE LINING

- Following the instructions on page 50, trace off the top sleeve pattern onto a separate piece of paper.
- Remove 1cm from the lower edge of the sleeve, leaving a 2cm facing.
- From the crown point measure up 0.5cm and mark.
- From the front shoulder point measure out 0.5cm and up 0.5cm and mark.
- From the back shoulder point measure out 0.5cm and mark. Using the sleeve head shape as a template, join these points at the crown with a curved line.
- From the new shoulder points redraw the lines down to blend in with the new sleeve hemline.

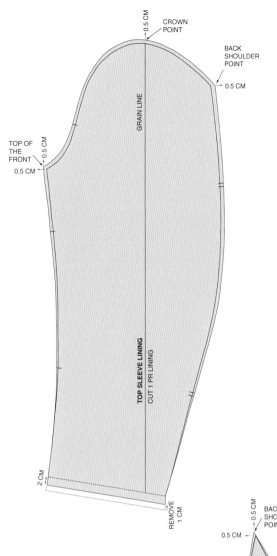

## STEP 27
### DEVELOPING THE UNDER SLEEVE LINING

- Following the instructions on page 50, trace off the undersleeve pattern onto a separate piece of paper.
- Remove 1cm from the lower edge of the sleeve, leaving a 2cm facing.
- From the front shoulder point measure out 0.5cm and up 0.5cm and mark.
- From the back shoulder point measure up 0.5cm and then out 0.5cm and mark.
- Join these points along the underarm with a curved line.
- From the new shoulder points redraw the lines down to blend in with the new sleeve hem.

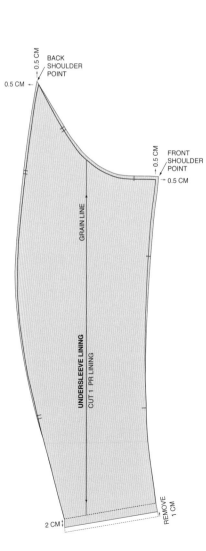

## STEP 28
### DEVELOPING THE FRONT BODY LINING

- Following the instructions on page 50, trace off a copy of the front body panel without the facing.
- Remove 2.5cm from the lower edge of the hem facing.
- From the shoulder point square out and up 0.5cm, find the new shoulder point and blend back to the front facing line along the shoulder.
- From the top of the front style line, measure 0.5cm out into the armhole and continue this line and the style line up to a point and mark where they intersect.
- Join this point with the new shoulder point by drawing a curved line following the shape of the armhole.

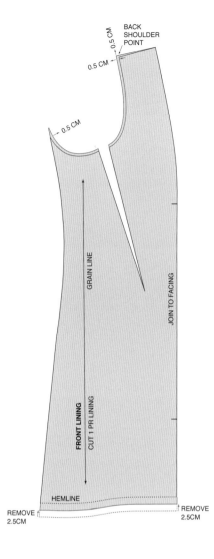

## STEP 29
### DEVELOPING THE BACK NECK FACING

**Back neck facing**
The back neck facing is added to give strength and to stabilise the collar. It is connected to the front facing at the shoulder and is cut from facing fabric and fused.

Here it is illustrated as a half pattern to be traced off before you make the adaptations for the ease in the lining.

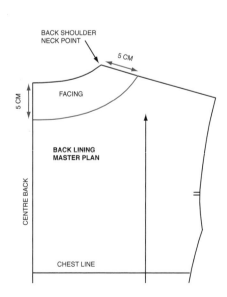

- Following the instructions on page 50, trace the left back pattern onto a separate piece of paper. Measure 5cm down the centre back and 5cm down the shoulder seam from the shoulder neck point. Connect these points with a curve following the shape of the neckline.

## STEP 30
### BACK NECK FACING PATTERN

- Trace off the back neck facing onto a new piece of paper and, following the instructions on page 50, create the full pattern shape.

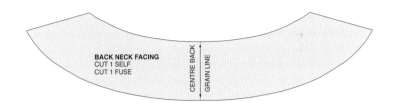

BACK NECK FACING
CUT 1 SELF
CUT 1 FUSE

CENTRE BACK

GRAIN LINE

## STEP 31
### DEVELOPING THE LEFT BACK BODY LINING

- Using the tracing of the back pattern on which you drew the neck facing, create half of the back lining pleat to introduce ease. From the centre back measure out 1.5cm below the facing line and mark, and from the chest line measure out 1.5cm and mark. Join these two points and then blend the line back to the original centre back line at the waist with a slight curve. Notch the centre back along this new line.
- From the shoulder point measure out 0.5cm and up 0.5cm and find the new shoulder point. Draw a straight line back to the outer edge of the neck facing.
- At the underarm point square out 0.5cm. Join this point back to the new shoulder point using a curved line following the original armhole shape.
- Because the vent on the left side of the back pattern is folded in when constructed, remove the vent shape from the lining together with a negative of the vent shape in the back panel lining itself.
- Remove 2.5cm from the lower edge of the hem facing. This will leave enough fabric to allow for an overlap, or ease, in the lining at the hem.

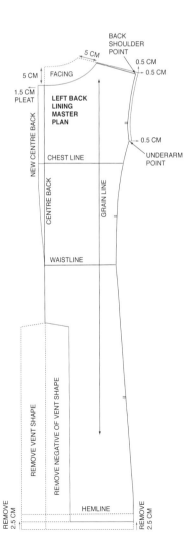

## STEP 32
### DEVELOPING THE RIGHT BACK LINING

- Trace off the right back panel pattern, from the left back panel pattern you have just developed and reverse.
- Add the negative vent shape back into the pattern to create a straight centre back line.
- As you are still working on a left back panel shape, you need to turn it over before adding the annotations for the right back lining.

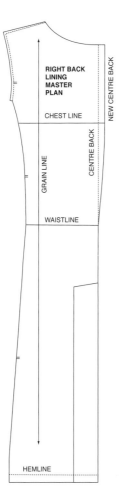

## STEP 33
### BACK LINING PATTERNS

- Following the instructions on page 50, trace off the back panel lining patterns.

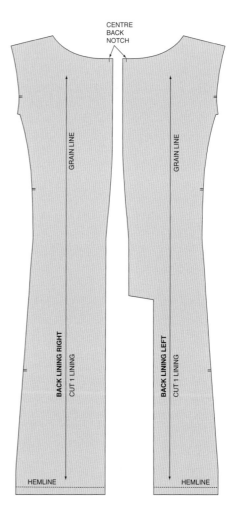

# PATTERN
# SINGLE-BREASTED JACKET

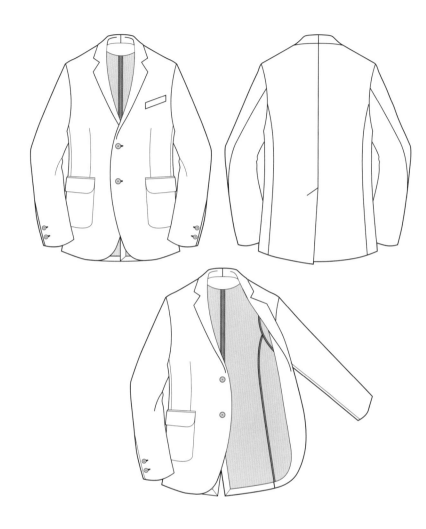

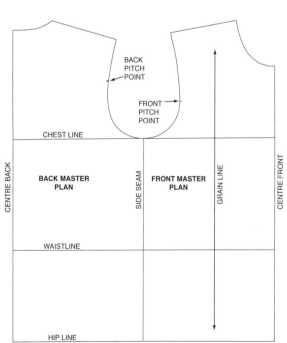

**This pattern includes development
of the following features:**

Shaping the body panels and creating a side panel

Extending the front and shaping the breast with added volume

Extending the hemline

Creating a centre back vent

Moving the shoulder slope towards the back

Creating a welted breast pocket

Developing a patch pocket with flap

Developing a roll collar with lapel

Developing a tailored two-piece sleeve with cuff vent

Developing taped internal seams with no lining

## STEP 1
## DEVELOPING THE MASTER PLAN

Start by selecting the basic men's body block, or by drafting
the basic block according to the instructions on page 40. Cut
a large piece of drafting paper slightly longer than the length
of the shirt you want to develop and transfer the shape of
the block and all marks, labels and instructions, following the
directions on page 48.

## STEP 2
### DEVELOPING THE HEMLINE

- From the hemline square down 8cm at the centre front, side seam and centre back lines.
- Join these three points with a straight horizontal line.

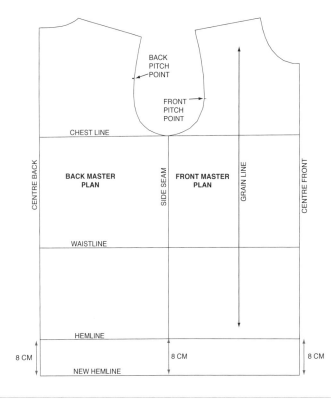

## STEP 3
### DEVELOPING THE INTERNAL SHAPING

When determining suit panel sizes it is important to do some market research, investigating similar garments and comparing measurements with the style you may be developing. Use your fit model or mannequin to gain the correct proportions for the panelling as this will ultimately affect the balance of the jacket.

- To create the front internal dart, at the centre front chest, waist and original hemlines square in 12.8cm and mark.
- From the chest line mark square down 10.5cm, and from the hemline mark square up 12.8cm; these two points are the ends of the dart.
- From the waistline mark measure out 0.7cm to each side, making the dart width 1.4cm.
- Connect all these points with curved lines.
- For the centre back shaping: from the centre back, measure in 0.7cm at the new hemline and the original hemline; at the waistline measure in 1.5cm, and at the centre back neck point measure in 0.5cm.
- From the chest line draw a curved line up to meet the new centre back neck point and then down to join the new point on the waistline, then down further to connect the points on the hemlines.
- Taking volume from the side seam gives a fitted silhouette and will also help you to develop the side panel. From the side seam at the waistline measure out 1.7cm in each direction and mark. Connect these two points with a curved line up to the underarm and down to the original hemline.

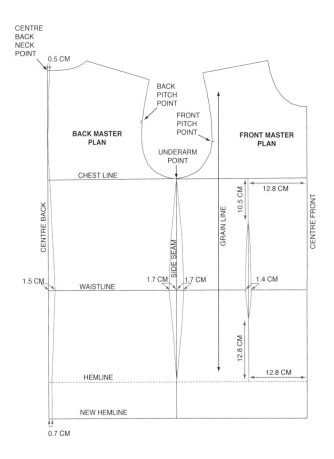

## DEVELOPING THE SIDE PANEL

### Side panels

On the front and back blocks you are going to create style lines that will separate the panel into front, side and back, as in the classic three-piece suit. In the previous step you took away volume from the side seam back and front. To create the side panel you need to combine these to gather and redraw them as a single shape. Having removed volume at the side seam, you then need to remove additional volume from the back panel, to finish the fitted shape of the jacket. You do this between the new back and side panel.

- Start with the front style line: from the centre back measure 17cm along the new hemline towards the centre front and mark; continue measuring 2cm and mark, and a further 12.5cm and mark. These points are the ends of the three new shaping lines.
- From the new side seam measure 3.3cm towards the front along the waistline and mark; from the underarm point measure 1cm along the armhole towards the front and mark; from the side seam measure 5cm along the old hemline towards the front and mark.
- Join the marks at the new and the old hemlines to the waistline mark with a straight line and continue up to the chest and front armhole with a graduated curve; this is the side front style line, which separates the new side panel from the front panel.
- To create the back style lines, from the centre back measure 16cm along the waistline and mark, and then a further 3cm and mark.
- From the underarm point measure 6.3cm towards the centre back and mark, and a further 2cm and mark.
- The back style lines start from a point on the back armhole below the pitch point; to find this measure 5cm from the chest line up the centre back and then square across to the back armhole and mark.
- From this point draw the back style lines, intersecting the chest and waist at the marks you made earlier, crossing over each other 9cm above the original hemline and continuing down to the new hem in a straight line.

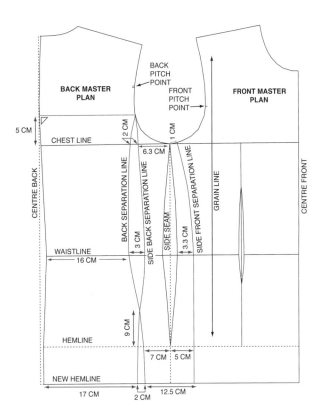

## DEVELOPING THE NEW SHOULDER SLOPE AND FRONT HEM STYLING

**Shoulder slope**

Move the angle of the shoulder seam
before you open up the front: this
will prevent the shoulder seam from
being seen from the front, giving
a seamless silhouette.

- From the back shoulder point measure 1cm down the armhole and mark; from the front shoulder point extend the armhole up 1cm and mark. From these two new points draw in the new shoulder seams back up to the shoulder neck points.
- To add style shaping to the centre front hem, measure 2cm down from the hemline at the centre front and connect back to the side seam with a smooth curve.

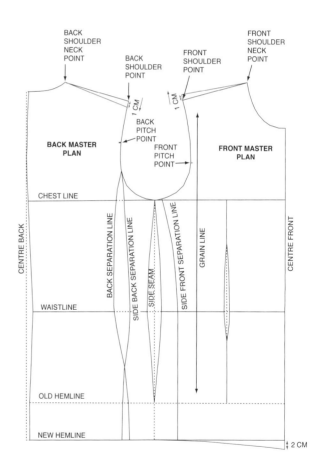

## STEP 6
## DEVELOPING THE FRONT EXTENSION

- Trace off the front panel onto a separate piece of paper and following the instructions on page 50 reverse the shape to create the left-hand side panel, which will eventually also contain the breast pocket shape.
- Extend out 2.5cm horizontally from the centre front neck point and at the hem; connect these points with a straight line to create the front extension.

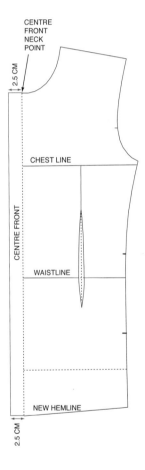

## STEP 7
## DEVELOPING THE FRONT BREAST SHAPING

**Lapel shape**
Pitching back and opening the front breast shape will enable the straight block front to follow the contours of a male chest.

- From the chest line measure up 4cm and square a line across; repeat four times.

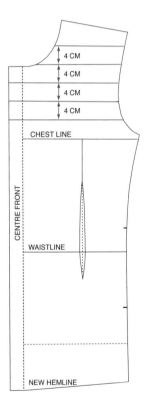

## STEP 8
### DEVELOPING THE WELTED BREAST AND PATCH POCKETS

- For the breast pocket placement, from the top of the waist dart measure 5cm along the chest line towards the centre front; this will be the bottom corner of the rectangular welt opening.
- Measure 6cm in the opposite direction and mark; from this point square up 1.8cm; this is the opposite corner of the rectangle.
- Join these points with an 11cm straight line, square up 1.5cm at each end and draw a rectangular box.
- The patch pocket runs off the front panel into the side panel and covers the waist dart; when plotting the pocket measurement do not include the dart width.
- From the waist dart measure 2cm along the waistline towards the centre front, and from this point square down 1.5cm and mark; this is the starting point for the pocket depth.
- Measure down another 1.5cm for the welt opening, then measure down a further 16.5cm (the pocket depth).
- The pocket width is 15cm. which will run over onto the side panel.
- Round off the bottom corners of the pocket.

## STEP 9
### ADDING IN THE VOLUME ON THE FRONT BREAST PANEL

- Cut along the horizontal lines you drew across the chest and neck from the centre front and neck into the shoulder; open each 0.4cm upwards at the front, creating a wedge shape, adding in a total of 2cm.
- Tape against another piece paper and redraw the front panel, blending through the open steps.

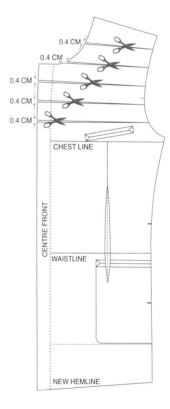

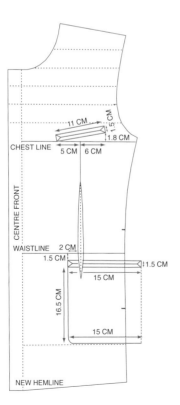

## DEVELOPING THE ROLL COLLAR

### Break point and roll line

Locate on the pattern where you want your collar to break on the new front edge line of the body panel. Consider the proportion of your design and silhouette length. The point at which the front will turn over to create a lapel is called the break point (BP) and the line that it turns on is the roll line. The lower down the front your BP is, the wider an opening you will have around the neck silhouette.

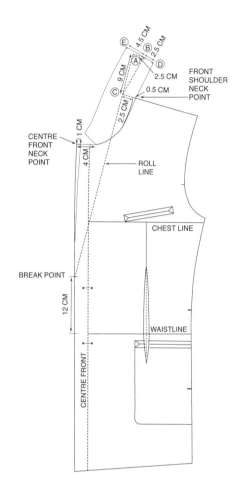

- From the front shoulder neck point measure out 2.5cm and mark point (C).
- You will run the roll line through point (C); from the waistline measure 12cm up the front, mark and name as the *break point*.
- Draw a straight line from here up through (C), continue for 9cm and mark point (A).
- From (A) square 2.5cm back towards the shoulder and mark point (B).
- Draw a line from (B) to (C); square out 2.5cm from the top of this line and mark point (D).
- From (B) extend the line out 4.5cm and mark point (E). This is the width of the collar (7cm) at the centre back neckline.
- From (E), starting at a right angle, draw out the collar shape that you require, finishing the collar notch 4cm in from the extended front.
- To shape the front of the jacket lapel, measure in 1cm from the centre front neck point. From this point draw a graduated line back down the centre front to give shape.
- From (D) draw a line back towards the shoulder line, crossing it 0.5cm back from the front shoulder neck point, and blend in to the curved neck shape.

### Checking the shape

It is always important to check the shape you have created by folding back the paper on the roll line to assess it; redraw and develop until you are satisfied. The sequence above is a method widely used to draft a basic tailored collar. Variations can be found in many pattern cutting books available, old and new; choose the one that you prefer.

## STEP 11
### DEVELOPING THE FACING

- From the collar measure back 4cm along the shoulder seam; this is the width of the facing.
- From the jacket front measure in 9cm along the waistline and mark, and measure in 9.5cm along the hemline and mark.
- From the waistline measure 10cm down the front edge of the jacket and continue down to the point you marked on the hemline with a deep curve; this is the lower front jacket shaping.
- From the hemline measure 4cm up the side seam and from here square in 10cm; from this point draw a graduated curve up to meet the point you marked on the waistline, continue up in a straight line to the chest line and blend back to the shoulder with another curved line.

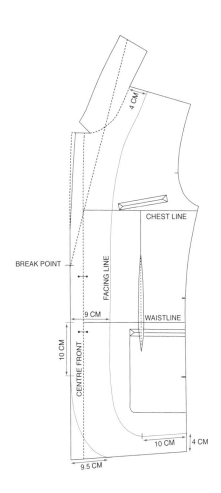

## STEP 12
### FINAL FRONT PATTERN

- Following the instructions on page 50, trace off the left and right front panels.
- Mark the breast pocket on the left side only, and the patch pocket position on both sides.

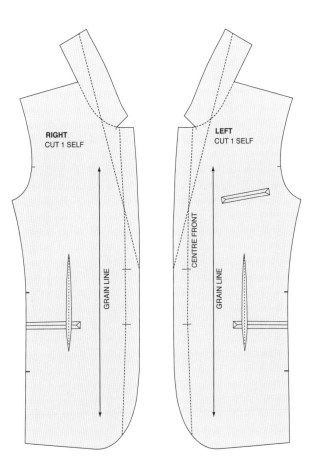

## STEP 13
### FRONT FACING PATTERN

- Following the instructions on page 50, trace off the front facing pattern.

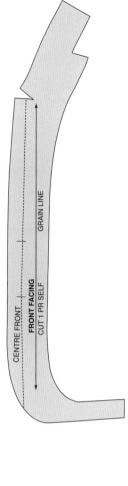

## STEP 14
### DEVELOPING THE SIDE PANEL AND HEM FACING

- Following the instructions on page 50, trace off the side panel onto a separate piece of paper.
- Next you need to remove the internal volume by closing the dart shapes in the side seam. Cut down both sides of the side seam to the bottom of the shaping and out along the waistline, making sure to leave the shapes connected by a sliver of paper at the edges so that the side lengths do not change when manipulated.
- Reposition by closing up the shape and tape together.
- Measure 4cm down on both sides at the hemline and square across to create a rectangular box; this is the hem facing.

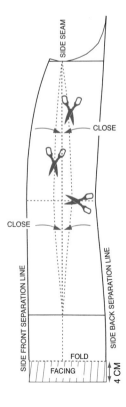

## STEP 15
### COMBINING THE SIDE PANEL

- Trace off the closed side panel onto a separate piece of paper.
- Match up the front panel at the waist and hemlines to the new side panel at the side front style line.
- Transcribe across the position for the remainder of the welted opening for the patch pocket.

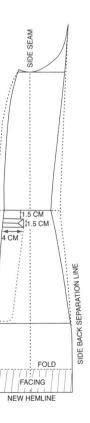

## STEP 16
### DEVELOPING THE CENTRE BACK VENT AND BACK NECK FACING

- Following the instructions on page 50, trace off the back panel onto a separate piece of paper.
- From the hemline at the centre back and side seams square down 4cm and square across to form a rectangular box, extending it 4cm past the centre back; this is the hem facing.
- From the bottom of the hem facing measure up 20cm and then square back into the centre back. From this point measure up 1.5cm on the centre back and draw an angled line back to the top corner of the vent shape.
- The centre back neck facing is 4cm in width to match the front; measure 4cm down from the centre back neck point and 4cm down the shoulder from the back shoulder neck point and connect these two points with a curved line.

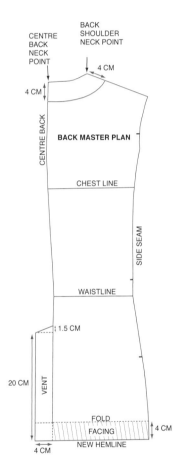

## STEP 17
### BACK PATTERN

- Following the instructions on page 50, trace off the back panel pattern.

## STEP 18
### BACK NECK FACING PATTERN

- Trace off the back neck facing onto a separate piece of paper and, following the instructions on page 50, create the full pattern shape.

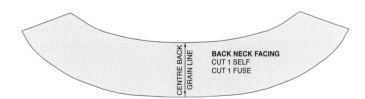

## STEP 19

### DEVELOPING THE WELTED BREAST POCKET TOP AND BOTTOM BAG

- From the front left final pattern in Step 12, trace off the breast pocket opening onto a separate piece of paper so that you have a rectangle 11cm long by 1.5cm wide drawn at an angle to the grain line.
- Extend the top stitch line by 1.5cm to the right and 1cm to the left, and extend the bottom stitch line by 1.5cm to the left and 1cm to the right.
- Connecting these points on the left, draw a 13.5cm vertical line down. Connecting the points on the right, draw a 15.5cm vertical line down. Square across 13.5cm at the bottom to connect these two lines (the width of the pocket bag).

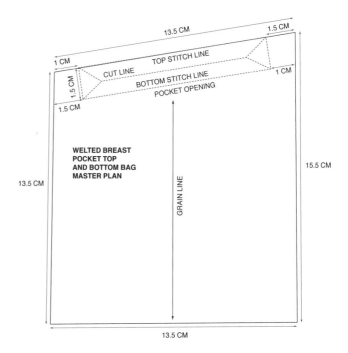

## STEP 20

### BREAST POCKET BAG PATTERNS

- Following the instructions on page 50, trace off the pocket bag shape and add a 1cm seam allowance above the top stitch line to create the final top pocket bag pattern.
- Trace off the pocket bag shape again as far as the bottom stitch line, then add a 1cm seam allowance on top of the stitch line to create the final bottom pocket bag pattern.

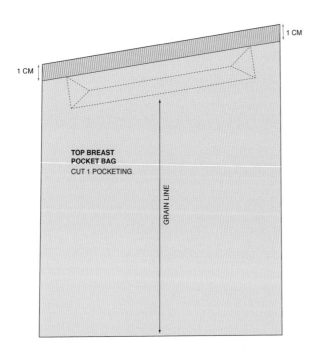

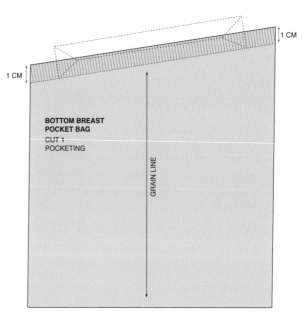

## STEP 21
### DEVELOPING THE BREAST POCKET WELT

**Welts**

If your welted pocket is angled then the welt's shape will need to reflect this. Welts can be the same size or larger than pocket openings and are doubled over so they have two layers of fabric, with a fusing layer in between for rigidity.

- From the front left pattern in Step 12, trace one long side of the breast pocket opening onto a separate piece of paper so that you have a line 11cm long at the same angle as the breast pocket itself. This will become the centre fold line. Copy the direction of the grain line across, too.
- Parallel to the grain line, draw 2.5cm lines up from both ends of the line and mark. Connect these marks to create a parallelogram.

- Mirror this parallelogram along the fold line.
- Add a 1.5cm seam allowance to both long sides of the shape and a 1cm allowance to the shorter sides.

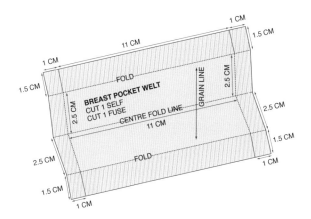

## STEP 22
### DEVELOPING THE FINAL PATCH POCKET

- On a separate piece of paper draw a rectangular box 15cm wide by 19.5cm tall.
- From the top measure 3cm down each side and square across with a broken line, naming it *fold*; this will become the facing for the pocket bag.
- Round off both bottom corners and add a 1cm seam allowance to create the final pattern.

## STEP 23
### DEVELOPING THE FINAL PATCH POCKET FLAP

- On a separate piece of paper draw a rectangular box 15.5cm wide by 6cm tall.
- From the top measure 1.5cm down each side and square across with a broken line, naming it *fold*; this will be sewn in to the welt opening construction.
- Round off both bottom corners and add a 1cm seam allowance to create the final pattern.

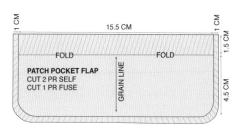

## STEP 24
### DEVELOPING THE PATCH POCKET PIPING

**Piping**

The piping is sewn between the pocket flap as decoration to the opening. In this example it is only 0.5cm wide.

- On separate piece of paper, draw a horizontal box 15cm long by 2cm wide to create a rectangular-shape for the piping.
- Divide the box in half lengthways, draw a line down the centre and label it *fold*.
- Add a 0.5cm seam allowance to both long sides and a 1cm seam allowance to each end to create the final pattern.

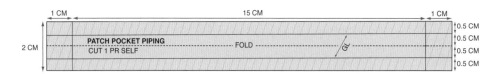

## STEP 25
### DEVELOPING THE TWO-PIECE TAILORED SLEEVE

**Measurements required to develop the sleeve**
- Armhole 51cm + 2cm ease = 53cm. (Take this measurement from the basic body block.)
- Sleeve length to wrist = 64cm. (This measurement is taken from the crown point, running down the back of the elbow to the wrist; extra length can be added at this point to suit your design.)
- Crown point to elbow length = 35cm.
- Upper biceps circumference = 40.8cm. (This measurement is taken round the upper arm; extra width 'ease' can be added for movement.)
- Cuff measurement = 30cm. Remove 2cm as 1cm from each side to reduce the cuff width from the basic tapered block, which is 32cm.
- Sleeve head height = 17cm.

- Cut a large piece of drafting paper slightly longer than the length of your sleeve or the arm length of your fit model.
- Draw a 64cm vertical line down the centre and label it *centre line*; label the top of this line (1) and the bottom (2). This is the length of the sleeve.
- From (1) measure down 17cm (the sleeve head height, or one third of the armhole measurement not including ease) and label point (3).
- From (1) measure down 35cm (the elbow length) and label point (4).

- Divide the armhole measurement (53cm) by 6 to give 8.8cm and add 1cm ease to give 9.8cm. From (1) square out 9.8cm to the left and to the right and label these points (5) and (6).
- From (2) measure out 9.8cm to the left and to the right and label these points (7) and (8).
- Connect all points (5), (6), (7), (8) to form a rectangle.
- Divide the sleeve head length (17cm) by 3 to give 5.6cm. From (6) measure down 5.6cm, make a mark and label it *back pitch point*. From the back pitch point square in 2.5cm and mark point (A); this is the top point of the back seam on the undersleeve.
- From (3) square out to the left to intersect the line from (5) to (7) and mark point (B), and square out to the right to intersect the line from (6) to (8) and mark point (C). This is the underarm line.
- From (B) measure out 2.5cm and mark point (D), and measure in 2.5cm and mark point (E). From (C) measure in 1cm and mark point (F), and measure out 1cm and mark point (G).
- To establish the front pitch point on the armhole divide the sleeve head height (17cm) by 2 to give 8.5cm, and subtract 2cm to give 6.5cm. This will ensure a rectangular shape to the sleeve head instead of the square shape that would occur if the sleeve head were just divided in half. From (B) measure up 6.5cm, make a mark and label it *front pitch point*.
- From (4) square out to the left to intersect the line from (5) to (7) and mark point (H), and square out to the right to intersect the line from (6) to (8) and mark point (I). This is the elbow line.
- From (H) measure out 1cm and mark point (J), and measure in 4cm and mark point (K).

- From (7) measure up 2cm and from this point measure out 2cm and mark point (L); this is the top sleeve cuff point. Measure in 2cm and mark point (M); this is the undersleeve cuff point.
- The cuff circumference is 30cm. Divide this between the top and undersleeve so that the top sleeve cuff width is 17cm and the undersleeve is 13cm. This allows the top sleeve seams to fall towards the back of the arm, slightly out of view.
- From (L) draw a line 17cm long to intersect the line from (7) to (8) and mark point (N). From (M) draw a line 13cm long to intersect the line from (7) to (8), also at point (N). These are the cuff hemlines.

- Draw in the top sleeve front seam by drawing a blended line connecting the points from (L) through (J) to (D).
- Draw in the undersleeve front seam by drawing a blended line connecting the points from (M) through (K) to (E).
- Using a French curve, draw in the top sleeve head starting at (D) with a concave curve through the front pitch point where you reverse the curve to a convex curve up to (1) and back down to the back pitch point with a similar convex curve.
- Measure the length of this line and compare it to the measurement of the armhole on the front and back patterns. Adjust the curves until the line is the same length as the armhole.
- Using a French curve, draw in the top of the undersleeve starting with a convex curve starting at (E) up to (A).
- Again, measure this line and adjust it until it is the same measurement as the armhole on the front and back patterns.
- Draw in the back seam of the top sleeve with a blended line from the back pitch point through points (G) to (I) and continue down to (N).
- Draw in the back seam of the undersleeve with a blended line from (A) through (F) to (I) and also continue with this seam on the same line as the top sleeve down to (N).

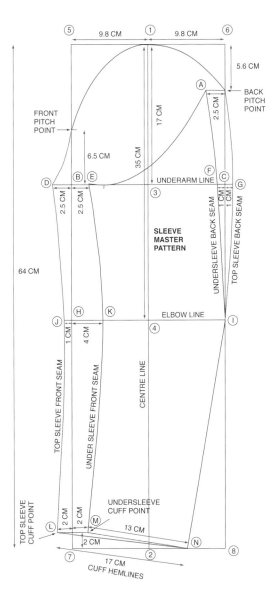

## STEP 26
### DEVELOPING THE FINAL TOP SLEEVE PATTERN WITH CUFF VENT

- Following the instructions on page 50, trace off the top sleeve onto a separate piece of paper.
- From the bottom of the sleeve measure down 3cm and draw a rectangular box to create the facing strip.
- Extend the length of the cuff facing by 3cm at the back seam line and square up 10cm to create a rectangular box 3cm in width. This is the cuff extension.
- Measure a further 1.5cm up the back seam and join this point to the outer corner of the box, creating an angle and shape similar to the centre back vent.
- The corner is then folded to create a mitred corner during construction.

## STEP 27
### DEVELOPING THE FINAL UNDERSLEEVE PATTERN WITH CUFF VENT

- Trace off the undersleeve onto a separate piece of paper and, following the instructions on page 50, reverse it over.
- From the bottom of the sleeve measure down 3cm and draw a rectangular box to create the facing strip. Extend the length of the cuff facing by 3cm at the back seam line.
- On top of this extension square up 10cm from the facing and create a rectangular box 3cm in width.
- Measure a further 1.5cm up the back seam and join this point to the outer corner of your rectangular box, creating an angle and shape similar to the centre back vent.
- The corner is then folded to create a mitred corner during construction.

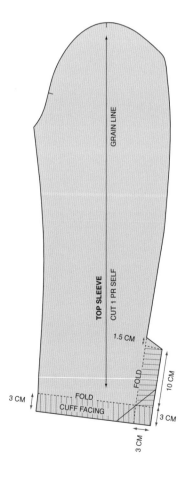

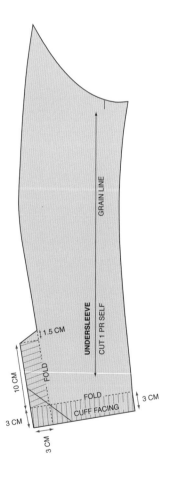

# PATTERN
# DOUBLE-BREASTED JACKET

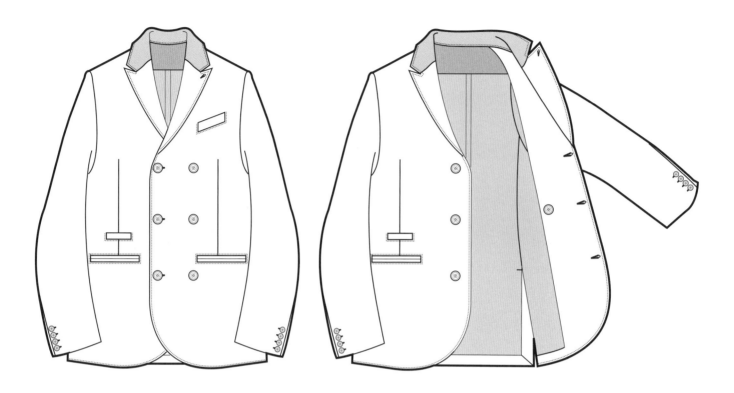

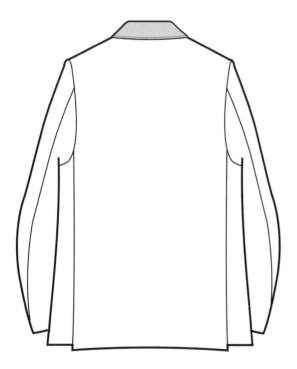

**This pattern includes development of the following features:**
Shaping the body panels and creating a side panel
Creating a double-breasted extension and shaping the breast
 with added volume
Extending the hemline
Creating side vents
Moving the shoulder slope towards the back
Lowering the armhole
Developing a welted breast pocket
Developing jetted side pockets
Developing a coin pocket
Developing a shaped convertible collar with hidden stand
 and lapel
Developing a tailored two-piece sleeve with cuff vent
Developing a full body lining

## STEP 1
### DEVELOPING THE MASTER PLAN

Start by selecting the basic men's body block, or by drafting the basic block according to the instructions on page 40. Cut a large piece of drafting paper slightly longer than the length of the jacket you want to develop and transfer the shape of the block and all marks, labels and instructions, following the directions on page 48.

**Creating the jacket block**
To create a suit jacket block from the basic block, you need to make some shape adaptations to the front, side, back and shoulder areas of the pattern, building on the techniques learned in the single-breasted jacket development (pages 252-67).

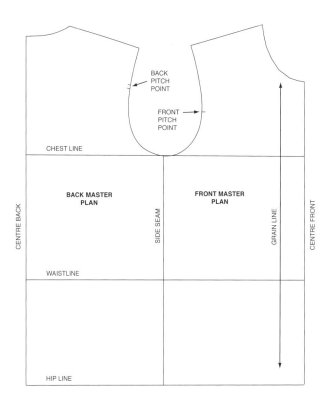

## STEP 2
### DEVELOPING THE HEMLINE

- From the hemline square down 5cm at the centre front, side seam and centre back lines.
- Join these three points to form the new hemline.

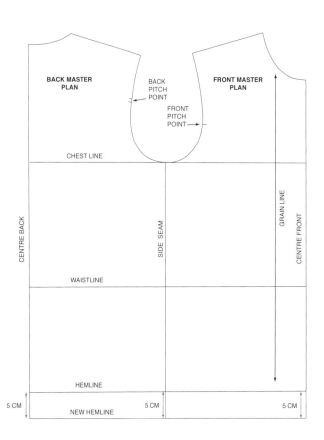

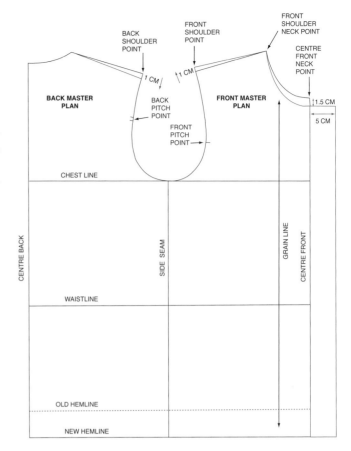

## STEP 3

### DEVELOPING THE NEW SHOULDER SLOPE AND FRONT DOUBLE-BREASTED EXTENSION

- From the back shoulder point measure 1cm down the armhole and mark; from the front shoulder point extend the armhole up 1cm and mark. From these two new points draw in the new shoulder lines back up to the shoulder neck points.
- From the centre front neck point measure down 1.5cm and draw in the new neckline up to the front shoulder neck point.
- From the new centre front neck point square out 5cm; repeat this at the new hemline. Connect these two points to create the double-breasted extension.

## STEP 4

### LOWERING THE ARMHOLE AND DEVELOPING THE INTERNAL SHAPING

- From the underarm point measure 2cm down the side seam and using the front and back body blocks as a template redraw the armhole from this point, connecting it back up to the shoulder on either side. Draw in the new pitch points on the lowered armhole.
- To shape the centre back, measure in 0.5cm at the new hemline, measure in 1.5cm at the waistline and measure in 0.5cm at the centre back neck point.
- Connect these points with straight lines to create the new centre back line.

## STEP 5
### DEVELOPING THE SIDE PANEL

- Taking volume from the side seam gives a fitted silhouette and will also help you to develop the side panel. From the original side seam at the waistline measure out 1cm into the front and back body panels.
- Connect these two points with straight lines up to the new underarm point and down to the point where the original side seam line intersects the old hemline.
- For the front style line, from the original side seam measure 5cm along the new hemline towards the front and mark, and measure 4cm along the waistline towards the front and mark. At the new underarm point square in 1.5cm towards the front and mark.
- Join up the three points with straight lines. This is the front style line which separates the new side panel from the front panel.
- Having removed volume at the side seam, you then need to remove additional volume from the back panel, to finish the fitted shape of the jacket. You do this between the new back and side panels.
- To create the back style lines, from the centre back measure 16.5cm along the waistline and mark, and continue to measure 1cm and a further 1cm and mark both points.
- From the centre back measure 19cm along the chest line and mark, and measure a further 1cm and mark. Measure in 18cm along the original hemline and mark.
- The back side seams start from a point on the back armhole below the pitch point; measure up 4.5cm from the chest line on the centre back and then square across to the back armhole and mark the point where the line intersects the armhole.
- From this point, starting with a shallow curve, draw the back style lines, intersecting the points marked on the chest line, waistline and original hemline and continuing down to the new hemline.

## STEP 6
### DEVELOPING THE FRONT LAPEL SHAPING

**Lapel shape**
Pitching back and opening the front chest/lapel shape will enable the straight block front to follow the contours of a male chest.

From the chest line measure up 4cm and square a line across; repeat four times.

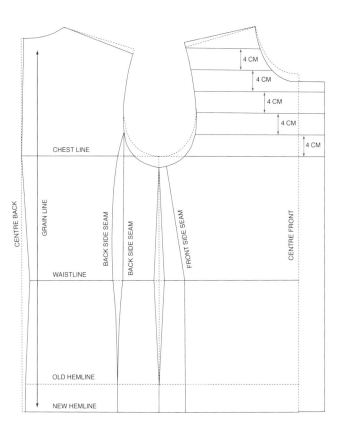

## STEP 7
### DEVELOPING THE WELTED BREAST POCKET AND SIDE JETTED POCKET

- For the breast pocket placement, from the centre front square in 8.5cm along the chest line; this is the bottom corner of the rectangular welt opening.
- From this point, draw a line 9cm long at an angle, ending 1.5cm above the chest line. Create a rectangle 1.5cm wide by 9cm long.
- A centre dart is created to run down into the side jetted pocket to give shape to the lower chest. This pocket runs off the front panel into the front style line; when plotting the pocket measurement do not include the dart width, which will be added next.
- From the centre front measure in 12.5cm along the chest line and from here square down to the old hemline. Mark a point on this line 5cm below the chest line; this is the top of the dart.
- From the front side seam measure in 9cm along the waistline and mark; measure a further 1.5cm and mark; this is the dart width. From these points draw two straight lines up to the dart top.
- The pocket opening sits 1.5cm below the waistline. Create a rectangle 14.5cm long and 1.5cm wide; this is the pocket opening.

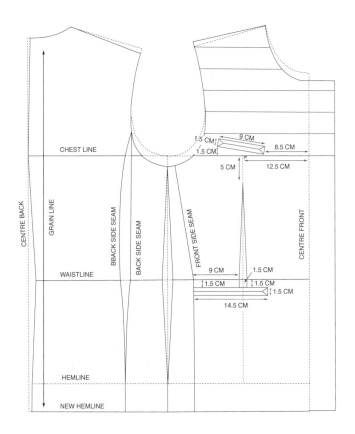

## STEP 8
### ADDING IN THE VOLUME ON THE FRONT LAPEL / CHEST PANEL, CREATING THE CENTRE DART VOLUME AND FRONT HEM STYLING

- From the master plan trace off the front panel only onto a separate piece of paper including all the development in Steps 6 and 7.
- Cut along the horizontal lines you drew across the chest and neck from the centre front and neck into the shoulder; open each 0.4cm upwards at the front, creating a wedge shape, adding in a total of 2cm.
- Tape against a new piece of paper and redraw the front panel blending through the open steps.
- When the centre dart is sewn up, this will reduce the length of the top of the jetted pocket. To add back this volume, square out 1.5cm (the width of the dart) from the top of the pocket opening. From here blend a line back up into the front style line finishing at the armhole.
- To add style shaping to the centre front hem, measure down 2cm from the hemline at the new front edge and connect back to the front style line with a smooth curve.
- Cut another piece of paper and trace off a new front master plan.

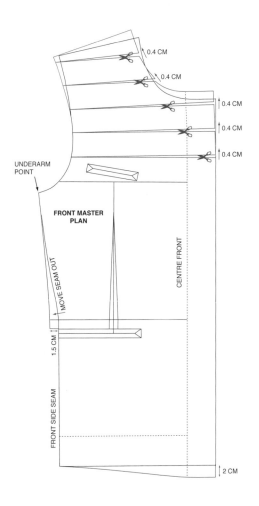

## DEVELOPING THE SHAPED CONVERTIBLE COLLAR, COIN POCKET AND HEM SHAPING

### Break point and roll line

Locate on the pattern the position where you want the collar to break on the new front edge line of the body panel. Consider the proportion of your design and silhouette length. The point at which the front turns over to create a lapel is called the break point (BP) and the line that it turns on is the roll line. The lower down the front your BP is, the wider an opening you will have around the neck silhouette.

- From the shoulder neck point measure out 2.5cm and mark point (C).
- You will run your roll line through (C); from the waistline measure 17cm up the front, mark and mark *break point*.
- Draw a straight line from here up through (C), continue for 8cm and mark point (A).
- From (A) square 2.5cm back towards the shoulder and mark point (B).
- Draw a line from (B) to (C). Square out 3cm from the top of this line towards the shoulder and mark point (D).
- From (B) extend the line out 4cm and mark point (E). This is the width of the collar (7cm) at the centre back neckline.
- From (E), starting at a right angle, draw out the collar shape that you require, finishing the collar notch 6cm in from the extended front.
- To shape the front of the jacket lapel, measure in 1cm from the centre front neck point. From this point draw a graduated line back down the centre front to give shape, and draw up 3cm to create the collar point. Draw a line from the collar point back to the end of the collar notch.
- From (D) draw a line back towards the shoulder line, crossing it 1cm back from the shoulder neck point, and blend in to the curved neck shape – find the angle by measuring in 4.5cm from the collar notch and then up 3cm until it connects to the neckline.

- The welted coin pocket is developed just above the jetted pocket running across the centre dart. From the waistline square up 1cm, then create a rectangle 1.5cm wide by 6cm long, with the measurement split between each side of the dart so that 2cm is towards the centre front and 4cm towards the side seam.
- At the centre front hemline measure back 9.5cm towards the side seam and mark; measure 22cm up the centre front. Use a French curve to give a smooth rounded edge to the bottom corner.

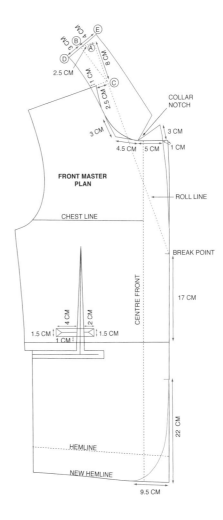

### Checking the shape

It is always important to check the shape you have created by folding back the paper on the roll line to assess it; redraw and develop until you are satisfied. The sequence above is a method widely used to draft a basic tailored collar. Variations can be found in many pattern cutting books, old and new.

## STEP 10
### FRONT RIGHT AND FRONT LEFT BODY PATTERNS

- Following the instructions on page 50, trace off the front panel to create the final front right pattern, excluding the welted breast pocket and the collar development.
- To trace off the left side final front pattern, reverse the master and copy the underside. Mark the breast pocket and omit the welted coin pocket.

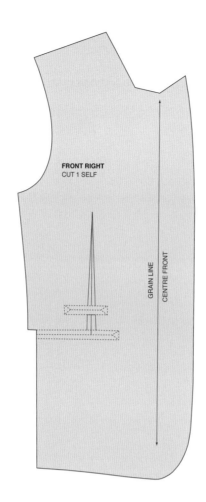

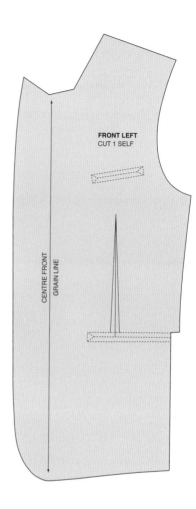

## STEP 11
### DEVELOPING THE FRONT FACING PATTERN

- Develop the front facing using the front right panel pattern.
- From the shoulder neck point, measure 4cm back along the shoulder seam; this is the width of the facing.
- From the jacket front, measure in 12cm along the chest line and mark, and repeat at the waistline.
- From the hemline, measure 4cm up the side seam and from here square across towards the centre front.
- Draw a blended line joining these points from the shoulder seam through the chest and waistlines and continue straight down towards the line you drew at the hem until the two intersect 4cm above the hemline.
- Following the instructions on page 50, trace off the final facing pattern.

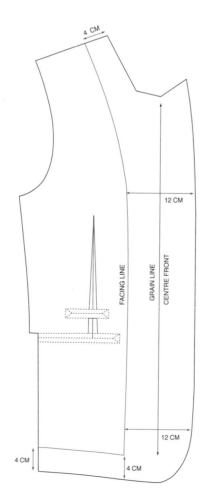

## DEVELOPING THE SHAPED CONVERTIBLE COLLAR AND HIDDEN STAND

- Trace off the half collar development from Step 9 onto a separate piece of paper.
- To develop half the concealed stand shape, measure 2cm up the centre back from the neckline and mark; measure 4cm in from the point at the angle of the front neckline and mark. Connect these points with a curved line.
- From the centre back measure 2cm along the neckline and 3.5cm along the outer edge and mark, repeat twice; divide the collar into four sections by connecting these points to form cut lines through the collar shape.

- Remove the stand shape from the development by tracing onto a separate piece of paper; double it over to create the full stand shape, indicating the vertical cut lines.
- Cut down the vertical lines on the full stand shape, leaving them attached at the neckline by a few millimetres. Overlap the sections along the top edge, moving them 0.3cm towards the centre back; this will bring the neckline up.
- Trace off the half top collar shape onto a separate piece of paper. Cut down the vertical lines from the outer edge, leaving them attached at the bottom by a few millimetres. Starting from the centre back, open out each line by 0.4cm, curving the top collar down.
- Remove 0.9cm from the centre back, which is the amount lost by closing the stand up.

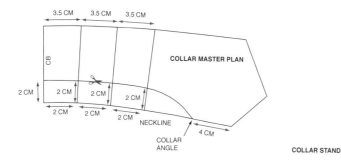

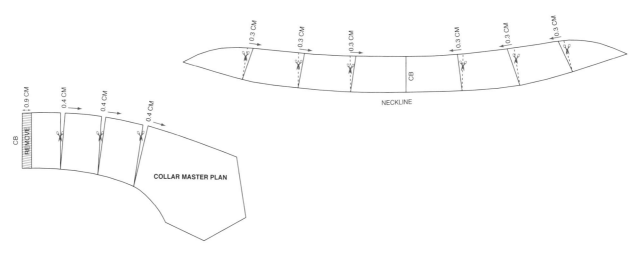

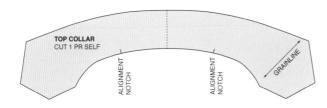

## COLLAR AND COLLAR STAND PATTERNS

- Trace off the top collar onto a new piece of paper and, following the instructions on page 50, create the full pattern shape.

- Following the instructions on page 50, trace off the full stand pattern.

## STEP 14
### DEVELOPING THE SIDE PANEL AND HEM FACING

- Following the instructions on page 50, trace off the side panel from Step 5 onto a separate piece of paper.
- Next you need to remove the internal volume by closing the dart in the side seam. Cut down both sides of the side seam to the bottom of the shaping and out along the waistline, making sure to leave the shapes connected by a sliver of paper at the edges so that the side lengths do not change when manipulated.
- Reposition by closing up the shape and tape together to redraw the new side panel shape.
- At the hemline measure 4cm down on both sides and square across to create a rectangular box; this is the hem facing.

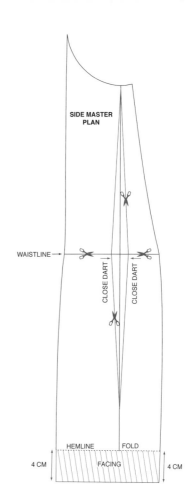

## STEP 15
### DEVELOPING THE SIDE VENT

**Parts of the vent**
The vent development has two parts. One is a side vent facing that sits under the back body panel, attached to the side panel. The vent shape is doubled so that it can be folded back on itself to create a facing with a mitred top. The second part is a facing that is developed on the back panel and sits over the side vent: this is a single shape that acts as a facing when turned in.

- To add the side vent to the side panel, square out 4cm from the back style line at the hemline and mark. Then measure out a further 4cm and mark. Square up 4cm (the hem facing width) and mark, then a further 20cm (the vent length) and square back into the back panel.
- Measure 4cm back along this line and square down to the mark on the hemline.
- Extend the 4cm facing line from the side panel across the vent.
- At the top of the vent, measure up 1.5cm on the outside line and again on the back style line. Connect these two points back down to the top of the centre line of the vent. This creates the mitred corner at the top of the vent.

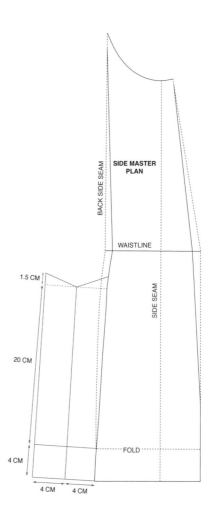

## STEP 16
## SIDE PATTERN

- Following the instructions on page 50, trace off the side panel pattern.

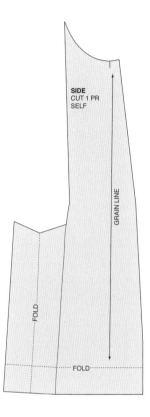

## STEP 17
## DEVELOPING THE BACK HEM, VENT AND BACK NECK FACING

- From the master plan trace the back panel onto a separate piece of paper.
- From the hemline measure down 4cm on both sides and square across to form a rectangle; this is the hem facing.
- From the bottom of the hem facing measure out a further 4cm from the front style line, then square up 4cm (the hem facing width), then a further 20cm (the vent length) and square back in to the side panel. From this point measure up 1.5cm on the side seam and draw an angled line back to the top corner of the vent shape.
- The back neck facing is 4cm in width to match the front; measure 4cm down from the centre back neck point and 4cm down the shoulder and connect these two points with a curved line following the shape of the neckline.

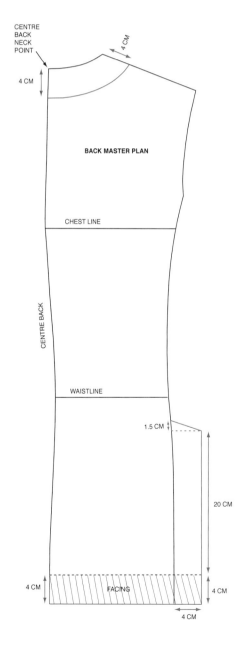

## STEP 18

### BACK PANEL AND BACK NECK FACING PATTERNS

- Following the instructions on page 50, trace off the back panel pattern.
- Trace off the back neck facing onto a new piece of paper and, following the instructions on page 50, create the full pattern shape.

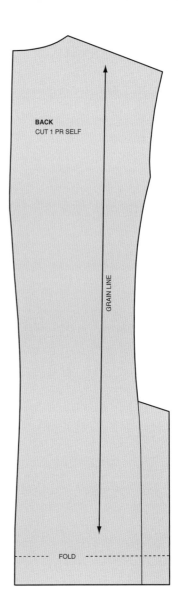

BACK
CUT 1 PR SELF

GRAIN LINE

FOLD

BACK NECK FACING
CUT 1 SELF

GRAIN LINE

## STEP 19

### DEVELOPING THE BREAST POCKET TOP AND BOTTOM BAGS

- From the front left final pattern in Step 9, trace off the breast pocket opening onto a separate piece of paper so that you have a rectangle 9cm long by 1.5cm wide drawn at an angle.
- Extend the top stitch line by 1.5cm to the right and 1cm to the left, and extend the bottom stitch line by 1.5cm to the left and 1cm to the right.
- Connecting these points on the left, draw a 12.5cm vertical line down. Connecting the points on the right, draw a 14.5cm vertical line down. Square across 11.5cm at the bottom to connect these two lines (the width of the pocket bag).

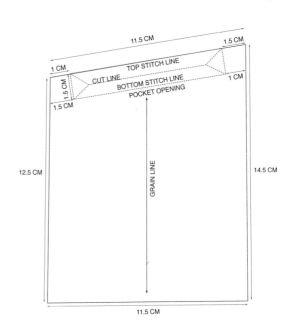

11.5 CM

1.5 CM

1 CM

1.5 CM

TOP STITCH LINE

CUT LINE

BOTTOM STITCH LINE

POCKET OPENING

1 CM

1.5 CM

12.5 CM

14.5 CM

GRAIN LINE

11.5 CM

## STEP 20
### BREAST POCKET BAG PATTERNS

- Following the instructions on page 50, trace off the pocket bag shape and add a 1cm seam allowance above the top stitch line to create the final top pocket bag pattern.
- Trace off the pocket bag shape again as far as the bottom stitch line, then add a 1cm seam allowance to create the final bottom pocket bag pattern.

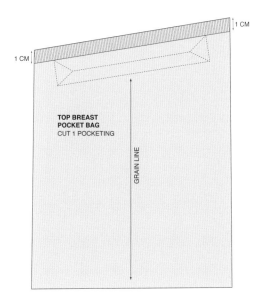

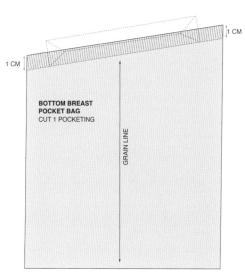

## STEP 21
### DEVELOPING THE BREAST POCKET WELT

**Welts**

If your welted pocket is angled, then the welt will need to reflect this. Welts can be the same size or larger than pocket openings and are doubled over so they have two layers of fabric, with a fusing layer in between for rigidity.

- From the front left pattern in Step 9, trace one long side of the breast pocket opening onto a separate piece of paper so that you have a line 9cm long at the same angle as the breast pocket itself. This will become the centre fold line. Copy the direction of the grain line across, too.
- Parallel to the grain line, draw 2.5cm lines up from both ends of the line and mark. Connect these marks to create a parallelogram.

- Mirror this parallelogram along the fold line.
- Add a 1.5cm seam allowance to both long sides of the shape and a 1cm allowance to the shorter sides.

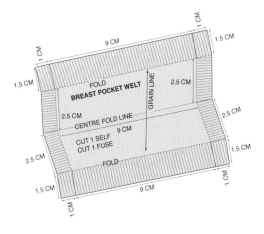

## STEP 22
### DEVELOPING THE COIN POCKET TOP AND BOTTOM BAG

- Draw a rectangle 6cm wide and 6.5cm tall (the size of the coin pocket bag). Label the top edge as the *bottom stitch line* and add a 1cm seam allowance to all sides. This is the bottom coin pocket bag.
- Draw another rectangle the same size and again label the top edge as the bottom stitch line.

- Square up 1.5cm on both sides and connect these points to create a second rectangle.
- Label the top edge of this rectangle as the *top stitch line*. Add a 1cm seam allowance on all sides. This is the top coin pocket bag.

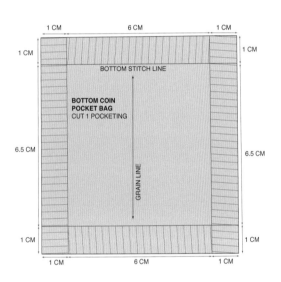

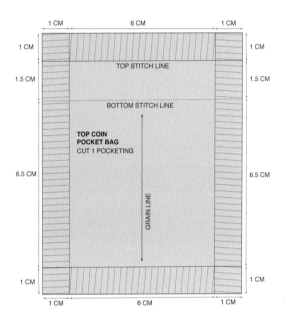

## STEP 23
### DEVELOPING THE COIN POCKET WELT

- On a separate piece of paper, draw a horizontal box 6cm long and 4cm wide to create a rectangular-shaped welt.
- Divide the box in half lengthways, draw a line down the centre and label it *fold*.
- Add a 1cm seam allowance to each end and a 1.5cm seam allowance to each long side to create the final pocket welt pattern.

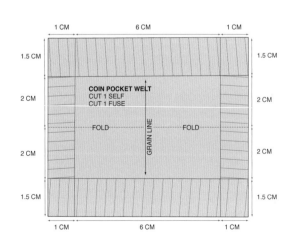

## STEP 24
### DEVELOPING THE TOP AND BOTTOM SIDE POCKET BAGS

- Draw a rectangle 14.5cm wide and 16cm tall (the size of the coin pocket bag). Label the top edge as the *bottom stitch line* and add a 1cm seam allowance to all sides. This is the bottom side pocket bag.
- Draw another rectangle the same size and again label the top edge as the *bottom stitch line*.

- Square up 1.5cm on both sides and connect these points to create a second rectangle. Label the top edge of this rectangle as the *top stitch line*. Add a 1cm seam allowance on all sides. This is the top side pocket bag.

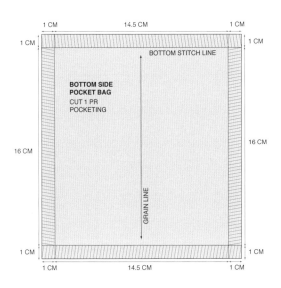

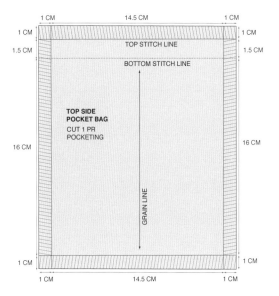

## STEP 25
### DEVELOPING THE SIDE POCKET JET

- On a separate piece of paper, draw a horizontal box 14.cm long (the width of the side pocket opening) by 1.5cm wide to create the side pocket jet.
- Divide the box in half lengthways, draw a line down the centre and label it *fold*.
- Add a 1cm seam allowance on all sides to create the final side pocket jet pattern.

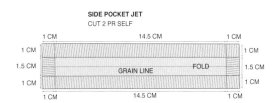

## STEP 26
### DEVELOPING THE FRONT LINING

- Following the instructions on page 50, trace off a copy of the front body panel from Step 9. Remove the facing shape from the front; the remaining shape will become the front lining.
- Next you need to add ease by increasing the armhole width to allow for movement. At the shoulder point measure out 0.5cm and mark, and up 0.5cm and mark. Find the new shoulder point, and draw a straight line back towards the front shoulder neck point.
- From the top of the front style line measure up 0.5cm and mark, and out 0.5cm and mark. Find the point and using a French curve draw a line 0.5cm out from the original armhole back up to the new shoulder point.
- From the new point blend the front side seam down to meet the original hemline.
- From the hemline extend the front style line and the front edge down by 2cm and square across; this will create an overlap to allow movement when bending over in the garment.
- Draw a fold line 1cm up from the new hemline.

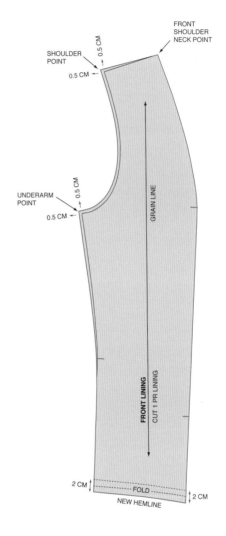

## STEP 27
### DEVELOPING THE BACK LINING

- Following the instructions on page 50, trace off a copy of the back body panel from Step 17. Remove the hem facing shape; the remaining shape will become the back lining.
- You need to add ease to the centre back to allow the lining to expand across the shoulder blades and also to increase the armhole to allow for movement.
- Fold over the vent shape onto the pattern, trace around it and then remove the vent and its negative shape from the back style line.
- From the centre back neck point measure out 2cm and then square down 31.5cm and square back in; this will become the pleat at the centre back.
- From the back shoulder point measure out 0.5cm and mark, and up 0.5cm and mark. Find the new back shoulder point and draw a straight line from here back towards the shoulder neck point.
- From the top of the back style line measure out 0.5cm and mark. From this new point, and using a French curve, draw a line 0.5cm out from the original armhole back up to the new shoulder point.
- From the new point blend the back style line down to meet the original hemline.
- From the hemline extend the centre back seam and the side vent seam down by 2cm and square across; this will create an overlap to allow movement when bending over in the garment.
- Draw a fold line 1cm up from the new hemline.

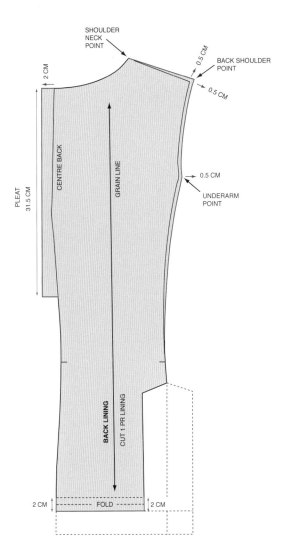

## STEP 28
### DEVELOPING THE SIDE LINING

- Following the instructions on page 50, trace off a copy of the side panel from Step 15. Remove the hem facing and the vent shape; the remaining shape will become the side lining.
- Next you need to add ease to the underarm shape to allow the lining to expand, giving increased movement to the armhole width. At the top of the front and back style lines measure up 0.5cm and mark, and measure out 0.5cm and mark. Find the new points (the front and back underarm points), and using a French curve connect them up at a distance of 0.5cm out from the original armhole.
- From the underarm points blend the style lines down to meet the original hemline.
- From the hemline extend the back and front style lines down by 2cm and square across; this will create an overlap to allow movement when bending over in the garment.
- Draw a fold line 1cm up from the new hemline.

## DEVELOPING THE TWO-PIECE TAILORED SLEEVE

**Measurements required to develop the sleeve**

Measurements required to draft the
tailored two-piece sleeve are as follows.

- Armhole 53cm + 4cm ease = 57cm.
  (Take this measurement from the
  basic body block.)
- Sleeve length to wrist = 64cm.
  (This measurement is taken from the
  crown point, running down the back
  of the elbow to the wrist; extra
  length can be added at this point
  to suit your design.)
- Crown point to elbow length = 35cm.
- Upper biceps circumference = 40.8cm.
  (This measurement is taken round the
  upper arm; extra width 'ease' can be
  added for movement.)
- Cuff measurement = 30cm. Remove 1cm
  from each side to reduce the cuff
  width from the basic tapered block,
  which is 32cm.
- Sleeve head height = 17.6cm.

- Cut a large piece of drafting paper slightly longer than the length of your sleeve or the arm length of your fit model.
- Draw a 64cm vertical line down the centre and label it *centre line*; label the top of this line (1) and the bottom (2). This is the length of the sleeve.
- From (1) measure down 17.6cm (the sleeve head height, or one third of the armhole measurement, not including ease) and label point (3).
- From (1) measure down 35cm (the elbow length) and label point (4).
- Divide the armhole measurement (57cm) by 6 to give 9.5cm cm and add 1cm volume to give 10.5cm. From (1) square out 10.5cm to the left and to the right and label these points (5) and (6).
- From (2) measure out 10.5cm to the left and to the right and label these points (7) and (8).
- Connect points (5), (6), (7), (8) to form a rectangle.
- Divide the sleeve head height (17.6cm) by 3 to give 5.8cm. From (6) measure down 5.8cm, make a mark and label it *back pitch point*. From the back pitch point square in 2.5cm and mark point (A); this is the top point of the back seam on the undersleeve.
- From (3) square out to the left to intersect the line from (5) to (7) and mark point (B), and square out to the right to intersect the line from (6) to (8) and mark point (C). This is the underarm line.

- From (B) measure out 2.5cm and mark point (D), and measure in 2.5cm and mark point (E). From (C) measure in 1cm and mark point (F), and measure out 1cm and mark point (G).
- To establish the front pitch point on the armhole divide the sleeve head height (17.6cm) by 2 to give 8.8cm, and subtract 2cm to give 6.8cm. This will ensure a rectangular shape to the sleeve head instead of the square shape that would occur if the sleeve head were just divided in half. From (B) measure up 6.8cm, make a mark and label it *front pitch point*.
- From (4) square out to the left to intersect the line from (5) to (7) and mark point (H), and square out to the right to intersect the line from (6) to (8) and mark point (I). This is the elbow line.
- From (H) measure out 1cm and mark point (J), and measure in 4cm and mark point (K).

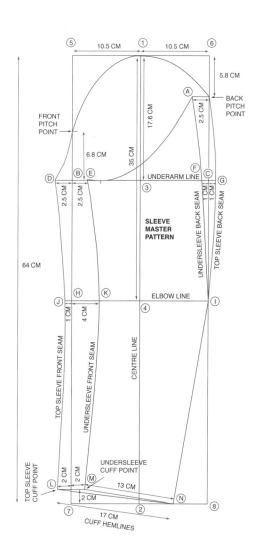

- From (7) measure up 2cm and from this point measure out 2cm and mark point (L); this is the top sleeve cuff point. Measure in 2cm and mark point (M); this is the undersleeve cuff point.
- The cuff circumference is 30cm. Divide this between the top and undersleeve so that the top sleeve cuff width is 17cm and the undersleeve is 13cm. This allows the top sleeve seams to fall towards the back of the arm, slightly out of view.
- From (L) draw a line 17cm long to intersect the line from (7) to (8) and mark point (N). From (M) draw a line 13cm long to intersect the line from (7) to (8), also at point (N). These are the cuff hemlines.
- Draw in the top sleeve front seam by drawing a blended line connecting the points from (L) through (J) to (D).
- Draw in the undersleeve front seam by drawing a blended line connecting the points from (M) through (K) to (E).
- Using a French curve, draw in the top sleeve head starting at (D) with a concave curve through the front pitch point where you reverse the curve to a convex curve up to (1) and back down to the back pitch point with a similar convex curve.

- Measure the length of this line and compare it to the measurement of the armhole on the front and back patterns. Here the length should be 35.2cm. Adjust the curves until the line is the correct measurement.
- Using a French curve, draw in the top of the undersleeve with convex curve starting at (E) up to (A).
- Again, measure this line and adjust it until it is the same measurement as the armhole on the front and back patterns – in this case 22.5cm.
- Draw in the back seam of the top sleeve with a blended line from the back pitch point through points (G) to (I) and continue down to (N).
- Draw in the back seam of the undersleeve with a blended line from (A) through (F) to (I) and also continue with this seam on the same line as the top sleeve down to (N).

## STEP 30
### DEVELOPING THE FINAL TOP SLEEVE PATTERN WITH CUFF VENT

- Following the instructions on page 50, trace off the top sleeve onto a separate piece of paper.
- From the bottom of the sleeve measure down 3cm and draw a rectangular box to create the facing strip.
- Extend the length of the cuff facing by 3cm at the back seam and square up 10cm to create a rectangular box 3cm in width. This is the cuff extension.
- Measure a further 1.5cm up the back seam and join this point to the outer corner of the box, creating an angle and shape similar to the centre back vent.
- The corner is folded to create a mitred corner during construction.

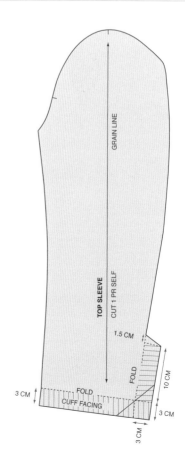

## STEP 31

### DEVELOPING THE FINAL UNDERSLEEVE PATTERN WITH CUFF VENT

- Trace off the undersleeve onto a separate piece of paper and, following the instructions on page 50, reverse it by turning it over.
- From the bottom of the sleeve measure down 3cm and draw a rectangular box to create the facing strip.
- Extend the length of the cuff facing by 3cm at the back seam and square up 10cm to create a rectangular box 3cm in width. This is the cuff extension.
- Measure a further 1.5cm up the back seam and join this point to the outer corner of your rectangular box, creating an angle and shape similar to the centre back vent.
- The corner is folded to create a mitred corner during construction.

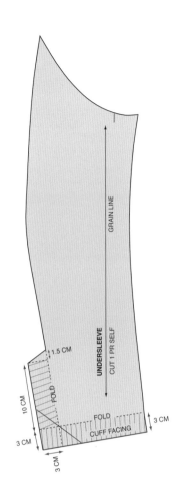

## STEP 32

### DEVELOPING THE FINAL TWO-PIECE SLEEVE LINING PATTERNS

**Matching the measurements**

Having enlarged the armhole of the body panel lining, we will now increase the sleeve head so that the measurements match. At the cuff hem we will increase the length of the lining so that when the arm is raised the lining will not pull the outer sleeve.

- Following the instructions on page 50, trace off a copy of the top sleeve from the sleeve master plan.
- From the crown point measure up 0.5cm and mark, and from the front and back shoulder points measure out 0.5cm and mark, and measure up 0.5cm and mark. Find the new points and connect these to new crown point with a curved line.
- From the new shoulder points draw a line down to blend in with the cuff hem.
- From the cuff hem measure down 2cm and square across to increase the length of the lining. Draw a fold line 1cm inside the new hemline.
- Following the instructions on page 50, trace off the undersleeve lining pattern.
- At the top of the front and back shoulder points measure up 0.5cm and mark, and measure out 0.5cm and mark; connect these points with a curved line.
- From the new shoulder points draw a line down to blend in with the cuff hem.
- From the cuff hem measure down 2cm and square across to increase the length of the lining. Draw a fold line 1cm inside the new hemline.

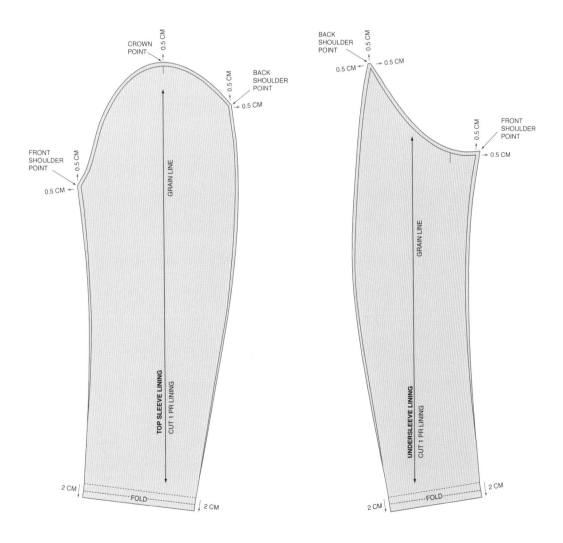

# PATTERN
# WAXED JACKET

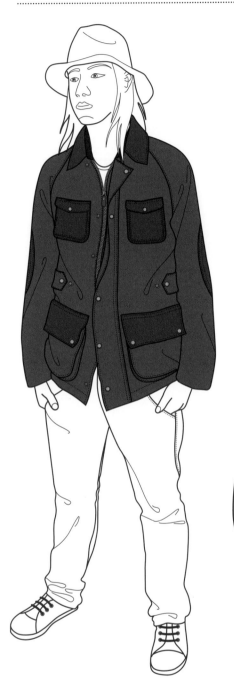

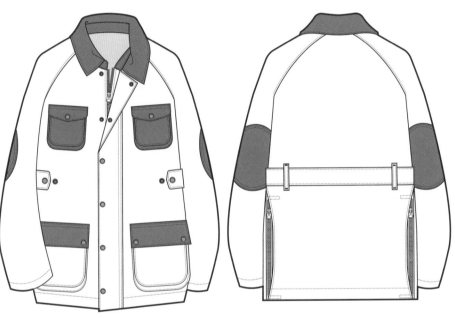

**This pattern includes development of the following features:**
Adding volume to the side seam
Enlarging the neckline
Creating a sewn-on front placket
Extending the hemline
Creating side vents
Developing a waist belt
Dropping the shoulder
Lowering the armhole
Developing breast and front patch pockets with gussets
    and flaps
Developing a back envelope pocket with side zip
Developing a shaped convertible collar with stand
Developing raglan sleeves with elbow patches
Developing a full body lining

## STEP 1

### DEVELOPING THE MASTER PLAN

Start by selecting the basic men's body block, or by drafting the basic block according to the instructions on page 40. Cut a large piece of drafting paper slightly longer than the length of the jacket you want to develop and transfer the shape of the block and all marks, labels and instructions, following the directions on page 48.

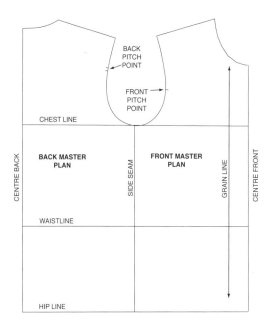

## STEP 2

### DEVELOPING THE ENLARGED NECK, DROPPED SHOULDER, LOWERED ARMHOLE AND EXTENDED HEM LENGTH AND ADDING VOLUME TO THE SIDE SEAM

- From the centre front neck point measure down 2cm and at the front shoulder neck point measure in 0.5cm; repeat at the back by measuring in 0.5cm from the back shoulder neck point. Using the basic body block as a template draw in the new front and back necklines.
- Open up the side seam by adding in 2cm between the front and back body panels and repositioning.
- From the front and back shoulder points measure up 0.5cm and out 1cm over the armhole and make a mark.
- From the chest line square down 3.5cm on each side and, starting from the new underarm point, redraw the new armhole shape using the basic body blocks as a template. Draw in the new pitch point positions on the lowered armhole.
- To create the jacket length, extend the centre front and centre back lines down by 11cm. Square across to create the new hemline and bring down the side seam line to meet it.

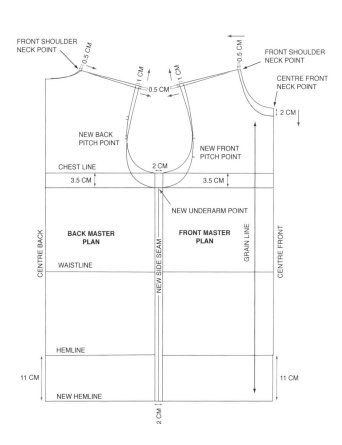

## STEP 3

### CREATING THE RAGLAN SHOULDER SHAPES AND FRONT PLACKET WIDTH

- From the shoulder neck point measure 4cm down the back neckline and 4cm down the front neckline and mark.
- From the new underarm point measure 9.5cm up the front armhole and make a mark, and measure 9.5cm up the back armhole and make a mark.
- From these points draw straight lines up to the marks you made on the front and back necklines.
- From the back neckline measure 13.5cm down this line and then square up 1cm. From the front neck measure 12cm down the line and then square up 1cm.
- With a shallow curve, draw another line from the points on the back and front necklines to the armholes, this time passing through the marks at 1cm.
- Trace off the shoulder shapes ready to transfer to the sleeve, adding front and back notches for alignment.
- To create the sewn-on placket, square out 3cm at the centre front neck point and mark and square in 3cm and mark. Repeat at the new hemline on the centre front and mark. Join these points to create the 6cm placket shape.

## STEP 4

### DEVELOPING THE PLACKET STITCH LINE, FOLDED HEM FACING, SIDE VENT AND WAIST BELT POSITION

- Trace off onto a separate piece of paper the front body pattern from the previous step without the raglan shape.
- To indicate the stitch line placement for the sewn-on placket draw a dotted line from the neckline to the hemline at a distance of 3cm in from the centre front.
- To indicate the facing stitch line draw a dotted line 3cm above the hemline.
- From the centre front measure in 5cm along the hem and then square down 3cm; this is the starting point for the facing.
- Extend the hem facing along to the side seam and square up. At this point measure out 4cm plus a further 4cm; this is the side vent width with a central fold line.
- From the top of the hem facing at the end of the side vent square up 25cm and then square back to the side seam; this is the side vent length.
- On top of the vent length measure up 2cm; from this point draw a line back to the side vent fold line and then angle back up to meet the side seam at the same 2cm height.
- To develop the waist belt position measure up and down 2.5cm on the side seam each side of the waistline; this is the belt width. From these points create a rectangle 5cm wide by 11.5cm long along the waistline. From the front of the rectangle, measure back 1cm either side and draw two lines back down to the centre to create the waist belt tip.

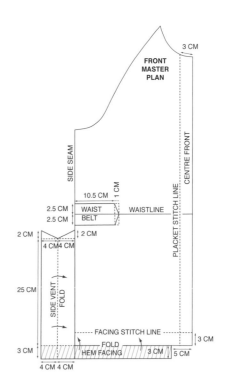

## STEP 5

## DEVELOPING FRONT PATCH POCKET PARTS AND POSITIONS

**Matching the measurements**
Having enlarged the armhole of the body panel lining, we will now increase the sleeve head so that the measurements match. At the cuff hem we will increase the length of the lining so that when the arm is raised the lining will not pull the outer sleeve.

- Trace off onto a separate piece of paper the front body pattern from the previous step.
- To establish the position of the front breast patch pocket bag, measure 9.5cm up from the waistline and 5.5cm in from the centre front and mark; this is the bottom right corner of your pocket bag.
- From this point create a rectangle 13cm high by 12cm wide; this is the pocket bag shape. Round off the bottom corners.
- The breast pocket flap position sits 1cm above the bag and is 0.5cm wider on each side. Measure up 1cm above the pocket bag and from this point create a rectangle 13cm long and 5cm wide sitting over the pocket bag. From the bottom line of the rectangle measure up 1.5cm on each side and draw two lines back down to the centre to create an envelope point to the pocket flap.
- To develop the lower waist pocket bag shape underneath the waistline, measure 1.5cm up from the facing stitch line and 5cm in from the centre front and make a mark; this is the bottom right corner of the pocket bag.

- From this point create a rectangle 17cm high by 19cm wide; this is your pocket bag shape. Round off the bottom corners by measuring 3cm up and in from each corner.
- The lower pocket flap position sits 1cm above the bag and is 0.5cm wider on each side edge. Measure up 1cm above the pocket bag and from this point create a rectangle 20cm long and 6.5cm wide sitting over the pocket bag.

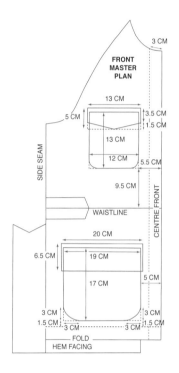

## STEP 6

## FRONT PATTERN AND DEVELOPING THE FRONT FACING

- Following the instructions on page 50, trace off the front body pattern, annotating all the positions needed for pockets and belt.
- Draw a vertical dotted line from the neckline to the hemline at a distance of 5cm from the centre front line; this will become the width of the facing pattern.

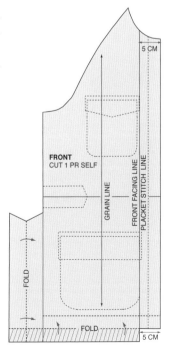

## STEP 7

## FRONT FACING PATTERN

- Following the instructions on page 50, trace off the front facing, adding alignment notches and a 1cm seam allowance on all sides to create the final pattern.

## STEP 8
### FRONT BREAST PATCH POCKET PATTERNS WITH GUSSET

- Following the instructions on page 50, trace off the breast pocket flap pattern, adding a 1cm seam allowance on all sides.
- Following the instructions on page 50, trace off the breast pocket bag pattern, adding a 1cm seam allowance all around the outside edge and a 2cm facing strip to the top opening edge, which will be folded into the bag.
- The measurements to develop the gusset on the breast patch pocket bag are taken by measuring around the outside

edge of the bag shape that will be stitched down to the jacket body - in this case 36cm. Draw the gusset as a long rectangular shape, 36cm long by 3cm wide, and add a 1cm seam allowance on all sides.

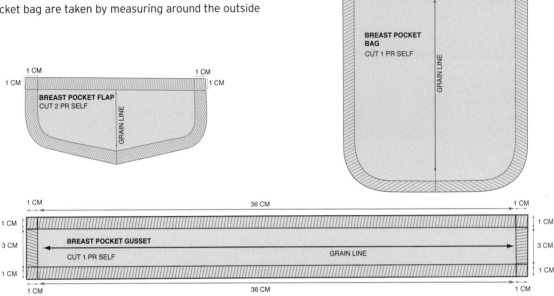

## STEP 9
### FRONT WAIST PATCH POCKET PATTERNS WITH GUSSET

- Following the instructions on page 50, trace off the waist pocket flap pattern, doubling it over along the length to make a folded pattern and adding a 1cm seam allowance on all sides.
- Following the instructions on page 50, trace off the waist pocket bag pattern, adding a 1cm seam allowance all around the outside edge and a 3cm facing strip to the top opening edge, which will be folded into the bag.

- The measurements to develop the gusset on the breast patch pocket bag are taken by measuring around the outside edge of the bag shape that will be stitched down to the jacket body - in this case 49.5cm. Draw the gusset as a long rectangular shape, 49.5cm long by 3cm wide, and add a 1cm seam allowance on all sides.

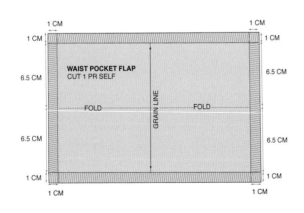
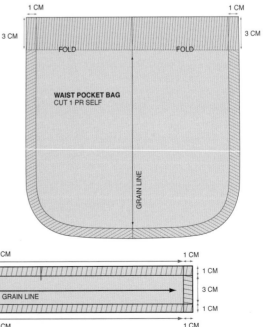

## STEP 10
### FRONT SEWN-ON PLACKET PATTERN

- On a separate piece of paper, draw a horizontal box 12cm wide by 67.5cm long (the length of the centre front) to create the rectangular-shaped placket.
- Divide the box in half lengthways, draw a line down the centre and label it *fold*. Add a 1cm seam allowance on all sides.

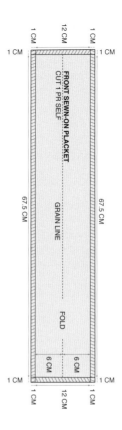

## STEP 11
### DEVELOPING THE BACK SIDE VENTS, HEM FACING AND WAIST BELT POSITION

- Trace off the back body without the raglan shape onto a new piece of paper and, following the instructions on page 50, create the full pattern shape.
- From the hemline corners square down 3cm and square across to create the facing.
- Repeat this above the hemline by squaring up 3cm, and indicate the facing stitch line with a dotted line.
- Extend the hem facing line and the hemline out from the side seam at both ends by 4cm; this is the vent width.
- From each end of the extended hemline square up 25cm and square back to the side seam; this is the vent length.
- On the top of the vent length measure 2cm up the side seam and from this point draw an angled line back down to the vent corner.
- To develop the waist belt position square up 2.5cm and down 2.5cm each side of the waistline to establish the belt width. From these points create a rectangle by connecting the points across the back.
- To position the belt loops, from the side seam on each side measure 7cm along the waistline and draw two rectangles 1.5cm wide by 7cm long centred over the waistline.

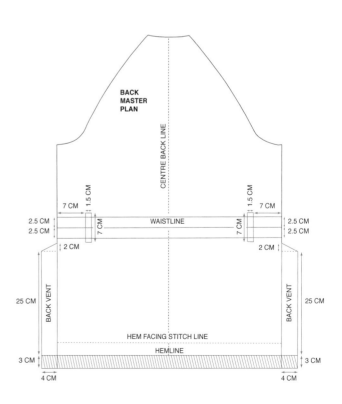

## STEP 12
### BACK BODY PANEL PATTERN

- Following the instructions on page 50, trace off the back body pattern without the side vents, which will be sewn on as part of the back envelope pocket bag, annotating all the positions for belt and loops.
- Add the position of the back envelope pocket by measuring 25cm up from the hemline on both sides and squaring across to create a rectangle 56cm wide by 25cm high.

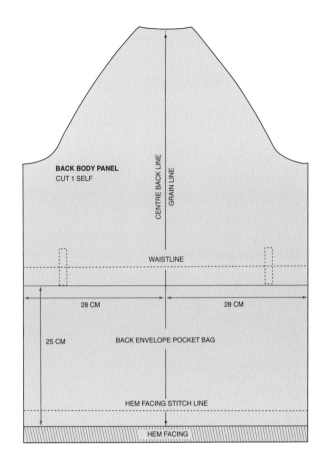

## STEP 13
### BACK SIDE VENT PATTERN

- Following the instructions on page 50, trace off the side vent pattern and add a 1cm seam allowance on all sides to create the final pattern.

## STEP 14
### DEVELOPING THE WAIST BELT PATTERN

- To create the waist belt trace off from Step 4 the front ends of the belt and from Step 11 the middle section, constructing a rectangle 5cm wide by 80cm long. Add a 1cm seam allowance on all sides to create the final pattern.

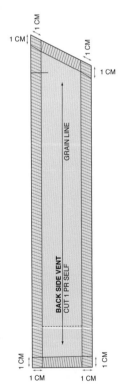

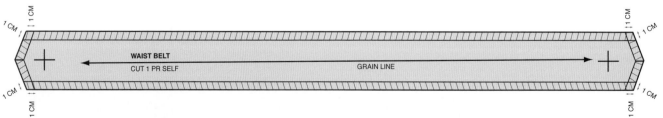

## STEP 15

### BACK ENVELOPE POCKET BAG PATTERN

- Following the instructions on page 50, trace off the final back envelope pocket bag from Step 12. Add a 1cm seam allowance on all sides.

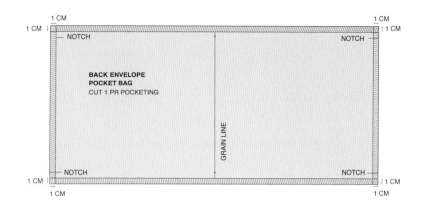

## STEP 16

### DEVELOPING THE TOP AND UNDER ENVELOPE POCKET FACING WITH ZIP OPENING

**Envelope pocket**

The envelope, or poacher's, pocket in this design has identical zipped openings on both the left- and right-hand sides so it can be used from either side of the jacket. The pocket openings have a folded facing with the zip attached to the under or lining side of the opening.

- The facing for the pocket's opening is constructed as a folding rectangle, 10cm wide by 25cm long. Divide in half lengthways adding a fold line down the middle.
- To divide again for the insertion of a 20cm closed-end zip, measure out 3cm from each end of the fold line and square across. Measure in 3cm along this line from the bottom and mark and 2cm from the top and mark. This is the opening for the zip.
- Create a stepped opening by drawing a rectangle 20cm long by 1cm wide, centred along the opening.

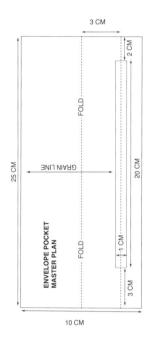

## STEP 17

### TOP AND UNDER ENVELOPE POCKET FACING PATTERNS

- Following the instructions on page 50, trace off the two parts of the back envelope facing patterns, and add a 1cm seam allowance on all sides on both patterns.

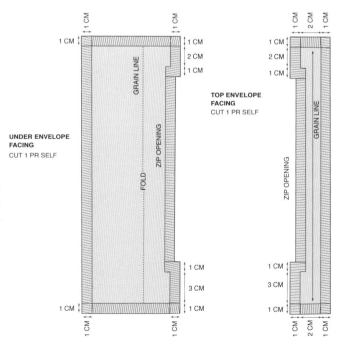

## STEP 18
### SLEEVE MASTER PLAN

Start this development by selecting the basic men's sleeve block, or by drafting the basic sleeve block according to the instructions on page 42. Cut a large piece of drafting paper slightly longer than the length of the shirt you want to develop and transfer the shape of the block and all marks, labels and instructions, following the directions on page 48.

## STEP 19
### DEVELOPING THE SLEEVE MASTER PLAN

- Draw round the basic sleeve block, opening it up along the centre line by 1cm.
- From the crown point measure down 1cm, the amount by which you extended the shoulder on the body panel.
- From the underarm line square down 1.5cm, half of the amount by which you dropped the armhole; redraw the new underarm line position, extending it by 2.5cm on each side.
- Using the basic sleeve block as a template, redraw the new sleeve head indicating the lowered pitch points.
- To shape the sleeve hemline, measure 1cm up each underarm seam and 1.5cm in on each side and mark.
- From these points draw in the new underarm seams, connecting them back up to the extended underarm line.
- From the new sleeve hemline square down 3cm to create the facing shape, pitching out at each side to reflect the sleeve seams when folded.

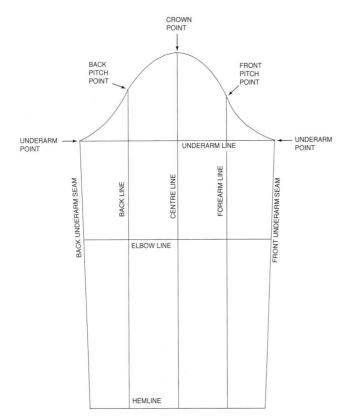

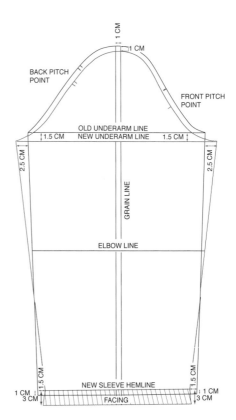

## STEP 20
### DEVELOPING THE ELBOW PATCH PATTERN

- Construct a rectangle 18cm long by 14cm wide. Divide the shape into four quarters, each 9cm by 7cm. Using a French curve create an oval-shaped elbow patch.

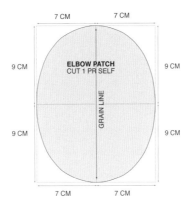

## STEP 21
### DEVELOPING THE RAGLAN PANEL SLEEVE

- Before you can separate the sleeve for the raglan you need to establish the elbow patch position. Trace off the sleeve pattern from Step 19. From the centre line along the elbow line measure 11cm out into the back sleeve and mark. Align one side of the elbow patch pattern to this point and, using the pattern as a template, draw in the patch position.
- Separate the sleeve into two halves, naming them front and back.
- Trace off the back raglan shape from Step 3. Add to the sleeve head by placing the shoulder points together at the new crown point and aligning the tips of the raglan to the sleeve head lines.

- Trace off the front raglan shape from Step 3. Add to the sleeve head by placing the shoulder points together at the new crown point and aligning the tips of the raglan to the sleeve head lines.
- It is important that the raglan sleeve panels have a fluid line. To do this, shape the crown point and the points where the raglan shapes join the sleeve head with shallow curves.

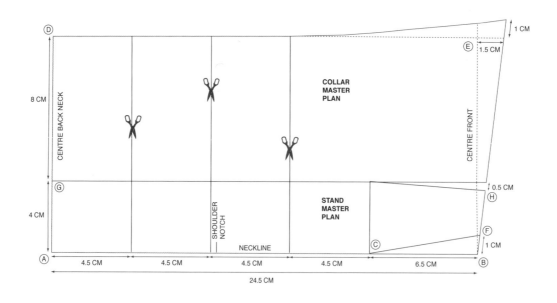

## STEP 22
### RAGLAN PANEL SLEEVE PATTERNS

- Following the instructions on page 50, trace off the front and back raglan panels as separate patterns.

## STEP 23
### DEVELOPING THE SHAPED CONVERTIBLE COLLAR WITH STAND

- On a new piece of paper draw a 24.5cm horizontal line and mark the left end (A) and the right end (B). This is the neckline.
- From (A) square up 4cm and mark (G), and a further 8cm and mark (D). This is the centre back neck.
- Finish drawing the rectangle by marking the top right corner (E) and connecting it down to (B).
- To shape the stand, measure up 1cm from (B) and mark (F). From (B) square in 6.5cm and mark (C). Join to (F) with an angled line.

- From (E) square out 1.5cm and draw an angled  line down to (F). Measure a further 1cm up to create the collar point. From the collar point draw a curved line back towards (D).
- From (G) square across to the angled front edge, and from (C) square up to this horizontal line. Measure down 0.5cm from where the line from (G) intersects the angled front edge and mark (H). Connect (H) back to the point above (C) with a slight curve.
- Starting from (A) make three marks along the neckline at a distance of 4.5cm apart, and square up from each mark to the top line of the rectangle to make three cut lines.

## STEP 24
### SEPARATING AND SHAPING THE STAND AND COLLAR

- Remove the stand shape from the development by tracing onto a separate piece of paper, including the vertical cut lines.
- Remove the collar shape from the development by tracing onto a separate piece of paper. Trace across the cut lines from the stand.

- Cut down the vertical lines on the collar shape, leaving them attached at the bottom by millimetres. Starting from the centre back open out each line by 0.4cm, curving down the collar. From the centre back remove 0.9cm width, which is the amount lost by closing the stand up.
- Cut down the vertical lines on the stand shape, leaving them attached at the bottom by millimetres. Overlap the tops by 0.3cm towards the centre back so that it brings up the neckline.

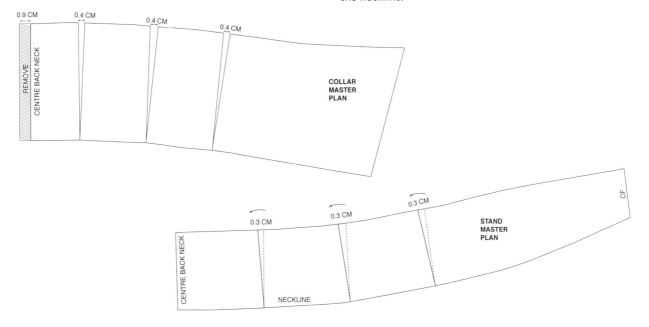

## STEP 25
### COLLAR STAND AND COLLAR PATTERNS

- Trace off the collar stand and, following the instructions on page 50, create the full pattern shape.

- Trace off the collar pattern and, following the instructions on page 50, create the full pattern shape.

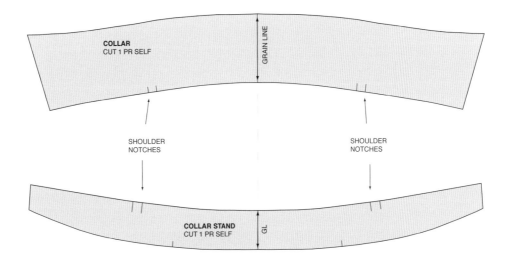

## STEP 26
### DEVELOPING THE FRONT LINING

- Following the instructions on page 50, trace off a copy of the front body from the pattern in Step 6. Remove the side vent, placket shape and hem facing.
- Next you need to add ease by increasing the armhole width to allow for movement. From the underarm point measure up 0.5cm and mark, and out 0.5cm and mark. Find the new underarm point and draw a line, blending it back up to the shoulder neck point.
- To extend the length and give the lining an overlap at the hemline measure down 1cm from the hemline and square across, labelling the line *fold*, and measure down a further 1cm and square across, to give a 2cm overlap.
- From the new underarm point blend the side seam down to meet the original hemline.

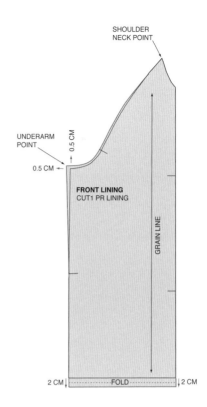

## STEP 27
### DEVELOPING THE BACK LINING

- Following the instructions on page 50, trace off a copy of the half back body from Step 12. Before mirroring the shape over to create a full pattern, you need to add ease to the centre back to allow the lining to expand across the shoulder blades and also to increase the armhole to allow for movement.
- From the centre back neck point measure out 2cm and connect this point to the hemline; this will become the pleat at the centre back neck.
- Double over the shape to create the full pattern. Remove the side vent and its negative shape in the body of the lining itself.
- On each side, from the underarm point measure up 0.5cm and mark, and out 0.5cm and mark. Find the new underarm point and connect back up to the shoulder neck point.
- To extend the length and give the lining an overlap at the hemline measure down 1cm from the hemline and square across, labelling the line *fold*, and measure down a further 1cm and square across, to give a 2cm overlap.
- From the new underarm point blend the side seam down to meet the vent.

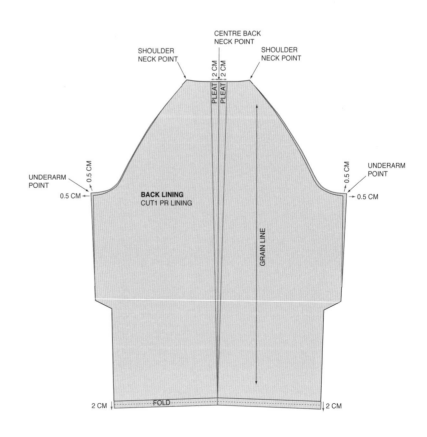

# DEVELOPING THE SLEEVE LINING

### Matching the measurements

Having enlarged the armhole lining, we will now increase the sleeve head so that the measurements match. At the cuff hem we will increase the length of the lining so that when the arm is raised the lining will not pull the outer sleeve.

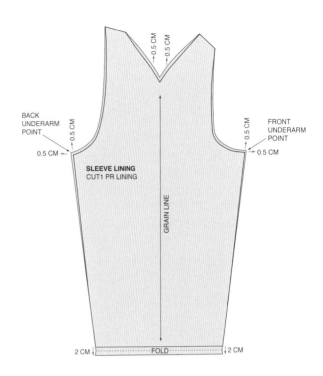

- Trace off a copy of the front and back sleeve patterns from step 21. Join the two separate patterns back together at the centre line so you can make a full lining pattern.
- From the front underarm point measure out 0.5cm and up 0.5cm and mark, and from the back underarm point measure out 0.5cm and up 0.5cm and mark; find the new underarm points and draw lines back up to the shoulder seam.
- From the new front and back underarm points blend the side seams down to meet the sleeve hemline.
- From the sleeve hemline measure down 1cm and square across and label the line *fold*, and measure down a further 1cm and square across, to give a 2cm overlap.

# PATTERN
# PARKA

**This pattern includes development of the following features:**

Adding volume to the side seam, front and back panels

Enlarging the neckline

Creating a grown-on placket

Extending and shaping the hemline with a fishtail at the back and a drawstring channel

Creating a drawstring channel at the waistline

Lowering the armhole

Developing front patch pockets with flaps

Developing a two-piece casual sleeve

Developing a collared hood with centre zip and fur panel

Developing a full body lining

## STEP 1
### DEVELOPING THE MASTER PLAN

Start by selecting the basic men's body block, or by drafting the basic block according to the instructions on page 40. Cut a large piece of drafting paper slightly longer than the length of the coat you want to develop and transfer the shape of the block and all marks, labels and instructions, following the directions on page 48.

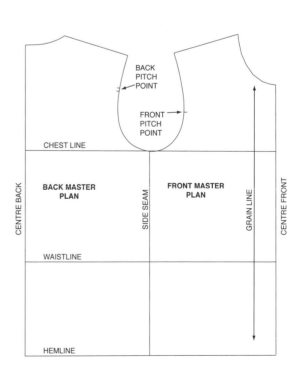

## STEP 2

### DEVELOPING THE ENLARGED NECK, DROPPED SHOULDER, LOWERED ARMHOLE AND EXTENDED HEMLINE, AND SHAPING THE HEM LENGTH WITH VOLUME ADDED TO THE SIDE SEAM

- From the centre front neck point measure down 2cm and from the front shoulder neck point measure in 1cm; repeat at the back by measuring in 1cm from the back shoulder neck point and 0.5cm down the centre back from the centre back neck point. Using the basic body block as a template draw in the new necklines.
- From the front and back shoulder points measure up 0.5cm and out 2cm over the armhole and mark.
- Open up the side seam by adding in 4cm between the front and back body panels and repositioning.
- From the underarm point square down 4cm and starting from this point draw in the new armhole, connecting back up to the new dropped shoulder seam, using the basic body block as a template. Draw in the new pitch point positions on the lowered armhole.
- To extend the length, from the lowered neck measure 82cm down the centre front. Square across to create the new hemline and extend the side seam and the centre back line.
- To shape the new hemline measure down a further 3cm at the centre front and square across to the centre back.
- To develop the parka fishtail design at the centre back, measure down a further 15cm and square across to the side seam to create a rectangle.
- Starting at the bottom of the extended rectangle at the centre back measure up 12cm and mark, and measure in 5cm towards the side seam and mark. Join these points with an angled line 10cm long. Using a French curve draw an arc from the 5cm point up to the side seam and curve down towards the centre front.

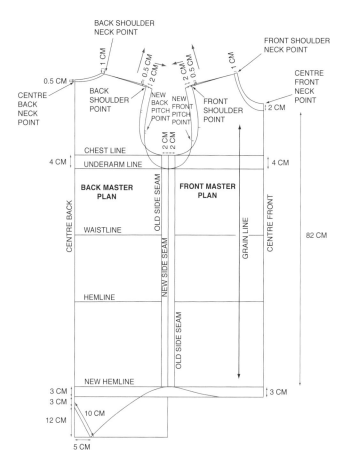

## STEP 3

### ADDING VOLUME TO THE FRONT TO CREATE THE SILHOUETTE

- Following the instructions on page 50, trace off the front body shape from the master plan onto a separate piece of paper.
- From the centre front at the hemline, measure in 14.5cm (half the width of the panel) and mark. From the side seam measure in 14.5cm along the waistline and from here square up 10cm and mark.
- From the underarm point measure 5cm up the armhole and from this point draw a line down to meet the mark made above and then a straight line down to the hemline. This is the cut line.
- From the hemline cut up along the cut line to just under the armhole.
- Keeping the centre front vertical, open the cut line 5cm at the hem to add in the volume.
- Redraw the hemline.

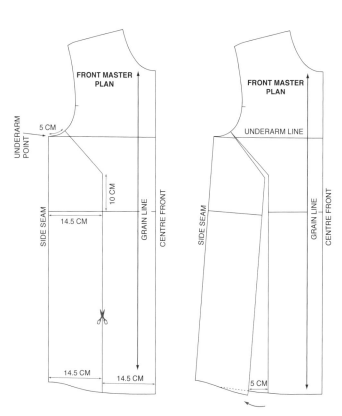

## STEP 4

### DEVELOPING THE FRONT PLACKET, FRONT PLACKET FACING AND HEMLINE FACING

- Develop the front placket on the pattern shape developed in the previous step. From the centre front neck point square out 2.25cm and square in 2.25cm. Repeat at the hemline and connect the points with vertical lines to form the 4.5cm-wide placket.
- From the new placket line at the centre front neck point measure 6cm in to the body, and repeat at the hemline; join with a vertical line. This will be the width of the facing pattern.
- To develop the hemline facing measure up 4cm from the hemline at the front facing width line and at the side seam; join these points with a line following the shape of the hem.

## STEP 5

### DEVELOPING THE DRAWSTRING CHANNEL LINE AND POCKET POSITION

- From the underarm point measure 19.5cm down the side seam and mark, and a further 2cm and mark. Square in to the front and create a rectangle 15cm long and 2cm wide; this will become the drawstring channel.
- Developing the pocket flap and pocket bag shape on the master plan itself allows you to assess the proportions in relation to the body front.
- Measure a further 9cm down the side seam and mark; this is the top of the pocket flap positioned over the side seam.
- From this point square in 22.5cm and square out 3.5cm. To develop the rectangle that will become the pocket flap shape, measure down 10cm on both sides and connect these points with a straight line.
- Make a mark halfway along the bottom line (13cm); measure up 2cm on each side and draw lines back to the centre of the bottom line to create an envelope point to the pocket flap.
- The pocket bag sits 1cm underneath the flap: first, measure 1cm down the side seam and mark.
- From this point square in 22cm and square out 3cm to create a line 25cm long.
- To develop the pocket bag shape square down 27cm on each side and connect these points with a straight line.

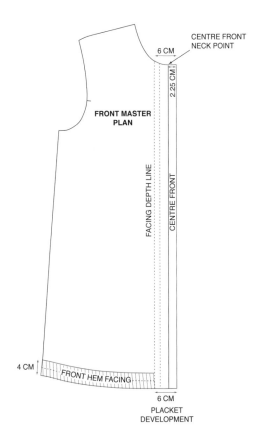

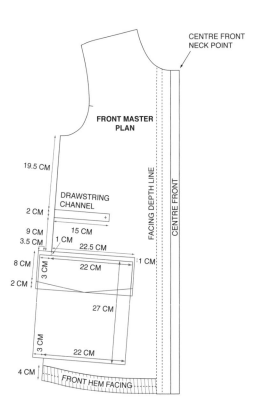

## STEP 6
### FRONT BODY PATTERN

- Following the instructions on page 50, trace off the front body pattern, indicating all the placement positions for the drawstring channel, pocket and front placket facing.

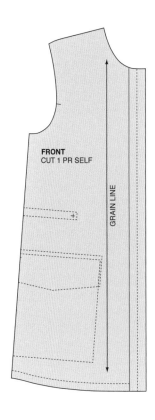

FRONT
CUT 1 PR SELF

GRAIN LINE

## STEP 7
### FRONT PLACKET FACING AND HEM FACING PATTERNS

- Following the instructions on page 50, trace off the final front placket facing pattern and the front hem facing pattern, adding a 1cm seam allowance on all sides.

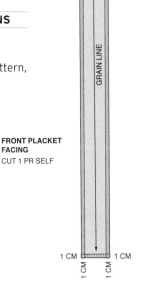

1 CM   1 CM
1 CM          1 CM

GRAIN LINE

FRONT PLACKET
FACING
CUT 1 PR SELF

1 CM   1 CM

1 CM   1 CM

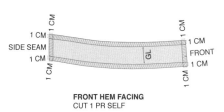

1 CM
1 CM
SIDE SEAM
1 CM
1 CM
GL
1 CM
FRONT
1 CM
1 CM

FRONT HEM FACING
CUT 1 PR SELF

## STEP 8
### ADDING BACK VOLUME TO CREATE THE SILHOUETTE

- Following the instructions on page 50, trace off the back body shape from the master plan onto a separate piece of paper.
- From the centre back at the hemline, measure in 14.5cm (half the width of the panel). From the side seam measure in 14.5cm along the waistline and from here square up 10cm and mark.
- From the underarm point measure 5cm up the armhole and from this point draw a line down to meet the mark made above and then a straight line down to the hemline. This is the cut line.
- Keeping the centre back vertical, open the cut line 6cm at the hem to add in the volume.
- Redraw the hemline.

## STEP 9
### DEVELOPING THE HEMLINE FACING AND DRAWSTRING CHANNEL LINE

- Develop the hemline facing on the pattern shape developed in the previous step. To develop the back hemline facing, measure up 4cm from the hemline at the centre back and at the side seam. Join these points with a line following the shape of the hem.
- From the underarm point measure 19.5cm down the side seam and mark, and a further 2cm and mark. From both points square across to the centre back; this will become the drawstring channel.

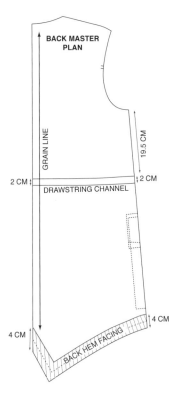

## STEP 10
### BACK, BACK HEM FACING AND DRAWSTRING CHANNEL PATTERNS

- Following the instructions on page 50, trace off the back pattern. Indicate the placement positions for the drawstring and hem facing. Indicate the position of the pocket by lining up this back pattern with the front from Step 5 at the side seam; trace the pocket position onto the back pattern with dotted lines.
- Trace off the back hem facing onto a new piece of paper and, following the instructions on page 50, create the full pattern shape. Add a 1cm seam allowance on all sides.
- Align the front and back body patterns at the side seam and trace off the drawstring channel and, following the instructions on page 50, create the full pattern shape. Add a 1cm seam allowance on all sides.

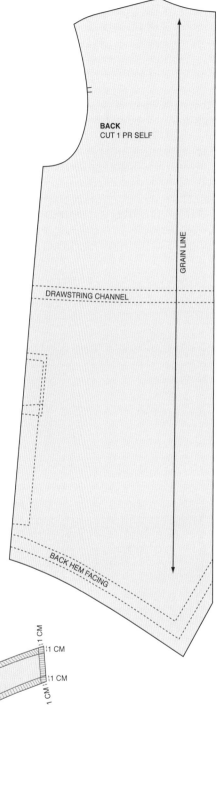

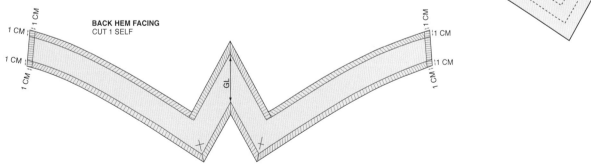

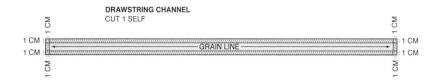

## STEP 11
### FRONT POCKET FLAP AND BAG PATTERNS

- Following the instructions on page 50, trace off the front pocket flap pattern and add a 1cm seam allowance on all sides.
- Following the instructions on page 50, trace off the front pocket bag pattern. Add a 1cm seam allowance on three sides and a 3cm facing to the top.

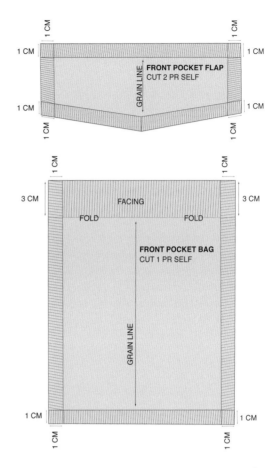

## STEP 12
### SLEEVE MASTER PLAN

Start this development by selecting the basic men's sleeve block, or by drafting the basic sleeve block according to the instructions on page 42. Cut a large piece of drafting paper slightly longer than the length of the shirt you want to develop and transfer the shape of the block and all marks, labels and instructions, following the directions on page 48. The design will be altered to reflect the dropped shoulder and the lowered armhole.

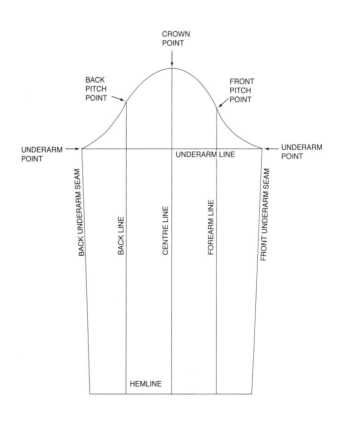

## STEP 13
### DEVELOPING THE SLEEVE

- Open the sleeve up along the centre line by 2cm.
- From the crown point measure down 2cm, the same amount you dropped the shoulder on the body block.
- From the underarm line measure down 2cm, half the amount by which you dropped the armhole; redraw the new underarm line position, extending it by 2.5cm each side.
- Using the basic sleeve block head shape as a template, redraw the new sleeve head, indicating the lowered pitch points.
- Draw the new underarm seams down to the sleeve hemline.
- From the sleeve hemline square down 4cm to create the facing shape, pitching out at each side to reflect the underarm seams when folded.

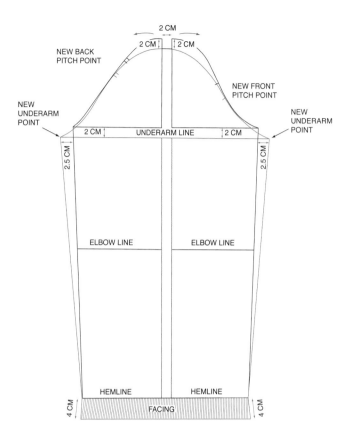

## STEP 14
### SLEEVE PATTERN

- Following the instructions on page 50, trace off the final sleeve pattern.

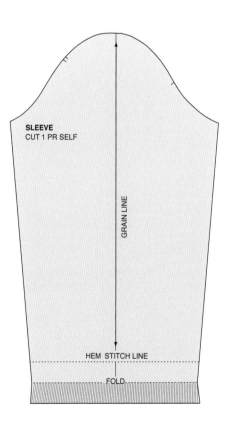

## DEVELOPING THE COLLARED HOOD

There are three measurements you need to create the pattern for the hood:

1. The front and back neck measurements, taken from the pattern - here they are 12.5cm and 12.5cm. If you are developing a hood with a centre back panel, remember to deduct the panel width from the final neck measurement as well as from the crown and front opening.

2. The front and back neck height, found by placing the front pattern on top of the back pattern and aligning them at the chest line, then measuring the distance between the front and back neck heights - here it is 6.5cm.

3. The vertical circumference of the head, taken for the hood opening by measuring around the face of the model's head, starting and finishing at the centre front neck point - here it is 80cm.

- Starting at the bottom right side of your paper mark point (A) and draw a 25cm horizontal line left (the length of the combined neck measurement) and mark point (B).
- From (A) square up 40cm (half the head circumference) and mark point (C). Complete the rectangle and mark point (F).
- From (B) square up 6.5cm (the neck height) and mark point (D). Square in 2cm and mark; label this point *centre back neck*.
- From (D) measure up 10cm and mark point (E). Square in 2cm and mark.
- Using a French curve draw in the neckline from (A) up to the centre back line 2cm in from (D). Measure 12.5cm (the front neck measurement) along this line from (A) and mark the shoulder notch.
- To shape the front opening, from (A) add on the front placket width, which is 4.5cm. To do this, extend the neckline by 2.25cm (half the placket width) and then square up 7cm; from this point square back 4.5cm and mark.
- From (C) measure down 5cm and then square out 5cm and mark; this is the top of the front opening. Using a French curve, draw in the curved front opening from the mark you made at the top of the placket to the top of the front opening.
- From the front opening draw the hood shape (determined by the design, head size, neck opening and usage) back around to the mark 2cm out from (E).
- To enlarge the hood, draw a cut line at a slight angle from the crown point through the hood down to finish just in front of the shoulder point notch.

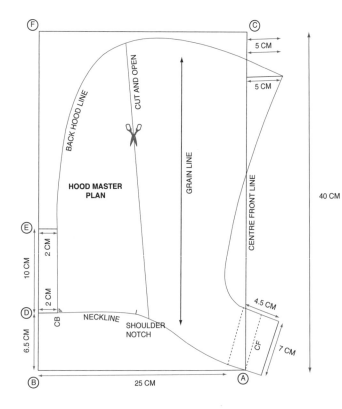

## STEP 16
### ADDING VOLUME TO THE HOOD

- Cut along the cut line from the top, leaving the shape connected by a few millimetres.
- Moving it clockwise, open the front by 8.5cm, which will pitch down the centre front. Redraw the top of the hood.

- From the new front opening position measure out 2.5cm and mark. From this point square back to the top of the hood panel; then from the same point square back down to the bottom of the opening, finishing with a slight curve to meet the front placket. This creates a straight front for the addition of the fur panel.

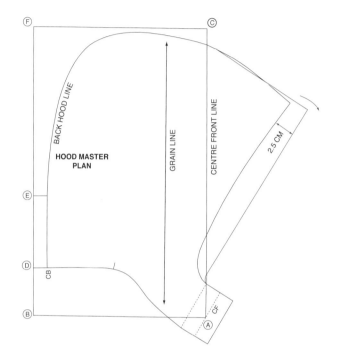

## STEP 17
### DEVELOPING THE FULL HOOD, NECK FACING, ZIP AND FUR PANEL

- Trace off the hood shape and, following the instructions on page 50, double it along the centre back neck to create a mirrored shape.
- To develop the facing shape, measure up 7cm from the neckline at the centre front and centre back and join these points with a line following the shape of the neckline.
- To remove the centre back hood panel, in which the zip is sandwiched, measure in 2cm along the back hood line on both sides, finishing 3cm from the new facing strip.
- The fur panel is attached to the hood along the front opening and will need a separate pattern. Measure 8cm back from the front opening and create a rectangular panel on both sides.

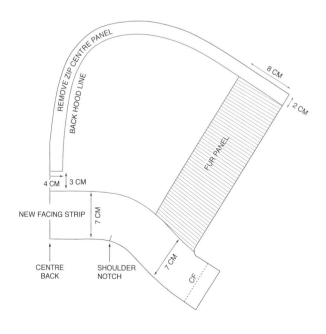

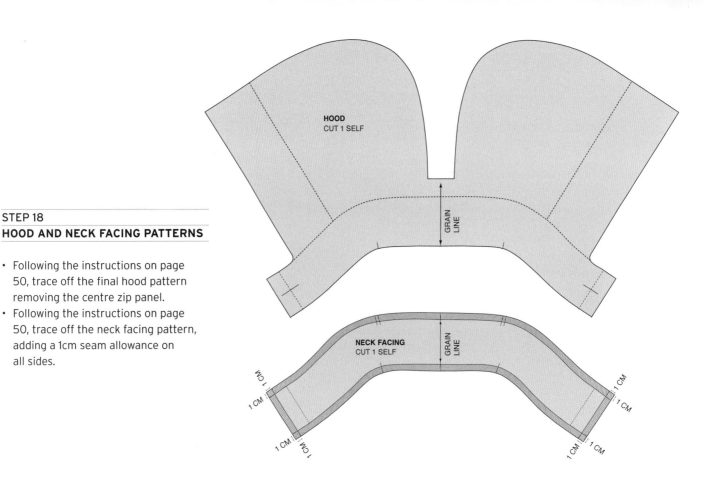

## STEP 18
### HOOD AND NECK FACING PATTERNS

- Following the instructions on page 50, trace off the final hood pattern removing the centre zip panel.
- Following the instructions on page 50, trace off the neck facing pattern, adding a 1cm seam allowance on all sides.

## STEP 19
### CENTRE BACK HOOD AND FUR PANEL PATTERNS

- Construct the final centre zip panel as a rectangle 4cm wide by the length of the back hood line measured from Step 17, adding a 1cm seam allowance on all sides.
- Following the instructions on page 50, trace off the fur panel from one side of the hood from Step 17, doubling the shape along the front opening. Add a 1cm seam allowance on all sides to create the final pattern.

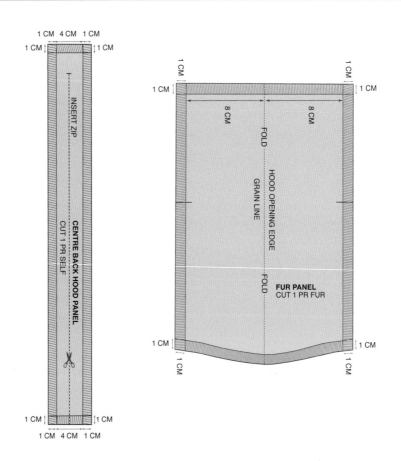

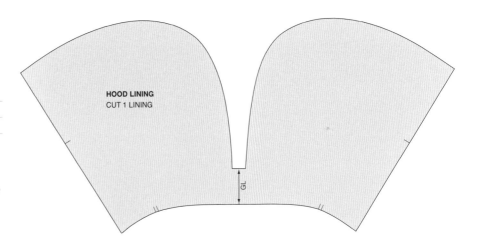

HOOD LINING
CUT 1 LINING

## STEP 20
### FINAL HOOD LINING PATTERN

- Following the instructions on page 50, trace off the hood lining pattern from Step 17 without the neck facing, centre zip and fur panels.

## STEP 21
### DEVELOPING THE FRONT LINING

- Following the instructions on page 50, trace off a copy of the front body shape from Step 6. Remove the facing shape from the front. The remaining shape will become the front lining.
- Next, you need to add ease by increasing the armhole width to allow for movement. From the shoulder point measure out 0.5cm and mark, and up 0.5cm and mark. Find the new shoulder point, and from this point draw a line following the curve of the shoulder back to the front shoulder neck point.
- From the underarm point measure up 0.5cm and mark, and out 0.5cm and mark. Find the new underarm point and draw a line 0.5cm out from the original armhole back up to the new shoulder point.
- To extend the length and give the lining an overlap at the waistline, cut it in half and open it up by moving the panels apart by 2cm.
- From the new underarm point blend the side seam down to meet the original hemline.

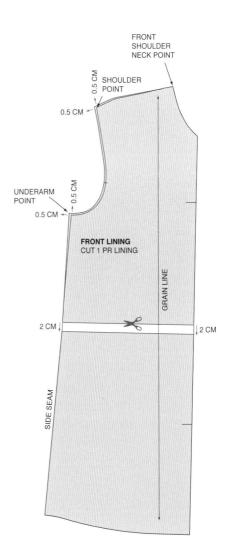

FRONT SHOULDER NECK POINT

0.5 CM
SHOULDER POINT
0.5 CM

UNDERARM POINT
0.5 CM
0.5 CM

FRONT LINING
CUT 1 PR LINING

GRAIN LINE

2 CM
2 CM

SIDE SEAM

## STEP 22
### DEVELOPING THE BACK LINING

- Following the instructions on page 50, trace off a copy of the back body from Step 9.
- You will need to add ease to the centre back to allow the lining to expand across the shoulder blades and also to increase the armhole to allow for movement. From the centre back neck point measure out 1.5cm and connect this point to the waistline; this will become the pleat.
- From the back shoulder point measure out 0.5cm and mark, and up 0.5cm and mark. Find the new shoulder point and draw a line following the curve of the shoulder back to the back shoulder neck point.
- From the underarm point measure up 0.5cm and mark, and out 0.5cm and mark. Find the new underarm point and draw a line 0.5cm out from the original armhole back up to the new shoulder point.
- To extend the length and give the lining an overlap at the waistline, cut it in half and open it by moving up by moving the panels apart by 2cm.
- From the new underarm point blend the side seam down to meet the original hemline.

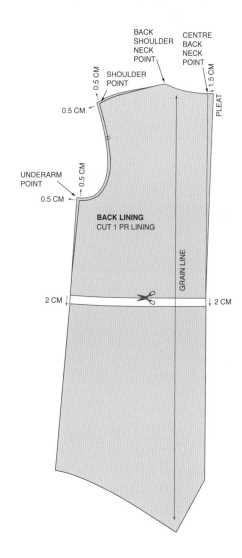

## STEP 23
### DEVELOPING THE SLEEVE LINING

**Matching the measurements**
Having enlarged the armhole lining, we will now increase the sleeve head so that the measurements match. At the sleeve hemline we will increase the length of the lining so that when the arm is raised the lining will not pull the outer sleeve.

- Following the instructions on page 50, trace off a copy of the sleeve from Step 14.
- From the crown point measure up 0.5cm and mark, and from the front and back underarm points measure out 0.5cm and mark and up 0.5cm and mark. Find the new underarm points and connect the front, the crown and the back with a curved line.
- From the new front and back underarm points draw a line down to blend in with the sleeve hemline.
- From the sleeve hemline measure down 2cm and square across to increase the length of the lining, pitching out at each side to reflect the underarm seams when folded.

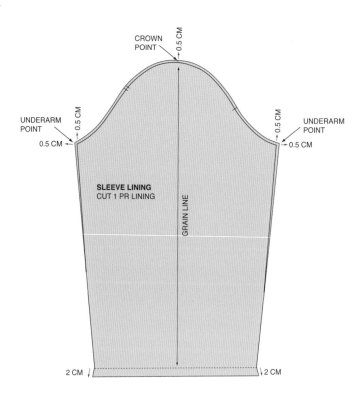

# GLOSSARY

**Annotation** Label or instruction added to a pattern to indicate grain line, piece name, season, cut ratio, internal features and fabric used.

**Awl** Wooden- or plastic-handled metal spike used to puncture small holes through pattern card, paper or fabric.

**Back shoulder neck point** Point where the shoulder line and the back neckline meet.

**Back shoulder point** Point where the shoulder line and the armhole line meet.

**Back shoulder seam** Line between the neck and armhole that rests along the shoulder on the final garment.

**Back underarm point** Lowest point of the armhole, usually where it meets the top of the side seam line.

**Balance marks** *See* notches.

**Bias grain** Line taken across the fabric at a 45-degree angle to the weft and warp threads.

**Biceps level** The largest circumference around the upper arm.

**Block** A basic pattern shape that represents an area of the body, usually the torso (body block), arms (sleeve block) or legs (trouser block).

**Body block** (bodice block/torso block) Basic pattern of the torso in a particular size that has no design features.

**Box pleat** A pleat made by making two folds in a piece of fabric, their edges facing in different directions.

**Button stand** A column of fabric at the front of a shirt or garment that holds buttons and buttonholes.

**CAD** Computer-aided design.

**Calico** Unbleached, raw cotton fabric used to test garment designs.

**CAM** Computer-aided manufacture.

**Centre back (CB)** Central line that vertically divides the back body into two halves.

**Centre back neck** Point at the top of the spinal column where the neck joins the body.

**Centre back rise** Line running between the waist and the centre crotch point that divides the back lower torso into two halves.

**Centre front (CF)** Central line that vertically divides the front body into two halves.

**Centre front neck point** Point in the centre of the ribcage where the front of the neck joins the body.

**Centre front rise** Line running between the waist and the centre crotch point that divides the front lower torso into two halves.

**Centre line** Line running down from the crown point to the cuff hem that divides the front and back halves of the sleeve.

**Chest line** The largest circumference of the chest horizontal to the floor.

**Collar point** The lowest external edge of the collar shape when folded down on the garment neckline.

**Collar stand** Rectangular band that is sewn to the neckline of a garment and lifts the collar.

**Crotch line** Line where the lower torso ends and the legs begin.

**Crotch point** Point where the front and back rises meet the inside leg seam.

**Crown point** The highest point of the sleeve head with a prominent curve where the arm joins the shoulder.

**Cuff guard** Fabric band that encases the slit opening at the bottom of the sleeve through which the hand passes.

**Dart** Stitched fold of fabric placed in a garment to fit it to the curves of the body.

**Dart point** The end of the stitched fold of fabric.

**Dart leg** The sides of the dart length.

**Dart line** The central line between the dart legs.

**Digitising** Digitally tracing the outline of a pattern piece to render the shape as computer mapping data.

**Drafting paper** Specialist paper or Manila card used to construct a pattern.

**Drill holes** Holes punched through a pattern card to allow the positions of pockets, buttonholes and design features to be marked on the fabric.

**Drop** The difference between the chest and waist circumferences.

**Ease** Measurement of space between the body and the garment added to the pattern to allow a proper fit.

**Elbow line** Line that denotes the level of the elbow within the sleeve length.

**Facing** Section of fabric used to finish hems and openings of garments; also used to give support to an area of fabric.

**Fit model** A model who is the size and shape of a fashion label's typical customer; clothes are fitted to their body shape.

**Flare** Volume added to a garment by pivoting or the insertion of a separate panel.

**Fold line** Label attached to a drawn line with bent arrows at each end to indicate a section of the pattern that needs replicating by folding the fabric over.

**Forearm line** Line running down the front sleeve denoting the front aspect of the arm.

**French curve** Flat drawing tool shaped in a graduating curve to give a template for drawing curves of the body.

**Front neckline** The length of the area made by the front neck opening in a garment.

**Front shoulder neck point** Point where the shoulder line and the back neckline meet.

**Front shoulder point** Point where the shoulder line and the armhole line meet.

**Front shoulder seam** Line that runs between the neck and armhole on a pattern; it rests along the shoulder of the body on the constructed garment.

**Front underarm point** Lowest point of the armhole, usually where it meets the top of the side seam line.

**Fullness** Extra volume to a pattern area in width, length, or both.

**Fuse** Interfacing material with an adhesive side used to stiffen or support internal sections of a garment.

**Gathers** Pulled together fabric, its length reduced to fit a smaller measurement.

**Grading** Process of enlarging or reducing the dimensions of a pattern proportionally to create a larger or smaller pattern size.

**Grain line** Direction of the warp and weft threads in a piece of fabric.

**Half back neck measurement** Distance between the centre back seam and the back shoulder seam.

**Half front neck measurement** Distance between the centre front seam and the front shoulder seam.

**Hem facing** Extended section of the garment body that is folded up to create a finished edge to the garment body.

**Hemline** Bottom edge of the garment body.

**Hip line** The largest circumference of the hips and buttocks horizontal to the floor.

**Horizontal grain** Direction of the weft threads that run horizontally across the fabric from selvedge to selvedge.

**Inside leg seam** The inner seam of the trouser legs.

**Knee line** Line of the knee on a trouser or pant leg pattern.

**Lapel** Constructed fabric panel that connects the collar and front opening of a jacket or shirt and gives a finished appearance; also used for strength and support.

**Made-to-measure** Describes a custom-made garment that is fitted to individual measurements.
**Marker** Gridded paper onto which patterns are traced, for fabric to be cut out.

**Neckline** Opening in a garment where the head passes through.
**Notches** Small incisions made to indicate a position when aligning patterns, seams, hems, CF and CB.

**Outside seam** Seam of the garment down the outside of a trouser leg.

**Pitch points (back and front)** Alignment point used when joining sleeves or pattern pieces that need to be positioned to hang at an angle or in a certain direction.
**Pivoting** Rotation of a pattern from a fixed point.
**Placket** Fabric band that encases a slit or opening at the neck or centre front of a garment and holds a closer of buttons or zips.
**Pleat** Fold in fabric that when repeated creates volume in a design.
**Plotter** Large-scale paper printer that plots digitised patterns.
**PR** = pair of patterns.

**Raglan sleeve** Sleeve that extends from under the arm towards the neck line.
**Roll line** Folded line where the lapel turns over from the collar down to the centre front opening.
**RSU** = right side up.

**Seam allowance** Extra volume added to the stitch line that allows seams to be sewn together.

**Set-in sleeve** Sleeve that is set or attached to a circular opening (armhole) that encases the arm around the shoulder down through the underarm pit.
**Shoulder neck point** Point where the front and back shoulder seams meet the neckline.
**Shoulder notch** Aligning notch on a collar to control fabric spread when inserting the collar; it is matched with the shoulder seams.
**Shoulder point** Point where the sleeve head and the front and back shoulder seams meet.
**Slash and spread** Pattern-making technique that involves cutting open a pattern to introduce or remove volume.
**Side seam** Seam of garment that runs down the side of the body, coats and trousers.
**Sleeve head (crown)** Upper part of the sleeve that is sewn into the armhole.
**Style line** Seams that separate the pattern piece of a design.
**Suppression** Removal of fabric to introduce shape to the curves of the human body.

**Toile** Sample garment made from calico and used to test the fit and proportional balance of a design on the human body.
**Tolerance** The amount of movement in woven fabric structure.
**Top stitch** Lock stitch that is placed along the edge of seams to secure them together.
**Torso** The trunk of the human body between the shoulders and the crotch.
**Tuck** Fold in fabric secured to seams; like pleats, tucks create volume.
**Two-piece sleeve** Sleeve shape made of two pattern pieces that take the natural hanging shape of the arm. The upper part attaches to the sleeve head / crown of the armhole; the lower part attaches to the underarm section of the armhole. It is generally used in tailored suits and coats, and the sleeve is set high under the arm for mobility.

**Under collar** Copy of the faced collar pattern that is reduced in size to enable the collar edge seam to turn under itself so that it is not visible.
**Underarm line** Line that runs across the width of the sleeve below the shaped head; it is usually the widest circumference of the sleeve as it encapsulates the bicep muscle.
**Underarm point** The lowest point where the side seams of the front and back body blocks meet with the armhole seams when sewn together.
**Underarm seam** Vertical seams of a set-in sleeve that, when sewn together, create the cylindrical tube of the sleeve.

**Vent** Vertical slit in the back or side back hem seams of coats or jackets that allows body movement when the garment is worn.

**Waistband** Band of faced fabric attached to the top of trousers to give finish and support or inserted in a jacket as a design feature to denote the waist level.
**Waistline** Circumference around the torso of the body between the hips and the bottom of the rib cage.
**Warp** Holding yarn that runs parallel to the edges of the loom.
**Weft** Filling yarn woven across the loom, perpendicular to the holding yarn.
**Wrist line** The smallest circumference of the arm.

**Yoke** Panel created in the top front or back area of a garment, coat or jacket. Also applied to a panel across the top of trousers.

# INDEX

**A**ccuMark software (Gerber) 68, 69, 70
Alcega, Juan de 8
anatomy *see* human anatomy
annotation 38, 39, 51
anthropometer 26
armholes 41, 42, 55, 59, 66;
    adjusting 81, 85, 90, 105, 127, 144, 233, 270, 289, 303
avatars *see* virtual avatars
awl 18, 19

**B**alance 31, 61, 62
'Balmac' trench coat 7
band collar 62
baseball hemlines 117, 127
basting (loose stitching) 8
bellows pockets 193
belts *see* waist belts
bespoke tailoring 21, 22, 59
bias grain 57
bib shirt 138-47
body blocks 20, 21, 36-37, 40-41;
    creation of master plans from 48, 74, 80, 89, 104, 116, 126, 138, 140, 206-8, 212, 220, 233, 252, 289, 302, 306; grading 53
body growth 55
    *see also* grading
body mapping 24
    *see also* 3D body scanning technology
boot-cut silhouette 199
boundary lines 24, 36
box-pleat 192-93
braces 156
branding 14, 20, 31, 68, 71
break point 273
breast pockets 106, 107, 118, 121, 221-22, 224, 225, 257, 262-63, 272, 278-79, 292
Browne, Thom 11, 12-13
button stand 162, 163, 190

**C**. P. Company 11
cagoules 50-51, 57, 68;
    pattern 206-19
Cambridge boating collar 64
capes 8
cargo pants 186-95
cargo pockets 188, 193
cassocks 8
casual styles 14, 63, 67, 95, 97:
    jackets 67, 220-31;
    shirts 62, 104-15, 135
chinos 158-67
club collar 64
coat linings 66, 248, 249-50
coats 7, 8, 14, 232-51
coin pocket 201, 273, 280
collar shapes 62-63, 64
collar stands 62, 64, 108, 120, 132, 298-99;
    hidden 62, 227-28, 236, 238, 275;
    patterns 84, 122, 133, 228, 238, 240, 275, 299
collars 50, 63-64, 84, 108, 120, 122 132-33;
    convertible 62, 227-28, 236, 238-40, 273, 275, 298-99;
    mandarin 62, 142-43
    *see also* neck sizes
compasses 18
computer-aided design (CAD) 7, 68-70
computer-aided manufacture (CAM) 68
computer-aided pattern-cutting 14, 22, 68-69
concealed pockets 65, 121
convertible collars 62, 227-28, 236, 238-40, 273, 275, 298-99
coronal plane 24
Coutts, J. 10
cross grain *see* horizontal grain
crotch line 45-47, 49, 61
    *see also* dropped crotch
crotch measurements 28, 33, 45, 58
cuff guards 67, 112, 113-14, 124-25, 146
cuff hemlines 111, 123, 136, 144, 245
cuff point 265, 285
cuff styles 67

cuff vents 246, 266, 285-86
cuffs 44, 113, 124, 145, 285-86;
    ribbed 86, 101, 174

**D**arts 105, 119, 127, 151, 188, 236-37, 253, 272
denim jacket 220-31
design development 36-39;
    and technology 14, 68-71
design development patterns 38
design drawings 20, 22
designer patterns 38
digital grading 70
digitising patterns 69-70
double-breasted styles 233, 268-87
doublets 8
drafter's pencils 18
draping 8, 20
drawstrings 174, 304, 306-7
drill holes 51
drop 31
dropped crotch 159, 160, 169, 176, 187
dyeing 60

**E**ase 58, 59, 95;
    for knitted fabrics 78, 85;
    applied to linings 66, 249, 283, 300, 313, 314;
    applied to sleeves 43, 59, 95, 110, 135, 144, 214, 244, 264, 284;
    applied to trousers 171
    *see also* darts; pleating
elasticated gathering 174, 209, 213
elbow patches 297
Engineered Garments 14
English neckline 63
envelope pockets 221-22, 224, 225, 295
epaulettes 134, 243-44
eyelet punch *see* pattern drill

**F**ace, The 14
facings: cuff 266, 286;
    fly 153, 162, 179, 190, 191;
    front 240, 259, 260, 274, 276, 291;
    hem 66, 209, 213, 234, 260, 290, 304, 306;
    hood opening 100;
    neck 209, 210, 212, 213, 249, 261, 277, 278, 311, 312;
    placket 77, 83, 304, 305;
    pocket 93, 107, 121, 155-56, 165, 170, 295;
    sleeve 246;
    vent 276;
    waistband 194
fit models 31
fitting 61
fleece 78
flies 151, 153, 159, 162-63, 169, 179, 180, 188, 190, 198, 200;
    extension 154, 157, 166, 179, 184, 191, 200, 203
French curves 18, 19, 41
French-style neckline 63
funnel collar 63

**G**arsault, M. de 8
geometry curves 18, 19
*GQ* 14
grading 52-55, 70
grain lines 46, 49, 51, 57
grandad vest 74-79
gusseted pockets 65, 292

**H**aute couture 20
hemlines: baseball 117, 127;
    cuff 111, 123, 144, 245, 265, 285; elasticated 213;
    facings 234, 304, 306;
    shaping 75, 127, 140, 207, 233, 253, 255, 269, 271, 273, 303;
    sleeve 44, 78, 214, 229, 230, 246, 287; trouser 46
hems 66
high-waisted trousers 150-57
hip curves 18, 19
hooded sweatshirt 88-103
hoods 88, 98-100, 216-19, 310-13
horizontal grain 57
human anatomy 24-27

**I**llustrations *see* design drawings
*Improved Tailor's Art, The* (Jacksons) 10

industrialisation 8
inside leg 28, 33, 45, 46, 47
internet, the 68
Italian loose neckline 63

**J**acket linings 66, 282-83, 287, 300-1, 313-14
jackets 8, 11, 61, 66;
    denim 220-31;
    double-breasted 62, 233, 268-87;
    single-breasted 63, 252-67
Jacksons, J. 10
jeans 196-203
jersey 78
jetted pockets 65, 272, 281

**'K**ASANE' 8
Kawakubo, Rei 14
knitted fabrics 58, 59, 78, 84, 85

**L**'*Art du Tailleur* (Garsault) 8
landmark points 25-27, 70
lapels 236, 256, 271
lay planning 70
layering 8
Lemonnier, Elisa 10
*Libro de Geometría Práctica y Traça* (Alcega) 8
line 62
linings 66;
    coat 66, 248-50;
    hood 313;
    jackets 66, 282-83, 287, 300-1, 313-14; sleeve 66, 247, 291, 301, 314
long-sleeved shirt 104-15
lumberjack shirt 116-25
Lycra 78

**M**ade-to-measure *see* bespoke
mandarin collar 62, 142-43
mannequins 30, 49, 71
Margiela, Martin 14
marker making 70
mass production 10, 22-23, 39
master plans 7, 37-38, 48-51, 74;
    for collars 227-28, 238-39, 275, 298-99;
    for coats/jackets 48, 206-8, 212, 220-21, 233-37, 252-55, 289-90, 302-4, 306;
    for epaulettes 243;
    for flies 163;
    for hoods 99, 216, 310-11;
    for pockets 161, 164, 172, 178, 181, 191, 201-2, 211, 222, 241, 262, 278, 291, 295; for shirts/tops 74-76, 80-1, 89-93, 104-6, 116-19, 126-28, 138-39, 140;
    for shorts 176-77, 180;
    for sleeves 48, 77-78, 85-86, 94-97, 110-12, 123, 134-36, 143-44, 214, 229-30, 244-45, 264-65, 269-73, 284-85, 296-97, 308-9;
    for storm flaps 243;
    for trousers 150-1, 158, 168-69, 170, 171, 186-88, 197-99
Maxima Poplin 7
measurement taking 7, 8, 21, 24-29, 40-1; armholes 41, 42;
    collars 236;
    hoods 98-100, 217-18, 310;
    inside leg 46, 47;
    neck 26, 41, 61, 62, 227;
    necklines 41, 120;
    sleeves 42-44, 59, 94, 244, 264, 284;
    tools for 10, 18, 26-29;
    trousers 45-47
    *see also* grading; size charts
median plane 24
military styles 8, 11, 12
mirroring 37, 38, 50
Miyake, Issey 8, 14
modelling *see* draping
moulage *see* draping
muff pockets 93, 94

**N**eck sizes 32, 33, 62, 98, 120, 132, 227
necklines 41, 63-64
notched waistbands 156-57, 166, 171, 174
notcher 18
notches 38, 48, 51, 70, 156, 171, 174, 238, 246;

alignment 91, 92, 156, 216, 218, 223, 226, 229, 231;
   collar 258, 273;
   shoulder 299, 310

**O**fficer collar 64
Owens, Rick 14

**P**arka 302-15
patch fly 180
patch pockets 65, 129-30, 192, 202, 209, 211, 257, 263-64, 291-92
pattern blocks 7, 26, 36;
   adapting 56
   see also body blocks; sleeve blocks; trouser blocks
pattern cutting 20, 36-39;
   history of 8-14;
   use of computers in 14;
   tools/equipment for 18-19, 39;
   training in 7, 8, 10
pattern design systems (PDS) 70-1
pattern drill 18, 19
pattern hole punch 18
pattern hooks 18
pattern masters 18, 19
pattern tracing 50-1
   see also under individual patterns
pattern weights 18
patterns: bib shirt 138-47;
   cagoule 206-19;
   cargo pants 186-95;
   chinos 158-67;
   denim jacket 220-31;
   digitising 69-70;
   grandad vest 74-79;
   high-waisted trousers 150-57;
   hooded sweatshirt 88-103;
   jeans 196-203;
   long-sleeved shirt 104-15;
   lumberjack shirt 116-25;
   parka 302-15;
   polo shirt 80-7;
   safari shirt 126-37;
   shorts 176-85;
   sweatpants 168-175;
   trench coat 232-51;
   waxed jacket 288-301
Peter Pan collar 63
pins 18
piping 264
pivoting 38, 56, 237
plackets 76, 81, 121;
   concealed 65, 139;
   facings 77, 83, 305;
   grown-on 65, 106, 127;
   sewn-on 65, 117, 127, 131, 221, 222, 290, 293, 304
pleating 141-42, 159, 169, 170, 176, 197, 199
pocket bearer 162, 192, 201
pocket flaps 121
pocket stands 65
pocket welts 65, 151, 153, 154-55, 156, 160, 164-65, 170, 172, 181-82, 221, 224, 234, 241, 257, 263, 272, 274, 279, 280
pockets 65, 93, 241-42, 304, 308;
   bellows 193;
   breast 106, 107, 118, 121, 221-22, 224, 225, 257, 262-63, 272, 278-79, 292;
   cargo 180, 193;
   coat 234, 241-42;
   coin 201, 273, 280;
   concealed 65, 121;
   envelope 221-22, 224, 225, 295;
   gusseted 65, 292;
   jeans 201-2;
   jetted 65, 272, 281;
   muff 93, 94;
   patch 65, 129-30, 192, 202, 209, 211, 257, 263-64, 291-92;
   shorts 178-79, 181-82;
   side 281;
   trouser 151-53, 154-55, 159, 160-62, 163-65, 169, 170, 172-73, 191-93
Poell, Carol Christian 14
polo shirt 80-87
posture 31, 61

*Practical Guide for the Tailor's Cutting-Room* (Coutts) 10
Prêt-à-porter see ready-to-wear
production line processes 20-23
production patterns 39
proportion 62
Prostyle 22

**Q**C (Quality Control) 23

**R**aeburn, Christopher 14
raglan shoulder shaping 290
raglan sleeves 89, 90-91, 94-97, 297-98
ready-to-wear 10, 14, 20, 22-23, 31, 52
ribbing 174
roll collar 62, 258, 273
   see also convertible collars
roll line 273
rulers 18, 19, 26

**S**afari shirt 126-37
sailor collar 62, 63
sample size 22 see also sizing systems
samples 22, 38
scalpels 18
*Science Completed in the Art of Cutting* (Walker) 10
scissors 18, 19
seam allowances 18, 38, 50, 51, 60
seams 18, 136
self-facing strips 155, 156, 165, 170, 181, 182
semi-bespoke 21, 22
set squares 18, 19, 26
set-in sleeve 67, 123-24
sewing 23
shaped pockets 241-42
shirts: long-sleeved 104-25, 138-47;
   short-sleeved 126-37
   see also polo shirt
shorts 176-85
shoulder slope 31, 61, 255, 270
shrink test 196
shrinkage 18, 60, 196
side pockets 281
silhouettes 7, 8, 10, 11, 20, 31, 62;
   fitted 119, 237, 253;
   leg 171, 187, 198-99
single-breasted styles 252-67
size charts 7, 10-11, 20, 24, 32-33;
   standardised 10-11, 22, 37
   see also grading; measurement taking; sizing systems
sizing systems 10-11, 52
   see also grading; neck sizes; 3D body scanning technology
slash and spread 38, 56, 239
sleeve blocks 37, 42-44;
   grading 54;
   creation of master plan from 48, 77, 85, 94, 110, 123, 134, 143, 214, 229, 244, 264, 269, 284, 296, 308
   see also under individual patterns
sleeve head ease 43, 59, 95
sleeve heads 43, 66, 78, 291;
   adjusting 95, 111, 135, 287, 301;
   and knitted fabrics 85
sleeve linings 66, 247, 291, 301, 314
sleeves 66-67, 296, 308-9;
   hemlines 44, 78;
   long 77-79, 89, 104, 110-15, 123-24, 143-45, 214-15, 229-31;
   raglan 89, 90-91, 94-97, 297-98;
   short 85-86, 126-37, 134-37;
   tailored 67, 244-47, 264-66, 284-87;
   two-piece 37, 67, 229-31, 284-87
   see also sleeve blocks
sportswear 11, 14, 58, 62
   see also hooded sweatshirt; sweatpants
standardisation of sizes 10-11, 22, 37
storm flap 243-44
straight collar 62
straight grain 57
Suzuki, Daiki 14
sweatpants 168-75

**T**ailor's chalk 18, 19, 26
tailored shorts 176-85
tailored sleeves 67, 244-47, 264-66, 284-87
tailoring 8, 10, 21;
   training in 10
   see also bespoke tailoring
Takada, Kenzo 14
tape measures 10, 18, 19, 26
*Taylor's Complete Guide* or *Comprehensive Analysis of Beauty and Elegance in Dress* 8
technology:
   and design development 14, 68-71;
   and measurement taking 29, 30, 52, 68, 71;
   and textiles 11, 14
3D body scanning technology 29, 30, 71
3D flattening technology 70-71
Throup, Aitor, 14
toiles 21, 30, 37, 38, 61, 62, 64
tolerance 59
tools 18-19, 26, 39
top collars 108, 120, 122, 132-33, 229, 240
tracing wheel 18, 19
transverse horizontal planes 24
trench coats 7;
   pattern 232-51
trend research 22
trouser blocks 37, 45-47;
   creation of master plan from 49, 150, 168, 170, 176, 180, 186, 197;
   grading 54-55
trousers: cargo pants 186-95;
   chinos 158-67;
   high-waisted 150-57;
   jeans 196-203;
   sweatpants 168-75;
   see also shorts; trouser blocks
turned-down collar 62, 63
turtleneck collar 63
two-piece sleeves 37, 67, 229-31, 244, 284-87

**U**ndersleeves 229, 230-31, 246, 265-66, 285, 286
unpicker 18, 19
*Uomo Vogue* 14

**V**an Beirendonck, Walter 14
vents 234, 249, 250, 261, 276-77, 283, 290, 293, 294
   see also cuff vents
virtual avatars 29, 71
volume, adding/removing 61, 207, 208, 212, 272, 289;
   to coats/jackets 209, 235, 253, 254, 257, 260, 271, 272, 276, 303, 306; hoods 311;
   to sleeves 67, 96;
   to trousers 170, 189
   see also pivoting; pleating; slash and spread

**W**aist belts 290, 293, 294
waistband tab 226
waistbands 102, 184-85, 194, 203, 226; notched 156-57, 166, 171, 174;
   sizing 174
waistlines 45, 46, 48;
   and darts 47, 49, 105, 119, 127, 129, 154, 169, 171, 181, 253, 257, 260;
   high 150-57
Walker, W. 10
Watanabe, Junya 63
waxed jackets 288-301
welt stands 65, 221, 241
   see also pocket welts
welts see pocket welts
WGSN 22
wide-spread cutaway collar 64
wing-tip collar 64
wool see knitted fabrics
Woolrich Woolen Mill 7

**Y**amamoto, Yohji 11, 14, 31
yokes:
   back 106, 107, 119, 121, 128, 187, 189, 199, 200;
   front 118, 121, 128, 221, 223, 229

**Z**ips 153, 211, 295, 311

# FURTHER READING

Aldrich, Winifred, *Metric Pattern Cutting for Menswear*, Blackwell, Oxford, (4th edition) 2006

Baudot, François, *The Allure of Men*, Assouline, New York/Paris, 2002

Blackman, Cally, *One Hundred Years of Menswear*, Laurence King, London, 2009

Boucher, François, *The History of Costume in the West*, Thames & Hudson, London, 1996

Chenoune, Farid, *A History of Men's Fashion*, Flammarion, Paris, 1993

Cicolini, Alice, *The New English Dandy*, Thames & Hudson, London, 2007

Cooklin, Gerry, *Pattern Grading for Men's Clothes: The Technology of Sizing*, John Wiley & Sons, 1992

Davies, Hywel, *Modern Menswear*, Laurence King, London, 2008

Gavenas, Mary Lisa, *The Fairchild Encyclopedia of Menswear*, Fairchild Publications, Inc, New York, 2008

Gieve, David W., *Gieves & Hawkes: 1785-1985 The Story of a Tradition*, Gieves & Hawkes, Portsmouth, 1985

Jobling, Paul, *Man Appeal: Advertising, Modernism and Menswear*, Berg, Oxford/New York, 2005

Knowles, Lori A., *The Practical Guide to Patternmaking for Fashion Designers: Menswear*, Fairchild Books, New York, 2005

McNeil, Peter and Karaminas, Vicki (editors), *The Men's Fashion Reader*, Berg, New York, 2009

Peacock, John, *Men's Fashion: The Complete Sourcebook*, Thames & Hudson, London, 1996

Shoben, Martin and Hallett, Clive, *Essential Shirt Work Book*, LCFS Fashion Media, 2001

Waugh, Norah, *The Cut of Men's Clothes 1600-1900*, Faber, London 1964/ Routledge 1987

Whife, A. A. and Brigland, A. S., *The Modern Tailor*, Outfitter and Clothier, Caxton, London, (4th edition) 1949

Whife, A. A., *A First Course in Gentlemen's Garment Cutting*, Tailor & Cutter, London, 1952

Whife, A. A., *Cutting from Block Patterns: Gentlemen's Jackets, Waistcoats, Trousers, etc.*, Tailor & Cutter, London, 1960

# PICTURE CREDITS

Fashion illustrations at the beginning of each pattern are by Thom Davies. All other technical drawings, diagrams and illustrations are by Elisha Camilleri. All toile photography is by Simon Pask Photography (model for the trouser patterns: Stuart Dando).

The author and publisher would like to thank the following individuals and institutions who provided images for use in this book. In all cases, every effort has been made to trace the copyright holders but should there be any errors or omissions, the publisher would be happy to insert corrections in any subsequent editions of the book.

2 © Alasdair McLellan, model: Roc Barbot at Models1,
   with thanks to Margaret Howell
6 Photo by Tim Barber www.woolrichwoolenmills.com
   www.wplavori.com
9 © WWD/Condé Nast/Corbis
10 l: © WWD/Condé Nast/Corbis; r: © WWD/Condé Nast/Corbis
11 l: © WWD/Condé Nast/Corbis; r: © WWD/Condé Nast/Corbis
12-13 © WWD/Condé Nast/Corbis
15 Engineered Garments SS12/model Jay Alaimo
18-19 Photography by Packshot.com
20 © Helen King/Corbis
21 John Lund/Paula Zacharias/Getty Images
23 © Qilai Shen/In Pictures/Corbis
25 Philip Dowell/Dorling Kindersley/Getty Images
27-29 Photography by Simon Pask, model: Raphael Sander for NEVS
30 Karina Lax
31 © WWD/Condé Nast/Corbis
39 b: © Helen King/Corbis
60 Gary Ombler/Dorling Kindersley/Getty Image
63 © WWD/Condé Nast/Corbis
70 Screen shots created in Gerber's AccuMark Pattern Design System (PDS)
   software 71 t: Screen shots created in Browzwear 3D Design Software; b:
   Screen shots taken in [TC]+'s (Textile Clothing Corp)3D body scanning
   program. Thanks to Dr Simeon Gill
73 © WWD/Condé Nast/Corbis (Issey Miyake Spring 2011)
148 © WWD/Condé Nast/Corbis (Junya Watanabe Man Fall 2012)
204 © Benoit Tessier/Reuters/Corbis (Issey Miyake Men Fall 2012)

All other photography by the author and staff at the Department of Apparel, Manchester Metropolitan University.

# AUTHOR'S ACKNOWLEDGEMENTS

Self-belief is a powerful creative tool: I am eternally grateful to Laurence King, Helen Evans, Anne Townley, Peter Jones and Lizzie Ballantyne whose enthusiasm and patience have allowed the book to evolve and develop into its present form.

Also to Nicole, Phoebe and River for their continuing support, patience and love throughout this process.

Special thanks to Elisha Camilleri and Thom Davies for sharing my passion for fashion and for their invaluable technical and creative contributions throughout the project.

I would like to thank all my colleagues and students past and present who have inspired the writing of this book through their invaluable comments and contributions. Many thanks to all the designers, fashion companies and educational institutions who generously gave their time during the research of this book.

Huge thanks to Dr Simeon Gill for his guidance and expertise in developing the anthropometrical sizing profiles and procedures, and to the staff at Manchester Metropolitan University who have supported this project.

Dedicated to the memory of my family who toiled in the cotton mills of Lancashire.

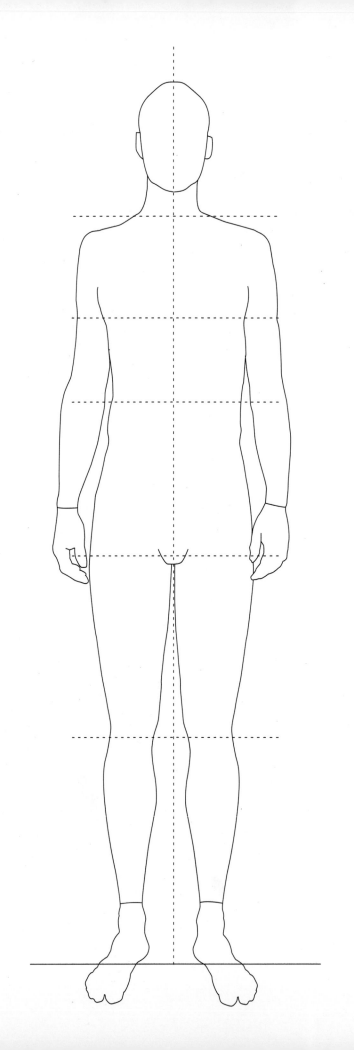